Advance Praise for
Ike in Love and War

"*Ike in Love and War* is a dazzlingly bold penetration of Dwight D. Eisenhower's mind. The author beautifully captures the emotional and intellectual drama of Eisenhower's quest for his historical destiny. He was a leader whom people admired, loved and respected everywhere, both as a warrior and a peacemaker. This book is a groundbreaking step forward in understanding the hidden dimensions of Eisenhower's leadership."

—**Brig. Gen. Carl W. Reddel**, USAF (Ret.), Executive Director
of the Dwight D. Eisenhower Memorial Commission

"Americans have good reason today to be interested in the way President Eisenhower united the nation in the 1950s. They can start by reading Richard Striner's insightful new history of Ike's careers in war and peace. The author delves deeply and originally into the emotional development of this remarkable leader."

—**Louis Galambos,** Editor of *The Papers of Dwight D. Eisenhower*

"Richard Striner is an unapologetic admirer of the man humbly reared in Abilene, Kansas, and who rose to become the most important wartime commander in American history. Eisenhower served two terms as president at the height of the Cold War and was, Striner concludes, 'a masterful president.' Striner's rigorous research and lively writing produce a compelling case for Ike's leadership, in a book that itself is 'masterful.'"

—**David A. Nichols**, Author of *A Matter of Justice: Eisenhower and the Civil Rights Revolution, Eisenhower 1956: The President's Year of Crisis,* and *Ike and McCarthy: Dwight Eisenhower's Secret Campaign Against Joseph McCarthy*

"Richard Striner's new biographical study, *Ike in Love and War*, breaks new ground in depicting Dwight D. Eisenhower as the tragic hero of America's modern democracy. Deeply researched and accessible, as well as provocative, it fits old facts into new perspectives and, most useful of all, broadens our understanding of the shrewd, complex, principled, often-misunderstood man who was the preeminent soldier-statesman of our times."

—**Philip Terzian**, author of *Architects of Power:
Roosevelt, Eisenhower, and the American Century*

"Richard Striner's new book on Dwight Eisenhower presents a ground-breaking look into this genuinely great American leader's sense of self and how and why he is such a defining historical figure. Striner pursues the depths of how Ike accomplished so much for America and the world - much of it unrecognized at the time. Who was this soldier-statesman and who and what shaped and motivated him? These questions and more are answered in this superbly engaging book of great consequence. A book that is especially relevant in our dangerously complicated and volatile world of today. Eisenhower's quiet insightful and courageous leadership is the hallmark of leadership... all leadership."

—**Chuck Hagel**, Vietnam Veteran, Former U.S. Senator and Former Secretary of Defense

IKE IN
Love AND *War*

How Dwight D. Eisenhower
Sacrificed Himself to
Keep the Peace

RICHARD STRINER

Post Hill
PRESS

A POST HILL PRESS BOOK

Ike in Love and War:
How Dwight D. Eisenhower Sacrificed Himself to Keep the Peace
© 2023 by Richard Striner
All Rights Reserved

ISBN: 978-1-63758-422-4
ISBN (eBook): 978-1-63758-423-1

Portrait on the cover courtesy of The White House Historical Association
Cover design by Conroy Accord
Interior design and composition by Greg Johnson, Textbook Perfect

Post Hill Press
New York • Nashville
posthillpress.com

Published in the United States of America
1 2 3 4 5 6 7 8 9 10

To Carl Reddel,
Without whom the Dwight D. Eisenhower Memorial
would not exist.

Contents

Preface

The world of Dwight D. Eisenhower seems distant these days, and for millions he is nothing but a name.

Yet the things that he achieved still matter.

Ike was a president who strove with great success to heal a stricken nation, to make decision-making more rational, to curb the influence of a demagogue, to make a huge investment in infrastructure without causing economic dislocations, and to counteract Russian aggression without bringing nuclear war.

Do these themes sound familiar?

There is much we can learn about the world that Ike made—and the complicated man who made it. We can profit from the study of Ike and his times—so different from ours, but so alike.

This book provides a new commentary on Eisenhower. It is the story of a life that was coherent but also mysterious. Ike left a record of consistencies mixed with contradictions, but his achievements look better and better over time.

This is a story of a man who drove himself relentlessly while doing his best to seem relaxed, a man who kept some of his greatest accomplishments secret and who paid the price of being undervalued. It is a story of burning ambition and excruciating sacrifice.

Decades ago, the political scientist Fred Greenstein argued convincingly that Eisenhower solved a central problem of the presidency. He was able to combine the functions that in other societies are split between a symbolic "head of state" who is largely a figurehead—whether a constitutional monarch or a president whose function is to float "above politics"—and the deal-maker who wields the levers of power: the "prime minister."[1]

Ike was able to combine these roles for two reasons. First, he was a military hero who projected a sunny and relaxed personality. That made him enormously popular. Second, he protected his popularity by engaging in machinations behind the scenes—by using "hidden hand" techniques.

And these techniques were often very crafty.

He was brilliant at concocting deceptions to create maneuvering room for himself. There were times when he would even try to seem befuddled—"out of touch." He paid a price for this when detractors said that he was old and past his prime. But in a strange sort of way, he got a kick from the deception since his mind was razor-sharp.

When press secretary James Hagerty warned him that a delicate issue might be raised at an upcoming press conference, Ike quipped, "Don't worry, Jim, I'll just confuse them."[2]

Here was a quintessential "foxy grandpa." Louis Galambos, who edited the Eisenhower *Papers*, called him "Machiavellian."[3]

This presidential achievement was in some respects unique to his times—and to the man. The closest thing we have seen in recent years to a military hero who was interested in presidential politics was Colin Powell, who considered a run for the Republican presidential nomination in 2000 but decided against it. With Powell, of course, there was the issue of race—an issue that continues to afflict us. Barack Obama broke the racial barrier in presidential politics, but the racist backlash against his achievement has been brutally apparent.

Ike's record on the issue of race is very interesting.

He sought to advance the cause of racial equality by measured degrees while containing the threat of white supremacist violence. He succeeded—his record of civil rights achievements behind the scenes is impressive—but the impatience of African Americans with the pace of change during his administration was understandable. We can learn a lot from the trade-offs that Ike engineered.

Of great interest at this point in our history is the way that Ike diminished the hysteria that was threatening the nation. This achievement was a deeply personal one: for most of his life he had been struggling to control the terrible temper he inherited from his father by employing techniques of self-control that he learned from his mother.

Just after he retired from the presidency, he revealed in an interview with CBS anchorman Walter Cronkite that in his own opinion his greatest presidential achievement was to bring a much-needed serenity to America.

No doubt the most formidable challenge in doing so was to undermine Senator Joseph McCarthy of Wisconsin—one of the foulest demagogues in American history, a scoundrel whose lies and abuse were making decent governance impossible. Ike's goal was to engineer the downfall of McCarthy without worsening the plague of irrationality that this demagogue spawned.

With his soaring popularity—based heavily upon his patriotic standing as the hero of D-Day—Ike could have chosen to confront McCarthy directly. But that was precisely what he chose *not* to do. His method was to sabotage his enemy behind the scenes in ways that were consistent with the dignity of the presidential office. He sought to calm the nation down.

He said that one of his most important responsibilities as president was to present "a respectable image of American life before the world."[4]

As he took on McCarthy, he was laying the groundwork for a cold new rationality in national security. He terminated the unwinnable war in Korea by forcing an armistice, and he quenched calls from his cabinet for Cold War escalation—such as proposals from Secretary of State John Foster Dulles to "roll back" Soviet power. He refused to get into another land war in Asia when others were calling for American intervention in Vietnam.

He developed a strategy for national security that was based in cost-effective deterrence, augmented by a secret program to develop the capacity for space-based reconnaissance of the Soviet Union.

His aim was to gather *objective facts* as the basis for decision-making—thus ensuring his responses to challenges would avoid either underreaction or overreaction.

A Republican who espoused conservative values, he advanced a left-right synthesis that he often called the "Middle Way." Here again, he was seeking to establish a common-sense political climate of balance and reason.

But beyond common sense, he was practicing a brand of centrist politics that was highly sophisticated—and not without precedent. Decades earlier, Theodore Roosevelt told an admirer that his work as a Republican leader was "to take hold of the conservative party and turn it into what it had been under Lincoln, that is, a party of progressive conservatism, or conservative radicalism; for of course wise radicalism and wise conservatism go hand in hand."[5]

Ike's achievement as a centrist is well-known, but the *story* of how he developed into a centrist is not. The evolution of his thinking in political and economic matters is a subject that few have taken on, not least of all because so much of his intellectual development remains mysterious. This book will seek to shed new light on these subjects.

Because the facts at hand raise tantalizing questions.

Ike was a *Democrat* in high school. Later on, he was privately pleased when FDR won the presidential election of 1932. His brother Milton was a New Dealer. His brother Edgar was an ultraconservative. After World War II, Ike warned against the dangers of socialism, and he revealed that he was a Republican.

Exactly *when* did he become a Republican, and *when* did conservative values capture his allegiance? Both parties had been courting him as a presidential candidate after World War II, and his popularity among liberals was considerable.

It appears he had a foot in both camps all along.

As president, he swore that he would cut back on excessive federal spending, and he warned about the danger of America becoming "insolvent." Nonetheless, he resisted all proposals to roll back the New Deal legacy.

He launched the greatest public-works project in American history, the Interstate Highway System, whose purpose went beyond the goal of providing America with up-to-date transportation infrastructure. Ike intended it to function as a program that could counteract recessions. Though he never admitted it, he was something of a Keynesian.

Here was a man whose ideological statecraft defies easy generalizations.

His views about political issues evolved dynamically. However steady his *instincts* were, his *perceptions* shifted as history progressed, and as his own personality developed.

Before the end of his first term in the presidency, he fulminated against the radical right. He said he wanted the Republican Party to be "progressive," and expressed his scorn for "reactionaries." The supporters of Barry

Goldwater began to revile him as a "socialist." Self-styled "liberal" Republicans perceived him as an ally.

Things had changed quite a lot since he had warned about the dangers of socialism in the late 1940s.

If Ike was indeed a conservative, what kind of a conservative was he? How much of his political and economic rhetoric was posturing? How much of it was based in deep conviction? And how much did his views in these matters keep changing and evolving through the years? How much of what he did was *calculation* as he sought to enlarge the political base of the Republican Party among middle-of-the-road independents?

The same sorts of questions should be asked about the evolution of his fiscal and economic views. These views are extremely important nowadays as Americans debate not only what the nation needs, but *how to pay for it.*

What can we learn from Ike's understanding of these matters?

During World War II, he advocated unlimited spending to underwrite the war. America, he said, should spend whatever it took to give its fighting men and women what they needed. And the country would have to generate economic superabundance to do so. At the beginning of the war, Ike told Army Chief of Staff George Marshall that "we must take great risks and spend any amount of money required."[6]

But in the aftermath of war, he began to preach fiscal austerity.

Why?

In 1949, he told Defense Secretary James Forrestal that "we must hold our position of strength without bankrupting ourselves."[7] He expressed this same point of view consistently throughout the 1950s—and beyond.

Few have sought to question the way in which his economic thinking developed. But questions should be asked, and this book will be the one to ask them. Because answers, however tentative, could be enlightening.

For example:

Was Ike aware of the fact that the money supply of the United States was *doubled* during World War II through the hidden methods of the Federal Reserve system? According to economic historian Allan H. Meltzer, America's "monetary base doubled in the four years ending in fourth quarter 1945."[8]

Did Ike understand such things? Did FDR understand them?

In the 1980s, the president of the Federal Reserve Bank of New York observed that when it comes to the innermost "secrets" of money and banking, "no president really understands these things."[9]

Ike was a master of deception when he took the big plunge and became a presidential candidate. So how much of his political rhetoric on behalf of financial austerity was meant to create a political *effect*, and how much of it was based in conviction?

We need to know.

There is much that we do *not* really know—much, no doubt, that we will never really know—as we seek to understand the way that Ike's thinking in political and economic matters developed over time.

Great strides have been made in recent times by historians and journalists to shed new light upon the hidden dimensions of Eisenhower's leadership. This book will attempt to convey these new findings, and—wherever possible—add to them.

After Ike's death, his widow, Mamie, supposedly mused that she could never be sure whether anyone had truly understood her late husband—not least of all herself.[10]

How much further can we go in attempting to understand this strong and complicated man—a man so underestimated at the height of his powers and so venerated later by historians? There is much to be gained in our current situation through a brand-new reckoning with Ike.

Above all, we need to ask ourselves this: How did Ike become a guarantor of *peace*?

He stood firm against advisers who could never grasp the risks of their advice. He controlled them. He gave America protection with *peace*, and he told his subordinates to sober up if they were reckless. In 1956, he put a stop to a war in the Middle East by standing up to America's allies and making them relent.

As he lived with these tensions, he forced himself and others to be calm and he kept the nation calm.

How did Ike become such a man?

CHAPTER ONE

Ike Himself

Writer Eric Larrabee once said that Dwight D. Eisenhower "gravitated upward as naturally as a sunflower seeks the sun."

His "disarming grin" made people feel good, and his relaxed appearance was charming. But few suspected what was hidden below: a cold strength that never let up.

In Larrabee's view, Ike possessed "an intelligence as icy as has ever risen to the higher reaches of American life."[1] Robert Donovan of the *Los Angeles Times* believed that Ike was "a cold man," despite his radiant smile.[2] He was a master of illusion that way, a cunning maestro, a calculating genius.

He was a person in possession of *total self-command*—"cold" beneath his superficial "warmth."

Or was he?

There is something missing from this overview of Ike's personality: *passions*. He had a fiery temper that could stun new acquaintances as soon as they came within its range. He had a burning ambition that drove him to exceed every previous achievement. His White House physician believed that without the relaxation of golf, Ike would "be like a caged lion, with all those tensions building up inside of him. If this fellow couldn't play golf, I'd have a nut case on my hands."[3]

Most importantly, his capacity for *love* was a quality he strove down the years to conceal. He often stated his aversion to "sentiment," and people took him at his word. But his love letters show how he felt in the grip of ardent *longing*.

It consumed him.

Fire and ice: these were the qualities beneath the easy charm and the captivating grin that Ike displayed.

But there is one more quality that needs to be acknowledged in Ike: his *mischievous* nature. He pulled pranks and had a fun-loving side.

He was very complicated.

Childhood

He emerged from obscurity.

David Dwight Eisenhower—that was the name he was given by his mother at birth—was born in Denison, Texas, on October 14, 1890, as a thunderstorm rolled overhead. His names David and Dwight would be reversed later on by his mother. The name Dwight was inspired by Dwight Moody, an evangelist.

Ida Stover Eisenhower and her husband, David Eisenhower, were both religious, and both of their families hailed from Germany. The first "Eisenhauer" arrived in colonial Pennsylvania in 1741. He was recruited by none other than William Penn, who needed farmers to provide more food in the Quaker colony.

By the middle of the 1800s, the Eisenhowers had settled around Harrisburg, and they belonged to a German Protestant sect called the "River Brethren," an offshoot of the Mennonites. Like the Amish, these people were known far and wide as the "Pennsylvania Dutch" (a corruption of "Deutsch"), and they were all committed pacifists.

Ike's grandfather, Jacob Eisenhower, prospered, as did many of the River Brethren, and in 1878 he led a migration to Kansas. A charismatic elder of the River Brethren, he was influential. He saw the opportunity for land acquisitions in Kansas, where the land was both fertile and cheap. So he and his followers—enough of them to pile their belongings into fifteen freight cars—set out for Kansas by train.

They decided to settle near the Smoky Hill River, near Abilene, a town that was dramatically changing. A decade before, it was the epicenter of the early Wild West, a "cow town" notorious for violence. Texas ranchers drove their cattle up the Chisholm Trail to the railroad that ran through Abilene. After the cowboys were paid, they got drunk and raised holy hell.

Only the action of lawmen like Thomas J. Smith and Wild Bill Hickok brought the town a modicum of order.

By the time that Jacob and his followers arrived, the town of Abilene was transformed. The frontier moved further west. Abilene's wild days were over, and the town became a peaceful oasis in the middle of the Kansas wheat belt.

Jacob thrived as his farming expanded, and with some of the other River Brethren, he founded a business, the Belle Springs Creamery.

Ike's father David—who was Jacob's eldest surviving son—was born in the middle of the Civil War. He was devoutly religious like his father, but that was where the similarities ended. David didn't want to be a farmer. Whereas Jacob was gregarious and generous, David was taciturn and moody. He enrolled at Lane University, a denominational college in Lecompton, Kansas, that was run by the United Brethren in Christ.

Two years after he enrolled, he met Ida Elizabeth Stover and they fell in love. They dropped out of college and got married.

Ida was devout, like David, but their personalities were different—to put it mildly. She was lively and witty, at times precocious, and her decision to go to college was a challenge to the period's norms.

She was friendly, captivating, and clever, while her husband was humorless. But somehow—in a way that will always remain their secret—they got along.

With help from his father, David opened a store in the town of Hope, Kansas. The town was selected for a simple reason: Jacob owned land there. David opened his store with a loan from Jacob, and his plan was to run the business in partnership with a salesman named Milton Good. The men and their families would live upstairs.

It didn't work. David couldn't get along with people, and he never learned to manage money. Good walked away, and David turned to his younger brother Abraham to help run the store. But then David quit the business and turned it over to Abraham.

An Eisenhower legend developed: David and Ida told the world that Milton Good absconded with money, thus ruining the business. But historians discovered decades ago that this story was a fiction.[4]

David never recovered from this failure. Even though he was a father—he and Ida had a son named Arthur who was two years old—he moved away by himself, leaving Ida, who was pregnant with their second child, in the care of his brother Abraham. David wandered down to Texas in search of a job.

Some biographers have speculated that David moved away because he felt disgraced. He was descending from the status of a businessman to working-class penury.[5]

He got a job in Denison, Texas, a railroad town, as a mechanic—an "engine wiper" who cleaned locomotives. Ida stayed on in Hope until she gave birth to their second son, Edgar.

Then she came to join David, and the two of them lived with their two little boys in a decrepit and sooty house near the railroad yard.

They were miserable.

And it was here, in Denison, that Dwight David Eisenhower—christened David Dwight—came into the world in 1890.

Jacob came to take a look at this appalling situation, and he made things right. He found a job for David in the Belle Springs Creamery, so David, Ida, and their three boys were brought to Abilene.

David worked at the creamery as a so-called "engineer"—he was really a mechanic—and his taciturnity deepened. He withdrew into himself, except for times when he led his children in Bible recitations or meted out harsh corporal punishment, his pacifism notwithstanding.

Ida carried on valiantly. Her friendliness, intelligence, and skill as a parent made up for some of David's deficiencies, but Ike and his brothers grew up in the gaze of a father who was very hard to love. "Lord High Executioner" was what Ike called his brooding father in a short book of memoirs that he wrote in old age.

David and Ida had six sons: Arthur, Edgar, Dwight, Roy, Earl, and Milton, in their order of birth. A seventh son, Paul, died in infancy, and this loss was such a blow to the parents that Ida lost her faith in the River Brethren, and she sought consolation elsewhere. In time she joined the "Bible Student" movement, which later evolved into the Jehovah's Witnesses.

The Eisenhower household was drenched in religion, but aside from a generalized belief in a higher power, Ike never took religion very seriously and he never joined a church until he became president.

The family lived in a tiny rented house on "the wrong side of the railroad tracks" until Ike was eight. There was no disguising the fact that they were poor, but the parents gave the boys a strong dose of the Protestant work ethic, with an emphasis on thrift. "'Waste not, want not' and 'a penny saved is a penny earned' were the rule of life," Ike remembered, and every cent mattered in those days: "the Indian on our penny would have screamed if we could possibly have held it tighter."[6]

Eventually, David's brother Abraham sold David and Ida a larger home on easy terms—a two-story house with enough space behind it for a small farm. So the Eisenhowers raised crops and tended livestock, which led to a daily chore load for the boys.

Ida worked out the arrangements. "Each morning before school," Ike remembered, "there were items on the agenda—milking cows, feeding chickens and horses, putting the stalls and the chicken house shipshape."[7]

That was just the beginning. The boys had to prune the orchard, harvest and store the fruit, weed the garden, hoe the corn, and put hay in the barn. Ida rotated these chores so that "none felt discriminated against," showing "insight, imagination, and managerial skill."[8]

To their credit, David and Ida encouraged their boys to get a good education, go to college, and seek their fortunes in a wider world—beyond Abilene.

Ike remembered Abilene as a town that was so quiet at night that "the whistle and rumble of a train could be heard rising and falling away across miles of country."[9] It was a town where "paving was unknown" until he was a teenager and where "after a heavy summer rain the streets became almost impassable because of mud."[10] In dry weather the dust would float above the street.

It was "just another rural town, undistinguishable from scores of others dotting the plains."[11]

Snow in the winter would "immobilize the community," except for games like "skating and hooking a sled behind a horse; the rider, lying flat on his belly, took a fair amount of snow from the horse's hoofs."[12]

This was the way of life that would be immortalized in American culture during Eisenhower's presidency in paintings by Norman Rockwell for the *Saturday Evening Post* and in plays like Meredith Willson's *The Music Man*.

Abilene, Kansas, as it looked when Ike was a boy.

The shops of Abilene were humdrum affairs, all business and no-nonsense; "shopkeepers assumed that customers came to buy only what was needed," Ike said, so the "window displays were amateurish," "goods were stored on shelves," and "nothing was done to encourage the casual browser."[13] This side of doing business in Abilene was dry as dust.

Just the same, there was a gaudy spirit of "civic puffery" in the Abilene business community, a boosterism arising from the "effervescent optimism" that was a "flourishing local industry." Abilene leaders entertained "dreams of what might lie ahead—the transfer of the state capital to the town, for example"—and Ike quoted text years later from an 1887 advertising brochure that lauded Abilene as "A GEM—The City of the Plains."[14]

Ike had a roving intelligence, and he loved to read. His favorite subject was ancient military history. Ida kept a good library, and he often stole time from his chores to regale himself with stories of battles and generals. "The battles of Marathon, Zama, Salamis, and Cannae became as familiar to me as the games (and battles) I enjoyed with my brothers and friends in the school yard," he recalled.[15]

But elementary school bored him, and he was justified in feeling bored. The teaching was rote recitation. "The darkness of the classrooms on a winter's day," he remembered, bred tedium, "and the monotonous hum of recitations, offset only occasionally by the excitement of a spelling bee or the suppression of a disorderly boy, are my sole surviving memories. I was either a lackluster student or involved in a lackluster program."[16]

He did enjoy arithmetic and the study of the English language, since both of these subjects appealed to his love of *precision*. "In grammar school," he remembered, "spelling was probably my favorite subject, because the contest aroused my competitive instincts or because I had learned that a single letter could make a vast difference in the meaning of a word."[17] Words and numbers and their denotations intrigued him.

Chores at home were as tedious as schoolwork, but Ida found ways to build her boys' morale and to emphasize teamwork. Ike adored his mother. To the end of his life, he considered her the finest person he had ever known. "Her serenity, her open smile, her gentleness with all and her tolerance of their ways, despite an inflexible loyalty to her religious convictions and her own strict pattern of personal conduct," he recalled in old age, "made even a brief visit with Ida Eisenhower memorable for a stranger."[18]

But his father—Lord High Executioner—was memorable for different reasons. He was a savage disciplinarian. Once, when he found out that Ike's older brother Edgar had been cutting classes, he grabbed a leather harness, and, as Ike recalled it, whipped the boy like a dog. Ike was outraged. But he inherited his father's terrible temper, so he struggled all his life to find ways to keep it under control. He would never achieve complete success in this endeavor, but Ida gave him the inspiration to keep trying—to persevere in the struggle to develop self-command.

One Halloween night, his parents refused to allow him to go trick-or-treating with his older brothers because he was too young. Ike threw a tantrum—he started beating his fists against an apple tree until his hands were bloody. David came out with a hickory switch, and after dishing out the standard punishment, he sent Ike to bed.

Ida came into the room and sat silently in a rocking chair for a long time. At last, she quoted the Bible, saying, "He that conquereth his own soul is greater than he who taketh a city." She also told him that feelings of vengeance were a total waste of time. Then she bandaged his wounded hands.

"I have always looked back on that conversation as one of the most valuable moments of my life," Ike remembered.[19]

In spite of Ida's pacifism, her boys learned to fight and defend themselves, and some of the toughest fights were the ones between Ike and his older brother Edgar, who became rivals. Both went by the nickname "Ike" for a while: Edgar was "Big Ike" and Dwight was known as "Little Ike." Though "Ike" was a traditional nickname for Isaac, people used it as a handy one-syllable abbreviation for the Eisenhowers' multisyllabic last name.

"Ike" would remain Dwight's nickname for the rest of his life.

In spite of David's pacifism, he taught Ike some things about fighting. On one occasion, Ike recalled, "I came in from the school grounds on the run, chased by a belligerent boy of about my own size." His father said, "Chase that boy out of here," and Ike discovered, as he turned on the boy, that the speed and surprise of his about-face startled his attacker into headlong flight. "I was rapidly learning," Ike wrote, "that domination of others in this world often comes about or is sought through bluff."[20]

One day just before he turned five, he was prowling around the farm of some relatives during a family gathering near Topeka. In the barnyard he encountered a nasty and bad-tempered goose who kept chasing him away. Determined not to be thwarted, he yelled and charged in mounting frustration at the bird until his uncle Luther Stover gave him a broom and suggested that he use it to teach the goose a lesson. "I learned," he wrote later, "never to negotiate with an adversary except from a position of strength."[21]

In general terms, his father, David, was a sorry role model, so Ike discovered a surrogate father in a local hunter and trapper named Bob Davis. With his parents' permission, he spent weekends camping with Davis, who taught him how to "rough it," how to cook over a campfire, how to shoot, how to play poker—and how to bluff at poker. This naturally augmented his new quest for self-control. And the poker lessons were a tonic for Ike because they stimulated an innate gift for mathematics.

Davis was a memorable teacher, an illiterate practitioner of John Dewey's creed of "learning by doing."

Ike described the method years later: "He would ask me whether I had a pair. 'Yes, nines.' 'All right,' he would say, 'how many nines are there out of the forty-seven cards that you have not yet seen?' Of course the answer was two. 'Well then, the chance of your drawing a nine as you take each card is two out of forty-seven'.... He dinned percentages into my head night after night around a campfire, using for the lessons a greasy old pack of nicked cards."

"Since I was fascinated by the game," Ike recalled, "I really studied hard to keep it going. Often, he would pick up part of the pack and snap it across my fingers to underscore the classic lesson that in a two-handed game one does not draw to a four-card straight or a four-card flush against the man who has openers."[22]

The shooting lessons that Ike received from Davis were augmented by lessons from other men who were good with guns, one of them a neighbor who claimed to have been a deputy to Wild Bill Hickok. "Across the street from our house," Ike recalled, "lived a man named Dudley, who claimed he had served for a time as a young deputy under Wild Bill. His tales of the man's prowess with a revolver were entrancing."[23]

One thing led to another, and before very long shooting practice was a part of Ike's routine. Three men practiced shooting on the flats of Mud Creek, a tributary of the Smoky Hill River: Dudley (Hickok's deputy), Henny Engle (Abilene's marshal), and a Mr. Gish, who was the local Wells Fargo agent. Eventually, they invited Ike to come along with them.

"Each man carried his revolver differently," Ike recalled. "Gish wore his in a shoulder holster under his left arm. Henny Engle used a conventional holster on his right side. Mr. Dudley slipped his revolver inside his belt, the barrel pointing toward his left foot and the grip handy to his right hand. I would watch intently as they would draw and shoot."[24]

Over time, they let Ike join in.

Many people have wondered about the way that Ike chose to join the military—devoting himself to the art of war—when the mother he revered was a *pacifist*.

Is it really very hard to guess the way in which he reconciled this seeming contradiction?

He had loved the study of ancient military history since early childhood. As he grew up, he learned to shoot, and he learned from his surrogate fathers and role models like Mr. Dudley what Abilene was like when it was terrorized by drunk killers—and what it took to make Abilene a safe place for decent people.

He learned about Hickok, and he learned about his predecessor, Marshal Thomas Smith, who gave his life to make the town safe. Smith's tombstone, which Ike visited, lauded the

> Fearless Hero of Frontier Days
> Who in Cowboy Chaos
> Established the Supremacy of Law.[25]

Ike read western fiction to the end of his life, and his wife sent him western pulp stories to read at night during World War II. In his presidential years, he loved the western productions of Hollywood, especially *High Noon*.

What better way to reconcile a life devoted to the military art, a life so at odds with the ideals of his pacifist mother, than to *use* the military art as the foremost way to *keep the peace*?

He would learn the military art and then use it to *bring the world peace*. If peace were the object, he was true to his mother's ideals—in a way—and he would project the use of force through control, unlike his father, whose violence was nothing better than an outburst of uncontrolled temper.

He would always be a warrior devoted to peace—*a guardian of peace*— and, as he and brother Edgar put their fisticuffs to use in the schoolyard brawls, it was *Ike* to whom the other kids would always look for protection.

A classmate named John E. Long recalled a day when a bully terrorized the schoolyard by swinging a cord with a heavy nut attached. Ike subdued this bully, and forever after, wrote Long, "students always wailed 'Ike, Ike, Ike'...whenever there was any kind of trouble on the school grounds."[26] The kids called for *Ike*—and *peace* was restored. They knew that he would always protect them.

He was already the protector of peace that he would be in his presidential future. He was a wild boy from the south side, true, but he was also a guarantor of order—a preserver of the peace.

He was like Wild Bill Hickok.

High School to West Point

But his future was not at all clear when he finished high school.

His yearbook—the Abilene High School *Helianthus*—predicted that he would go on to be a history professor at Yale.[27] His immediate plan was to follow his brother Edgar to the University of Michigan.

In high school he devoted himself to sports and student leadership. He and Edgar were rivals, and he was jealous when the high school yearbook hailed Edgar as the football star of the school. But Ike had the consolation of being president of the Abilene High School Athletic Association, set up to do fundraising for varsity athletics.

He also organized two-week camping trips in which his cooking and forestry skills could be displayed. His leadership flair was apparent.

His intellectual abilities were demonstrated in mathematics, especially when his skills in impromptu conceptualizing were tested. He disliked algebra, but "the introduction of plane geometry was an intellectual adventure, one that entranced me," he wrote in old age. The principal and Ike's math teacher dared him to try to solve some geometry problems without using the textbook, and he found the challenge "delightful because it meant that no advance study was required."[28]

He was also paying close attention to national politics in high school.

It would be interesting to know whether he noticed that the statecraft of President Theodore Roosevelt was keeping the peace in Ike's teenage years: it prefigured what he would do later in the 1950s. "Teddy" mediated the Russo-Japanese War, and he sponsored the Algeciras Conference to defuse Franco-German rivalries. He won the Nobel Peace Prize for such work. We will never know if these events made any impression on Ike at the time—but it would not have been surprising if they did. He was keenly aware of current events.

Shortly after Ike's graduation, he revealed that he favored the *Democratic Party*.

Six months after his high school graduation, he gave an oration to the Dickinson County Young Men's Democratic Club, and this address—"The Student in Politics"—was printed on the front page of the *Dickinson County News*.

He attacked the Republican Party because it was the friend of corporations—the protector of privilege—and its leaders opposed the direct election of United States senators, a major reform goal at the time. Ike observed that this proposed progressive reform would make it "harder for the interests (the rich corporations) to control congress, and…this is the reason the Republicans oppose such a plan."

And even though some reform-minded Republicans "have become disgusted with the policies and the actions of the party proper and branched off into, Square Dealers, Insurgents, Progressives, and Reformers," Ike observed, they continued to "cling to the name Republican," whereas they ought to switch parties, because "they are fighting for many of the principles which the Democrat party advocates."

Consequently, he concluded, an observant young man might decide that "with the Republican Party splitting up and a number of honest and fearless ones tending towards the Democracy, that the Democrat party deserves his first vote."[29]

Ike began to hang around the offices of the *Dickinson County News*. Before very long he became close friends with the editor, Joseph W. Howe.

Howe encouraged Ike's intellectuality, and the mischievous streak that it could generate. He recalled that Ike "liked to debate subjects and had the faculty of asking controversial questions…to confuse his opponent." When challenged, Ike "would come forth with some witticism and put on his best smile. In that way he generally ended the debate by disposing of his opponent's argument."[30]

It would often be asserted down the years that Ike, while extremely intelligent, was "no intellectual." Howe's reminiscences make that assertion dubious. It was true that Ike would never develop the sensibilities of the literary and academic elite, but the reason for this is obvious: his career choice. If he had gone on to be a history professor, as his high school friends predicted, things would have been different.

Just the same, he possessed the qualities that elevate intellectuality above the level of ordinary intelligence: a propensity to step back from propositions, scrutinize them, and apply the methods of critical analysis to sort out the tricky ambiguities—the nuances.

Ike could do such things.

Ike and Edgar had planned to take turns attending classes at the University of Michigan. While one brother took courses, the other one would be working to earn tuition money. Then they would switch places for a spell.

Edgar set off for Ann Arbor, and Ike went to work at the Belle Springs Creamery—doing manual labor. But then a high school friend, a boy named Everett "Swede" Hazlett, approached him with a striking proposition: they would both apply to the Naval Academy, where midshipmen could attend tuition-free.

A congressional sponsor was necessary, so Ike sent a letter to United States Senator Joseph L. Bristow, and followed up by eliciting support letters from influential citizens in Abilene. After Ike passed the entrance exam that both of the military academies used, Bristow sent him to West Point instead of Annapolis.

"Swede" went into the navy, and he and Ike kept up an avid correspondence until Hazlett's death in 1958.

Ike was admitted to the West Point Class of 1915, and told to report to the military academy in June 1911. His mother bade him a stoical goodbye: she said, "It's your choice," as he left for the train. But then her stoicism collapsed.

She went to her bedroom and wept.[31]

On the way to West Point, Ike took time to visit Edgar at Ann Arbor, and the two of them had a double date, which Ike remembered thus: "He hired a canoe and we set out on the river...with a couple of college girls. We took along a phonograph and played the popular songs. Paddling in the moonlight, we passed canoe-loads of other students, enjoying the pleasant June evening." Then they paid for the canoe and walked the girls back to the dorms.[32]

Ike also made a stop in Chicago to visit Ruby Norman, a girl whom he had dated for a while in high school. They were long since platonic friends.

At last, he arrived at West Point on the Hudson and gazed up at the campus of the United States Military Academy. He climbed up the hill, and soon he was immersed in the introductory hazing that was standard at West Point:

> Orders were not given with any serious attempt at instruction or intended for easy comprehension. They were a series of shouts and barks.... Here we were, the cream of the crop, shouted at all day long

by self-important upper-classmen, telling us to run here and run there.... No one was allowed to do anything at ordinary quick-time; everything was on the double.[33]

Then things became solemn as Ike and the rest of the "plebes" (freshmen) were sworn in at the initiation ceremony that evening.

Ike remembered this event for the rest of his life, because "a feeling came over me that the expression 'The United States of America' would now and henceforth mean something different than it ever had before. From here on it would be the nation I would be serving, not myself."[34]

But this feeling of reverence wore off, as Ike settled into a routine that made him rueful as he looked back upon it: instead of paying attention to his studies, he immersed himself in competitive sports, which he pursued relentlessly—when he was not building his reputation as a prankster who piled up a record number of demerits.

The tales of Ike's mischievous behavior would take on the status of West Point legends: He broke one rule after another. He smoked cigarettes (forbidden), he played poker for money (forbidden)—he also learned bridge—he danced with girls at cadet dances in a manner that the stodgy rules of the academy forbade.

His most serious offense—he got away with it—was recorded years later by a fellow cadet named Charles C. Herrick:

one of the worst offenses at the Point was to get caught off the reservation. But somehow it never worried Ike and some of the others. They'd sneak out the lavatory windows, and past the sentry post and off they'd go up the Hudson in a rented boat to Newburgh for coffee and sandwiches. Imagine, they'd travel 30 miles—15 there and 15 back—just for chow. If any of those guys had been caught they'd have been thrown right out of the academy.[35]

Why was Ike so reckless?

Different explanations have been offered, and one of the most convincing is the explanation of Eisenhower biographer Michael Korda, who suggests that Ike "was kicking up his heels at being away from home, and above all at no longer being subject to his father's rather dour view of life, or his mother's intensely religious sense of right and wrong."[36]

But there was probably something more to it; he was rebelling against the lackluster learning environment at West Point, whose antediluvian teaching methods used the same sort of rote recitation that had killed his enthusiasm for learning in elementary school. Even his enthusiasm for military history turned sour.

Here is the way, according to Ike, that the battle of Gettysburg was presented as an object for study:

> We were required to remember the name of every general officer or acting general officer in the entire opposing forces. You also had to learn what the officer commanded—the exact character of the command. Then you had to remember the situation or position of each of these commands at such and such an hour on such and such a day.... But this wasn't the kind of thing that interested me, so I didn't pay attention.[37]

West Point's lesson on the battle of Gettysburg was (according to Ike) completely stale: there was no critical analysis, no study of the options Lee and Meade confronted, no probing into strategy and tactics, no teaching of any kind that would be *useful* in war.

Was it any wonder that he turned away from academics?

The same dismal teaching methods ruined another of his favorite subjects: mathematics. One day in a course on integral calculus, "the instructor said that on the following day the problem would be one of the most difficult of all. Because he was giving us, on the orders of the head of the Mathematics Department, an explanation of the approach to the problem and the answer."

Ike remembered that the explanation was "long and involved" and that the teacher "was doing his task completely by rote and without any real understanding of what he was talking about." So Ike's attention drifted.

The next day he was ordered to recite the whole exercise, and while he could remember the solution to the problem, he had to do more: he had to recite the procedure that led to the solution. And he had paid no attention to that.

So he improvised: he worked out an approach that made sense and led straight to the solution of the problem.

His instructor was furious. He said, "Mr. Eisenhower, it is obvious that you know nothing whatsoever about this problem. You memorized the answer, put down a lot of figures and steps that have no meaning."

Ike was about to lose his temper when a senior professor dropped by to conduct a "routine inspection." "Just a minute, Captain," said J. Franklin Bell, a math professor who ranked as a major; "please have Mr. Eisenhower go through the solution again." On hearing Ike's procedure, Bell announced that "Mr. Eisenhower's solution is more logical and easier than the one we've been using. I'm surprised that none of us, supposedly good mathematicians, has stumbled on it. It will be incorporated in our procedures from now on."[38]

If Bell had not entered the room, Ike would probably have been tried for insubordination, for he was ready to explode with anger. He revealed this in a letter that he sent to Bell decades later.[39]

So he plunged into *sports* and neglected his studies. He played baseball and football, both of which fired his competitive instincts, but it was in football that he became a star. Coach Ernest "Pot" Graves called him "the best line plunger and linebacker I've ever seen at West Point."[40]

Then disaster struck: in a game with Tufts a week before the big army–navy game, he got tackled hard and hurt his knee badly when he hit the ground wrong. After several days in the hospital, he reported to a riding class and the instructor ordered him to perform a very difficult maneuver on horseback. He lost his balance and fell to the ground with such force that his injured knee was almost torn apart. That knee would be disabled for the rest of his life, and he would never play football again.

He sank into a very deep depression. But he rallied and decided to become a cheerleader, then a coach, thus managing to stay involved in football through creativity and flexibility. He was a success, and he could probably feel his leadership talent on the rise.

And something else was being inculcated in Ike: an instinct for *teamwork* that would make him an exceptional senior officer later. He became skilled in preparing, training, and organizing men.

In a letter to Ruby Norman after a victory over navy in 1913, Ike gave vent to the joyous exuberance that he was feeling at the time:

We surely turned the trick—22-9. Oh you beautiful doll! Some game, some game! Just a small crowd saw us do it, you know. Just 45,000 people. Sure was sad!... You should have seen us after the game. Oh! Oh! Oh! Believe me, girl, I *enjoyed* myself. Course I couldn't raise a riot for I was in uniform—but I went down to Murray's in a crowd of four—and we danced and ate—and oh say—the joy of the thing is too much—I feel my reason toppling.[41]

Ike was long since one of the most fun-loving cadets at West Point. Classmate Joseph Haw recalled that while "there were some remarkable conversationalists in the class," even "the best of them had to talk fast to keep up with Ike. He could and did talk at the drop of a hat about anything, anywhere, anytime."[42]

Ike's growing interest in the female sex got him labeled as a "parlor snake," for he was frisky. He told Ruby Norman, who was playing in an all-girl concert orchestra in New York City, that if he dropped down to visit during Christmas leave "we don't know *what might* happen.... I'm not going to open up and tell you all I'd really like to this evening.... I've changed my views concerning matrimony. I saw in the paper it was 'kisstomary to cuss the bride' so me for it."[43]

Later on, a Brooklyn girl named Dorothy Mills would teasingly call him a "fresh masher."[44] Ike met her in his senior year—when she was dating his roommate.

When Ike got to New York on his Christmas break, he stayed at the magnificent Hotel Astor, a huge beaux arts classical establishment that was located on Times Square. The public rooms were immense, ornate, and splendidly embellished. This hotel had established a special policy for West Point cadets: they could wait until they graduated to pay their accumulated bills and they all got a 25 percent discount.

And Ike loved to dance.

Cadet dances were a feature of the West Point social life, and at one of these events, Ike danced with a girl who was the daughter of a professor. West Point had a prescribed repertoire of dances, with the two-step, the waltz, and the polka predominating. But Ike and his dancing partner defied the rules, and his behavior was observed and reported.

Ballroom dancing was a craze among the young, and new dances were appearing all the time. The bunny hug and turkey trot had appeared when Ike was in high school, and teenagers danced them to ragtime. In 1912, the dancing couple Vernon and Irene Castle became a national sensation in the United States, and the precedent they set would be replicated in the 1930s by Fred Astaire and Ginger Rogers. In 1913, the tango made its debut in the United States.

Ike enjoyed reminiscing about what happened after he had asked the professor's daughter to dance:

> This girl and I liked to whirl; to just whirl around the room as rapidly as we could. I suppose the exercise probably showed a little more of the girl's ankles, possibly even her knees, than the sharp-eyed authorities thought was seemly. I was warned not to dance that way anymore.[45]

But

> I met the girl again and forgot entirely the warning issued earlier. The exuberant sensation of swinging around the room was too much for me to ignore and so, in due course, I was brought before the Commandant. He informed me that I not only danced improperly, but had done so after a warning. For this offense I was demoted from sergeant to private, was awarded a month on the area.[46]

A month "on the area" meant confinement to barracks with "punishment tours"—tedious mandatory work routines—several afternoons a week.

It so happened that Ike had to be in the hospital and on crutches during the month in question due to another injury. So after his release, he had to make up the missed "punishment tours," no less than twenty-two of them.

The giddiness in Ike's behavior at West Point would alternate with moods of deep reflectiveness. At night he would wander out to the ruins of Fort Putnam, built in 1778 by soldiers of the Continental army. He gazed upon the terrain as a military commander would look at it—rehearsing the possibilities for attack and for defense.[47] On a summertime furlough in Abilene, he would take long walks at night by himself, lost in meditation.

18

Eisenhower Presidential Library

Ike at West Point.

As graduation approached, it looked as if Ike might be declared unfit for service and denied a commission in the army because of his knee injury. Lt. Col. Henry A. Shaw, the academy's medical officer, was willing to recommend him for coastal artillery duty, but Ike dismissed that kind of service as unbearably dull. He told Shaw that he would rather move to Argentina and live as a gaucho, and he said that he was taking a look at some travel literature.

So Shaw decided to overrule the academy's medical board, which had voted down a commission for Ike, and appeal to the surgeon general of the War Department. Ike knew nothing of this until years later.

After Shaw got his way, he told Ike that he could recommend him for infantry duty if he avoided service on horseback—in light of the knee injury. Ike agreed, and so he graduated with the class of 1915, awaiting further action by President Woodrow Wilson to give him his army commission.[48]

Looking back, he recalled that throughout his years at West Point, he would often ask himself, "What am I doing here?" He "sometimes wondered—where did I come from, by what route and why; by what chance arrangement of fate did I come by this uniform?"[49]

Well before graduation, he applied for service in the Philippines for a less-than-inspirational reason: military attire in the tropics would require fewer uniforms, so he could save money. Since army officers had to purchase their own uniforms—money was deducted for this reason from the stipends that cadets received—he would get a big refund, and afterward use the money to go on some sort of a spree.

First Love

On a summertime furlough in 1913, Ike looked up an Abilene girl named Gladys Harding. He had a crush on her in high school, and before long he was spending many evenings at the Harding home. He wore his summer white cadet uniform to impress her.[50]

They met again at Christmastime, 1914, when she came to New York with the Apollo Concert Company in which she was a pianist. After Ike's graduation in 1915, she was back in Abilene—waiting for him.

In a few weeks, he was ardently in love, and he proposed to Gladys, who by all accounts was very beautiful. She didn't answer immediately, for two reasons: her father, a well-to-do businessman, took a dim view of marriage to an army officer, since officers in the peacetime army were ill-paid and bored, waiting endlessly for promotions that didn't come for years. In the second place, Gladys was a serious musician. She was about to leave on another concert tour, and she was not at all sure that she was prepared to give up a musical career to be an army wife.

But she thought about it.

Years after she had married someone else, Gladys gave her diary and Ike's letters to her son, with a prohibition on releasing the documents until she, Ike, and Mamie Eisenhower were dead. Years later, her son gave these records to an army officer and historian named Cole Kingseed, who made them available to Eisenhower biographer Carlo D'Este.

Among Eisenhower authors, only D'Este and Merle Miller have seen the full significance of this early experience for Ike.

In the cover note for the packet of letters from Eisenhower that she still retained in 1957, Gladys wrote, "Letters—from Dwight D. Eisenhower—that I rec'd, when we were *young* and *happy!*" On August 5, 1915, she wrote in her diary, "D. asked me to marry him."

She was scheduled to leave for New York on another concert tour on September 1, and they had little time. In mid-August, Ike's commission arrived, and instead of being sent to the Philippines, he was ordered to report to San Antonio, Texas, due to border tensions with Mexico.

Ike was agonized as his amorous feelings grew stronger and could find no satisfying outlet.

I "need and hunger for you," he wrote to Gladys, avowing that "your soldier boy really *loves* you." As September 1 approached, he told her that "this parting is going to be the hardest of my life." He traveled with her to Kansas City, where she was to catch a train to New York, and it appears that in the course of this trip she told him that she loved him.

"My heart seems to choke me," he wrote in a letter just after she had left, because he missed her so. And yet "even while seeing you—I know that you love me—me!" And that knowledge would "help me through the coming year and bring you to me again—to claim you forever and always and now sweetheart good night. Your devoted Dwight."[51]

His torment continued after he arrived at Fort Sam Houston in San Antonio, Texas, one of the army's most magnificent peacetime posts, with its splendid officers' quarters, its handsome quadrangle and parade grounds, its many dozens of military buildings serving multiple uses, and its soaring stone clock tower.

Amid all this military splendor, he was despondent—desolate because of his distance from Gladys. He seems to have been waiting for a final answer on his marriage proposal, and it appears that Gladys was thinking about whether she could give up her musical career and follow Ike wherever the United States Army might send him.

She was trying to sort out her feelings—to make up her mind.

"I can't enjoy life at all," he wrote to her in the autumn months of 1915 in an undated letter. "I was so happy last summer. And now—seems that you are sort of 'drifting'—as you said you would." "With me," he continued, "it's the same old routine day after day, and I have all my evenings to just *think* of you."[52]

In time, however, he reverted to his old West Point routine, playing poker for money, engaging in hijinks, and getting to know his commanders: Colonel Millard Waltz, a veteran of the Spanish-American War, and the base commander, General Frederick Funston, a swashbuckling combat veteran, controversial because of his outspoken advocacy of American imperialism.

Then one day in October, a lady named Lulu Harris, the wife of a major at "Fort Sam," called Ike as he was inspecting guard posts. Ike set down the following recollection:

> "Ike," she called, "won't you come over here? I have some people I'd like you to meet." "Sorry, Mrs. Harris," I called back, "I'm on guard duty and have to start an inspection trip." She then turned to one young girl, as I discovered later, and said, "Humph! The woman-hater of the post." Naturally this caught the attention of the girl, who said something to Mrs. Harris that caused her to call once more. "We didn't ask you to come over to *stay*. Just come over here and meet these friends of mine."[53]

The friends were the Douds, a wealthy Denver family who spent their winters in San Antonio. And the girl—Mary Geneva Doud, who was nicknamed Mamie—revealed later that Ike was the handsomest man she had ever seen.

So it started.

Within months, they were dating: having dinners at a Mexican restaurant called "The Original" by the banks of the San Antonio River, and going to vaudeville performances at an Orpheum theatre.

We will never know what Ike was thinking and feeling about the two women in his life—Gladys and Mamie—in the final months of 1915. While he had proposed to Gladys, she had not committed herself. She told him she loved him, and his ardent passion for her is obvious from his surviving letters.

And we naturally ask ourselves: Were his feelings for Mamie as strong?

In a letter that he sent to Ruby Norman on January 17, 1916, he told his old female friend that "the girl I run around with is named Miss Doud, from Denver. Winters here. Pretty nice—but awful strong for society—which often bores me. But we get along well together."[54]

Faint emotions, compared to his desperate longing for Gladys. But perhaps Ike adopted this tone in the hope that Ruby would notify Gladys (they were friends) that Ike was dating someone else—a maneuver designed to arouse jealousy in Gladys, which might drive her to commit herself.

We will never know.

Ike and Gladys were pulled away from each other by powerful momentum. They were bound for different destinations. It is easy to say that they should have waited for one another—but for how long?

Ike's amorous feelings had been strained to fever pitch in the summer. After parting with Gladys, he had nothing to fall back upon except idle fun—fun with the guys. He had proposed to Gladys, asked her to become his wife. And she had not answered yes or no. She was still not saying yes or no.

And now this new girl had entered his life.

How could he have known at that time that Gladys Harding was developing the settled conviction that she and Ike should get married?

Choices

Mamie was petite, vivacious, insouciant. She was dating other fellows, but she happily went out with Ike, and they had fun.

Was it really as intense as the kind of love that he had experienced the summer before? The question is legitimate as the Eisenhowers' marriage would later be troubled, and the troubles were deep and complex.

It is possible that if Gladys had said yes to Ike's proposal, their relationship might also have succumbed to stresses and strains—the life of an army wife might not have suited Gladys at all.

Still we wonder: Was Ike head over heels in love with Mamie Doud by Valentine's Day, 1916, when they got engaged? Or was Mamie—cute and entertaining as she was at that time—a consolation prize?

Perhaps Ike settled for a *pleasant* instead of a passionate relationship, embraced it for a simple but overpowering reason: *it worked*, and he needed to move on with his life, get over Gladys if she couldn't conquer indecision. If so, he had progressed to a more advanced stage of self-control.

And paid a price for it.

In any case, Gladys was heartbroken when she heard from Ruby Norman that Ike was engaged to someone else. For Gladys had decided to give it all up for Ike. Distraught, she impulsively married Cecil Brooks, a suitor she had once before rebuffed, and the marriage, according to Ruby Norman and her daughter, was loveless.[55]

She still remembered Ike and the summer of 1915, when "we were *young and happy!*"

In 1953, when Ike returned to Abilene in the course of his first year in the presidency, a lady ran out to the motorcade. Ike ordered the driver to halt, and he reached out to embrace his first love. Mamie was reportedly furious.[56]

The memories of what might have been had never gone away.

CHAPTER TWO

Ike the Soldier

Ike's marriage gave him a glimpse of an exciting new world—a world of wealth—for Mamie's family was rich.

John Sheldon Doud, Ike's father-in-law, was a millionaire, and his ancestors came to America in the 1630s. His wealth derived from a meatpacking business that his father created in the 1870s, and he lived with his wife and daughters in a six-bedroom mansion in the affluent Capitol Hill section of Denver. Mamie grew up with servants waiting on her, and she finished her education in finishing school, not high school.

She was a fashionable belle, spoiled by a generous father, but in no way haughty or aloof: she was lively and fun.

Doud and his wife embraced Ike as the son they never had, and the feelings were mutual: his father-in-law became another of Ike's surrogate fathers, as friendly and supportive as "Lord High Executioner" had been distant and cold.

Doud was generous and he gave the young couple financial assistance. His wealth could be summoned, but the couple subsisted for the most part on Ike's army salary.

War and its Aftermath

During his engagement to Mamie, Ike decided it was time to "take a more serious attitude toward life." He had "been too prone to lead a carefree" existence, and it was time "to set my sights on becoming the finest army officer I could."[1]

For Mamie, something comparable happened: she took her role as an army wife seriously, and she strove to be a loyal spouse for a second lieutenant. She braced herself for the relative hardships of living in officers' quarters, and she tried to accompany Ike where he was sent—unless he was given "field duty."

She and Ike planned to get married in November 1916, but in light of the dangers facing America, they got married in July. Tensions on the Mexican border had led to fighting: Pancho Villa staged his raid on Columbus, New Mexico, on March 9, and U.S. forces under the command of General John J. Pershing were sent on a "punitive expedition" to pursue him. If Germany's leaders resumed unrestricted submarine warfare, the United States would have to enter World War I.

President Wilson called units of the National Guard into federal service at the Mexican border, so Ike and other regular army officers were dispatched in "cadres" to train them. Ike was sent to "Camp Wilson"—a tent encampment—to serve as an "inspector instructor" for the Seventh Illinois Infantry Regiment. This gave him his first experience in preparing troops for the possibility of combat, and he was good at it.

After returning to "Fort Sam," he asked General Funston for leave to get married. Funston granted him ten days' leave—an exceptional favor under the circumstances—so Ike and Mamie raced off to Denver by train. After getting married on July 1, they had a brief honeymoon at a mountain resort called Eldorado Springs, then raced back to San Antonio via Abilene, where Ida insisted on cooking them an elaborate fried chicken meal.

Ike and Mamie set up housekeeping in his bachelor quarters at Fort Sam. At first, they ate in the officers' mess, but the mediocre food prompted Ike to cook, using kitchen gear that the couple received as wedding presents. He taught Mamie to cook, and with money provided by the Douds, they bought a small icebox—and a used car.

Ike served briefly as provost marshal for Fort Sam, which meant that he prowled San Antonio to inspect bars—and other locations—to stop regulars and National Guardsmen from fighting. One night, an obviously drunken guardsman took a shot at him.

A month later, he was sent back to Camp Wilson and his marriage with Mamie experienced its first strain.

Eisenhower Presidential Library

A studio portrait of Mamie Eisenhower on her wedding day, 1916.

Mamie didn't like the fact that she was being left by herself so often—even though Ike had given her a gun to protect herself—so they quarreled. Ike told her that duty would always come first, and he said this in such a matter-of-fact way that she felt deeply hurt. Indeed, in Michael Korda's opinion, his statement "could not have been better calculated to chill a romantic and distraught young woman to the bone."[2]

After Germany resumed submarine warfare, Wilson asked Congress for a declaration of war, and on April 2, 1917, the United States entered World War I.

The size of the American peacetime army was small, and so the nation was completely unprepared. When the war broke out in 1914, Theodore Roosevelt urged Wilson to begin a preparedness program.

Wilson stubbornly refused until 1916, and by then the legislative mill was so jammed—and antiwar sentiment in the Democratic Party was so strong—that the appropriations bogged down in Congress for months. The ink was barely dry on the legislation when the war crisis hit.

For this reason, the nation's mobilization in 1917 was a nightmare.[3] Everything was in short supply, the raw draftees needed months of training, and America's European allies were clamoring for troops.

Fort Sam Houston's commander, General Funston, was in line to command the American Expeditionary Forces that would go to France, but then he died of a heart attack, and the command was given to General Pershing.

Eisenhower's newly revealed talents for training and administration would be pushed to the limit. All through 1917 and the year that followed, the army brass would use him as a trainer and logistician. The long-term result for Ike would be an administrative specialization with a lack of combat experience. That would lead to profound results for Ike in the Second World War, and it made him impatient and resentful in the First World War.

He was consumed with the aspiration to get overseas and into action. His ambition "to set my sights on becoming the finest army officer I could" had a logical culmination: leading troops into battle. But he was kept at home because his skills in preparation were so valuable.

He resented it. Many of the officers who would loom large in his military career later on—George C. Marshall, Douglas MacArthur, George Patton—went to France with Pershing and got command or even combat experience. Patton and MacArthur were both wounded and decorated. They were war heroes.

But not Ike.

He was shunted back and forth during 1917 from one location to another, training new recruits. He was also assigned to train new officers. Now as never before, his talent as an operational and logistical planner was revealed.

These experiences revealed something important about Ike: he possessed a *holistic* mind that could see the big picture and relate the parts to the whole. Over time, this capability would be intrinsic to his rise to global fame.

In the meantime, he was an excellent trainer, and that was all that the army brass wanted as far as Captain Eisenhower (he was newly promoted) was concerned.

First, he went to Leon Springs, Texas, north of San Antonio, to create a new tent encampment. A new 57th Infantry Regiment was to be formed at this place, with Ike as the supply officer. He had an unsettling experience: he was struck by lightning in a rainstorm. "All that I was conscious of," he recalled, "was a sort of ball of fire in front of my eyes."[4] He was knocked out, but then recovered.

In September, he was sent to Fort Oglethorpe, in Georgia. Meanwhile, Mamie was pregnant, and she had to stay behind because Ike was on "field duty." Her mother came from Denver to help with the delivery because Fort Sam had no maternity facilities.

The baby, a boy, was born on September 24, 1917, and he was christened Doud Dwight, a name Mamie thought up. She began to call him "Ikey," which eventually devolved into baby talk and became "Icky."

Ike was overcome with emotion. "You could have knocked me over with a feather," he wrote to her. "Why you sweet little old girl, somehow it doesn't seem possible." He signed the telegram, "Your lover—YOU BET."[5] He was granted a three-day leave to see his wife and newborn son, who were just about to leave for Denver.

In December he was sent to a new training operation at Fort Leavenworth, Kansas, with a Christmas leave to visit Mamie and her parents, who were "wintering" in San Antonio, as they did in the old days.

As soon as he arrived, he heard that a machine-gun battalion was being formed at Fort Sam to go to France. He volunteered, and he received an immediate reply from the War Department directing him to follow orders and proceed to Fort Leavenworth.

When he got there, a reprimand was waiting for him. The authorities were displeased by the fact that he was questioning their judgment as to the best use of his abilities.

So he decided to plunge into his work and make the best of it. One of the men he trained called him "a corker" who "has put more fight into us in three days than we got in all the previous time we were here…. He knows his job, is enthusiastic, can tell us what he wants us to do, and is pretty human, though wickedly harsh and abrupt.... He gets the fellows' imaginations worked up and hollers and yells and makes us shout and stomp until we go tearing into the air as if we meant business."[6]

At Leavenworth, Eisenhower took a course himself—about tanks, the new fighting vehicles that were destined to change the course of military history. The concept of an all-terrain military vehicle had been circulating for years, and one of the people who played a key role in developing the tank was the young Winston Churchill. A major breakthrough in the development of tanks had been the invention of the caterpillar tread.

Tanks were in use on the battlefields of France by 1917. The British Mark VI was a lumbering behemoth that crawled in front of infantry and battered down machine-gun emplacements. The French designed a smaller, lighter, and more maneuverable tank, built by Renault.

Strategists and tacticians were turning their minds to the long-term potential of tank warfare. Among the most promising of these theorists were Charles de Gaulle, Heinz Guderian, and George Patton, who commanded the U.S. tank school in France and who would lead American tank units into combat—when Americans finally got into battle by the summer of 1918.

Because he had taken a tank training course at Fort Leavenworth, Ike was rewarded with a change of assignment in February 1918. He was sent to Camp Meade, Maryland—later Fort Meade—to join the 65th Engineers, from which the 301st Heavy Tank Battalion was being developed. This battalion would ship out to France in June. To his delight, Ike was informed that he would command the 301st. While no American tanks were in production yet, French Renault tanks were being shipped to Camp Meade.

But then his orders were changed and his desire to get into combat was foiled again.

Instead of going to France, he would go to Gettysburg, Pennsylvania, to create a new tank training center from the ground up. The army established an independent tank corps, and Ike would be in charge of setting up a camp where recruits would learn about tanks before they went overseas.

This training camp—Camp Colt—would be set up in the middle of the Civil War battlefield. As the troops walked around the encampment, they would see Big Round Top, Little Round Top, Cemetery Ridge, and all the other features of the old battlefield in the background.

Ike did a magnificent job at Camp Colt from the moment he arrived on March 24, 1918. He swung into action to obtain tents, food, and uniforms. "I was very much on my own," he remembered. "There were no precedents…and I was the only regular officer in the command."[7]

This was a major assignment, and he figured out creative ways to simulate tank action using other vehicles—flatbed trucks, for example, with machine guns mounted on top of them—until the Renault tanks arrived. There were ten thousand men and six hundred officers under his command, and he had been promoted to major. Mamie and Icky came to Gettysburg in April, and the family set up quarters in a fraternity house of Gettysburg College.

When the Spanish flu—the dreaded killer flu of the 1918–1919 global pandemic—struck in September, Ike established a quarantine with systematic cleaning of floors with Lysol and kerosene. By the end of October, the emergency was over, and fatalities at Camp Colt were far lower than at other installations.

On October 14, Ike was promoted to lieutenant colonel, and two weeks later he was given orders to ship out to France on November 18. Once in France, he would command an armored regiment.

Then sad news arrived: Mamie's younger sister Edda Mae, nicknamed "Buster," died of a kidney infection at the age of seventeen. Mamie and Icky prepared to return to Denver, and Ike drove them to the Pennsylvania Railroad Station in Harrisburg on November 10.

And the next day…the war was over. Armistice was declared on November 11, and when Ike heard the news, he was enraged. "I suppose we'll spend the rest of our lives explaining why we didn't get into this war," he told another officer. "By God, from now on I am cutting a swath that will make up for this."[8]

The Wilson administration's unplanned demobilization was every bit as chaotic as its ill-planned mobilization. Ike had to hastily dismantle Camp Colt and begin the process of demobilizing the men.

This was a miserable experience.

He and his men were ordered to proceed to Fort Dix, New Jersey. The disassembly of Camp Colt was laborious: "endless hours of planning were required so that we would not find ourselves still camped at Colt, with our kitchen stoves on some railroad siding, and with the other fundamental impedimenta of all military organizations highballing toward New Jersey."[9]

After proceeding to Dix in December, most of the five thousand to six thousand men under Ike's command were given medical exams, paid bonuses, and sent home. Ike was ordered to take enough men to constitute the nucleus of a tank corps—around three hundred men, plus three Renault tanks—to Fort Benning, Georgia, by railroad.

This trip was a nightmare, one of the very worst things that Ike had ever experienced.

The railroad system had been nationalized during World War I under the terms of the Railway Administration Act. The railroads would be returned to private ownership within twenty-one months after a peace treaty was signed, with compensation for the use of the corporations' property.

The U.S. Railway Administration charged fares, and the army rates were low. But during the demobilization, troop trains were given low priority for budgetary reasons. With the war over, railroad officials were eager to bring in the higher-priced fares, and they prioritized service accordingly.

So every other kind of train had the right of way as the troop trains waited their turn. Ike and his men had to wait at whistle stops while passenger trains, freight trains, and milk trains passed them by.

"The trip lasted four days, each about a year long," Ike recalled, as the train languished for hours on railroad sidings, with the men using candlelight for warmth and illumination, since "there were no lights, no heat, no hot water."[10]

When Ike and his troops arrived at Fort Benning after this freezing journey, they had to stay until officials of the War Department decided what to do with the tank corps. He and Mamie could not yet be reunited. There was no way to know when new orders would arrive or what Ike's destination would be. Meanwhile, his temporary promotion in rank would, per army policy, expire because peace had arrived. He would soon be a captain again.

Permanent rank in the army was based upon the seniority system; to be moved up in rank, someone else had to die or retire. It did not matter how good you were or how much you had earned promotion. You stayed where you were until a slot opened up, and you waited your turn based upon longevity of service.

In March, Ike was sent from Fort Benning back to Camp Meade, which would remain the home of the tank corps. He and Mamie stayed separated, for Meade did not have quarters to accommodate families. The nearest cities, Baltimore and Washington, were distant enough that Ike deemed commuting impractical.

Alone, he contemplated what appeared to be a dismal future. He envisioned himself "putting on weight in a meaningless, chair-bound assignment, shuffling papers and filling out forms." He resented the fact that the war had passed him by, and he contemplated resigning from the army to seek work in the private sector.[11]

He did not know how lucky he was.

Many veterans of the First World War would have no jobs at all when they emerged from the army in 1919. One of the most preventable side effects of Wilson's inattention to demobilization was a depression that lasted from 1919 until 1921. This is a forgotten depression in American memory today, but people still remembered it in the Great Depression of the 1930s.

Advisers in Wilson's entourage had recommended public-works programs to generate jobs in the emergency they foresaw. American industries would be shutting down to retool for civilian production. For the duration, jobs would be scarce.

Wilson did nothing.

To compound this problem, Wilson decided to lift the wartime price controls. He did it without any planning. Consequently, the price of civilian commodities—already scarce due to wartime rationing—skyrocketed. The result was sudden inflation.

Here was an early example of what some economists would call "stagflation" in the 1970s: high unemployment combined with high inflation. And since *wage* controls were also lifted, the wages of the people who still had jobs began falling.

People would remember this episode during World War II, and the result would be the passage by Congress in 1944 of the G.I. Bill, a program whose intention was to take returning veterans out of the workforce by paying for them to go to college, even grad school, with stipends for themselves and their families. There might have been another depression after World War II if Americans had not learned from experience.

1919 was a year of mass suffering, with catastrophic strikes by labor unions, riots, and free-floating hatred—including a white supremacist backlash against Black veterans seeking the vote in return for their service to "make the world safe for democracy." Race riots and lynchings led to what some called the "Red Summer" of 1919—red for all the blood that was being shed in peacetime. Both Truman and Eisenhower would face the challenge of preventing a repetition of such things after World War II.

As these horrible events were unfolding, Ike was given an opportunity to get away and have an adventure.

Secretary of War Newton Baker organized a transcontinental convoy of tanks and trucks. The convoy would travel from Washington, D.C., to San Francisco, and Ike volunteered. For once, his superiors in the War Department went along with his wishes.

The purpose of this convoy was to demonstrate the inadequacy of America's road system in motor-age conditions.

A broad-based campaign for better roads had been underway for a decade or more. An organization was established in 1913 to promote a transcontinental "Lincoln Highway," but things had not gotten very far. There were insufficient paved roads to accommodate the burgeoning motor age, and only half of the roads that would be used in the Lincoln Highway project were "improved" by 1919. This meant that roughly half of them were dirt.

"Motoring" for Americans was often nerve-racking. Bad weather conditions turned unpaved roads into obstacle courses or muddy quagmires. One of the selling points for the Model T Ford—in addition to its low price—was its ruggedness, for with the use of vanadium steel and with a brilliantly suspended chassis, the "flivver" could navigate roads that would break the axles and springs of many other cars. But even flivvers had their limits.

Eisenhower Presidential Library

The 1919 motor convoy in perilous terrain.

The War Department's convoy set out on July 7, 1919, from a new "Zero Milestone" on the Mall in Washington. The first leg of the trip was to Frederick, Maryland, and while the roads were decent, the state of the art in 1919 motor vehicle design left much to be desired. Fan belts kept breaking, spark plug casings cracked, tires punctured, valves stuck, and the list of mechanical mishaps for the convoy went on and on.

Ike calculated that the average hourly speed of the convoy was only five and two-thirds miles per hour because of such problems. And as the convoy moved westward, the roads became nonexistent.

But Ike had a wonderful time. At night, he and the others pitched tents and broke out cards for a bridge game. Ike was "roughing it" again. He and a buddy named Sereno Brett played pranks, including a hoax of an Indian attack in Wyoming.

Mamie and the Douds joined the convoy for a leg of the trip in Nebraska. They went back to Denver when the convoy reached Wyoming. At last, the convoy arrived at its destination on September 6.

Ike never forgot the experience, and it inspired him later to create the Interstate Highway System.[12] But another experience from 1919 would also figure in the conceptualization of Ike's interstate program. As conceived in 1954, the program was deliberately designed to reverse economic contractions that could lead to joblessness.

Peers and Mentors

Ike was meeting some of the officers who would serve with him in the next world war: Omar Bradley and Mark Clark, both of whom he met at West Point, Leonard "Gee" Gerow and Wade Haislip, whom he met at Fort Sam Houston, and George Patton, whom he met when he returned to Camp Meade after the motor convoy.

Ike and Patton had a number of things in common, mostly their expertise in tanks. They both enjoyed profane humor, they both had terrible tempers, and they both liked to ride and to shoot. They were both ambitious. They got along well in the autumn of 1919, and before long they were friends.

Patton, however, was strikingly different from Ike. He was wealthy. He bred horses, played polo, drove expensive cars, and showed aristocratic good manners with a special flair for charming women when he was not demonstrating the profane "blood and guts" behavior for which he would become famous.

He was a born warrior, and he extolled the joy of battle. His grandfather was a colonel in the Confederate army, and his lineage and heritage obsessed him.

It wasn't just the fact that he was descended from English nobility. He believed—or so he said—that he was the reincarnation of military geniuses from antiquity, and that he had a supernatural destiny to fulfill through warfare.

This very strange man became a boon companion to Ike. And their friendship centered on *the tank*. Ike, who had run the army's domestic tank training center at Camp Colt, was eager to learn what the tank had been like in battle. Patton could tell him.

They both believed that another world war was coming, and they talked about serving together. Patton envisioned a partnership for them along these lines: "This is what we'll do," he said. "I'll be Jackson, you'll be Lee. I don't want to do the heavy thinking; you do that and I'll get loose among our #96&%$# enemies."[13]

Before long, they were developing visionary ideas about tank designs for future wars and the role of tanks in the strategic thinking of the future. They disassembled tanks one bolt at a time and then put them back together. Army tank doctrine was mired in the notion that the role of the tank would stay the same: tanks would crawl in front of infantry to clear the way.

Ike and Patton wanted tanks that were built for *speed* to transform the nature of modern war.

"George and I," wrote Ike years later, believed that tanks could have "a more valuable and spectacular" role in war. "We believed that they should be speedy, that they should attack by surprise and in mass. [They could] cause confusion, and by taking the enemy's front line in reverse, make possible not only an advance of infantry, but envelopments of, or actual breakthroughs in, whole defensive positions."[14]

They conducted experiments at Camp Meade, making use of the tanks that they had—big Mark VIIIs as well as the small Renault tanks—to simulate the sorts of maneuvers they envisioned.

They had adventures that bonded them because the things that they did were dangerous. One day they were using a Mark VIII to tow smaller Renaults that were attached by cables. Ike remembered the experience because he and Patton could have died when a cable snapped:

> In the midst of the racket we heard a ripping sound and we looked around just in time to see one of the cables part. As it broke, the front half whirled around like a striking black snake and the flying end, at machine-gun bullet speed, snapped past our faces, cutting off brush and saplings as if the ground had been shaved with a sharp razor. We were too startled at the moment to realize what had happened but then we looked at each other. I'm sure I was just as pale as George. That evening, after dinner, he said: "Ike, were you as scared as I was?"[15]

They had other adventures too. One night, they drove off base packing Colt automatics. They were looking for a fight. Years later, Ike recalled that he and Patton "had been told that the road was full of highwaymen. We wanted to run into one so we could see the guy's face when he found himself looking down the barrels of two guns."[16]

Eventually, Ike and Patton took their tank theories to a higher level. "We analyzed tactical problems...used at Leavenworth in Command and General Staff School courses," Ike recalled. "After comparing our solutions with those approved by the Leavenworth faculty, we would add... our dream tanks and solve it again. The troops supported by tanks always 'won,' in our revised solution."[17]

They wrote up their doctrine and submitted articles to *Infantry Journal* extolling the potential of the tank to revolutionize war.

They were both...reprimanded.

Ike was called into the presence of Major General Charles S. Farnsworth, the army's chief of infantry. He was told to desist from advocating doctrines that challenged the army's standard method or face a court-martial. So he and Patton were peremptorily silenced.

Decades later, he would have the power not only to envision newer ways of waging war but to *command* them.

Resistance to innovation at the War Department went beyond mere stodginess in the 1920s. There was a higher politics. The army was facing a wave of isolationism, antiwar sentiment, and shrinking military budgets. Progressive thinking in military circles ran the risk of being condemned as "warmongering."

Farnsworth's threat of a court-martial was not an idle one, as events would prove. In 1925, Brigadier General William L. "Billy" Mitchell would be court-martialed for warning that America was falling behind in military aviation.

The backlash of American isolationism between the world wars— strong in both political parties—derived from bitter feelings combined with exhaustion after all the hysteria, violence, and division in 1919. It was no accident that Warren G. Harding won the 1920 presidential election with the slogan "Back to Normalcy."

America had not joined the new League of Nations, and this fueled a sense of letdown after the "war to end wars." By 1920, there was a widespread sense that the war had been futile—a sense that all those men had "died for nothing."

If Woodrow Wilson had played his cards differently, America might have entered the League with bipartisan support. Former President William Howard Taft led a group called the "League to Enforce Peace" (LEP) that supported the League of Nations and even Senator Henry Cabot Lodge was ready to negotiate on terms for America's participation.

But Wilson would not negotiate. His refusal to compromise derived in part from mental impairment, for well before the stroke that he suffered in October 1919, he suffered from arteriosclerosis, first diagnosed in 1906, which can lead to episodic dementia.

In any case, more and more Americans were convinced in the 1920s that America should never again get "suckered" into meddling in "Old World" problems.

Ike took note of these things. And his resolution to stave off a new wave of isolationism would be one of the reasons why he chose to run for the Republican presidential nomination in 1952.

Both Ike and Mamie wanted their episodic separations to come to an end.

Mamie scouted out locations in and around Washington, D.C., and discovered that she could rent a room in Laurel, Maryland, well within an hour's commuting time from Camp Meade. But she couldn't take the cramped quarters after she and Ike lived there for a month, so she went back to Denver.[18]

In May 1920, the War Department began to permit the expansion of officers' quarters to accommodate families provided that the officers covered the cost of the renovations themselves. So Ike and Patton became neighbors in renovated barracks. Mamie came up and sent for Icky, who had been living with an aunt in Boone, Iowa. He was three years old in the autumn of 1920.

He began playing with the Patton children, and Mamie got to know Patton's wife Beatrice. Meanwhile, Ike and Patton were enjoying themselves producing bootleg liquor in defiance of Prohibition.

Patton and his wife entertained at their new abode, and one evening they invited Ike to come for dinner so that he could meet Brigadier General Fox Conner, who had served as operations officer for Pershing in France.

This encounter would change Ike's life.

Like Patton, Conner came from a wealthy background—in his case, the planter class of Mississippi. Soft-spoken and scholarly, Conner was an intellectual, a student of history, and a visionary. Like Ike, Patton, and Billy Mitchell, he was interested in the technological advances that would change the face of battle.

After dinner, Conner asked Ike to brief him on the new tank doctrines. After the briefing, Conner said he found it extremely interesting, gave his thanks, and departed. A few months later, he notified Ike that he was being sent to the Panama Canal Zone to command an infantry brigade. He asked Ike to come along as his executive officer.

Ike was overjoyed, but, as usual, the War Department bureaucrats rejected this latest in a series of requests for a different assignment.

Yet Fox Conner was not a man to be easily thwarted when he wanted something. He and others knew that another world war was coming, and they were on the lookout for young officers with leadership potential.

Ike had been promoted from captain to major when Icky arrived at Camp Meade. These months were the happiest that Ike could remember, for he wanted the family life that his field duty had prevented. He was eager to plunge into parenthood and become a doting father, not only for the happiness but also to make up for his own father's coldness. He would give his little boy what he had been denied.

Icky was a happy child at age three, and Ike reveled in his cute antics.

Before long, the Eisenhowers were entertaining, and, according to granddaughter Susan Eisenhower, their quarters were "a second home for young officers who were tank zealots." They "adopted the Doud tradition of a Sunday buffet open house," which became known as "Club Eisenhower."[19]

Then tragedy struck.

They decided to hire a local girl to help Mamie with the housekeeping. They didn't know that she was suffering from asymptomatic scarlet fever. Icky caught it. The doctor at Camp Meade brought specialists from Johns Hopkins Hospital, but little could be done. At the end of the year, Icky died.

Ike would always proclaim that this disaster was the worst of his life. "We were completely crushed," he wrote. "Even now as I write of it," he reflected two years before his own death, "the keenness of our loss comes back to me as fresh and as terrible as it was in that long dark day soon after Christmas, 1920."[20]

Sometimes couples are brought together by shared sorrow. But in the opinion of biographer Jean Edward Smith, that did not happen for Mamie and Ike. "Instead of drawing closer together, each retreated into a private world of sorrow," he concluded.[21] This conclusion is affirmed by Julie Nixon Eisenhower, who wrote that "the loss of their beloved son closed a chapter in the marriage."[22]

Ike began to develop gastrointestinal problems, a health condition that would plague him for the rest of his life, and there can be little doubt that depression and stress were the triggers.

Fox Conner, who would play the role of Eisenhower's guardian angel, pulled strings, and he soon got his way.

Conner was close to John Pershing, who had just become the new chief of staff. So he paid a call upon the general. Suddenly, orders came down from the War Department for Ike to join Conner in Panama. Ike was about to have the time of his life.

And Mamie would hit rock bottom. This would be the greatest ordeal to which their marriage had yet been subjected.

Some believed they were close to a divorce before it was over.

They traveled to Panama on the troopship *San Miguel* and arrived on January 7, 1922. Ike remembered that "the accommodations were miserable."[23] The passengers were packed together like sardines, the ship was caught in a gale, and Mamie, pregnant with their second child, suffered from morning sickness, seasickness, and claustrophobia.

When they got to Panama, they faced stifling heat, oppressive humidity, insects, lizards, mildew, and the sorts of diseases that had cost so many lives in the building of the Panama Canal. They had to walk across the Canal itself on a narrow catwalk over one of the locks to reach Camp Gaillard, the army's post.

They found that their quarters consisted of a broken-down, decrepit, infested house on stilts that was built by the French decades earlier.

Conner and his wife were in a house next door, but the general's wealth had permitted him to renovate it. Ike and Mamie would be living in a place that had to be reclaimed from the inhabitants: rats, snakes, insects (including disease-infested mosquitos), lizards, and bats. The rainforest was encroaching on the side porches.

And here was Mamie Doud, young belle of the Denver Douds—pregnant in these stygian conditions. Ike admitted that the place had its problems, but for him it was just another challenge of...roughing it. For her it was nothing less than purgatory.

Virginia Conner, the general's wife, believed that "the marriage was clearly in danger.... Ike was spending less and less time with Mamie, and there was no warmth between them. They seemed like two people moving in different directions."[24]

Mamie's parents came to visit in June, and they decided this was no place for their daughter. So Mamie was whisked back to Denver on the next steamer. The baby was born on August 3, and Ike was there, thanks to Conner, who granted him leave. The baby, a boy, was christened John Sheldon Doud Eisenhower, after Mamie's father.

Mamie stayed in Denver for several months, while Ike returned to Panama. She rejoined him in the fall, having decided to try again. But this time she brought along a nurse to help care for the baby.

In light of what happened to Icky, it is interesting that she chose to return at all.

She was willing to give it another try, and her determination showed; Virginia Conner reported that "after Johnny was born and Mamie felt better, she began to change. I had the delight of seeing a rather callow young woman turn into the person to whom everyone turned. I have seen her, with her gay laugh and personality, smooth out Ike's irritability."[25] This was an interesting turn of events—but more twists and turns were on the way.

For Ike, Fox Conner was the mentor of his dreams—a teacher who gave him the kind of instruction he should have received at West Point. But this was even better because the instruction was coming in a personal tutorial. Conner was grooming Ike as a protégé who would rise in the high command.

Together, they rekindled Ike's enthusiasm for military history. Conner gave him historical novels, then moved right along to the classics like Caesar's *Commentaries* and Tacitus. He added Plato and Shakespeare. Returning to military topics, they covered the campaigns of Frederick the Great and Napoleon. They studied the American Civil War with an emphasis on strategy.

"General Conner questioned me closely about the decisions made— why were they made and under what conditions," Ike recalled. "'What do you think would have been the outcome if this decision had been just the opposite?' 'What were the alternatives?'"[26]

Conner made Ike read Clausewitz's *On War* three times, then quizzed him.

They moved on to the problems of coalition warfare, a sore point in World War I. They discussed the uses of psychology to get allies to work like a team. Ike recalled that "he laid great stress in his instruction to me on what he called 'the art of persuasion.'" Conner even got out "a book of applied psychology and we would talk it over."

Here was preparation for the role that Ike would play as supreme commander of Allied forces in Europe during World War II.

They went out together on horseback, camped at night in the jungle, discussed strategy over the campfire. Every geographical feature they encountered would be used for instructional purposes: How would Ike handle such terrain from the standpoints of attack and defense? Conner also taught Ike how to write out orders as commanders write them out.

Is it any wonder that Ike would revere Conner for the rest of his life? This instruction was *perfectly* adapted to his sensibilities.

And Mamie...sank back into despondency.

"I was down to skin and bones and hollow-eyed," she remembered, so she went back to Denver again, taking John and the nursemaid with her.[27] According to Susan Eisenhower, Mamie took a look at her marriage and compared it to the marriages of friends she could observe in Denver. She decided Ike was better as a husband than most of the others, so she went back to Panama and stayed there with Ike until his tour of duty ended in September 1924.

Michael Korda has concluded that while Mamie probably "learned from Mrs. Conner, apparently a perfect example of an army wife, just what it took to push a husband's career in the narrow world of the old peacetime army," it "also seems likely that she laid down some conditions of her own."[28] Korda guessed that a tough new quid pro quo was established in the marriage as Mamie learned how to stand up to Ike and make him pay more attention to her needs.

"She does not say outright that she was contemplating divorce" as she recovered her health and took stock of her marriage, Korda muses, "but when one reads between the lines it seems likely that the thought had crossed her mind."[29]

Tough love is what it took to preserve their evolving relationship.

Conner was ordered to Washington in the summer of 1924. He would serve as deputy chief of staff for logistics. Pershing's term as chief of staff was coming to an end.

It was obvious that Conner had been grooming Ike for the high command, and a transition in his self-image was underway. Even though he continued to express the desire to be commanding troops—rather than occupying a "desk job"—he had already started to imagine himself working at a higher level.

But the same old dreary routine was awaiting him when he returned from Panama. He was sent to Camp Meade to be assistant coach of the III Corps Area football team. After that, he would go to Fort Benning to command the 15th Light Tank Battalion. At least he would have the direct command of troops that he said he wanted.

But this wasn't enough anymore, and he knew it.

He decided "it was high time I was getting to one of the established army schools."[30] He wanted to begin at the Infantry School, which the army created in 1921 to provide advanced training for infantry commanders. If successful, he might go on to attend the Command and General Staff School (CGSS) at Fort Leavenworth.

The Infantry School came under the authority of Ike's old nemesis, General Farnsworth. But it just so happened that the school was located at Fort Benning, where Ike would be sent in any case. So he made an appointment with Farnsworth to plead his case—to request advanced training when the football coaching was over.

The result was entirely predictable; Farnsworth told Ike to carry out his orders and sent him on his way.

Some have theorized that Farnsworth might have been giving Ike dead-end assignments as punishment for being insubordinate.

They also theorize that Ike paid a call upon Conner after meeting with Farnsworth. As he made his way out of the old State, War, and Navy Department building—an enormous Victorian edifice next to the White House that still exists and is now named in Eisenhower's honor—he may have knocked upon Conner's door.

In any case, Conner dashed off the following telegram to Ike: "NO MATTER WHAT ORDERS YOU RECEIVE FROM THE WAR DEPARTMENT, MAKE NO PROTEST. ACCEPT THEM WITHOUT QUESTION. SIGNED CONNER."[31] In Ike's memoirs, he called this telegram "cryptic in the extreme."

But he probably knew why Conner sent it.

Conner was covering himself, for he would go on working behind the scenes for Ike. He was also seizing an opportunity for more postgraduate instruction. His message (between the lines) was simple: keep a poker face and don't reveal your intentions to opponents. Ike had long ago learned to keep a poker face, and it was time to put this knowledge to higher use.

Within months, he was transferred to Fort Logan, Colorado, to serve as an army recruiter. It dawned upon him that this was one more move on the chessboard by Conner.

The method was to take Ike out of Farnsworth's jurisdiction—long enough to get him sent to Fort Leavenworth—since recruiting was completely outside of Farnsworth's authority. In the meantime, Fort Logan was seven miles from the Doud home in Denver, giving Ike a chance to be with his family. Conner seemed to think of everything.

And then in April, 1925, Ike was suddenly ordered to attend...the Command and General Staff School at Fort Leavenworth. Farnsworth had been outmaneuvered again. Patton, who had graduated with honors from CGSS, sent Ike a hundred pages of notes from his coursework.[32]

One of Ike's fellow students at Fort Leavenworth was a friend from Fort Sam, Leonard "Gee" Gerow. Mamie became good friends with Gerow's wife, who taught her how army wives advanced their husbands'

Ike, his parents, and his brothers at their Abilene home, 1925.

careers. She also regaled Mamie with the satisfactions of the social whirl in army politics. Under the influence of Katie Gerow, the belle of the Denver Douds decided that such a life might not be so bad after all. This would mark an upward turn in the marriage.

Meanwhile, Ike graduated first in his class.

After his superb performance, he was back under the jurisdiction of Farnsworth, who naturally struck back. He ordered Ike to report to Fort Benning and command the 24th Infantry Regiment. Among other things, he would be coaching football again.

Biographer Jean Edward Smith was the first to point out that the 24th was an all-Black outfit. He suggested that Farnsworth might have been attempting to lower Ike's stature in the racially segregated army.[33] Pershing had commanded the 24th before his service in the First World War, and his nickname "Black Jack" was not intended as a compliment. It was intended as a stigma. The upper echelons of government were rife with bigotry.

Mamie and Ike went down to Fort Benning, but Conner—right on schedule—outmaneuvered Farnsworth again.

On December 15, 1926, Ike was ordered to report to the American Battle Monuments Commission in Washington. He would be working for Pershing, and his task would be to help compile a record of America's participation in World War I. Conner was sending Ike to his next career-building assignment under a new mentor: Pershing, the commander of the American Expeditionary Forces in the First World War. The next few years would be extraordinarily pleasant.

Ike and Mamie moved to Washington, and a graceful way of life awaited them. Ike worked in the State, War, and Navy Building—a federal office building rather than a military base—and so the Eisenhowers lived like the other well-to-do residents of the nation's capital and Ike could wear business suits instead of a uniform. Mamie went shopping at Washington department stores, and she and Ike paid calls upon well-connected Washingtonians. Mamie loved it.

They rented a suite at the luxurious Wyoming apartment house, a beaux arts masterpiece in the ritzy Kalorama neighborhood above Dupont Circle. The building, constructed in 1905, still exists.

Club Eisenhower was back in operation.

Ike's younger brother Milton, an intellectual destined to achieve great things in the world of higher education, was working in Washington at the same time. He was a staff assistant to the secretary of agriculture, so he and Ike saw each other regularly.

Biographer Stephen Ambrose, who claimed that he interviewed Ike and Milton in the 1960s, tried to shed some light upon Ike's political and ideological development. In recent years, historians have questioned whether Ambrose really conducted these interviews—one of several unpleasant footnotes in the life of this scholar who became a celebrity author.[34] But for what it may be worth, according to Ambrose, Ike

discovered he was more conservative than Milton. His brother...was chiefly concerned with what the government could do for the people (in his own case, especially farmers), while Dwight in both their theoretical and practical discussions, found that he put the emphasis on the duty of citizens toward the government. In general, Milton saw a positive role for government and wanted it to grow, while Dwight saw a negative role and wanted it to shrink (except, obviously, in the military).[35]

It bears noting that laissez-faire—the creed of minimal government—was the order of the day in the Republican administration of Calvin Coolidge, but farmers were struggling in the 1920s, since crop prices were collapsing and farm income dropped. This foreshadowed the great farm crisis of the 1930s. And such things were of great interest to Milton.

Farm lobbyists persuaded Congress to pass a relief bill, the McNary–Haugen Act of 1927, which would have boosted crop prices through government purchases of "surplus" crops, which would then be sold overseas. This would alter the flow of supply and demand in the farmers' favor. Coolidge vetoed the bill.

Such issues prefigured Ike's proposal in his presidential years of a "Soil Bank" that would take land out of cultivation to raise crop prices and help out the farmers.

The American Battle Monuments Commission was created by Congress in 1923 at Pershing's request. Its task was to "beautify" the cemeteries in France where Americans who died in battle during World War I were buried. To make these sites more significant for visitors, Pershing commissioned Ike to write a "battlefield guide." The result was entitled *A Guide to the American Battlefields in Europe*, and it comprised a history of American participation in World War I.

This was a plum assignment for Ike, as he lived in posh surroundings with Mamie.

Ike's exultation must surely have increased when Pershing lauded his "splendid service."[36] Then another opportunity arrived: Ike was selected to attend the prestigious Army War College in southwest Washington, D.C. There were no tests or grades at the war college; students wrote papers, and Ike chose the potent topic of mobilization, another demonstration of his interest and skill in logistics.

The school commandant rated Ike's accomplishments "superior," calling him "a young officer of great promise."[37] Ike was soon invited to join the War Department general staff.

But Pershing offered him a different reward: a tour of duty in France to inspect the battlefields and cemeteries. Ike was at first reluctant to go: he was eager to move up the ladder and receive the promotion to lieutenant colonel that would come with his service for the general staff.

But Mamie was in favor of accepting Pershing's invitation. "Honey, let's go to Europe," she begged; "this gives us an opportunity to see the Old World and travel."[38] Ike went along in a morose state of mind and then enjoyed one of his most memorable larks to date.

Ike, Mamie, and John embarked for France in August 1928 aboard the ocean liner *America*, accompanied by Mamie's parents.

Mamie did an excellent job of finding them accommodations in Paris; she booked a hotel and scouted out apartments to rent. She found a nice one on the right bank of the Seine on the Quai d'Auteuil, and she also found a school for John.

So they settled down in the radiant city where American sophisticates were flocking to escape Prohibition. The Eisenhowers moved in different circles from Jazz Age luminaries like Scott and Zelda Fitzgerald, Ernest Hemingway, Gertrude Stein, James Joyce, and all the other literati in Paris. But their abode, the latest "Club Eisenhower," was a place of revelry, bridge games, and cocktails.

Ike traveled through the French countryside, making friends with ordinary people (his driver served as interpreter), and he studied the terrain where so many millions had been killed a decade before. Here was the terrain where he had not been allowed to fight. He took his son John along on many of these trips.

As he took in the cemeteries, especially the one at the Somme—that slaughterhouse where thousands of British soldiers were massacred in 1916—he saw headstones stretching almost to the horizon. The French were at work on the Maginot Line to defend themselves against the future onslaught that Marshal Ferdinand Foch and Georges Clemenceau had warned them was coming. And there was no guarantee that the British or Americans would come to their assistance again when they needed it.

Ike asked for leave and took Mamie and some friends on a seventeen-day automobile trip through Belgium, Germany, and Switzerland.

He was pleased to be seeing Germany, the land of his ancestors, for the first time. In five years, Hitler would be chancellor.

Ike's relationship with his son was taking on a strain that would vary over time. John would sometimes feel insecure around him. Perhaps Ike was compensating for Mamie's behavior, for after losing Icky, she subjected John to overprotective "smother love," and Ike strove to make sure that his son was growing up *tough*.

He became a tough disciplinarian—never punitive in physical terms as his father had been, but inclined to scold. He was close to reenacting the cold father-son relationship from which he had suffered. "Dad was a terrifying figure to a small boy," John recalled, and while they grew closer to each other in some ways, John always felt he had to measure up.[39]

There were obviously tensions at work—tensions that were seeking an outlet.

It bears noting that *Pershing* was a distant sort of person himself—aloof and austere. After Ike finished the guidebook, Pershing asked him to help with the drafting of his war memoirs. Pershing scrutinized every punctuation mark, and Ike had to be extremely diplomatic—delicate, if not deferential—in expressing opinions since he differed with Pershing as to the best literary format.

Pershing was inclined to present his diary entries verbatim, whereas Ike believed this would frustrate readers and cause them to put the book aside. With great tact—with all the diplomacy he could muster—Ike persuaded Pershing to let him take a crack at composing some narrative text, and Pershing gave him the go-ahead.

Pershing was impressed, but he wanted to solicit the opinion of a colonel who had served him as one of his closest aides in the war: George Catlett Marshall. Ike recognized the name, since Conner told him Marshall was "a genius" whom he ought to try to meet and cultivate.[40]

Marshall, renowned for his razor-sharp mind and his stern dedication to duty, sized up Ike's composition. He liked what he saw, but he counseled Ike to let Pershing have his way and write his memoirs just the way it pleased him.

Ike saw the wisdom of that, and Marshall saw the potentiality of Ike as a promising officer with greater things in store for him.

Ike was becoming a master of tact in the presence of men who could advance his career. The insouciant attitude of earlier years was replaced by a new calculation for the sake of career-building. There was a new willingness to suppress disagreements—even angry ones—if necessary. Some of this was military discipline, but some of it bespoke a new fluency in the art of political maneuver.

Something had changed in Ike's outlook, and there can be no doubt that Fox Conner and his lessons in psychology made it happen.

In his memoirs, Ike commented on the belief of "cynics" that "it's not *what* you know, it's *who* you know." He admitted there was "just enough truth in that phrase" to accord it some respect.

Looking back, he offered readers this advice: "Always try to associate yourself closely with and learn as much as you can from those who know more than you, who do better than you, who see more clearly than you. Don't be afraid to reach upward. Apart from the rewards of friendship, the association might pay off at some unforeseen time."[41]

In the parlance of our own times, he was recommending the art of networking—an art that he had learned from Conner.

Many people down the years would be impressed by the finesse Ike had at his disposal. He was supremely diplomatic when he needed to be, and he could seem deferential as he scrutinized people and came to his own conclusions.

A memorable demonstration of this finesse was recorded years later by one of his former speechwriters. The scene was the Eisenhower farm at Gettysburg, where Ike was receiving a visitor, General Harold K. Johnson, a former army chief of staff. In the course of their conversation, Ike's visitor declared: "Herodotus wrote about the Peloponnesian War that one cannot be an armchair general twenty miles from the front." After Johnson departed, Ike's speechwriter asked him to recite the quotation again.

Ike replied, "First, it wasn't Herodotus, but Aemilius Paullus. Second, it wasn't the Peloponnesian War, but the Punic War with Carthage. And third, he misquoted." Asked why he didn't say anything, Ike answered this way: "I got where I did by knowing how to hide my ego and hide my intelligence. I knew the actual quote, but why should I embarrass him?"[42]

Within a few years, he would need every bit of this self-restraint when he went to work for one of the most arrogant, tyrannical, and insufferable people to wear the uniform of a general since the days of George B. McClellan in the Civil War.

We are speaking of Douglas MacArthur, but more on that momentarily.

After spending a year in Paris, Ike was anxious to recover the opportunity to serve the War Department's general staff. Major Xenophon Price, Pershing's executive officer, tried to keep him in France, so Ike cabled—who else?—Fox Conner, whose latest tour of duty had sent him to Hawaii.

Ike was ordered back to America.

The Eisenhowers sailed aboard the SS *Leviathan* from Cherbourg on September 17, 1929—just as the Wall Street crash was beginning.

Ike's work for the general staff would build upon the mobilization paper he wrote at the War College. Wilson's ill-planned mobilization of 1917 still rankled in the memories of influential people, though the antiwar moods of the 1920s made it risky politics to speak of such things.

One of the people who proposed to do something to prevent a repetition of that fiasco was Ike's new boss: Major General George Van Horn Moseley, the principal military adviser to Assistant Secretary of War Frederick Payne.

Moseley wanted a plan for the mobilization of industry in the event of a future war, and he entrusted this task to Ike. "I am particularly pleased with this detail," Ike wrote in his diary.[43]

To receive more training for this assignment, Ike attended the Army Industrial College, established in 1924 and successively renamed the Industrial College of the Armed Forces and then, most recently, the Dwight D. Eisenhower School for National Security and Resource Strategy.

Eisenhower attended the college from 1930 to 1933, and he consulted with people like the international financier Bernard Baruch, who had played a key role in the World War I mobilization.

Ike's flair for administrative operations and logistics was further developed in the course of this work—developed to the point where he was becoming a master of systems analysis.

System Failure: The Economy Contracts

In ideological terms, there was something ironic in this situation, something that forced Ike later—much later—to revisit the minimal-government doctrines he espoused in his talks with brother Milton.

Stephen Ambrose noted the irony years ago in his comments about Ike's mobilization study for the War Department:

> A job more out of joint with the times could hardly be imagined. Over the next three years, the worst years of the Great Depression, Eisenhower's task was to plan for plant expansion, at a time when factories all across the land were closing their doors; to plan for material shortages, at a time when no buyers could be found anywhere for enormous quantities of goods already stockpiled; to anticipate a manpower crisis, at a time when one-third of the American work force was unemployed; to draft legislation for an explosion of government expenditures and deficit financing, at a time when the Hoover Administration was trying to reduce government costs and activities in order to balance the budget.[44]

Ike told Milton that he favored smaller government—except in war. But what about emergencies in *peacetime*?

Ike was on his way to becoming an organizational wizard. He was achieving this status at a time when America's economy was going through a massive *systemic breakdown*. An out-of-control chain reaction was sucking financial relations down a vortex. Irresistible force was pulling everything inward and downward.

Any student of systems analysis could see what was happening if they took the time to analyze it.

Economic historians still argue about the causes of the Great Depression, and the disappearance of corporate records makes their work difficult. Moreover, the catastrophe was global. But the records that do survive make the following reconstruction plausible.

The 1929 crash put tremendous pressure on banks—banks that overextended themselves by lending money for stock speculation. Most of the Wall Street speculators bought their stocks with borrowed money. This was called buying "on margin."

Many of these borrowers defaulted on their loans because they lost everything. So what did the bankers do? Here is what they did: they started calling in other sorts of loans to stave off insolvency.

As this happened, corporations had to speed up repayment of bank debt. They diverted funds they would otherwise have used for operations—including payrolls. They laid off workers and suspended operations. As unemployment spread, the customer base of the economy shrank, because people with no income could no longer purchase goods. Shrinking sales caused layoffs of more workers, and the chain reaction fed on itself. Meanwhile, a wave of commercial bank failures beginning in 1930 threatened the complete collapse of commercial banking by 1933.[45]

Here was a study in *systems analysis*—a study in *systemic implosion*.

By 1933, the level of unemployment in the United States had risen to thirteen million, with no end in sight.[46]

In 1932, the British economist John Maynard Keynes predicted—on the basis of the wipeout of purchasing power—that only government could reverse the chain reaction through projects that put people to work, put money in their pockets, and persuaded businessmen to resume hiring, since the purchasing power that was necessary to sell the goods had been restored.

In an article for *Atlantic Monthly*, Keynes wrote that "there will be no… escape from prolonged and perhaps interminable depression except by direct state intervention to promote and subsidize new investment." Governments must, he wrote, "be ready to spend on the enterprises of peace what the financial maxims of the past would only allow us to spend on the devastations of war. At any rate, I predict with an assured confidence that the only way out for us is to discover *some* object which is admitted even by the deadheads to be a legitimate excuse for largely increasing the expenditure of someone on something!"[47]

There can be little doubt that Ike was observing this situation in the years between 1930 and 1933.

Early in his presidency he advocated a massive public-works project to counteract a recession: the Interstate Highway System.

In the meantime, did he still believe in the small-government maxims he shared with Milton? If so, *to what extent* did he still believe in them? It is important to ask these questions as we track his ideological and political development.

Conservatism and Liberalism in the Great Depression

Small-government maxims were consistent with Democratic Party doctrine before the 1930s. From Andrew Jackson's time onward, Democrats viewed government as the friend and protector of *the rich*.

So it was consistent for Ike to tell Milton that he favored small government in light of the sympathy he expressed for the Democratic Party in his 1909 speech to the Young Men's Democratic Club.

The *Republicans* in Lincoln's day were the ones who supported "big government." *Republicans* built the transcontinental railroad and created the land-grant college system in the Civil War. In Theodore Roosevelt's day, such attitudes still survived in the Republican Party.

But in the twentieth century, the Republican Party became divided—and so did the Democratic Party.

In a slow transformation that Jacques Barzun once called "the great switch," the creed of small government crossed ideologies—it ceased to be a "liberal" doctrine and became a "conservative" doctrine—and it moved across party lines. By the 1920s, conservatives within the Republican Party opposed "big government."

Meanwhile, Democrats were moving toward the stance that would be adopted under FDR: that big government could serve the poor and help the unemployed.

These issues are important as we track the evolution of Ike's political and ideological views. The culture of the officer corps in the years before World War II tended toward conservatism—even ultraconservatism.

In the view of Eisenhower biographer Jean Edward Smith, "Ike shared the Regular army officers' animosity to 'socialism.'"[48] And some of the members of the officer corps harbored attitudes that went beyond "conservative" and merged with the culture of the extreme far right.

Smith characterized Patton's outlook, for instance, as "ultra-conservative, bigoted, and racist." He observed that Ike's new boss at the War Department—George Van Horn Moseley—"stood out as the exemplar of racist xenophobia, white supremacy, anti-Semitism, and political repression."[49]

A study of anti-Semitism in the pre-World War II United States Army—*The "Jewish Threat:" Anti-Semitic Politics in the U.S. Army* by Joseph W. Bendersky—has documented the extent of such views in the officer corps, although Moseley's opinions were extreme. In World War II, he welcomed the Holocaust as something that he felt Jews deserved "for the crucifixion of Christ."[50] He said that Jewish refugees fleeing to America should be accepted only "with the distinct understanding that they all be sterilized before being permitted to embark."[51]

Against this sinister background, it might seem alarming that Ike and Moseley got along. What are we to make of this?

Moseley was a competent officer. Even such a paragon of decency as George Marshall praised Moseley's abilities upon his retirement in 1938.[52]

So the fact that Ike got along with Moseley proves nothing in regard to his own political views. As it so happened, Ike sympathized with the European Jews, and he even considered taking part in a plan that might have rescued them—as we shall see.

But the Ike-Moseley relationship does suggest that Ike was starting to develop the power to get along with people while turning a blind eye to their faults. And this sheds important light upon the power of mental compartmentalization that Ike was developing.

In his diary, Ike called Moseley "a wonderful officer—a splendid gentleman and a true friend."[53] In Jean Edward Smith's opinion, the psychology was obvious: "Moseley had become a surrogate for Fox Conner."[54]

Speaking of Moseley in his memoirs, Ike wrote that his "outspoken reaction to public questions, often political, got him a bad press. Many who did not know the man himself may have thought him a reactionary or a militarist. The impression he created was a distortion, I am sure."[55]

Was Ike really unaware of how evil a man Moseley was? Perhaps. There were things he didn't care to know.

In any case, his need for father figures would come to an end with the outrageous behavior of his new boss, Douglas MacArthur.

Servitude Under Macarthur

President Herbert Hoover appointed General Douglas MacArthur as the army's new chief of staff in 1930. Moseley and Ike were both pleased by the change, since the departing chief of staff, Charles Summerall, had not been enthusiastic about their mobilization study. MacArthur was enthusiastic.

A new episode in Ike's career was beginning, one that would plunge him into the politics of the Depression and subject him to the whims of a boss so capricious that Ike was led to the brink of emotional and physical breakdown by the end of the decade.

MacArthur was a legendary figure. He had earned great renown, and he dramatized himself so effectively that people who yielded to the power of his charisma often looked upon him as a god-like figure. He came from a wealthy background, like Patton—but his ambitions and delusions of grandeur exceeded anything that Patton's personality could have generated.

His father, Arthur MacArthur, won the Medal of Honor in the Civil War, and he served as governor-general of the Philippines in 1900 and 1901. Douglas MacArthur's mother idolized her son and built his ego to stupendous proportions.

She told him to grow up like Robert E. Lee, and she stayed in a hotel at West Point so he could feel her very presence. He graduated as the valedictorian of his West Point class in 1903, and then he served as an aide-de-camp to President Theodore Roosevelt.

In World War I, he was wounded in combat and won the Distinguished Service Cross, the Silver Star, the Purple Heart, the French Legion of Honor, and the Croix de Guerre. He was a war hero. And his egotism swelled as he prepared himself for what he felt to be a world-historical destiny. He believed himself to be a genius.

Some people grew faint in his presence, for he knew how to gather around him a cohort of weak personalities. Stronger people were disgusted by his affectations and his swagger. He sometimes knew he was going too far, and so he learned how to flatter and be charming. His theatricality spanned the range, but his penchant for excess never left him.

His actual skills as a commander in wartime have been fiercely disputed by military historians and others.

In 1919, he was appointed superintendent of the U.S. Military Academy at West Point. He retained his wartime rank as major general, instead of being restored to his peacetime rank like Ike and most other officers.

In 1922, he married Louise Cromwell Brooks, an extremely wealthy heiress. Rumor had it that Pershing was his rival in the courtship. The two men grew to dislike one another—intensely. Pershing thought that MacArthur was a damnable egotist, and MacArthur resented what he called the "Chaumont crowd": those who had served with Pershing at AEF headquarters instead of fighting at the front, like himself.

After their wedding, MacArthur and his wife departed for the Philippines, where he would serve as commander of the military district of Manila. By 1930, the marriage ended in divorce, and he was back in Washington.

This was the man who would be Ike's new boss, and they got along splendidly at first. Ike was dazzled by MacArthur's prestige and his access to the power players in Washington.

MacArthur made Moseley his deputy chief of staff, and he promoted Ike to take Moseley's place as an adviser to the assistant secretary of war, Frederick Payne.

Ike's talents came to MacArthur's attention, and so MacArthur decided to reassign Ike to himself.

Ike's industriousness was useful to MacArthur, who depended on a busy staff to carry out his wishes—not least of all because of his long absences from the office in midday. He was absent for trysts with a beautiful Filipina actress named Elizabeth Cooper, who was born Isabel Rosario Cooper. He got her an expensive apartment in the Chastleton apartment house on Sixteenth Street north of the White House.[56]

To make up for these absences, MacArthur worked far into the night, and he forced the members of his staff to keep the same hours.

The first of Ike's assignments for MacArthur was to draft a recommendation to Congress. In response to antiwar sentiment, Congress created a War Policies Commission. Isolationists were claiming that America was duped into War I by munitions makers and war profiteers. This new commission, to be chaired by War Secretary Patrick Hurley, would make recommendations. Ike was assigned by MacArthur to work with the commission.

Ike wrote the final report, which recommended a constitutional amendment clarifying Congress's power to prevent profiteering. MacArthur delivered this recommendation in congressional hearings, and he expressed his gratitude to Ike with a special commendation, lauding him for "excellent work," for "successful accomplishment in the highest degree," and for his overall display of "outstanding talents."[57]

Before long, those talents were being demanded by Payne, Moseley, and MacArthur all at once, and Ike began to work six-day weeks. He often stayed in the office until eight or nine o'clock at night. The stress took a toll on his health, and he began to experience flare-ups of the gastrointestinal problems that appeared after Icky's death.

In December 1931, Ike decided he was tired of doing high-level staff work in Washington. He and Mamie agreed that it might be a good idea to request a tour of duty back at Fort Sam Houston, so he applied for it. He needed a break from the relentless Washington grind, and he was not at all certain what he wanted in his army career: the old longing to be in direct command of troops retained its allure.

But MacArthur requested him to stay, and the flattery was more than Ike could withstand. "Gen MacA was very nice to me," he wrote in his diary, "and after all I know of no greater compliment the bosses can give you than I want you hanging around."[58]

So he stayed.

By the summer of 1932, he was MacArthur's man-of-all-work. He made his servitude vivid in his memoirs. "My office was next to his," Ike recalled, and he was always at MacArthur's beck and call; "only a slatted door separated us. He called me to his office by raising his voice."

And "on any subject he chose to discuss, his knowledge [was] poured out in a torrent of words. 'Discuss' is hardly the correct word; discussion suggests dialogue and the General's conversations were usually monologues."[59]

Moreover, his monologues were often political. "Most of the senior officers I had known always drew a clear-cut line between the military and the political," Ike recalled, "but if General MacArthur ever recognized the existence of that line, he usually chose to ignore it."[60] MacArthur's political convictions were ultraconservative.

At MacArthur's side, Ike learned more and more about politics in Washington. His initiation into politics began a long time before the presidential kingmakers sought him out. As Michael Korda has said, "Ike was never the simple soldier he made himself out to be, certainly not after his return to Washington ... and his apprenticeship in military politics beside Douglas MacArthur."[61] Before long, this newest apprenticeship would extend to civilian politics as well.

The Bonus Army

In the summer of 1932, Ike was still under MacArthur's spell, and he played a role in an incident that made the name of Douglas MacArthur notorious.

Economic conditions for millions hit rock bottom in 1932. From an estimated 1.5 million unemployed men in 1929, the ranks of the unemployed had swollen to 4.3 million in 1930, and that figure doubled to eight million by 1931. By 1932, it was twelve million.[62] From all indications, this trend would continue, and the reason was simple: there was no counterforce in existence to propel things back in the other direction.

This is purely a matter of systems analysis.

People in the nation's capital were comparatively insulated from the crisis because the jobs of federal workers remained secure.

But in other American cities, the situation was horrendous. By October 1931, over 40 percent of the workforce in Chicago was unemployed.[63] Chicago social worker Louise Armstrong remembered seeing "a crowd of some fifty men fighting over a barrel of garbage that had been set outside the back door of a restaurant. American citizens fighting for scraps of food like animals."[64]

In the countryside, things were often worse: in Pennsylvania coalfields, another social worker reported seeing families "freezing in rickety one-room houses, subsisting on wild weed roots and dandelions."[65]

In 1924, Congress had voted to pay an old-age bonus to the veterans of World War I. This bonus would be paid two decades later—in 1945. In 1929, Congressman Wright Patman of Texas introduced a bill to pay the bonus immediately. President Hoover opposed the legislation because it would unbalance the budget.

In May 1932, several hundred unemployed veterans on the West Coast organized a march on Washington. Calling themselves the "Bonus Expeditionary Force" or Bonus Army, they were led by a veteran named

Walter Waters, and they traveled through American cities holding out a big flag as they marched down the main thoroughfare, so that people who were looking at them from windows could throw down nickels and dimes to help them pay for gasoline and food. Other marchers rode the rails in boxcars to get to Washington.

By summer, around twenty thousand unemployed veterans were in Washington, and Police Superintendent Pelham Glassford appealed to the federal government to help the city feed and house them. Hoover quietly agreed to a loan that permitted the construction across the Anacostia River—in a place called Anacostia Flats—of a tent encampment equipped with field kitchens. He also allowed the marchers to camp out in some abandoned buildings. The marchers augmented their tents with huts constructed of plywood. They built some of these huts on the National Mall.

On June 15, the House of Representatives passed the Patman bill, but it stalled in the Senate. On June 17, the Senate defeated it.

In response, some of the Bonus marchers turned angry and violent. Some of them stoned the cars of senators who voted against the bill, and many of the marchers remained in Washington.

In July, the local authorities began cutting off the humanitarian support, and Hoover got Congress to authorize a loan that would help the marchers get home.

On July 28, federal and local officials ordered the police to clear the marchers out of abandoned buildings and return them to their encampment across the Anacostia. Violence broke out. Superintendent Glassford requested federal assistance, and Hoover ordered MacArthur as army chief of staff to take charge of returning the marchers to their encampment and to do so without excessive force.

MacArthur took charge of the operation in person.

As early as May, he and Moseley had agreed that the Bonus marchers were a communistic rabble. Moseley activated "Plan White," a contingency plan to protect the federal government against domestic insurrection.

So when MacArthur received Hoover's orders on July 28, he put on his uniform and ordered Ike to do the same. He took command of the operation in the streets of Washington and brought Ike along.

Library of Congress

Douglas MacArthur on the streets of Washington routing the Bonus Army, 1932.

George Patton brought cavalry and tanks from Fort Myer across the Potomac River and assembled his forces on the Ellipse, south of the White House.

In the action that followed, infantry used bayonets and tear gas and Patton's cavalry used sabers and tanks to force the veterans back across the bridge. Hoover ordered MacArthur to halt at the bridge—and under no circumstances to pursue the veterans back into their encampment.

Hoover sent that order twice. Moseley delivered it the first time, and then Col. Clement B. Wright, secretary of the army general staff, delivered it the second time.

MacArthur disobeyed these orders.

He directed his troops to cross the bridge and enter the veterans' encampment.[66] Newsreel cameramen recorded the scene, and it was shown in movie theaters all over the country. The encampment was set afire, and the veterans and their families fled the city. Several people had been killed, including children.

Hoover declined to do what Harry Truman would do roughly twenty years later: relieve MacArthur of command. MacArthur claimed that his disobedience of orders resulted from some miscommunication.

He was lying.

In his memoirs, Ike sought to distance himself from what MacArthur had done. He claimed that he told MacArthur that "the matter could easily become a riot and I thought it highly inappropriate for the Chief of Staff of the army to be involved in anything like a local or street corner embroilment." He even went so far as to claim in an interview with biographer Stephen Ambrose that "I told that dumb son-of-a-bitch that he had no business going down there."[67]

In his memoirs, Ike expressed sympathy for the Bonus Marchers, stating that "restraint and a reasonable amount of good humor marked the veterans' attitude."[68]

And though Ike soft-pedaled MacArthur's disobedience, he did it in a manner so ironic that it bordered on sarcasm.

He wrote that when Moseley and Wright delivered Hoover's orders, "in neither instance did MacArthur hear these instructions. He said he was too busy and did not want either himself or his staff bothered by people coming down and pretending to bring orders."[69]

Biographers Geoffrey Perret, Merle Miller, Carlo D'Este, and Jean Edward Smith believe that Ike was sugarcoating his memories. They assert that he was far more in sympathy with MacArthur's actions than he claimed to have been in later years.[70]

In the aftermath of the Bonus Army rout, Ike wrote in his diary on August 10, 1932, that "a lot of furor has been stirred up but mostly to make political capital."[71]

Ike drafted MacArthur's official report on the incident. In this report, MacArthur (in Ike's words) claimed that "the troops largely avoided actual physical contact with rioting elements," and that "at no time did I give orders" for "initiating the destruction of the encampments." Ike's draft for MacArthur claimed that the fires must have broken out spontaneously.[72]

Eyewitness accounts accused the soldiers of torching the encampment, and some photographic corroboration exists. A newsreel documentary shows soldiers battering down some plywood huts in the encampment.

And then a soldier can be seen tossing a sheet of plywood from a demolished shack onto a bonfire.[73]

In the months that followed, journalists Drew Pearson and Robert Allen wrote columns attacking MacArthur for the way the incident was handled. Ike was outraged. He wrote in his diary that "the two men are innately cowards" engaging in "ceaseless attempts to belittle a man recognized as courageous, if nothing else."[74]

MacArthur sued the journalists. But he was forced to drop the suit when they threatened to reveal his affair with Elizabeth Cooper.

"Dictator Ike"

Notwithstanding all this, Ike was *not* in support of the policies of President Hoover.

And this is of the utmost importance.

Looking back upon the Depression in his memoirs, Ike acknowledged that "the government had to alleviate distress and minimize hardships."[75] And when FDR won the presidential election in 1932, Ike was pleased. "I believe it is a good thing the Democrats won," he wrote in his diary.[76]

He had no particular ideas about what FDR ought to do, but he did proclaim something startling. "Things are not going to take an upward turn," he wrote, "until more power is centered in one man's hands. Only in that way will confidence be inspired; will it be possible to do some of the obvious things for speeding recovery, and will we be freed from the pernicious influence of noisy and selfish minorities. For two years I have been called 'Dictator Ike' because I believe that virtual dictatorship must be exercised by our President. So now I keep still—but I still believe it!"[77]

This statement was not in most respects as bad as it might seem today.

It is important to understand such opinions in historical context. When Ike wrote those words, Hitler had been chancellor of Germany for less than a month. The horrors of the Third Reich had barely started. True, Mussolini had established his fascist dictatorship in Italy and Joseph Stalin was effectively the dictator of the Soviet Union. But most of the horrors of Stalinist rule—the famine he created in Ukraine, for example, to enforce the collectivization of farms—were effectively covered up, so they did not come to the world's attention until later. Visitors to the Soviet Union like George Bernard Shaw sent back glowing accounts.

Many people in those days took Latin in high school, and they read the ancient classics, including Titus Livy's account of what "dictatorship" meant in the ancient Roman republic. In times of emergency, the elected leaders of Rome would sometimes lay down their powers and summon a man universally renowned for his courage, intelligence, and trustworthiness. Such a man was the hero-dictator Lucius Quinctius Cincinnatus, who, after rescuing Rome, stepped down and let things return to normal.

Early in 1933, a Hollywood film called *Gabriel Over the White House* was shown in movie theaters. The film told the story of a president named Judson Hammond, played by Walter Huston, who decides that heroic action is imperative to save the American people from the Depression.

When a march of unemployed veterans descends on the nation's capital, Hammond goes forth to greet them. He says they will be inducted into a magnificent "army of construction" that will bring back prosperity. After Congress refuses to carry out his proposals, Hammond declares martial law, adjourns Congress, assumes dictatorial powers, and then... saves America. After doing so, he dies—conveniently for all, since his mission has been accomplished—and things return to normal.

At the end of FDR's first year in office, Ike set down his thoughts about Roosevelt's performance. "Only history can render a verdict as to the wisdom of Pres. Roosevelt's policies," Ike wrote. "But as definitely as has ever been done in this country...the people gave the Pres. a mandate to revise our economic processes and to take charge of our nation in leading it out of the wilderness of depression. The only chance for success is to follow where the Pres. leads."[78]

Ike was keeping an open mind as he watched the New Deal unfold.

Over time, his instinctive distrust of "big government" reasserted itself. But his conviction that government must counteract depressions grew stronger.

FDR was no dictator. But he was very much afraid that a real dictator might oust him and seize power if he could not bring recovery. One of the men he feared most in this way was Senator Huey P. Long of Louisiana.

Biographer William Manchester relates that just after the Bonus Army incident FDR was at Hyde Park, conferring with Rexford Guy Tugwell, a professor who would soon become a member of his "Brain Trust." The telephone rang, and it was Senator Huey Long on the phone.

Long had established a near dictatorial rule in his home state, which he veritably ran by remote control from the Senate. He was touting a plan to redistribute the nation's wealth, and he clearly had his eye on the White House. When Roosevelt put down the phone, he expressed the opinion that Long was one of the two most dangerous men in the country. Who was the other one, asked Tugwell, guessing it was probably Father Charles Coughlin, a demagogic priest whose radio broadcasts had given him a huge following.

"Oh no," replied FDR. "The other one is Douglas MacArthur."[79]

In November 1934, retired Marine Corps General Smedley Butler told the Special Committee on Un-American Activities of the House of Representatives that he had been approached by a corporate executive with the following proposition: he would create a fascist organization of veterans to conduct a coup d'état that would oust Roosevelt and create a dictatorship.

Butler's story was corroborated by James E. Van Zandt, the national commander of the Veterans of Foreign Wars, who said that he had been approached with the very same proposition.[80]

MacArthur's term as chief of staff would come to an end in November 1934. FDR offered the position to Fox Conner, who declined. The next eligible candidate was George Moseley, and FDR knew all about Moseley's far-right politics.

MacArthur requested an extension of his term as chief of staff, and FDR pondered the matter. He urgently wanted to get MacArthur out of the country.

So he invited the general to Hyde Park, and he made the following offer: he would extend MacArthur's term as chief of staff into 1935, until his successor was appointed. MacArthur would go to the Philippines, where he would help prepare the archipelago for national autonomy, which Congress had determined should be phased in by 1946. In the interim, the Philippines would have its own "commonwealth" government under the military protection of the United States.

MacArthur would be the American proconsul, the first American high commissioner for the Commonwealth of the Philippines.

FDR turned on the flattery, an art in which he excelled MacArthur many times over. He had secretly loathed MacArthur for years.

Roosevelt piled on the following incentives: MacArthur would remain on active duty while becoming the commander of the Philippine army. He would be provided with a rent-free suite at the lavish Manila Hotel, plus a monthly stipend that would exceed $40,000 in today's values.

MacArthur agreed right away. And then he invited Ike to join him in the Philippines as his deputy.

Ike himself would get a suite at the Manila Hotel plus a monthly stipend that would make him the second highest-paid officer in the army.

Neither he nor Mamie really wanted to go to the Philippines—notwithstanding his earlier and quixotic application to go there when he graduated from West Point. Once again, he was weary of the bureaucratic grind, and he longed for the simpler duty of commanding some troops.

Or so he told himself.

On the other hand, his service with MacArthur had given him a vast amount of knowledge concerning politics and government. He had accompanied MacArthur when he testified before Congress and met with the president. He had even heard FDR rebuke MacArthur in comparatively gentle terms when MacArthur expressed himself too vehemently. "You must not talk that way to the president," said FDR, and some have speculated that Ike would remember that scene when Bernard Law Montgomery was rude to him after D-Day. "You can't speak to me like that," Ike said, "I'm your boss."[81]

For all the stress of working for MacArthur, Ike's vistas had continued to broaden. And he had learned enough about power politics to know that, for better or worse, he was known as "MacArthur's man." As Michael Korda has observed, he had also learned what the disfavor of MacArthur could mean. Consider the following example.

Pershing had requested MacArthur to promote George Marshall to brigadier general, and MacArthur had refused. He had nothing but contempt for Pershing and his entourage. Instead of promoting Marshall—one of the most gifted young officers in the army—MacArthur sent him to a dead-end assignment, into exile as an instructor for the Illinois National

Guard. That was exactly the sort of thing that Charles Farnsworth had once done to Ike.

Korda argues convincingly that "Ike, as a mere major, was well aware that MacArthur could make or break him.... After all, if an officer as distinguished as Colonel George C. Marshall could be sent to Chicago to instruct the Illinois National Guard, there were plenty of other remote army posts in which Major Eisenhower could look forward to years of coaching the football team until he reached retirement age."[82]

So Ike agreed to go with MacArthur to the Philippines.

And thus began one of the worst ordeals of his life.

In the Philippines

MacArthur told Ike that he could bring along an officer of his own choice to be his deputy, and Ike chose a friend from West Point, Major James B. "Jimmy" Ord, who had worked with him in Washington and who was also fluent in Spanish.

FDR promised MacArthur that he would remain chief of staff until December 15, 1935. It was important to MacArthur that he retain the four-star rank that went along with that position when he came to Manila.

So he prepared to ship out.

And FDR would soon be rid of a dangerous general—a general whom he regarded as one the two most dangerous men in America. He was rid of the other one already, since Huey Long had been assassinated in September 1935.

On October 1, 1935, MacArthur and the rest of his party—his still-adoring mother, Ike, Ord, and several others—left Washington, heading to San Francisco, where they would board the steamship *President Hoover* for the voyage to the Philippines. MacArthur, divorced from his first wife in 1929, was about to meet his future wife, Jean Faircloth, in the course of this voyage.

Mamie Eisenhower refused to come along.

She said she was afraid of the tropics, afraid of contracting some disease that might kill her—or kill their son. "Gee" and Katie Gerow had just returned from the Philippines, and Katie was deathly ill. She soon passed away. And though the disease that killed her turned out to be cancer, Mamie feared she might have died of a pestilential disease from the tropics.

Mamie did not want a repetition of the wretched Panama experience. She confessed in a letter to her parents that while "I hate to let him go alone," she was "*scared*." And there was more to it than that.

She wanted their son John to finish the 1935–1936 school year. She was also reluctant to leave the Wyoming apartment building, the only secure home that she had ever known in her marriage with Ike.

After all, she reasoned, "This job may peter out or Ike might not be able to stand the climate."[83] So she would wait.

She enjoyed the way of life they had shared at the Wyoming; she liked entertaining at home surrounded by her favorite things; she liked dressing up and going out to call upon Washington socialites.

She had no idea of the fury her decision would kindle in Ike. He felt betrayed.

He was bitter, but he kept his feelings hidden. Mamie had no way of knowing the costliness of her decision.

As the train with MacArthur and his party reached Cheyenne, Wyoming, MacArthur got a nasty surprise, and it arrived by telegram.

FDR was savoring the exquisite pleasure of double-crossing Mac-Arthur. He broke his promise that MacArthur would retain his rank and would remain chief of staff when the ship arrived in the Philippines.

FDR went ahead and appointed someone else to be army chief of staff: Malin Craig, a member of the Pershing circle whom MacArthur detested.

When MacArthur found out, he was livid—overcome with wrath. But he pulled himself together and dashed off a telegram congratulating FDR on a good choice.

Jean Edward Smith got it right when he summed up the episode this way: "MacArthur needed the support of Craig and FDR in the Philippines, and he groveled accordingly. For Eisenhower, it was an unforgettable insight into the nature of Washington politics at its highest level."[84]

As Ike settled into his new routine in Manila, his friendship with "Jimmy" Ord deepened. Their mission was to prepare a defense plan for the Philippines to be used in case of Japanese attack.

During Hoover's presidency, Japan had attacked Manchuria without provocation and converted it into a puppet state. World War II had already broken out in Asia when MacArthur and Eisenhower set foot in the Philippines. In 1937, Japan unleashed a ferocious attack upon China and accounts of the Japanese atrocities horrified the world.

In the 1920s, a defense plan for the Pacific had been drawn up: Joint Army–Navy Basic War Plan Orange, which provided for deployment of troops to the Philippines if war broke out. But dwindling congressional appropriations had forced a contraction of the plan. By the mid-1930s, Plan Orange drew the American defense perimeter from Alaska to Hawaii to Panama—leaving the Philippines out.

MacArthur was confronting an impossible mission in the Philippines because of these realities. But instead of confronting the facts, he sank into avoidance. He established vague policy guidelines, and left Ike and others to carry on while he stayed at home in his hotel.

Ike noticed MacArthur's inattention. "We are at a loss to determine what the question of policy may be," he wrote in his diary on January 20, 1936.[85]

MacArthur declined to consult with President Manuel Quezon of the Philippines. "Things happen," wrote Ike on May 29, 1936, "and we know nothing of them. We're constantly wondering whether the President [Quezon] will approve or disapprove. We ought to know. We could if the general would take the trouble to see Q weekly—but apparently he thinks it would not be in keeping with his rank and position for him to do so!!!!"[86]

Consultations with Quezon were important, since most of the Philippine army's expenses were paid by the Philippine government. Budgetary planning with Quezon was necessary, but MacArthur neglected it—or else he made plans that were based upon wildly inflated and overoptimistic presumptions.

Ike's early admiration of MacArthur—admiration that extended at times to the brink of hero-worship—was turning to disdain. Within the next few years, this disdain would turn to outright disgust, and eventually to hatred.

As MacArthur neglected the substance of his military duties, he obsessed about the pomp and ceremony of his office. Early in 1936, Ike was appalled to discover that MacArthur was considering the possibility of becoming a field marshal in the Philippine army. Ike expressed his opposition to this idea, and he suffered the consequences. "Oh Jesus! He just gave me hell," Ike recalled.[87]

MacArthur continued to retreat into a world of fantasy. "From late 1935 to 1938," recalled Robert Eichelberger, who worked for Malin Craig at the War Department, MacArthur boasted that "'the Japanese would not invade the Philippines, but if they do, in case of war, we shall meet them on the beaches and destroy them.'"[88]

Ike began to detach himself from MacArthur's orbit. And he found new ways to divert himself. He took flying lessons, something he had wanted to do for a long time. He began to play golf at the army-navy club. He paid calls upon President Quezon, making up for MacArthur's negligence, and before very long he had an office at the presidential palace. He discovered that Quezon loved to play poker and bridge, and he was soon attending parties on the presidential yacht, the *Cassiano*.

He was living the life of a bachelor, and his anger at Mamie deepened.

Granddaughter Susan Eisenhower has affirmed that Mamie was maintaining an active social life in Ike's absence, "and word of her apparent independence and resourcefulness no doubt made its way to Manila."[89] Ike was seen playing bridge and golf with Marian Huff, the pretty wife of a naval aide to MacArthur. Jean Edward Smith has ventured to suggest that "whether there was anything more than golf and bridge between Ike and Marian Huff is a matter of conjecture."[90]

Another crisis in the Eisenhower marriage was underway.

Having failed to hear from Ike for many weeks, Mamie finally decided to close the apartment in Washington and move with John to Manila. Ike met them at the dock. On the way to the hotel, he said that "I gather I have reason for a divorce, if I want one."[91]

The resentment was mutual. Even though Mamie discovered that her fears about living in the Philippines had been exaggerated—and she also discovered that a highly satisfactory social life had been awaiting her—she could not help informing her parents that "the only way I can get along" with Ike "is to give him his own way *constantly*."[92]

Even so, she did try to fix things. She took golf lessons in the hope of displacing Marian Huff as Ike's partner on the golf course. But she didn't like the game, and so she turned her mind to other things.

She was aware of how much her husband liked Marian Huff, because he talked about it. Ike and Mamie were harboring an insidious amount of anger toward one another, and this would have consequences.

In late summer 1937, Chief of Staff Malin Craig advised MacArthur that his regular tour of duty in the Philippines would be coming to an end. MacArthur threw a tantrum. He wrote to Craig that "your letter has amazed me. The action suggested would constitute my summary relief… Considering rank and position it can only be interpreted as constituting disciplinary action." He "found the thought repugnant of resuming to a subordinate command after having been military head of the army."[93]

So he requested retirement.

MacArthur's request was approved, effective December 31, 1937. Even so, he would remain in the Philippines as a field marshal in the Philippine army. FDR's reasons for keeping him far away had not changed. The upshot was that Ike would become the senior United States officer on active duty in the Philippines, though he would not be in *command*.

He had finally been promoted to lieutenant colonel.

He was not at all sure that he wanted to stay. MacArthur's behavior remained insufferable. On October 8, 1937, he wrote in his diary that "now I'm at a cross road. If the Marshal is to persist in making things unpleasant…then I'm for home…. I'm disgusted." He poured out this disgust as follows:

He was raised in the conception of Douglas MacArthur superiority. Actually he has become only pathetic. The barest mention of his name in the gossip column…sends him into hysterical delight or deepest despair…. I shall never forget the time in Washington when receipt of instructions to report to the President led him to conclude, in the greatest seriousness, that he was to be invited to be the President's running mate in the succeeding election.[94]

Meanwhile, an instance of MacArthur's duplicity had arisen, and Ike recorded it in the same pages of his diary.

MacArthur foisted a budgetary overrun on Quezon, despite the objections of Ike and Jimmy Ord. Then he shifted the blame to Ike and Ord when Quezon found out. "I've got to decide," Ike wrote, "whether I can go much further with a person who, either consciously or unconsciously, deceives his boss, his subordinates, and himself (probably) so incessantly as he does."[95]

In January 1938, Ike was hospitalized with a severe intestinal obstruction. Then his friend Jimmy Ord was killed in a plane crash. For the sake of his sanity and health, he would soon have to extricate himself from his servitude to MacArthur.

Ike's tour of duty was set to expire in October 1938. At the request of Quezon and MacArthur, he asked for a one-year extension, provided that he and Mamie could return to the United States for three months. To take Ord's place, Ike appointed Major Richard K. Sutherland, whom he and Mamie had known when they lived in Wyoming.

Why did he agree to stay on in the Philippines? He was probably experiencing doubt about the options available. He needed time to assess his situation, and a trip to the United States might help him to size things up.

Besides, the mission of preparing the Filipinos to defend themselves was of interest to Ike, no matter how unrealistic the prospects were. He was held in high esteem by Quezon. He was heavily involved in the buildup of Filipino forces, and he found the work inspiring.

But as he flew above the Philippines in his plane, it was obvious to his strategic mind that defense against Japanese attack required the kind of air and naval forces that could not at that time be assembled because of the existing priorities in Washington.

And the Japanese were becoming more belligerent all the time. An air of unreality pervaded the scintillating social life of Manila. People avoided the thought of their approaching doom by yielding to escapism.

During Ike's visit to the United States, he lobbied Malin Craig for more arms and supplies for Philippine defense. And he made the convincing argument that defense of the Philippines could constitute a holding action that would buy time for mobilization in the event of war. Craig was impressed.

On the return trip, Ike visited Lieutenant Colonel Mark Clark, his old friend from West Point, who was stationed at Fort Lewis, Washington. Ike expressed an interest in getting an assignment to serve at Fort Lewis after his Philippine duty ended.

Upon returning to the Philippines, he discovered that Sutherland had stabbed him in the back. He convinced MacArthur that Ike was scheming to take his place as commander of the Philippine army.

So MacArthur promoted Sutherland to be his chief of staff and demoted Ike to operations officer.

At last, Ike's contempt for MacArthur boiled over. His diary entry of November 10, 1938, seethed with rage. MacArthur, he wrote, was "as stupid as he is crooked." He was "a fool, but worse he is a puking baby."

It was "incomprehensible that after 8 years of working for him, writing every word he publishes, keeping his secrets, preventing him from making too much of an ass of himself... he should suddenly turn on me." Especially stupid, wrote Ike, was the fact that MacArthur would "deliberately make enemies of anyone that he feared might in the future reveal the true story of his black and tan affair." This was an allusion to MacArthur's dalliance with the Eurasian mistress.

"Oh hell," Ike concluded, "what's the use? Now that I've jotted all this down I hope that it never again comes, even momentarily, to my mind."[96]

As he waited for his tour of duty to expire, a very interesting offer came his way in early 1939. The Nazi Kristallnacht pogrom—which had taken place November 10, 1938—quickened worldwide interest in helping German Jews to escape while there was still time. And it just so happened that a significant Jewish community existed in Manila. Ike had made friends among these Filipino Jews, many of whom were refugees from Nazi Germany.

"Through several friends," Ike recalled, "I was asked to take a job seeking in China, Southeast Asia, Indonesia, and every other country where they might be acceptable, a haven for Jewish refugees from Nazi Germany. The pay would be $60,000 a year."

He thought about resigning from the army to accept this job.

"But," he recalled, "I had become so committed to my profession that I declined."[97]

His fight against Hitler, the man who had defiled the land of his ancestors, would take a different form.

CHAPTER THREE

Ike the Commander

Late in 1938, Ike wrote to Mark Clark, asking him to use his influence to get him transferred to Fort Lewis, in Tacoma, Washington, as a battalion commander. Clark had connections with George Marshall, the incoming army chief of staff. On May 27, 1939, the orders came through: Ike would go to Fort Lewis.

The date for Ike's departure would be December 13, 1939. On September 23, Ike told Clark that he felt "like a boy who has been promised an electric train for Christmas."[1]

Several weeks earlier, Hitler had attacked Poland and World War II began in Europe. In his diary, Ike expressed his rage:

> For a long time, it has seemed ridiculous to refer to the world as civilized. It doesn't seem possible that people that proudly refer to themselves as intelligent could let the situation come about. Hundreds of millions will suffer privations and starvation, millions will be killed and wounded because one man so wills it. He is a power-drunk egocentric, but even so he would still not do this if he were sane. He is one of the criminally insane, but unfortunately he is the absolute master of 89,000,000 people.... Hitler's record with the Jews, his rape of Austria, of the Czechs, the Slovaks and now the Poles is as black as that of any barbarian of the Dark Ages.[2]

76

The Advent of George C. Marshall

George C. Marshall, army chief of staff from 1939 to 1945, was one of the principal architects of victory in World War II, and he and Ike became a team. They had a great many things in common, but their personalities were different.

Both of them were small-town boys, and their experiences in childhood were strangely similar.

Marshall was born in Uniontown, Pennsylvania, and his family relations were comparable to Ike's: he had a father who was hard to please, a mother who loved and supported him, and an older brother who became a rival.

He was ten years older than Ike.

Instead of attending West Point, Marshall went to the Virginia Military Institute in Lexington, Virginia—where he met his first love. His first romance was a head-over-heels experience, similar to Ike's. He would sneak out of his dorm room and scale the walls of the campus in order to walk into town and stand beneath the window of Elizabeth Carter "Lily" Coles, lost in rapture as she played the piano.

He succeeded in marrying the woman whom he felt to be the love of his life, and the two of them were extremely happy.

Marshall was commissioned a second lieutenant and was sent to the Philippines and then to Oklahoma territory. He attended the prestigious Command and General Staff School at Fort Leavenworth, and when America entered the First World War, his duties were similar to Ike's: he set up training camps.

But unlike Ike, he succeeded in going to France with Pershing as assistant chief of staff for the first division.

Marshall had a legendary encounter with Pershing in the course of the war that might have ruined his career. Pershing was bawling out a division commander when Marshall tugged at the general's sleeve and told him that the diatribe was unfair. Everyone expected Pershing to slap Marshall down and put an end to his tour of duty. But that was not what happened. Pershing was so impressed by Marshall's candor that he sought his advice in the future.

There was something magnificent about George Marshall that commanded respect.

Marshall became Pershing's chief of operations, and he planned the victorious campaign in the Meuse–Argonne that was America's single greatest contribution to winning the war. He was a brilliant planner, and when Pershing was appointed army chief of staff, Marshall served as his deputy. After that, he went off to China, where he learned to speak Chinese.

And then, back home in the United States... his beloved wife Lily died tragically young.

As Marshall grieved, he was sent to Fort Benning to be head of the Army Infantry School—the same school that Charles Farnsworth had kept Ike from attending in 1924.

Marshall led the school from 1927 to 1932, and he revamped the curriculum in what would be known as the "Benning Revolution." He instilled the idea that future wars would demand mobility. He insisted that officers think for themselves and *think quickly* in the heat of action. He invited officers to his home for lengthy conversations.

Here was a man who was cut from the very same cloth as Fox Conner.

While in Georgia, Marshall fell in love again, this time with a widow who had three children. Her name was Katherine Tupper Brown, and their marriage was an instant success. And Marshall was given an instant family. He became so close to his stepson Allen that he treated the lad as his own son, and Allen loved him accordingly.

Marshall and Katherine were such soulmates that she wrote a book about their marriage at the end of World War II, and its title was *Together*.

The difference between the romantic and marital experiences of Marshall and Ike was important. But the most important difference between the two was the difference in outlook that made Ike a politician. Marshall could manage the political aspects of his job, like relations with Capitol Hill. And he was deeply concerned with the problems of defending democracy.

But he could never have entered civilian politics or become president. Politics was too dirty a profession for a man of his blunt integrity and staunch rectitude. He was tough but *wholesome,* and he believed so firmly in the ethic of selfless dedication that he would never take credit for his accomplishments.

He had been inclined toward mischief in his early years, but that was no longer the case in adulthood. He lacked the guile that was essential to Ike's Machiavellian cunning.

FDR, on the other hand, was a man who was very much like Ike when it came to artful cunning. His feline capacity for hide-and-seek made him nimble in the art of double-crossing. He and Ike made an interesting duo during World War II.

With a man like Marshall, what you saw was what you got—plain truth. With Ike, you never knew what was going on behind the disarming façade that his easygoing grin—perfect for deception—led you to believe.

As the New Deal commenced, George Marshall was an eager participant in the development of FDR's "Civilian Conservation Corps," the "CCC." This program was placed under the oversight of the army, and Marshall was very glad to play a role in developing it.

After MacArthur's term as chief of staff ended—and after the Chicago exile that MacArthur inflicted on Marshall—promotion and advancement were possible, and Marshall moved up the ladder. He was promoted to brigadier general and ordered to Washington to become the deputy chief of staff to Malin Craig.

In 1938, Marshall stood up to FDR in a manner that was strikingly similar to his dustup with Pershing in World War I. In a preparedness meeting at the White House, FDR was arguing that in light of isolationist sentiment, an emphasis on aviation would be better for political reasons than a buildup of the land army.

Everyone in the room agreed with Roosevelt, except for Marshall, who told him he was dead wrong.

And everyone expected the worst for Marshall: they expected that his tour of duty would end. But FDR, like Pershing, was extremely impressed by the tough integrity of Marshall—so impressed that he made him chief of staff.

George Catlett Marshall was sworn in as army chief of staff on September 1, 1939—the very day that Hitler invaded Poland.

In election year 1940, the central issue of the campaign was the issue of war and peace. Hitler's blitzkrieg swept through Europe, and Denmark, Norway, the Netherlands, Belgium, and France were all conquered by

*General George
Catlett Marshall*

June. Everyone knew that Hitler's next move would be an attempt to invade England in the autumn.

A powerful bipartisan isolationist group was insisting that America should stay out: the "America First" Committee. The committee's celebrity spokesman was the aviator Charles Lindbergh. But many Americans were frightened as they contemplated the future in 1940—frightened by Adolf Hitler.

FDR was running for an unprecedented third term, and the stakes were enormous. In a sly move, he tried to get both the presidential and vice-presidential nominees from the 1936 Republican ticket—Alf Landon and Frank Knox—into his cabinet. Landon demurred, but Knox accepted and became the new secretary of the navy. In 1898, he had been a Rough Rider with Teddy Roosevelt.

The new secretary of war was Henry Stimson—a prominent Republican who had been introduced to public service by Theodore Roosevelt and who had served as secretary of state under Hoover.

Republican internationalists like Henry Luce—publisher of *Time* magazine—mounted a boisterous campaign to prevent the nomination of an isolationist candidate. They succeeded with the nomination of Wendell Willkie, a moderate-to-liberal Republican (and also an ardent champion of racial equality) as well as an internationalist in outlook.

FDR took to the radio to warn Americans about the impending worst-case wartime scenario: America alone in an Axis-dominated world.

Isolationists argued that America was capable of "going it alone" since "Fortress America" could hold its own. But the problem for the isolationists was simple: "Fortress America" did not yet exist, and America was ill-prepared to defend itself.

Since Fortress America would have to be *created*, the pretext for a gigantic mobilization—a mobilization for *defense*—had arrived, and FDR, Marshall, and the other internationalists made the most of it.

With grudging isolationist support, FDR pushed through a huge "defense" appropriation in 1940 that laid the groundwork for everything that followed. It also helped to end the Great Depression once and for all.

FDR set up a Defense Advisory Commission to coordinate the mobilization. He set up a National Defense Research Committee to investigate the cutting-edge scientific issues...like nuclear fission.

FDR and the new British prime minister Winston Churchill maintained steady and top-secret consultations about the Nazis' nuclear weapons research. The German program was coordinated by one of the world's top physicists: Werner Heisenberg.

There was no time to lose.

Meanwhile, something would have to be done to build up the strength of the army. The size of the United States Army was *number nineteen* in the world as of May 1940. The pitiful scale of America's peacetime army would no longer do.

In September 1940, army Chief of Staff Marshall got Congress to create the first peacetime draft in American history. It would last for only a year, so time was of the essence. Marshall inducted over a million men in the winter of 1940–1941, and they would all have to be trained.

After gaining authority from Congress to do so, he terminated the army's seniority system, forcing hundreds of officers to retire so he could identify, prepare, and promote new promising leaders.

This gave Ike his chance.

And FDR got his chance to be wartime commander in chief: he won an unprecedented third term.

He requested the War and Navy departments to develop a secret "Victory Plan" in 1941. The author was Major Albert Wedemeyer, a strategist whose thinking was in line with the doctrines of Marshall, Ike, and Patton.

He had studied as an exchange student at the German Kriegsakademie and had watched German field maneuvers in 1938 before returning to the United States and going to work at the army war plans division.

In 1941, he predicted that Britain and Russia—Hitler had invaded the Soviet Union in June—could never defeat the Germans by themselves.

Attacks in northwest Europe by American forces would be necessary to destroy the Wehrmacht, he said, and massive tank operations would be needed. America would have to put over eight million men in the field by 1943.

Joint army and navy contingency plans of different kinds had been developed down the years. Pursuant to the new Victory Plan, a contingency plan called "Rainbow Five" was written to encompass preparations for a war on multiple fronts against multiple enemies.

Ike's Meteoric Rise

In December 1939, Ike, Mamie, and John had arrived in San Francisco. Two months later, they came to Fort Lewis in Tacoma, Washington, and John was sent to the home of his uncle Edgar, Ike's older brother, who lived in Tacoma.

John had lived in boarding schools over the years, and in the summertime of 1940, he would go to Millard Preparatory School in Washington, D.C., to study for the West Point entrance exam, for he intended to follow in his father's footsteps.

As for Ike, he had the experience he had wanted for so many years: commanding troops.

The satisfaction was immense. After maneuvers at Fort Lewis, he and his men went to Camp Ord in California for summer training. He let John come along to see what field duty was like. Years later, John remembered Ike's tent, with its "two cots, two camp chairs, and a large folding camp desk. On the desk stood a couple of kerosene lamps that threw bright light and eerie shadows on the tent walls."[3]

During their stay in California, Ike helped create camps for the training of draftees and National Guard units from other parts of the country.

In August, he was back at Fort Lewis in command of a battalion. He marched his men through backwoods country in Washington State that had just been worked over by loggers. In a letter to "Gee" Gerow, Ike described the "stumps, fallen logs, tangled brush, holes, hummocks and hills" over which they passed. "The experience," he wrote in his memoirs later, "fortified my conviction that I belonged with troops; with them I was always happy."[4]

After FDR and Marshall got Congress to approve the peacetime draft, George Patton was sent to Fort Benning, and he prepared to command a new armored unit. He wrote to Ike in a state of exultation. "It seems highly probable," he said, "that I will get one of the next two armored divisions. If I do, I shall ask for you either as Chief of Staff, which I should prefer, or as a regimental commander. Hoping that we are together in a long and BLOODY war."[5]

Ike was thrilled at the prospect of serving under Patton—so thrilled that he asked Mark Clark to make it happen. But then he got some unwelcome news from "Gee" Gerow, now a brigadier general and head of the war plans division in the War Department. Gerow wanted Ike to come and serve under him...in a desk job.

Ike was so upset by this invitation that he broke out in shingles.

After he found a way to turn down the invitation, Mamie expressed her disappointment that he passed up a chance to return to Washington, where they had been so happy.

In the spring of 1941, thousands of newly drafted men began arriving for training as Marshall put his army-building operation into higher gear. As this happened, the word began to spread that Dwight Eisenhower was an extremely talented officer whose skills should be employed at higher levels.

He was assigned to be chief of staff for the IX Corps, commanded by Major General Kenyon Joyce at Fort Lewis. Joyce became a new mentor who taught Ike some fine points about commanding troops.

In the midst of maneuvers, General Joyce was summoned to the telephone. After he hung up, he told Ike to "start packing."[6] Ike was being sent to San Antonio as chief of staff for the Third Army, commanded by Lieutenant General Walter Krueger. The Third Army was going to participate in vast war games that Marshall ordered. Ike and Mamie would return to San Antonio, but this time they would have excellent accommodations.

Krueger would be one of the commanders in the great Louisiana war-games maneuvers of 1941. This would be the largest peacetime exercise of its kind in American history. Involving over five hundred thousand men, it would simulate war conditions in mock battles between two field armies. Marshall told members of Congress that he wanted the mistakes to be made in Louisiana, not in Europe.

Krueger had requested Ike by name, telling Marshall he wanted a chief of staff "possessing broad vision, progressive ideas, a thorough grasp of the magnitude of the problems involved in handling an army, and lots of initiative and resourcefulness. Lieutenant Colonel Dwight D. Eisenhower, Infantry, is such a man."[7]

Marshall approved the request immediately.

The Second and Third Armies would clash in a thirty-thousand-square-mile area stretching from Texas to the fields and bayous of Louisiana. The chief umpire for the war games would be General Lesley McNair, and his deputy umpire would be Mark Clark.

Krueger's Third Army would be designated the "Blue Army" during the exercise. The Second Army, commanded by General Ben Lear, would be the "Red Army." Krueger and Ike led their forces from Fort Sam Houston to Lake Charles, Louisiana, on August 11, 1941. The war games commenced on September 15.

In each exercise, one army would conduct the offensive while the other would defend. Then their roles would be reversed. The Red and Sabine Rivers would form obstacles as the armies maneuvered. The city of Shreveport would be one of the objectives. The most important feature of the games was to test which army made better use of tanks, and each commander—Krueger and Lear—would be given a chance to show what he could do with George Patton's 2nd Armored Division.

Krueger won the games hands down. "Had this been real war," wrote a *New York Times* reporter, "Lear's force would have been annihilated."[8]

Since the war games were covered by the press, Krueger made Ike his spokesman at press conferences. This made the name of "Eisenhower" better known on a national basis.

In light of the results that were reported to Marshall, deserving officers were given promotions. Those who failed were relieved of command.

Accordingly, President Roosevelt submitted a list to the United States Senate of officers to be promoted to general. Dwight D. Eisenhower was promoted to the rank of brigadier general, and Krueger pinned the stars on his epaulets back at Fort Sam Houston.

There had hardly been time for this good news to sink in when the Japanese attacked Pearl Harbor.

On December 12, 1941, Colonel Walter Bedell Smith, the secretary of the army general staff, placed a call to Fort Sam Houston and asked to speak to General Eisenhower immediately. "The Chief," he told Ike, "says for you to hop a plane and get up here right away. Tell your boss that formal orders will come through later."[9]

War Plans

"Gee" Gerow had been the head of the war plans division, but Marshall wanted someone else. "Toward the end of the Louisiana maneuvers," Krueger recalled, "General Marshall asked me whom I regarded as best fitted to head the war plans division .... I named Eisenhower, though I was loath to lose him."[10]

Ike flew to Washington and reported to Marshall, whose office was in the Munitions Building, a large but temporary building on the Mall that was built during World War I. The old State, War, and Navy building was no longer big enough for army staff. Before long, a gigantic new building would arise across the Potomac: the Pentagon.

Marshall got down to business immediately.

He talked about the war in the Pacific and the dreadful situation that confronted the United States: the battleship fleet was out of action; Hawaii was defenseless; the Philippines were being overrun. The invasion of the Philippines started on December 8, the day after Pearl Harbor, and MacArthur (whom FDR had recalled to active duty and made commander of all U.S. Army forces in the Far East) had bungled the defensive preparations.

The Philippines had received significant—albeit belated—reinforcements, including B-17 "Flying Fortress" bombers.

But MacArthur had not paid sufficient attention to the warnings sent out by the War and Navy departments before the Pearl Harbor attack: warnings that a Japanese attack upon American targets could be imminent. A few hours after the Pearl Harbor attack, Marshall ordered MacArthur to implement Plan Rainbow Five.

MacArthur waited.

His bombers got caught on the ground and destroyed.

General Walter Short, in charge of defending the Hawaiian Islands, also disregarded the warnings. If he had made more effective use of his land-based aircraft—keeping them aloft in rotation to maintain a constant patrol—the planes that were headed toward Pearl Harbor might have been spotted out at sea and engaged before they got within range of their target.

Short's career was destroyed by this failure. But MacArthur—always protected by his powerful connections and political access—kept his influence, rank, and reputation.

In any case, the Pacific situation was desperate when Ike walked into Marshall's office. So Marshall asked Ike this question: "What should be our general line of action?"

Ike knew that he was being tested, and he knew that his answer had to be excellent. "Give me a few hours," he requested, and the chief of staff agreed.[11]

Three hours later, he returned and presented his answer. The Philippines had to be defended, Ike said, though the mission was doomed from the beginning. "The people of China, of the Philippines, of the Dutch East Indies will be watching us," Ike explained. "They may excuse failure but they will not excuse abandonment. We must do what we can. Our base must be Australia…. We must take great risks, and spend any amount of money required."[12]

Ike's answer was a synthesis: it took political factors into account within the military framework.

Marshall agreed.

Then he turned the problem over to Ike. "Eisenhower," he said, "this department is filled with able men who analyze their problems well but feel compelled to always bring them to me for final solution. I must have assistants who will solve their own problems and tell me later what they have done. The Philippines are your responsibility. Do your best to save them."[13]

Marshall's test was moving to its crucial second phase: he would see for himself how Ike performed.

Ike swung into action, commandeering resources to be sent from Australia to the Philippines by blockade runners. With permission from the British, he sent troops aboard the Cunard liner *Queen Mary*—which the British had converted to a troopship—counting on its powerful engines to outrun U-boats.

Ike moved in with his brother Milton, who was living in Falls Church, Virginia. Mamie waited in San Antonio—waiting for news about the length of Ike's new assignment. John was a plebe at West Point, and so at Christmastime she went up to see him. At the end of December 1941, Ike's Washington assignment was made permanent.

Harry Butcher, a friend from Club Eisenhower days and also the manager of Washington's local CBS radio affiliate, found a suite for Ike and Mamie at the Wardman Park Hotel, further up Connecticut Avenue from their previous haunts at the Wyoming.

After winning his third presidential term, Franklin Roosevelt had done everything possible to help the British during 1941. The United States was technically neutral. But FDR insisted that Germany's actions were a threat to American security and the best *defense* would be to help the British. Isolationists raved, but FDR went right ahead.

He got Congress to pass the Lend-Lease Act, sending massive supplies to the British across the Atlantic. He met with Churchill in Newfoundland, aboard the USS *Augusta* in August 1941. The conversations continued aboard the HMS *Prince of Wales*. FDR and Churchill hammered out the "Atlantic Charter," a statement of unity in defense of democracy against the Nazi threat.

Well before the Japanese attacked Pearl Harbor, the United States and Great Britain were fighting Nazi Germany. Once FDR made his "day of infamy" speech and got Congress to declare war on Japan—and Hitler, per the terms of the Axis pact, followed up with a declaration of war on America—Churchill and the British high command flew to Washington to meet with their American counterparts and chart global strategy. The conference, which lasted from December 22, 1941, through January 14, 1942, was dubbed "ARCADIA" by Winston Churchill.

Ike attended these meetings as an aide to George Marshall.

To put it mildly, he was not enjoying himself, since he saw his new role as yet another detour into "desk work," while luckier colleagues would be leading men into battle. "Tempers are short," he wrote in a diary entry for January 4, 1942. "There are lots of amateur strategists on the job, and prima donnas everywhere. I'd give anything to be back in the field."[14]

One afternoon Marshall made it clear that Ike's skill as a planner precluded direct command of troops. "You are going to stay right here and fill your position," the chief of staff declared, adding that "while this may seem a sacrifice to you, that's the way it must be." Ike later confessed that this was like 1918 all over again.

He had still not worked out an inner conflict of ambitions. He had never gotten over the fact that he missed out on combat in World War I, and he was determined to make up for it. On the other hand, he had felt the allure of the higher intellectual challenges of command, and he had felt it ever since his days in Panama. His horizons had been steadily expanding in the course of twenty years, and he knew it—or half knew it. But events would have to force him to his destiny.

"General," Ike said to Marshall, "I'm interested in what you say, but I want you to know that I don't give a damn about your promotion plans as far as I'm concerned. I came into this office from the field and I am trying to do my duty. I expect to do so as long as you want me here. If that locks me to a desk for the rest of the war, so be it."

Ike recalled getting up from his chair in a resentful state of mind and striding to the door. But then he paused: "something impelled me to turn around just as I started out the door and, seeing his eyes on me intently, I had to grin a little bit at my own childishness. A tiny smile quirked the corner of his face."[15]

During the ARCADIA meetings, everyone agreed on a "Europe First" strategy. Nazi Germany was the greatest menace. The Germans had attacked the Soviet Union with staggering force in the summer of 1941, and if Russian resistance should collapse, Nazi power might become insurmountable.

But the follow-up issue was obvious: What strategy for defeating Nazi Germany should be used? The British had been fighting the Germans in northeast Africa, and Churchill was eager for American help. He envisioned a pincer operation by landing troops in French Northwest Africa. Calling the project "GYMNAST," he proposed it to Roosevelt right away. FDR showed interest, but concluded that the matter demanded further study. They agreed to take the first steps toward a buildup of American forces in England. This project was called "MAGNET."

Then FDR and Churchill got to work on creating an effective organizational basis for Anglo-American teamwork. They thought up a new and unprecedented arrangement: the Combined Chiefs of Staff (CCS).

The members of the American and British high commands would serve together as members of a single team—a challenging arrangement that would cause big problems while preventing even bigger ones. Friction between the American and British commanders would be a source of major tension during the war. But the integration of Anglo-American military force was essential to grand strategy.

The six members of the Combined Chiefs were General Sir Alan Brooke, chief of the imperial general staff; Admiral Sir Dudley Pound, first sea lord; Air Chief Marshal Sir Charles Portal; U.S. Army Chief of Staff George Marshall; Chief of Naval Operations Admiral Harold Stark (who would soon be replaced by Admiral Ernest King); and General Henry H. "Hap" Arnold, chief of the air corps, which would be reorganized later as the U.S. Army Air Forces.

The CCS would be headquartered in Washington, with its operations coordinated by Field Marshal Sir John Dill, who would live in Washington and communicate with the British chiefs in London as necessary. Dill would be joined later on by an American counterpart, Admiral William D. Leahy, who became (in effect) chairman of the American chiefs of staff.

In a crucial move, George Marshall suggested that every theater of the war should have its own supreme commander. "I am convinced," he said, "that there must be one man in command of the entire theater—air, ground, and ships.... If we can make a plan for unified command now, it will solve nine-tenths of our troubles."[16] To secure British support, Marshall proposed that the first supreme theater commander should be British: General Sir Archibald Wavell, whose theater would be the Southwest Pacific, including India and Burma.

Then Marshall turned to Ike and said, "Eisenhower, draft a letter of instruction for a supreme commander in the Southwest Pacific."[17] Ike's draft was so good that it won the immediate approval of Secretary of War Stimson and FDR. Then Marshall faced the task of convincing Churchill, which he did on December 28, 1941.

But Marshall was opposed to the North Africa campaign. He regarded it as a diversion that would delay preparations for attacking Nazi Germany on the European continent. He was afraid that the Russians might collapse without a "second front" in Europe.

This remained his settled point of view.

Ike was naturally preoccupied with the immediate task he had been given: relief of the Philippines. On New Year's Day, 1942, he wrote that the "Far East is critical, and no other sideshows should be undertaken until air and ground are in a satisfactory state. Instead, we're taking on Magnet, Gymnast, etc."[18]

But the fight in the Philippines was nothing more than the delaying action that Ike had described to Malin Craig back in 1938. So Ike's thoughts began turning to the global picture, and as soon as this occurred, he changed his mind about making the Pacific a short-term strategic priority. He committed himself to "Europe First."

On January 22, Ike wrote that "we've got to go to Europe and fight, and we've got to quit wasting resources all over the world, and still worse, wasting time. If we're to keep Russia in, save the Middle East, India, and Burma, we've got to begin slugging with air at West Europe, to be followed by a land attack as soon as possible."[19]

He quietly assembled a group of fellow officers who shared this view—a minority view, since "a majority believed that definite signs of cracking German morale would have to appear before it would be practicable to attempt such an enterprise" as a cross-channel invasion.[20]

That was the majority view, and Ike chose to take it on.

"A very few—initially a very, very few—took a contrary view," Ike recalled, and he set this group to work, making plans and developing projections. Marshall was kept informed, and he approved: "General Marshall, who had already been informed of the basic conception on which we were working, was one of the believers."[21]

He was a believer because of his fear that if the Soviet Union collapsed, the war would be unwinnable.

Since Ike took the initiative in studying a strategic concept that Marshall already believed in, the partnership between the two men was established definitively.

Ike would now be "Marshall's man." They would never become close friends, but they would be a team for the duration of the war.

And so George Marshall made the decision to put Ike in charge of war plans. "Gee" Gerow was given another assignment, and Ike took over the division, which would be renamed the operations division (OPD) on February 16, 1942. He was promoted to major general on March 27. Marshall told President Roosevelt that Ike would be responsible for "all dispositions of army forces on a global scale." He would be much more than a staff officer "in the accepted sense of the word." He was to be a "subordinate commander."[22]

When the promotion papers were sent through channels, the personnel officer at the War Department questioned whether Ike was to be known as a "commander." "He was chagrined," Ike recalled, "when he was called in to the Chief's office and icily told that the statement had been drafted by General Marshall himself."[23]

Commander.

On February 28, Ike presented his planning draft for a cross-channel invasion to Marshall.[24] He acknowledged that the plan depended on "overpowering air force," and "the airplanes we needed did not then exist."

Marshall listened patiently, and he said, "This is it. I approve."[25]

Hap Arnold and Admiral Ernest King (who had by then replaced Admiral Stark as chief of naval operations), approved also. And so Marshall got ready to present the plan to FDR and the Combined Chiefs of Staff.

The British, especially Churchill, would be tough to win over. They firmly believed that an early cross-channel invasion would be doomed. Moreover, as important new research by Nigel Hamilton has suggested, FDR was in secret agreement with the British because he was convinced that American troops would need to be tested in battle—battle-hardened by facing the Germans in North Africa—before taking on the Wehrmacht at Hitler's Atlantic Wall.[26] FDR kept this view to himself and let events play out.

His presidential modus operandi had developed as long ago as 1933: He recruited advisers with opposing points of view, and he let them battle it out. He would play devil's advocate. Even if he knew what he wanted, he would pose as undecided for a while.

At last he would settle the matter, through compromise if possible, or else through direct intervention. Either way, he would play the role of the honest broker, a leader who let all of his advisers have their say.

He was a master of foxy deception that way, and he would use such deceptions to buy himself time as he assessed the power realities.

He would use this same method in 1942 as the members of the British and American high commands took opposite positions on the best "Europe First" strategy.

Ike and Mamie moved into a handsome red-brick mansion, "Quarters 7," at Fort Myer, where the other members of the high command, including Marshall, were living in splendor.

Ike was rising to his global destiny.

Soon he and Marshall would be hammering out global strategy—with FDR, Churchill, and others. From commanding a battalion at Fort Lewis, he had risen with incredible swiftness. He rose from obscurity to power, and with power he would soon rise to fame. He would have the chance to change history.

And everything had happened so quickly.

Two weeks before his big promotion, Ike's father passed away in Abilene.

On March 25, Ike presented Marshall with a preliminary plan—in effect, a logistical prelude—for cross-channel invasion. It called for a buildup of

American forces in Britain, to be used against Germany and prioritized for the invasion of the European continent. This plan was codenamed "BOLERO." "The war plans division," Ike wrote, "believes that, unless this plan is adopted as the central aim of all our efforts, we must turn our backs upon the Eastern Atlantic and go, full out, as quickly as possible, against Japan."[27]

On April 1, he presented Marshall with the invasion plan itself. D-Day would occur in one year—on April 1, 1943.

Amphibious landings would be made on the French coast between Calais and Le Havre, with paratroopers dropped behind German lines. This invasion plan was codenamed "ROUNDUP."

An emergency plan for a fast 1942 invasion was developed and codenamed "SLEDGEHAMMER." This plan would be used in the event that the Soviet Union might collapse without it.

Marshall and Stimson reviewed the overall package and presented it to FDR, who probed for weaknesses. But since he found himself confronted by a unified position among the high command, he gave preliminary approval. He then instructed Marshall and his presidential aide Harry Hopkins to fly to England and present the plan to Churchill and the British chiefs of staff.

Churchill recalled that Marshall advocated SLEDGEHAMMER from the outset: in his memoirs, Churchill wrote that "General Marshall had advanced the proposal that we should attempt to seize Brest or Cherbourg, preferably the latter, or even both, during the early autumn of 1942."[28]

The British agreed to BOLERO—the buildup of troops in Great Britain—but they insisted on the simultaneous launching of the North African campaign. They agreed to ROUNDUP in principle, but only as a *best-case goal* for a 1943 cross-channel invasion. As for SLEDGE-HAMMER, they resisted. Alan Brooke regarded the proposal as dangerous nonsense. He said that a 1942 cross-channel invasion was out of the question.

Events would prove that he was right. Even in 1944, when the D-Day armada set forth against Nazi-held Europe, the risks would be tremendous. But to save face for the Americans, the British set forth their reactions to SLEDGEHAMMER in euphemistic terms. The plan would have to "await developments."

General Hastings Ismay, Churchill's personal chief of staff, reflected that "our American friends [Marshall and Hopkins] went happily homewards under the mistaken impression that we have committed ourselves to both Roundup and Sledgehammer. This misunderstanding was destined to have unfortunate results."[29]

Everything was going wrong in all theaters of the war by the spring of 1942. The Philippines were lost. The Japanese captured Singapore, depriving the British of their foremost bastion in the East. They were overrunning Indochina, the Dutch East Indies, and Malaya. Their next thrusts would be aimed at India and Australia. Meanwhile, the Germans conquered immense amounts of Russian territory and Leningrad was under siege. German atrocities in "Operation Barbarossa" were almost beyond description.

In May, Ike took a hard look at BOLERO, and the magnitude of the logistical task began to sink in. It was all very well to call for a rapid buildup of forces in Britain and to sketch the tasks as best-case goals. But what about the *worst-case* contingencies? Organizational wizards must anticipate problems. They must try to envision the possibility of set-backs and develop contingency plans. Ike began to draw upon lessons he had learned at the Army Industrial College.

Back in February, he had asked hard questions about the production of landing craft. Who would design them? Who would build them? How many were needed? And how soon could they be ready?

The navy would have to build them, he was told, but no one in the naval shipyards was making this top priority—yet. Admiral King, chief of naval operations, was not speeding up their production. He had other problems on his mind.

Inter-service rivalry was also a factor, and so in May Ike and Marshall met with FDR to discuss the landing craft issue.

Meanwhile, Marshall revealed that he was shocked by the condition of the American forces that he saw in London. He had grave doubts about the fitness of the American commander, Major General James E. Chaney. Everything was disorganized—chaotic.

On May 20, Marshall ordered Ike to fly to London, and assess the situation in detail. He would also confer with the British high command to assess their commitment to SLEDGEHAMMER.

Ike took a delegation of army officers with him, among them Mark Clark, Hap Arnold, Major General John C. H. Lee (head of the army's supply division), and others. They departed on May 23.

Before they left, Marshall asked Ike to draft a preliminary memorandum regarding the role of an American commander in an overall European Theater of Operations (ETO). This memo—which Ike later referred to as "the Bible"—recommended that such a theater commander should have power over all the American forces that would be engaged: on land, on the sea, and in the air.

Arriving in London on May 26, Ike and his delegation checked into Claridge's Hotel. Ike and Mark Clark were driven around London by a female driver who was a member of Britain's volunteer motor transport corps. Her name was Kay Summersby.

Born in Ireland, Kathleen Helen MacCarthy-Morrogh was a well-to-do former fashion model who came from a wealthy family. She was raised by the landed gentry, raised with governesses, rode to hounds, and moved in sophisticated circles. She had married a British army officer named Gordon Thomas Summersby, but the marriage didn't work. Nonetheless, she retained her married name after the divorce. After that, she got engaged to a U.S. Army captain named Richard Arnold.

The marriage was postponed because Arnold, too, was getting a divorce, and they were both awaiting the arrival of their final divorce papers.

Dick Arnold's orders kept him flying back and forth, so he and Kay seldom got the chance to see one another.

Ike was appalled by the condition of the American staff, and he decided right away that General Chaney would have to go. He met with British leaders, and he tried to cultivate them. He met General Bernard Law Montgomery, already a hero because his fighting retreat in the Dunkirk campaign saved thousands of lives. He was rude, arrogant, and peremptory. When Ike lit a cigarette, Montgomery snapped, "Who's smoking?" "I am, sir," Ike replied, and Monty said, "Stop it. I don't permit smoking in my office."[30]

Ike hated the man instantly.

Monty was nasty, but his commander Sir Alan Brooke was unpleasant on a higher plane. He was condescending, haughty, and aloof.

Ike did make a friend among the British—Lord Louis Mountbatten, whom Marshall singled out as a leader who deserved cultivation. Ike turned on the charm.

In presenting his scenario for an early cross-channel invasion, Ike stated that the perfect man to command it would be Mountbatten—who was sitting right across the table. Ike had never met him before, and so General Brooke made the introduction, smiling ironically. Ike and Mountbatten would become staunch friends.

But the meetings went badly. It was clear that the British commitment to ROUNDUP was tepid, and they looked upon SLEDGEHAMMER as a catastrophic fantasy.

On June 3, a British emissary arrived in Washington to express this point of view to FDR. Churchill's spokesman was none other than Lord Mountbatten, who told the president that Churchill was opposed to a 1942 cross-channel invasion.

Marshall was angry when Sir John Dill told him about this meeting—angry because he had not been invited to attend.

Before returning home, Ike relaxed over drinks with his colleagues at Claridge's and they discussed the question of who should be Chaney's replacement. Mark Clark got the definite impression that Ike wanted the job himself. "He never said so," Clark remembered, "but it was clear to me that he very much wanted the job, very much."[31]

Ike went to bed early, but Clark and Hap Arnold kept talking. As Arnold recalled it, "The two of us came to the conclusion that it should be Ike." Arnold volunteered to make this recommendation to Marshall.[32]

When Ike and his delegation returned, Marshall debriefed them. He met with Arnold and Clark, and he told them he had asked General Lesley McNair for his advice about a replacement for Chaney. McNair, said Marshall, had recommended the following candidates: George Patton, Joseph Stilwell, and Lloyd Fredendall. But perhaps, said Marshall, someone younger ought to command. Clark's immediate response was "Eisenhower."[33]

On June 3, it was Ike's turn to brief Marshall.

A new commander and a new command structure were needed, Ike said, and the new commander of American forces in England should take on all of the responsibilities that BOLERO and ROUNDUP would demand. Ike recommended a candidate: General Joseph T. McNarney, Marshall's deputy chief of staff, who helped Marshall reorganize the War Department's structure earlier in the year.[34]

Without commenting on this recommendation, Marshall told Ike to draft a more specific directive spelling out the role of a commander for the ETO. This directive would give more specificity to the terms of the earlier ETO memorandum (the Bible) that Ike had drafted in May. Ike submitted the new directive on June 8.[35]

Marshall reviewed the directive. Then he turned to Ike and asked if it would suit him personally. When Ike replied that he believed it satisfactory, Marshall told him that he might be the one to execute it.

He knew that he almost had the job. In his diary he wrote that "the chief of staff told me this morning that it's possible I may go to England to command. It's a big job, if the United States and the United Kingdom stay squarely behind Bolero, and go after it tooth and nail, it will be the biggest American job of the war."[36]

On June 11, Ike wrote that "the chief of staff says I'm the guy."[37] That night he told Mamie that he would "command the whole shebang."[38]

Theater Commander

Ike's only experience in commanding troops had been at the battalion level, and he had never seen combat. He always said that he wanted release from the "desk job" routine, that he wanted to command troops. He would now have the chance to command troops on the grand scale.

He was a theater commander.

He began to assemble his team. He said that he wanted Mark Clark, and he also asked for Walter Bedell Smith (universally known as "Beetle") to serve as chief of staff. Marshall said that Beetle could come later on after he had finished up some work in Washington. He would join Ike's staff in September.

Beetle was known as a bad-tempered disciplinarian, and that suited Ike perfectly. He would serve the function of being Ike's hatchet man.

Ike chose some other men who were selected for the support services they could render: Colonel T. J. Davis from the adjutant general's office—he and Ike had served together under MacArthur—Major Ernest R. "Tex" Lee, his executive assistant in the Louisiana war games, and Sergeant Mickey McKeogh, who had served as his orderly under Krueger's command. This team would be greatly expanded when Ike reached London.

He paid a call upon Admiral King because the naval forces in the ETO would be just as much under his command as the land forces. He asked if Admiral Stark could serve under him, and King agreed.

Ike also asked for the services of Harry Butcher, a lieutenant commander in the naval reserve—the old Club Eisenhower friend who ran the CBS radio station and who was skilled in public relations. King agreed to that as well. Ike had learned the value of good press relations when he worked for Krueger.

On June 23, 1942, Ike flew off to London with his team. Mamie and John were there to say farewell—John had come down from West Point, and he talked with his father. Then he stood at attention in his cadet uniform and saluted Ike. Mamie and John watched the plane lift off from Bolling Air Field.

Mamie would be staying home.

That was the nature of field duty, especially in *wartime*—army wives did not accompany their husbands.

Mamie would remove their belongings from Fort Myer, put the large items in storage, and decide where to live. Her parents wanted her to come back to Denver, but she chose to stay in Washington and live at the Wardman Park. Harry Butcher made all the arrangements.

Shortly before Ike's departure, Winston Churchill flew to the United States. Decisions about strategy were being made at the highest level, and Stalin was sending urgent requests for the opening of a second European front in 1942. He sent his foreign minister Vyacheslav Molotov to meet personally with both Churchill and FDR.

FDR and Churchill gave lip service to the principle of a second front, but they hedged their statements with disclaimers about feasibility.

Then Churchill flew to America at once. He was accompanied by Alan Brooke and Hastings Ismay.

His goal was to convince FDR that *peripheral* attacks should be made to give the Russians relief: the GYMNAST operation in North Africa along with a campaign to liberate northern Norway, codenamed JUPITER. He wished to have these operations take place simultaneously in the autumn.

As for the issue of a major cross-channel invasion in 1942, he agreed with Brooke that it was out of the question. In his memoirs, Churchill explained his reasoning.

Even if an amphibious cross-channel assault could be carried out in 1942—unlikely due to the shortage of landing craft—"the Allies would be penned up in Cherbourg and...would have to maintain themselves in this confined bomb and shell trap for nearly a year under ceaseless bombardment and assault.... The Germans had left twenty-five mobile divisions in France. We could not have more than nine ready by August for 'Sledgehammer.'"[39]

The very notion of SLEDGEHAMMER would lead to tragedy if the attempt were made.

Churchill arrived in the United States on June 18, and he flew straight to Hyde Park. Brooke and Ismay stayed in Washington, where they conferred with Marshall and Ike. Brooke made his opposition to SLEDGEHAMMER clear.

FDR and Churchill spent days discussing all the issues of the war at Hyde Park, not least of all the issue of nuclear weapons—the issue that would lead to the Manhattan Project.

Then they confronted the problem of SLEDGEHAMMER.

In a secret memo dated June 20, Churchill told FDR that an attempted 1942 cross-channel invasion would "lead to disaster." Instead, "within the general structure of BOLERO," a "French Northwest Africa operation ought to be studied."[40] FDR listened sympathetically. He told Churchill his arguments were strong, but he did not commit himself.

The men boarded a train for Washington, arriving on the morning of the 21. A telegram was waiting for them. FDR read it, then passed it to Churchill. The message: "Tobruk has surrendered, with twenty-five thousand men taken prisoners."[41] The British campaign in North Africa was going badly.

The defeat at Tobruk opened up a path for the German Afrika Korps to drive eastward into Egypt and capture the Suez Canal. And the larger prospects were worse. Hitler's African campaign had started out as an attempt help the Italians—who were being defeated by the British. But then the Afrika Korps campaign took on a life of its own.

It evolved into part of a much larger pincer movement: as the German invasion of Russia plunged on toward the oilfields of the Caucasus, German victory in Egypt would open up the Middle East. And the pincers would converge.

As early as 1940, Churchill had expressed great fear about the Jewish settlements in Palestine. "Should the war go heavily into Egypt," he warned, "the position of the Jewish colonists will be one of the greatest danger."[42] By 1942, when the Holocaust had started, there could be little doubt about what would happen in Palestine if Hitler controlled the Middle East.

And Hitler did intend to add the region to his empire. On May 23, 1941, he had sent orders to commence an airborne operation in Iraq, and Churchill took quick action to preempt it. British forces engaged and then defeated a Luftwaffe strike force.

Churchill recalled that "the Germans had at their disposal an airborne force which would have given them Syria, Iraq, and Persia, with their precious oilfields. Hitler's hand might have reached out very far toward India" if preemptive action had not been taken by the British.[43]

In 1942, Axis leaders were discussing the future partitioning of Asia after the collapse of the Soviet Union. Hitler approved an agreement that would give Japan not only China, India, and southeast Asia, but also… Siberia. The German empire would terminate at the Urals.

But the Germans would have complete control of the Middle East: Syria, Iraq, Iran, and … Palestine.[44] The anti-Semitic Palestinian leader Haj Amin al-Husseini—the mufti of Jerusalem—visited Hitler on November 21, 1941. The führer told him he would be "fighting the Jews without respite, and…the fight includes the fight against the so-called Jewish National Home in Palestine."[45]

During Churchill's visit, FDR brought Marshall and Admiral King to the White House. He invited them to join the discussion with Churchill, and

Marshall offered to send the British three hundred new Sherman tanks—the tank was just coming off the assembly lines—to bolster their forces in North Africa.

But then the conversation turned angry.

Marshall called the North African campaign a diversion that would hinder and delay the cross-channel invasion. He said that British opposition to a cross-channel invasion might compel the United States to abandon the "Europe First" strategy. King supported Marshall.

FDR rebuked them gently, observing that their threat was "a little like taking up your dishes and going away."[46]

The president could see that Marshall did not get along with the British and was less than diplomatic when expressing his opinions to foreign heads of state.

After this meeting, Harry Hopkins and Ismay were invited by Roosevelt and Churchill to help conduct a postmortem. FDR was still playing for time, and the "agreements" they reached were mere generalities about pursuing the exploration of all possible options with all possible speed.

When Ike arrived in London as the new American theater commander, he was greeted by Lord Mountbatten, who was accompanied by senior American officers: Major General Carl "Tooey" Spaatz, commander of the U.S. Eighth Air Force, and Major General John C. H. Lee, who was in charge of logistics.

The American headquarters was located at 20 Grosvenor Square near the ritzy Claridge's Hotel. When Ike found out that he would be staying at Claridge's again—he had stayed there during his last London visit—he revealed that he found the place ostentatious, so he moved to the slightly more sedate Dorchester, which would be his London home from then on.

He put Harry Butcher to work making contacts among the London press corps. He paid calls on the British high command, and he sought out Winston Churchill right away. He made such a good impression on Churchill that the two of them began to have lunch together several times a week, and before long Ike was visiting the prime minister's country estate, "Chequers."

Ike knew that the British were appalled by the SLEDGEHAMMER proposal. He put the matter in under-stated language when he cabled

Marshall on June 30 that "there seems to be some confusion of thought as to the extent of a British commitment."[47]

Then he looked up...Kay Summersby. He had been thinking about her in America, and he brought her a basket of fruit, which was a lovely gift in ration-starved Britain. He told "Tex" Lee to track her down.

When he discovered that she had become the chauffeur for "Tooey" Spaatz, Ike summarily reassigned her to himself.

In July, FDR took steps to resolve the strategic impasse without further delay. Marshall was continuing to recommend a Pacific-first strategy if the British refused to go along with SLEDGEHAMMER.

On the 16, FDR sent Harry Hopkins, Marshall, and King to London with orders to settle their differences with the British. Upon their arrival, Marshall ordered Ike to prepare a memorandum detailing the advantages of a 1942 cross-channel invasion and dismissing the case for a North African campaign.

Privately, Ike and Clark tried to take a realistic look at SLEDGEHAM-MER. "We have sat up nights on the problems involved," Ike wrote, "and have tried to open our eyes clearly to see all the difficulties." They concluded that "with wholehearted cooperation all the way round we have a fighting chance."[48] Ike actually believed that a cross-channel invasion could be launched in just a few months.

Marshall's interactions with the British high command were extremely unpleasant. The British war cabinet voted down a 1942 cross-channel invasion on July 22. When Ike was informed, he told Harry Butcher that "July 22, 1942 could well go down as the blackest day in history."[49] Looking back years later, he admitted that this had been a very foolish opinion.[50]

And its foolishness would soon be demonstrated.

A British commando raid on the French port city of Dieppe on August 19 proved that Hitler's Atlantic Wall was formidable. The experimental raid was a complete disaster, and the casualties were terrible. Ike acknowledged years later that "those who held the Sledgehammer operation to be unwise at the moment were correct."[51]

In any case, Hopkins cabled FDR for instructions, and Roosevelt replied that he favored the North African campaign. The president said that the proposal for SLEDGEHAMMER would have to be dropped and the Americans would have to agree with the British on "some operation which would involve American land forces being brought into action against the enemy in 1942."[52]

Hopkins relayed the president's wishes to Marshall, and on July 25, the Combined Chiefs of Staff agreed to an American-led North African landing in October. A cross-channel invasion could follow in the spring or summer of 1943.

Marshall told Ike that he would be the deputy commander of the North African invasion until the president named a commander. The operation was to bear the name TORCH.

On August 6, FDR informed Churchill that *Ike* would be the commander—"Commander in Chief of the Allied Expeditionary Force."[53] Ike had presumed that Marshall would be the commander, but that was not to be.

When Marshall and King returned to Washington, they had refused to behave themselves. At a meeting of the chiefs of staff chaired by Admiral Leahy on July 30, they declared that the decision to go ahead with TORCH was by no means final.

FDR summoned them into his presence and informed them that he, as commander in chief, was ordering that TORCH would be America's priority. The operation would go ahead. And further opposition must cease.[54]

By doing this, FDR proved that he was a wartime commander on a par with Lincoln, who overruled high-ranking officers—even Grant—when he deemed it necessary. FDR saw the big picture in 1942 more clearly than two other brilliant men: Marshall and Ike. Ike would learn a great deal in his interactions with FDR.

To give Marshall his due, his fear about the collapse of the Russians was well-grounded. The fighting that would soon begin at Stalingrad would prove to be a turning point in the war.

And his concerns about TORCH delaying the cross-channel invasion were justified. Marshall perceived that the TORCH operation might extend itself so far into 1943 as to preclude ROUNDUP. The cross-channel invasion might have to wait until 1944. Ike perceived this as well.

Marshall was also correct in his perception that Churchill would keep recommending one "peripheral" action after another because he was simply afraid of the cross-channel challenge.

Nonetheless, George Marshall had been acting rather strangely.

This leader who prided himself on rationality was petulant in his insistence on SLEDGEHAMMER. He minimized the odds against it to the point of recklessness.

Perhaps his emotions were out of control because he was feeling the same frustration that Ike had been feeling: the frustration of being in a desk job while others were getting the fame of leading men in battle. He knew that his performance as army chief of staff was invaluable, but he probably felt the way that Ike felt in 1918.

Mark Perry, who has written on the Ike-and-Marshall relationship, has called Marshall's behavior "the cry of a warrior for the smell of a battle that he had always believed he would command."[55]

Importantly, Marshall was handling problems in the Pacific that would exasperate a saint. Admiral King was engaged in a never-ending battle with Douglas MacArthur, whom FDR had evacuated from the Philippines, not least of all because of his dangerous histrionics. In the face of defeat, MacArthur found release in the prospect of going down a martyr. He might have forced his troops to keep fighting the Japanese until every single one of them was dead.

FDR sent him to Australia.

Torch

In August, the tough work of planning the TORCH operation began. The problems of invasion were compounded by a thorny issue that was latent in the operation when the British conceived it. The target area, French North Africa, comprised Morocco, Algeria, and Tunisia. All of these areas were controlled by the Vichy government—the French collaborationist regime that was cooperating with Hitler.

As soon as Churchill became prime minister, he urged the French to keep fighting. He refused to recognize the Vichy regime, and he welcomed Charles de Gaulle, who fled to London and established a "Free French" resistance movement.

But Churchill also ordered the bombing of French warships moored near Oran to prevent them from falling into Nazi hands. More than a thousand Frenchmen died.

Fearing there was no love for the British in French North Africa, Churchill was perfectly willing to make TORCH an American-led operation.

The United States, unlike Britain, had recognized the Vichy regime. One of the reasons was the politics of 1940, when Roosevelt was fighting so hard to win the unprecedented third presidential term. He was under incessant attack by isolationists who charged that he was luring the United States into a needless war.

Unlike Churchill, FDR was in no position to encourage the French to resist in 1940 or to recognize the Free French movement of de Gaulle. To have done so would have invited isolationist accusations that he was meddling with overseas affairs in a manner that would violate American neutrality.

Moreover, he believed that by recognizing Vichy, he was reducing the inclination of the Germans to occupy French North Africa themselves.

As the TORCH operation took shape, FDR hoped that by maintaining good will with Vichy, French resistance to the American invasion of their African colonies might be kept minimal.

That was what he *hoped*.

There was, of course, a price to pay for this dalliance, for Vichy was blatantly a fascist-leaning regime. American liberals protested FDR's policy, and this was embarrassing. But he let Secretary of State Cordell Hull take the blame as he kept his own options open.

A career American diplomat named Robert Murphy was FDR's representative in French North Africa. Highly conservative and in fact sympathetic to Vichy, Murphy despised de Gaulle and the Free French. He sold FDR on the idea that a military Vichy official might expedite the American landings and minimize resistance if such an official could be recruited.

Ike would be up to his neck in the politics of this situation before long.

The American foreign service was rife with the same kind of ultra-conservative attitudes—extending even to anti-Semitism—that were common in the prewar army high command. Many people in the State Department were pleased by the Vichy regime's anti-Semitism. In fact,

State Department officials went out of their way to prevent Jewish refugees from entering the United States.

Henry Morgenthau Jr., FDR's treasury secretary, was Jewish, and his outrage at State Department policies led him to commission a study that would be entitled *Report to the Secretary on the Acquiescence of this Government in the Murder of the Jews.* In response to this report, FDR created the War Refugee Board in 1944. The board commenced many operations that that would help Jewish refugees in Europe to escape.

Operation TORCH was an extraordinary challenge from the outset. It would constitute the greatest invasion armada that had ever been attempted. The operation would be thrown together in months with very little in the way of advanced planning or intelligence-gathering. The American troops had never been in combat, and Ike, their commander, had never been in combat either.

In the parlance of the times, this was a "seat-of-the-pants" operation.

In late August, FDR and Churchill reached agreement regarding the composition of TORCH: the majority of troops would be American, but British troops would also serve. FDR secured Churchill's agreement that Ike would be the theater commander.

But Ike did not have a free hand. The British resisted the unified command structure that they first supported at ARCADIA. They argued among themselves about the landing zones, and Ike had to accommodate their wishes. He had no say in the selection of the ground commander for the British troops who would participate in TORCH.

He persuaded General Krueger to send his own operations officer, Colonel Alfred Gruenther, to London as head of the planning team. And he chose Norfolk House in London as command headquarters.

Throughout the month of August, Ike struggled to determine how much naval support he could get. He had to determine the number of transport ships and assault craft (landing craft) that were available. The Atlantic crossing was a hazardous one because the U-boat menace had not yet been brought under control. And the logistical challenge was tremendous.

George Marshall helped to shape this plan—he insisted on shaping it—and his notions, once again, were sometimes odd. Ike and the British agreed at first that the invasion force should land on the Mediterranean coast of Algeria—as far to the east as possible.

This would put the troops close to Tunisia, which would have to be occupied quickly to prevent German reinforcements from being brought through Sicily as well as to draw Rommel's Afrika Korps away from Egypt.

"I decided," Ike wrote, "to make the entire attack inside the Mediterranean."[56] But the American chiefs of staff—including Marshall—wanted troops to be landed to the west near Casablanca, on the Atlantic coast of Morocco, far away from Tunisia and the Afrika Korps. Part of the reason was their fear that the Spanish might notice the invasion fleet moving through the Strait of Gibraltar. And they might tell the Germans.

The result was a messy compromise that FDR and Churchill had to broker. Allied troops would land in three separate zones: at Casablanca in French Morocco and simultaneously at Algiers and Oran in Algeria. Ike saw the problem: there would be a "long and insecure line of communications" between the western and eastern invasion points.[57]

But he would have to cope with this problem as best he could. He set the target date for TORCH as November 8, 1942.

The invasion plan that Ike devised called for two separate invasion fleets. One of them would sail from Great Britain through the Strait of Gibraltar and proceed to the coast of Algeria. The other would sail from Hampton Roads, Virginia, across the Atlantic to the coast of Morocco. The overall invasion force would comprise one hundred sixteen thousand men, to be carried in over four hundred ships, accompanied by over three hundred other naval vessels.

"We are undertaking something of a quite desperate nature," he wrote in his diary. "The extent of the unfavorable potentialities is vast, including not only the chances of a very bloody repulse but bringing into the ranks of our active enemies both France and Spain, which are now classed as neutrals.... We are sailing in a dangerous political sea, and this particular sea is one in which military skill and ability can do little in charting a safe course."[58]

The pressure on Ike in September and October 1942, was enormous. When Gruenther arrived, it appeared to him that Ike had almost "aged ten years," and he was no longer "the cheerful man I remembered."[59]

In addition to the urgency of overseeing TORCH, Ike was deluged with social invitations. He drew mixed reactions among the British: some, like Brooke, regarded him with ill-disguised contempt; others saw in him a war hero in the making. With little break in his work routine, he was smoking three packs of cigarettes a day.

His busy rounds included once-a-week lunches with Churchill and weekend meetings at Chequers.

So he asked Harry Butcher to find him a country retreat where he could get away from the stress. Butcher found a gabled house in Kingston, Surrey, only half an hour away from London. It was called Telegraph Cottage, and it soon became Ike's home away from home as opposed to the Dorchester Hotel.

Ike created a surrogate family to populate this home: Harry Butcher, T. J. Davis (Ike's adjutant general), and a cluster of NCOs who took care of the housekeeping and cooking: sergeants Mickey McKeogh, John Hunt, and John Alton Moaney. The latter two were African Americans.

"Butch says I'm human again," Ike wrote to Mamie. "This cottage is a godsend." He added that "when all this business is over and I come back, you'd better 'figger' where we'll go and how we'll live. Possibly a shack, but at least we should be free as air."[60]

As he wrote this letter to Mamie, he was preoccupied with thoughts about someone else: Kay Summersby. As Jean Edward Smith has affirmed, "Ike's feelings for Kay were hardly the normal ones of a three-star general for his driver."[61]

And she was no longer just his driver: he had made her his all-purpose assistant. She had become his overall "girl Friday" at the office as well as his chauffeur.

On the road, they got to know one another, and their innate attraction was intense. She became his bridge partner at the card games that were becoming regular features of evening life at Telegraph Cottage. As her bridge partner, Ike learned that the two of them were almost telepathic.

They seemed perfectly attuned to each other.

"Kay was very beautiful in those days," recalled a friend of hers; "she was charming and gracious, and she was gay and witty." She was "extremely capable," and, importantly, "close mouthed."[62] She was a woman who could be trusted with secrets and could keep her mouth shut.

Kay Summersby, Ike's chauffeur, adjusting the flag on his limousine.

She was lovely to look at.

Slender and statuesque, she had a classically beautiful face and charismatic ways. Trained at the Worth salon, she had the grace of a fashion model, which is just what she was before she joined the transport corps. She had dancing eyes and a pert nose and her long face made her highly arched brows magnificent. Her hair was coiffed in waves.

Having given Kay a gift already—the basket of fruit—Ike decided to give her another: a Scottish terrier. He had never owned a dog, so he left the selection of the pet to Kay and "Beetle" Smith, who was a dog lover.

Scotties had been popular in the 1930s. FDR owned a Scottie named "Fala." In the popular Hollywood *Thin Man* film series, the husband-and-wife detective team of Nick and Nora Charles (played by William Powell and Myrna Loy) owned a terrier named "Asta."

The name that Ike gave to the dog that Kay and "Beetle" selected was "Telek."

When people asked about the name, he would grin and say it was a secret.

But the meaning of the name was quite clear. The letters "tele" were a reference to Telegraph Cottage, and the "K" at the end stood for… Kay.

People started to talk about their relationship, about the time they spent together, about the way she was always at his side. He was married and she was engaged. All the more reason for lurid speculation.

Yes, people were beginning to talk.

As the planning for operation TORCH intensified, the specifics shaped up. Robert Murphy arrived on September 16, and he briefed Ike on the plan to enlist the assistance of one or more Vichy occupation officials.

Ike cabled Marshall asking him to clarify Murphy's place in the chain of command. The response came back: Murphy was the personal representative of the president of the United States. But Ike was assured that his role as theater commander would be unquestionable. He put Mark Clark in charge of developing the Vichy plan with Murphy.

In close consultation with Gruenther and Marshall, Ike selected commanders for the task forces that would hit the beaches in North Africa. He chose Patton to command the assault force that would sail from Virginia to Morocco and whose target area would center on Casablanca.

For command of the center task force—the one that would land at Oran—Ike chose Major General Russell "Scrappy" Hartle. But Marshall interfered and instructed Ike to make his selection from a list of other corps commanders. Ike asked Mark Clark to take a look at the list, and Clark chose General Lloyd Fredendall.[63]

Ike went along, and the choice would prove disastrous.

Over time, Ike discovered for himself that both Fredendall and Clark were incompetent field commanders.

The task force that would land at Algiers would be commanded initially by Major General Charles "Doc" Ryder, whom Ike remembered from his West Point days. After the landings, command of this task force would switch to a British officer: General Sir Kenneth Anderson, whom Ike did not know at all.

Ike's own command center for the operation would be Gibraltar.

Patton and his men sailed from Hampton Roads on October 24. The center and eastern task forces sailed from the Firth of Clyde in Scotland. The fleet was commanded by Admiral Sir Andrew Cunningham.

Before this fleet sailed on October 26, Ike travelled to Scotland to inspect their camp and meet the troops. Harry Butcher, Mickey McKeogh, and Kay Summersby came with him. Ike left the camp dejected. The troops "did not know what was expected of them," he cabled Marshall.[64]

But there was no time left to do anything about it; the high-risk gamble was in play, and Ike prepared for the worst.

To lighten his spirits, he asked Kay if she would like to come with him to North Africa—after the landings. "I'd give anything to go," she replied, and Ike said, "It's settled then. You'll be following us. It will probably be a month or two before the situation is stabilized. And Kay, you don't have to be told that this is top secret. Not a word to anyone."[65]

Feeling better, Ike cabled Marshall in a confident tone. "I fear nothing except bad weather and possibly large losses to submarines. Given a fair break in these two matters, you may rest assured that the entry will go as planned."[66]

Ike paid a courtesy call on King George VI, and then hosted a farewell dinner at Telegraph Cottage on October 31. He wrote to Mamie, telling her that "I've never wanted any other wife—you're mine, and for that reason I've been luckier than any other man."[67]

As psychological giveaways go, this letter was a classic specimen—the first in a very long series.

Ike left for Gibraltar.

Paying for the War

In his 1942 State of the Union address, President Roosevelt set enormous production goals for the year: sixty thousand planes, twenty-five thousand tanks, six million tons of merchant shipping. Conventional opinion regarded these goals as unattainable, but America was on the way to surpassing them by December 1942.

"Let no man say that it cannot be done," proclaimed FDR in those melodious tones that always soothed and uplifted the nation: "It must be done, and we have undertaken to do it."[68]

New classes of powerful warships were in production: the *Iowa* class of battleships and the *Essex* class of fast carriers. The enormous B-29 Superfortress bomber was being developed. By the end of the war, the United States was producing more armaments than all of its enemies.

New mobilization agencies were created: organizational entities akin to what Ike the logistician had contemplated back at the Army Industrial College, agencies like the War Production Board (WPB), National War Labor Board (NWLB), War Manpower Commission (WMC), Office of War Mobilization (OWM), Office of Price Administration (OPA), and the Office of Scientific Research and Development (OSRD).

Federal spending rose in astronomical progression: from $13.3 billion in 1941 to $34 billion in 1942, $79.4 billion in 1943, $95.1 billion in 1944, and $98.4 billion in 1945.[69] The Great Depression was a bad dream in hindsight. America was proving it had always had the power to generate superabundance. Every American who wanted a job during World War II had a job.

Economists took note of this fact.

Looking back in 1957, economist Alvin Hansen reflected that "the war put the American giant to work, and once fully employed, we found we were able to raise our standard of living...beyond any level previously achieved at the very time we were fighting a total war. This no one would have believed until it actually happened."[70]

The "economic miracle" of World War II was fundamental to the power of the American armed forces. It created the industrial and agricultural infrastructure that gave them their might and sustained them.

But how was it paid for? The superficial answer is simple enough: Treasury Secretary Morgenthau wanted roughly a fifty-fifty split between revenue brought in through taxation and revenue derived from deficit spending. So roughly half of the money came from taxes, and the other half from the sale of war bonds.

But this superficial answer begs another question—a question that was largely unasked at the time and ever since: Where did all this money come from in the first place?

This is not the time or place for a long lesson in the technics of money and banking. This is not the place for a long explanation of what economists call "fractional reserve banking." Anyone with time can look it up.

But this is the place to point out something that will probably seem unbelievable: most of the money came from thin air.

In 1939, the Federal Reserve Board published a guidebook explaining its system's operations. The title was *The Federal Reserve System: Its Purposes and Functions*. On page 85 is the following statement: "Federal Reserve bank credit...does not consist of funds that the Reserve authorities 'get' somewhere in order to lend, but constitutes funds that they are empowered to create."[71]

Empowered to create.

And that is still the case today.

As economist Seymour Harris declared two decades later, "In World War II...the task of the Federal Reserve was to manufacture money."[72]

The Federal Reserve system created money that was lent to commercial banks. The commercial banks lent the money to people who invested it by buying Uncle Sam's war bonds.

As simple as that.

The operational money supply of the United States was doubled during World War II through hocus-pocus.

Few people understood this process at the time that it was being employed, and few people understand it today. As previously noted, the chairman of the Federal Reserve Bank of New York proclaimed in the 1980s that "no president really understands these things."[73] That is an appalling assertion to contemplate. But is it true?

Did FDR understand these things?

There is reason to believe that he did not. A filmed interview that he gave near the end of the war suggests that someone tried to explain it to him—perhaps Marriner Eccles, the chairman of the Federal Reserve Board—but he found the subject incomprehensible.

So he turned it into light humor instead of worrying about it. He left it all...to the experts.

While joking with a group of reporters, FDR referred to an unnamed economics textbook filled with nonsense: "Cost of production—the stock argument of the stars. A control of prices by that means is inarguable, and with scientific money and the prevention of combines and monopolies, practically impossible. Another great thought." Reporter: "What book is that?" Roosevelt: "I don't know!"

He continued: "The possessor of money is entitled to a certain amount of worth, as divided by money."

"Now don't forget that, divided by money."[74]

CHAPTER FOUR

Supreme Commander

The Rock of Gibraltar was a dismal place when Ike arrived on November 5, 1942. His command center was six hundred feet underground in a network of dim, ill-ventilated, and damp tunnels. That was just the beginning: General Henri Giraud arrived, and he instantly demanded that Ike turn over the command of the TORCH operation to him.

He insisted on commanding it himself.

Robert Murphy had recruited Giraud in the hope that he could give the Allies control of French North Africa. But Giraud was semiretired and had no real influence. If Murphy thought he could substitute Giraud for Ike as the commander of TORCH, he was living in a fantasy world.

Granted, the cooperation of the French could be vastly helpful, since a swift advance on Tunisia was vital. French cooperation would have speeded things along. But relying on Murphy had not been a shining moment in FDR's presidential leadership.

Ike managed to handle the problem of Giraud.

Around 2 a.m. on November 8, the three TORCH task forces approached their destinations. Thus began a long campaign that would go so badly for Ike in the beginning that he was afraid he would be relieved of command and demoted.

Battle Shock

At first there was little information from the landing zones, and Ike was tense. Before long, he received grim news: heavy fighting had broken out in the ports of Oran and Algiers, and he was justifiably worried that the Allied advance into Tunisia would be slowed down.

That was exactly what would happen in the weeks ahead.

George Patton, the task force commander who was best qualified to handle this situation, was far away in Morocco. As yet there had been no word from Patton's task force. French resistance in Morocco had been formidable.

Ike eased the strain by turning his mind to other things, and it is a measure of how much Kay Summersby meant to him that he directed Beetle Smith to send "a company of fifteen or twenty secretaries and stenographers essential to the headquarters' effective operation."[1] This was obviously the signal to send Kay. Most of the male—as well as female—members of his entourage had received the message one way or another in regard to what Kay was beginning to mean to him. And the gossip was explicit.

Brigadier General Everett Hughes, an old Club Eisenhower friend who had known the Eisenhowers for years and who was serving as a deputy chief of staff at Ike's London headquarters, wrote in his diary, "I suspect from the females that Butch has his eye on a bit of **** for the CG [i.e., commanding general]."[2]

According to Jean Edward Smith's evidence, wartime extramarital affairs were common among Ike's married associates, with Hughes maintaining a liaison with his secretary Rosalind Prismal and with Harry Butcher spending time with Molly Jacobs, a Red Cross volunteer.[3] The rumors concerning the romantic relations—or the lack thereof—between Ike and Kay Summersby will be discussed shortly.

There is no place for squeamishness in the consideration of these matters, for biographers need to confront them and place them in historical context.

So let us begin.

It should be noted that mores concerning extramarital sex had been permissive in the smart set since the Roaring Twenties—especially within the upper class. Noël Coward's plays set the standard.

In the 1937 film *Topper*, the revelation of an infidelity propels the married couple *higher* in the social register. A socialite played by Hedda

Hopper tells the wife that she had hesitated to invite her and her "*deli-cious* husband" to social functions because she was afraid "you might not approve of our little crowd." But the scandal made everything OK.

"Never complain, never explain" was the motto of a frisky couple in the 1939 film *Ninotchka*.

One of Churchill's political allies, Viscount Alfred Duff Cooper, had countless affairs, and his wife didn't mind. Their relationship was roughly comparable to the famous "open marriage" between the duke and duchess of Devonshire in the late eighteenth century, another period of sexual permissiveness. Everyone knew that both the duke and the duchess were... "available." For a while, their marriage encompassed a "ménage à trois."

In 1934, Winston Churchill's wife took a cruise without Winston in the company of others. William Manchester, Churchill's biographer, confirmed that his wife "fell in love" with Terence Philip, a "handsome, wealthy art dealer seven years younger than she," and she "conceded that the initiative had been hers."[4]

FDR's prepresidential affair with his wife's social secretary will be discussed in another chapter.

The point is this: it is very important to put the matter of Ike and Kay Summersby in historical perspective. Kay was raised among the landed gentry.

The fighting in Oran and Algiers grew worse. French resistance was strong, and the fighting went on for three days. Many ships were sunk, and the casualties on each side were roughly three thousand killed or wounded.

At noon on November 8, General Alphonse Juin, the French commander in Algiers, agreed to an armistice. Ike sent Clark and Giraud to follow up, but Giraud's presence made no difference, because no one paid attention to him.

Juin's superior officer, Admiral Jean Louis Darlan—the commander of the Vichy armed forces, who happened to be in Algiers—refused to agree to a general cease-fire because of orders from the Vichy government's chief of state, Marshall Philippe Pétain. But then Darlan was captured by a pro-Allied group in Algiers.

On November 10, Hitler sent troops to occupy southern France, and Darlan decided to negotiate. Mark Clark, Robert Murphy, Darlan, and

Juin worked out a settlement that would be known as the Clark–Darlan agreement. French resistance would cease, Allied troops would be given access to military assets, and the remnants of the Vichy regime in North Africa would keep order.

Ike was overjoyed. "I approve of everything you have done," he cabled Clark.[5]

And that almost cost him his command.

The response in Britain was fury. Churchill's cabinet members were outraged. The British remained committed to de Gaulle and the Free French, and they had never agreed to Murphy's machinations. De Gaulle, who had not been informed about the TORCH landings, was disgusted. So were many Americans. Edward R. Murrow, the CBS radio commentator in London, asked, "Are we fighting Nazis or sleeping with them? Why this play with traitors?"[6]

George Marshall swung into action, explaining to members of Congress and the press that Ike was not to blame and that for military reasons the TORCH campaign was under pressure to move ahead swiftly.

On November 17, FDR tried to wash his hands of the matter, telling Ike that Darlan was not to stay in power longer than necessary. Ike's brother Milton, deputy director of the Office of War Information (OWI), came to Africa to reign Murphy in. Churchill sent Harold Macmillan to advise Ike on political issues.

Ike had been blindsided, and the lesson he learned in this debacle was the first of many mortifications. "From what I hear of what has been appearing in the newspapers," he wrote to John, "you are learning that it is easy enough for a man to be a newspaper hero one day and a bum the next."[7]

He sent a cable to the Combined Chiefs explaining that circumstances shaped his decisions. Robert Sherwood recalled that when FDR saw this cable, he read it aloud—with oratorical flourishes.[8]

Eric Larrabee has reflected on what surely impressed FDR the most: here was a general who "could think politically, with cool realism, and then act with an amorality worthy of the Old Master himself."[9]

However cool Ike's decisions might have been, his emotions were livid—and profane. During the Darlan negotiations, he told Beetle Smith that he was sick of "the petty intrigue and the necessity of dealing with little, selfish, conceited worms that call themselves men."[10] He sent the following message to Churchill: "I have too often listened to your sage advice to be completely handcuffed and blindfolded by all of the slickers with which this part of the world is so thickly populated."[11]

Jean Darlan was assassinated on December 24, 1942. Ike was ordered to put Giraud in his place.

In the weeks after the landings, the TORCH campaign went badly, and more humiliations were in store. Flaws in the preinvasion planning were revealed, and Ike's lack of combat experience was shown up for what it was: a major impediment.

Ike had been right to be angry over missing out on combat in World War I. He had lessons to learn, and the learning of them in North Africa would be excruciating.

Tunisia needed to be occupied quickly, and Patton was the one who should have been given the assignment. Beginning on November 9, Hitler sent massive concentrations of troops, planes, and tanks to Tunisia and gave command to Field Marshal Albert Kesselring, a general who excelled in defense. Kesselring established his headquarters in Rome.

When Ike's task force commander, the British general Sir Kenneth Anderson, set out from Algiers on November 11, he was hopelessly out-gunned in Tunisia. Ike, still ensconced at Gibraltar, had no first-hand knowledge of this situation. The aftereffects of the Darlan fiasco were consuming most of his time.

He did not move his headquarters to Algiers until November 23, and he did not visit the front until November 28.

Meanwhile, Bernard Law Montgomery, whom Churchill put in command of the British Eighth Army, won a stunning victory over the Afrika Korps in the second battle of El Alamein, which took place between October 23 and November 11. Monty became an authentic hero, and his judgment of the American performance was scornful as he chased Rommel's Afrika Korps westward.

George Patton was equally contemptuous. "Ike is not well," he wrote, "and keeps saying how hard it is to be so high and never to have heard a hostile shot. He could correct that very easily if he wanted to." Patton's guess was that Ike and Clark were both "on the way out," because "they have no knowledge of men or war."[12]

Alan Brooke joined the chorus. "It must be remembered," he wrote, "that Eisenhower had never even commanded a battalion in action when he found himself commanding a group of armies in North Africa. No wonder he was at a loss as to what to do."[13]

After Marshall warned him on December 22 that "German intentions against your right flank seem evident," Ike went to the front.[14] The winter rains had set in, and he was informed that the muddy conditions would probably last into February.

Thankfully, FDR had anticipated delays and setbacks of many kinds, and he even welcomed them. He believed that American troops and their commanders would need a great deal of combat experience—they would have to make many mistakes and learn from them—before the cross-channel invasion could be attempted.

On January 7, 1943, FDR met with the American chiefs of staff at the White House. Marshall brought Albert Wedemeyer, whom he had promoted to be head of war planning, to discuss the next steps in the war. The British, they said, would recommend continued Mediterranean-based activity, beginning with an invasion of Sicily and continuing northward from there. They would probably push for an invasion of Italy.

The preference of the chiefs would be a cross-channel invasion in August 1943.

The invasion would cross the channel at its widest point and land troops in Brittany. According to the minutes of this meeting, Marshall acknowledged that the losses would be heavy, but endurable. "He said that, to state it cruelly, we could replace troops whereas a heavy loss in shipping" with continued Mediterranean operations would destroy the opportunity to cross the English Channel in 1943.[15]

FDR did not like what he was hearing.

In December, the Canadian prime minister Mackenzie King had visited him at the White House, and King's diary notes reveal that FDR anticipated, and even desired, a prolongation of fighting in Africa and the Mediterranean until the American army was battle-worthy. "In many ways," FDR said, "he wished for nothing more than let the fighting in Africa continue indefinitely."[16]

This was greatly to Ike's advantage in early 1943.

Beetle Smith had sent Kay Summersby and other female staff members from Scotland in December. He sent them aboard a troopship, and the trip became harrowing when the ship was torpedoed by a German submarine off the coast of Algeria. Kay and the others got away in a lifeboat, and she arrived at Ike's headquarters just before Christmas.

Beetle Smith hosted a Christmas dinner. "Sat around with Ike after the party broke up," wrote Everett Hughes. "Discussed Kay. I don't know whether Ike is alibiing or not. Says he likes her. Says he wants to hold her hand. Doesn't sleep with her. He doth protest too much, especially in view of the gal's reputation in London."[17]

Ike had the little dog Telek sent over from England.

Meanwhile, Mamie was having a bad time back at home. She was suffering from an inner-ear condition that made it hard to travel. She wandered around the apartment at the Wardman Park, opening closets to look at Ike's suits, and she sought relief from loneliness in talks with Butcher's wife, Ruth, who lived across the hall.[18] Gradually, she began to spend time shopping or playing cards with other army wives. She did some Red Cross volunteer work. George Marshall paid calls upon her frequently to keep her informed about Ike.

She was lonely, worried, and frail. The effervescence of her youth was gone, and she shunned the attention of the press.

Ike wrote her letters as the holidays approached, and on New Year's Eve, he told her that "I've never *been in love with anyone but you*! I never will [original emphasis]."[19]

The first part of that declaration wasn't true, and he must have known it.

He had been deeply in love with Gladys Harding.

On January 14, 1943, FDR, Churchill, and their staffs met at Casablanca for a strategy conference. Stalin was invited, but he sent his regrets: he was preoccupied with the final stages of the Stalingrad battle.

Ike was invited to brief the Combined Chiefs of Staff on January 15. His journey from Algiers had been hair-raising: two engines on his

B-17 had conked out, and he was almost forced to parachute to safety. He was jittery.

But he had worked up a plan by which he hoped to regain the initiative.

His plan—codenamed SATIN—was to use Fredendall's force as a wedge to keep the Germans in Tunisia commanded by Colonel-General Hans-Jürgen von Arnim from joining forces with Rommel's Afrika Korps.

It only took Alan Brooke minutes to shoot down the plan by running the numbers: each of the two German forces outnumbered Fredendall's force by so vast a margin that the Americans would get ground between millstones if Ike's plan were attempted.

Neither George Marshall nor Ernest King nor Hap Arnold said anything one way or the other. Ike departed. He tried to retain his self-confidence, but he was deeply uncertain about his fate. And within a few weeks, he called off SATIN.

Harry Butcher put it succinctly: "His neck is in a noose, and he knows it."[20]

Ike was summoned to meet with FDR, who asked him how long it might take to achieve victory in Africa. Ike's estimate was June at the latest. He had no way of knowing it, but that suited FDR's purposes.

Even so, historians have differed in sizing up FDR's reaction to Ike at the Casablanca conference. When Marshall asked the president to promote Ike from lieutenant general to full general—four-star general— the president's reply, according to Harry Hopkins, was that "he would not promote Eisenhower until there was some damn good reason for it…. The president said he was going to make it a rule that promotions should go to people who had done some fighting."[21]

But FDR gave Ike the promotion before very long.

In Nigel Hamilton's opinion, FDR was content with Ike's performance from the standpoint of politics: "From the president's point of view," he has argued, "Eisenhower had done extremely well."[22] One of the most important things was Ike's skill in handing the challenges of coalition warfare. He worked patiently with impatient and difficult people: his British colleagues, for example, and the French.

It seems that this was of paramount importance to Roosevelt.

In Hamilton's view, "the young Allied commander in chief was not only learning on the job, but inventing a new kind of coalition command that might be messy and might result in many an upset or failure, but which brought together the collective *power* of Western arms—naval, air, and army—in a way that even the most disciplined of German troops could not stand up to, in the end."[23]

In Mark Perry's opinion, "Marshall chose Eisenhower as the linchpin of his delicate effort to forge an international military coalition because— unlike Patton, Clark, Bradley, MacArthur, Stilwell, Devers, or any other single officer then serving in uniform—Eisenhower understood and was willing to nurture the Atlantic alliance."[24]

The British members of the Combined Chiefs did not perceive this at Casablanca. But even their efforts to turn Ike into a figurehead hastened the process that would bring him to the mastery of coalition warfare.

For they definitely intended to kick him upstairs, and in the short run they succeeded.

On January 20, the Combined Chiefs decided that the British general Harold Alexander—who had become commander in chief of all British forces in North Africa—would become Ike's deputy. Montgomery's Eighth Army, when it reached Tunisia, would also be added to Ike's command.

Ike would remain the overall commander, but two seasoned and successful British deputies would *handle the fighting*. Ike would administer and coordinate. Alexander would be the commander of ground forces.

Notwithstanding this slight to Ike's ability, the rearrangement consolidated his status as a theater commander. As Korda has observed, "inadvertently, the British chiefs of staff, looking for a way to strip Ike of his military command, had made possible his promotion to a new role as the Anglo-American 'supremo' both they and the Prime Minister had been determined to avoid."[25]

Ike visited the front lines in Tunisia before the Casablanca conference ended. He reported to Marshall that the coordination between the forces of Fredendall, Anderson, and the French forces of Juin—which had joined the action—was not satisfactory. He would begin to take remedial measures.

Marshall advised him to get some rest: he was wearing himself down. He also advised Ike to maintain a high profile so the British would not be tempted to usurp his authority.

In Harry Butcher's opinion, Marshall and Ike had developed something like a father-son relationship. But that is not the way in which Eisenhower scholar Mark Perry views it. "For Marshall, Eisenhower was not a 'son' or a close friend," Perry has written. "He was an underclassman. For Eisenhower, Marshall was an upperclassman, whose last name must always be preceded by his rank."[26]

Marshall always addressed Ike as simply..."Eisenhower."

Kay Summersby remembered that Marshall "terrified me" when he visited Ike's headquarters. "He came to visit Ike in Algiers after the conference, and Telek and I got off on the wrong foot with him.... I always had the distinct impression that General Marshall would have been just as happy if I did not exist."[27]

Before the Casablanca conference broke up, the Allies reached agreement on several important matters. At FDR's insistence, the Allied goal would be to demand "unconditional surrender" of the Axis powers. The Darlan episode figured heavily in this far-reaching policy.

De Gaulle was present at Casablanca, and FDR coaxed him into having his picture taken shaking hands with Giraud. There was no love lost between the two, and there was no love lost between de Gaulle and FDR. In the months that followed, FDR tried to prevent de Gaulle from eclipsing Giraud as the presumptive leader of liberated France.

FDR's dislike of de Gaulle was perhaps an unconscious projection of his own deep embarrassment about Darlan. De Gaulle would rise steadily in 1943, and by midyear, he indeed eclipsed Giraud.

The most important decisions at Casablanca concerned grand strategy.

The next step after North Africa would be an invasion of Sicily. This operation would be codenamed HUSKY. After days of debate, and with Marshall threatening a Pacific-first strategy if the British malingered on the cross-channel invasion, an agreement was reached: the buildup for a cross-channel invasion would continue in England, while Mediterranean operations would continue in Sicily.

As an inducement to Churchill, FDR dropped hints that the supreme cross-channel commander might be British. Consequently, Churchill began to intimate to Alan Brooke that the command of the invasion might be his.

A general consensus was reached that the cross-channel operation would be launched in 1944. Everyone got a piece of what they wanted at Casablanca, and no one was really satisfied with the result.

On February 13, Ike informed the War Department that while Rommel's forces were approaching, the "Axis cannot risk at this moment to embark on an operation which might mean heavy losses of men and equipment."[28] Just the same, he was displeased with the deployment of Fredendall's forces: they were spread too thin, and their positions had not been fortified. During the night he began to confer with front-line commanders, noting that Fredendall had hidden himself away in "safe quarters" that had been drilled in the side of a cliff.

Ike meant to take remedial action, but it was too late: at dawn on February 14, a massive onslaught by Rommel's Afrika Korps destroyed Fredendall's position. Fredendall himself suffered a nervous breakdown. Then Arnim's forces joined the battle.

This was the Battle of Kasserine Pass, one of the most devastating American defeats of World War II. Ike raced back to headquarters to get whatever reinforcements were available, and then he returned to the battle zone, hurrying around the front in a scout car, rallying the men. He was finally getting a taste of combat.[29]

When General Alexander arrived, he took command at the front. His years of combat experience served him well. Meanwhile, Ike relieved Fredendall of command and offered his post to Mark Clark.

Clark declined.

This was the first sign of the weakness that had been lurking in Clark's leadership and judgment all along. This old West Point friend who appeared such a promising officer to Marshall and Ike would turn out to be a profound disappointment in battle.

Ike offered the command of Fredendall's demoralized forces to Patton, who of course accepted. And to serve as Ike's "eyes and ears," Marshall sent over General Omar Bradley, a shrewd observer, to be deputy chief of staff.

The defeat at Kasserine Pass did not matter very much in the long run, because America's wartime output was overwhelming Germany. The Germans could not keep up with the logistical challenge: their supplies in North Africa kept dwindling as more and more American planes and tanks and troops and men kept pouring in.

Alexander did an excellent job with the ground command, and Montgomery's performance was also effective.

On a trip to Washington in March, Harry Butcher was summoned to the Oval Office, where FDR queried him about Kasserine Pass. The president made it clear that the setback had not diminished his willingness to give Ike a chance.

In Hamilton's judgment, FDR regarded the American defeat as "proof of his wisdom in insisting American forces learn the skills of modern combat in a 'safe' region of the Mediterranean, where they could swiftly recover."[30]

After meeting with FDR on March 26, 1943, Butcher wrote in his diary that "the principal message the President asked me to convey—and he spoke repeatedly of the General as 'Ike'—was: 'Tell Ike that not only I but the whole country is proud of the job he has done.'"[31]

Ike worked hard to justify this confidence, and he was grateful to FDR for his understanding. "We are learning something every day, and in general do not make the same mistake twice," he wrote to a newspaper publisher back in Abilene.[32]

He had discovered that he needed to be a lot more tough-minded—less inclined to let personal attachments interfere with command decisions. "Officers that fail must be ruthlessly weeded out," he wrote in the aftermath of Kasserine Pass, and "considerations of friendship, family, kindness, and nice personality have nothing to do with the problem."[33]

As the fighting in Tunisia progressed, Alexander consigned the Americans to "mop up" operations. The British were doing the tough work, and Patton and Bradley resented their disdain for American fighting prowess.

Marshall noticed the situation as well. He told Ike to *order* Alexander to give American troops a bigger combat role.

Ike did, and the performance of the American troops began to improve.

All of these experiences added to Ike's political know-how. He saw the necessity of unified command, and he disciplined American officers who disparaged the British and pushed back against British officers who disparaged Americans.

He tried to project an optimistic demeanor, telling everyone that the war would be won by Anglo-American unity. He learned to project good cheer, while making tough moves behind the scenes. Did this prefigure his modus operandi in the "hidden-hand presidency?"

"Few figures in public life," wrote Jean Edward Smith, "have proved more adept at making a silk purse out of a sow's ear than Dwight Eisenhower."[34] Harold Macmillan called Ike "a jewel of broadmindedness and wisdom."[35]

Tunis fell to the combined Allied forces on May 8, and on the 13, the last German units surrendered. The Anglo-American victory in North Africa was stupendous: the Germans lost over two hundred ninety thousand killed or captured. Their presence in North Africa had been eradicated.

There is very good reason to believe that the North Africa campaign gave the Russians relief: many of the units that Hitler sent to North Africa—and later to Italy—were withdrawn from the eastern front. After the Russians prevailed at Stalingrad, Hitler tried another offensive in the summer of 1943 and the Soviets halted it decisively.

The battle of Kursk, which took place in July and August, was the largest tank battle of the war, and its massiveness dwarfed anything that the Americans and the British could have taken on at that point: over four and a half million troops, twelve thousand tanks, and eight thousand aircraft on both sides were involved.

The German defeat at Kursk would destroy Hitler's power to unleash any further offensives against the Red Army.

Ike and Kay

Margaret Bourke-White, the *Life* magazine photographer, was aboard the troopship when Kay Summersby and the others had to make for the lifeboat. Bourke-White took pictures, which were published in *Life*, and Mamie Eisenhower saw the pictures and the references to Ike's pretty young assistant.

She sized up the situation and wrote to Ike about it. We do not know what she said because most of her wartime letters to him were apparently destroyed. But she did save the letters that she received from him, and they reveal the growing strain in the marriage.

"So *Life* says that my old London driver came down," Ike wrote to her on March 2, 1943. "So she did—but the big reason she wanted to serve in this theater is that she is terribly in love with a young American colonel and is about to be married to him come June—assuming both are alive.... But I tell you only so that if anyone is banal and foolish enough to lift an eyebrow at an old duffer such as I am in connection with WACs—Red Cross workers—you will know that I've no emotional involvements and will have none."[36]

Before long, Kay's fiancé, Richard Arnold, would be killed while inspecting a minefield.

Harry Butcher found another getaway destination for Ike, a stucco villa with a red tile roof overlooking the Mediterranean. It had tennis courts and stables, and Ike and Kay would go horseback riding. Elspeth Duncan, another female aide, accompanied Ike and Kay. She told Everett Hughes that "she foresees a scandal. Wants to quit. I tell her to stick around. Maybe Kay will help Ike win the war."[37]

The rumor that Ike and Kay Summersby had an affair has persisted, and biographers have offered opinions. In Carlo D'Este's view, the rumors were unfounded. "When, where, or how," he inquired, "could Eisenhower and Kay Summersby have carried on an affair if they had so chosen? Eisenhower was constantly surrounded by a retinue of aides, friends, cooks, valets, drivers, WAACs, visitors, hangers-on, and others from whom such a relationship could not possibly have been hidden."[38]

Michael Korda took a worldlier view, observing that whenever "adults of the opposite sex are thrown into a tense and highly charged working atmosphere over a long period of time, they will always find a way to be alone with each other, however briefly, if that's what they want to do."[39]

"Where there is smoke, there is fire," Korda wrote, "and there was an awful lot of smoke around General Eisenhower and Kay Summersby, enough to convince plenty of people that they were lovers, whether they were or not." But "the truth of the matter is that nobody knows, and prurient speculation is out of place."[40]

It would be easy to agree that this is nobody's business except for what Harry Truman allegedly revealed. The writer Merle Miller participated in some interviews with Truman that were taped in 1961, and then he interviewed Truman by himself. Miller used this material in an oral history of Truman that was published in 1974, after Truman's death. The title of the book was *Plain Speaking*. Miller was present when the interviews were taped, and he also had lunch with Truman sometimes between the taping sessions.

Or so he claimed. "Mr. Truman and I had days, sometimes weeks, of conversations," Miller wrote, "many of them on tape, many not."[41]

Miller quoted Truman as saying that he knew for a fact that Ike wanted to divorce Mamie at the end of the war and marry Kay. He found correspondence between Ike and Marshall about this subject, and he said that he destroyed the correspondence before he left the presidency.[42]

Miller's claim has generated tremendous controversy. Eisenhower expert Robert Ferrell listened to the taped interviews—which he found at the Truman Library—and said that he heard nothing whatsoever about Ike and Kay. But he also acknowledged that Major General Harry H. Vaughan, an aide to Truman, confirmed the existence of the Ike–Marshall cables in an interview that he gave to the Associated Press after Miller's book was published.[43]

Truman allegedly heard about the cables in the course of the 1952 election, when operatives of Robert Taft, Ike's rival for the Republican presidential nomination, tried to get them for the purpose of embarrassing Ike. Truman got them first.

In biographer Jean Edward Smith's opinion, "much of the bitterness that developed during the 1952 campaign between Eisenhower and President Truman was attributable...to Ike's knowledge that he was hostage to the possible release of General Marshall's letter."[44]

Smith came across even more circumstantial evidence that seemed to confirm what Miller wrote—some of it in interviews with General Lucius Clay (Smith wrote a biography of Clay that was published in 1990) and some of it in the course of interviews with faculty at Columbia University.

Here is the gist of it.

A historian named Garrett Mattingly said that he read the very cables that had passed between Ike and Marshall—the cables that Truman supposedly destroyed. He read them during his service as a junior officer in Naval Intelligence.

Mattingly revealed this to colleagues in the history department at Columbia University when Ike was serving as the university's president.[45] And that was years before Harry Truman made the alleged disclosure. Another Columbia faculty member named Henry F. Graff told Smith about these conversations.[46]

It is easy to shrug away such tales of what someone allegedly told someone else, who in turn passed the word to someone else. What does it matter—when the people in question are dead and the evidence is questionable?

It matters a great deal.

Because if the Truman/Miller allegations were true, the implication for Ike's emotional development is obvious. The experience could have affected his state of mind profoundly in his presidential years—not least of all because he turned Kay loose in the end.

The magnitude of such a *sacrifice* is what matters.

When the book *Plain Speaking* was published, Kay Summersby found herself stunned. She had never known for certain whether Ike had intended to get a divorce and spend the rest of his life with her, though she had heard some rumors.

So she decided to tell her story to the world: the story about how she and Ike had had a torrid affair.

She was dying of cancer when she wrote her book *Past Forgetting— My Love Affair with Dwight D. Eisenhower*. She said that she wrote it as a tribute to the greatest adventure of her life because Ike was the love of her life.

Historians dismissed her claims as those of a hysteric—a woman who romanticized, exaggerated, even created imaginary memories to give herself some emotional relief as she was dying.

They presumed that her memories were nothing but fantasies— or lies.

But that was not the way General Omar Bradley viewed the matter. After reading Kay's book, he declared that "the close relationship" between the couple was "accurately portrayed, so far as my personal knowledge extends."[47] Others who were on the scene during World War II got the same impression about the bond between Ike and Kay. Their recollections are imbued with the knowledge of those who were on the scene—those who saw things.

On December 19, 1943, Anna Roosevelt told her husband that FDR "suspects that the man you first wrote to about going into the army is sleeping with his attractive driver."[48] General James Gavin was so curious about the matter that he asked a reporter from the *Chicago Tribune* for his opinion. "Well," the reporter replied, "I have never before seen a chauffeur get out of a car and kiss the General good morning."[49]

This is all circumstantial evidence—easy to dismiss as rumor-mongering.

But as the weight of the evidence grows, it appears that Kay Summersby was not fantasizing. Biographers need to consider the implications carefully—at least if the claims of this dying woman seem plausible.

And so it was that in 2013 biographer Jean Edward Smith concluded that while the question as to "whether he and Kay were intimate remains a matter of conjecture," there was "no question they were in love."[50] And Smith was right to come to that conclusion.

Because the whole thing made perfect sense from the standpoint of Ike's emotional development.

When he proposed to Mamie, he was on the rebound from Gladys Harding, for whom he had an ardent longing. The marriage with Mamie succeeded at first—succeeded on its own terms—but after the loss of Icky, something happened.

Strains and tensions began to appear: first the Panama episode and then the refusal of Mamie to accompany Ike to the Philippines. When she finally arrived, he declared that he deserved a divorce if he wanted one.

This marriage had been an on-and-off relationship, a marriage full of tension and disillusionment. It was a damaged relationship—one that could be put back together as needed, but Ike and Mamie bore deep grudges against one another. The underlying damage would never be fully mended.

Even so, the marriage comprised a quarter century's worth of shared experiences. Ike cared about Mamie—and he cared very much about John.

His wartime letters to her were more than just formulaic professions of a love that had gone stale. Anyone who reads these letters will be struck by the force of the continuing bond between this man and this woman.

In other words, Ike was *conflicted* about his feelings for Kay Summersby, and the only way he could handle the situation was to keep himself *tough* as he explored his fascination with Kay. Because everyone who witnessed his interactions with Kay could recognize at a glance that this was no mere "friendship." It was *romance*, and everybody who was on the scene and who recorded their impressions perceived it.

When Ike met Kay, he met a woman who apparently set him aflame the way that Gladys Harding had done. Kay thrilled him.

And unlike Mamie—unlike even Gladys—Kay was *adventurous*. Not only was she willing to follow him everywhere, she was *in a position to do so* because she was in uniform.

It was perfect.

For her, this was the adventure of her dreams, and she would not miss a moment. Whatever Ike wanted to do, she was ready.

For him, this was another chance to have what he had missed out on when he lost Gladys. But this was better—better because this woman was *committed* once the intimacy started. She let nothing interfere.

The spark of their encounter struck a powerful blaze, and the difference between their origins—poor and genteel—was catnip.

According to Kay, the affair began in earnest in Algeria following the death of her fiancé. After she heard the news, Ike "put his arms around my shoulders and led me over to the sofa," she recalled. "'Go ahead,' he said. 'Go ahead and cry. It's the only way.'"[51]

Weeks passed.

Ike was ordering new uniforms for himself, and he decided to order some for Kay. "'You can't possibly know how much I would like to do for you," he said—according to Kay. "There was a strange quality in his voice," she continued. "He was looking at me, his teeth clenched.... Then Ike took off those reading glasses of his and stretched out his hand. 'Kay, you are someone very special to me.' I felt tears rising in my eyes. He was someone very special to me, too. I had never realized how special before...., In my face, in my eyes, there was nothing but absolute naked adoration. I could not hide it."

Her mind moved quickly as she tried to understand what was happening.

"So this is love, I thought. I had been in love before, but it had never been like this—so completely logical, so right.... Love had grown so naturally that it was a part of our lives.... Yes, I loved this middle-aged man with his thinning hair, his eyeglasses, his drawn, tired face."[52]

She was not sure exactly what to do, especially in light of the fact that hours later Ike began to back away. He said, "'I'm sorry about this morning, Kay. That shouldn't have happened. I spoke out of turn. Please forget it.'" She felt hurt, at a loss, but she pulled herself together and told herself to be tough.[53]

One day it was time to get fitted for the new uniforms, and she tried to distance herself. She said it really wasn't necessary. Here is what she said happened next:

> He got so red in the face that I thought he would pop a blood vessel right then and there.... "You are a goddamned stubborn Irish mule," he said between his teeth. "You are going to get measured for those uniforms. And you're going to get measured tomorrow. That's an order." He glared at me. I was just as angry as he was. We stood there like two fighters, each daring the other to make a move. "Goddamnit, can't you tell I'm crazy about you?" he barked at me. It was like an explosion. We were suddenly in each other's arms. His kisses absolutely unraveled me.... And I responded every bit as passionately. He stopped, took my face between his hands. "Goddamnit," he said, "I love you."[54]

And that was how things became intimate—according to Kay.

How intimate? Very intimate, if her account should be believed, and opportunities for consummation would develop. At first, however, they encountered all the obstacles that Carlo D'Este summarized. They had to be careful.

"The cocktail hour was often a time we could count on for ourselves," she recalled. "In Algiers we would sit on the high-backed sofa in the living room, listen to some records, have a couple of drinks, smoke a few cigarettes and steal a few kisses—always conscious that someone might walk

in at any moment. We were more like teen-agers than a woman in her thir-
ties and a man in his fifties."[55]

If this is what happened, Ike had reached another turning point in his
life. He had found what he had lost: "absolute naked adoration."

Now consider the sequel.

To give up something like that at the end of World War II: What
would such a thing have meant to a man like Dwight D. Eisenhower?

As soon as *Past Forgetting* appeared, the members of the Eisenhower
family circled the wagons. Their attitude was perfectly understandable:
Mamie Eisenhower was still alive, and her feelings had to be protected.

As late as 1997, Ike's granddaughter Susan Eisenhower challenged
the veracity of Summersby's book. She even claimed that Kay had never
written it: "she had died within a month after signing the contract, so the
book was penned by a ghost writer," Susan said.[56]

Given the paucity of evidence, it is hard to reconstruct exactly how the
manuscript of *Past Forgetting* evolved, but the questions about its veracity
are important.

It seems that *two* different ghost writers, Sigrid Hedin and Barbara
Wyden, helped to put this manuscript together, and their employment
by a dying woman would not have been exceptional. Wyden was quite
reputable: she had been an editor at *Newsweek* as well as at the *New York
Times Magazine*.

The book's publisher, Simon and Schuster, had a reputation to protect,
and the editor in chief at that time was Michael Korda, the future Eisenhower biographer. Post-publication publicity claimed that Summersby
had read and approved 75 percent of the manuscript before she died.[57]

But the credibility of *Past Forgetting* must be probed by asking other
questions. First, is there circumstantial evidence to support the book's
overall narrative and some of its specific allegations? Second, does the
book shed light upon some of the unanswered questions—the myster-
ies—that continue to surround the life of Dwight D. Eisenhower?

The answer to both of these questions is yes, and accordingly three
major Eisenhower biographers—Stephen Ambrose, Michael Korda, and
Jean Edward Smith—have found the book compelling.

So did people like General Omar Bradley, who had the opportunity to watch Ike and Kay close up.

Some of the unanswered questions about Ike concern his behavior in the aftermath of World War II—in the "lost years" in between his military and presidential careers. His behavior in those years was very strange—as we shall see.

But if, for the sake of the argument, we presume that Kay Summersby was telling the truth, things make more sense.

They fit into a much larger pattern.

Because of this correspondence between Kay's account and Ike's behavior, *Past Forgetting* is credible. Readers, of course, will have to reserve judgment on this matter until the time comes to assess it.

In the meantime, the account of Kay will be presented on its merits, with due allowance made for the continuing controversy.

Sicily

The next conference between FDR, Churchill, and the Combined Chiefs of Staff took place in Washington between May 12 and May 25, 1943. It was codenamed TRIDENT.

In 1942, FDR had sided with Churchill and the British in resisting the impatience of the U.S. chiefs for a cross-channel invasion. A year later, he was ready to move in the opposite direction—ready to side with the U.S. high command and insist upon moving ahead with the invasion once the Sicily campaign had been concluded.[58]

But Churchill had no intention of allowing that to happen.

At TRIDENT, he made it clear that his preference was to keep Allied operations confined to the Mediterranean indefinitely.

Even though the British started planning for a cross-channel invasion quite early in the war, their memories of the slaughter at the Somme in 1916 were still vivid, and Churchill and his chiefs found endless reasons to procrastinate. Admiral Leahy recorded Churchill's position in his diary: "There was no indication in his talk of a British intention to undertake a cross channel invasion of Europe either in 1943 or 1944."[59]

Churchill and Alan Brooke started talking about the necessity of knocking Italy out of the war. They also touted the advantage of operations in the Balkans. When Marshall countered that the goal was to knock Nazi Germany—not Italy—out of the war, Brooke insisted that the "no major operations" across the channel "would be possible until 1945 or 1946."[60] To try the invasion sooner, he believed, would lead to a bloodbath.

FDR disagreed. It would be time to shift operations after Sicily, he said, time to get serious about the cross-channel invasion. American troops and their commanders would have had quite enough combat experience by then. So FDR began to side with the American high command—against Churchill.

He turned on the charm with the British, taking Churchill and the Combined Chiefs for a tour of Williamsburg, Virginia. Then he took Churchill off by himself to his presidential retreat in the Catoctin Mountains—"Shangri-La," the retreat that Dwight D. Eisenhower would later rechristen "Camp David."

Churchill remained resistant.

Indeed, he began to meet with U.S. congressional leaders behind FDR's back. He told some of them on May 19—according to Canadian prime minister Mackenzie King, who attended the meeting—that "the great objective now was to knock Italy out of the war."[61]

But it didn't work. Before Churchill started to double-cross FDR, the president went to work behind the scenes. The trip to Shangri-La was a diversion: by taking Churchill away, FDR made it hard for him to participate in the ongoing deliberations of the Combined Chiefs.

Field Marshall Dill went to work on Brooke and warned him of the consequences if the Anglo–American alliance broke down. He told him that Americans were impatient to defeat Japan, and they would simply not tolerate the prolongation of the war in Europe into 1946.

What would happen if the Americans shifted to a Pacific-first strategy?

On May 18, the Combined Chiefs reached a compromise: planning for a spring 1944 cross-channel invasion would go forward. After operation HUSKY, operations would be mounted in the Mediterranean for the purpose of eliminating Italy from the war, but with a strict limitation on resources: divisions would be transferred to England to join the great invasion force that would cross the channel in the spring.

Isolated, outnumbered, and outmaneuvered, Churchill played for time. Italy had become his idée fixe, his grand obsession.

On May 24, at a meeting in the Oval Office, he openly repudiated the Combined Chiefs' agreement.

FDR began to get stern—even angry.

After dinner, he told Churchill that the date for the cross-channel invasion would be set and that forces would have to be withdrawn from the Mediterranean by November 1.

Churchill still resisted, and FDR's composure broke down on May 25. According to Stimson, Churchill "acted like a spoiled boy...when he refused to give up on one of the points—Sardinia—that was an issue. He persisted and persisted until Roosevelt told him that he, Roosevelt, wasn't interested in the matter and that he had better shut up."[62]

After TRIDENT, Churchill insisted on visiting Ike with Marshall to discuss the best way to get Italy out of the war. The delegation, which by then included Brooke and Ismay, arrived in Algiers on May 28.

Churchill worked to get Ike committed to further Mediterranean operations. He implied that TRIDENT was not the last word on the matter. In Marshall's presence, Ike agreed that HUSKY might be followed up with a swift invasion of Italy. He had not been briefed, and so he spoke off the cuff.

Marshall said nothing.[63]

Planning for HUSKY—the invasion of Sicily—started while Ike was still preoccupied with Tunisia, and the plan was put together through a trans-Atlantic give-and-take that was messy. Like TORCH, this massive invasion would be thrown together in a hurry.

Planning was concluded on May 12, and the invasion was set for July 10. The Sicily armada would be bigger than the fleets that were used in the TORCH operation: more than three thousand vessels would head for Sicily. One hundred seventy-five thousand troops were committed. Most of the Axis troops defending the island would be Italian, but two German panzer divisions were also present.

On June 11, on Ike's initiative, the Allies captured the tiny island of Pantelleria, a rocky isle that Mussolini had fortified. Its radio direction finders might have interfered with Allied communications, so Ike wanted the island taken. Alexander was completely opposed because he deemed the island unassailable.

Ike overruled him. He ordered a massive naval bombardment of Pantelleria, and observed it aboard Admiral Cunningham's flagship, the HMS *Aurora*. The Italian garrison surrendered, and Ike had the satisfaction of acting as a battlefield commander at the front—a front-line commander whose instincts were vindicated.

The HUSKY invasion of Sicily would consist primarily of two task forces, one commanded by Montgomery, the other by Patton. Monty was given the lead role by Alexander: his mission was to move up the eastern side of the island and capture the city of Messina. Patton would play a supporting role to the west.

Two days before the invasion, a foul gale was blowing through the Mediterranean, and Ike had to decide whether to abort the operation. Based upon weather forecasting, he decided to proceed, and the forecasts proved accurate.

The Sicily campaign was successful, but it was marred by serious mishaps. Monty—who was often accused by his critics of moving too slowly—was delayed because he had underestimated the time it would take to get around Mount Etna, the massive volcano that stood athwart his path. Patton veered off to the northwest and took the city of Palermo, then veered east in a race to beat Monty to Messina.

German resistance was ferocious—Kesselring had sent in two additional divisions—but Patton pushed his men to the limit and took Messina on August 17. Along the way, Patton's histrionics got him into trouble that could have resulted in a court-martial. The scandal would force him to play a secondary role in future Allied operations for almost a year after Ike saved his career.

His lust for combat incited him to slap the faces of two American soldiers in field hospitals who were suffering from nervous breakdowns. He screamed that they were cowards, and he threatened to shoot them after he slapped them. Members of the press found out, and they confronted Ike, who reprimanded Patton and ordered him to apologize. Patton complied, so Ike tried to keep the matter confidential. But the incident resurfaced later on in the year when investigative journalist Drew Pearson started playing it up and members of Congress got enraged.

General George Patton, commanding the troops in Sicily, 1943.

Stimson and Marshall were able to save Patton's career, as well as the reputation of Ike, who was accused of being too lenient with Patton.

Ike would be criticized down the years for failing to prevent the escape of the German divisions from Sicily by blocking the strait of Messina. The problem with this criticism is political: no one had thought about this particular issue because HUSKY and related operations were stopgap measures whose broader objectives had never been properly conceptualized.

The general objective was to keep Allied troops in the Mediterranean active and to "take Italy out of the war," to use Churchill's slogan. The invasion of Sicily *did* precipitate a political upheaval in Italy, and Mussolini fell from power on July 25. His place was taken by Marshal Pietro Badoglio. In the months that followed, the political logic of the situation—such as it was—would lead Ike and others to negotiate for Italy's surrender, and the politics ushered in a replay of the Darlan fiasco, with charges that the Allies were dallying with fascists in a way that was at odds with the "unconditional surrender" pledge of Casablanca.

Italy

On August 9, FDR met with the American chiefs of staff, and he made his wishes clear. American troops could not sit idle, and the cross-channel invasion would not occur until May 1944. So he would indulge Churchill's Mediterranean strategy, but only to a limited extent: he would approve an operation to seize Italian airfields and keep German troops pinned down. But that was the limit: seven divisions would be shifted to England in the fall. "He was for going no further into Italy than Rome," wrote Henry Stimson.[64]

Two great questions loomed as the invasion of Italy was being planned. The first question was whether the Badoglio government would negotiate and surrender. The second was whether Hitler would muscle in and take over.

The Italian regime played a double-handed game: they played up to the Germans while exploring the issue of how much Allied force might be sent into Italy—and how fast. The negotiations occurred in Lisbon, and Ike sent representatives. He contemplated an airborne assault to seize Rome and its airfields, sending Brigadier General Maxwell Taylor and some intelligence operatives from the Office of Strategic Services (OSS) on a dangerous mission behind enemy lines to assess the situation.

Meanwhile, Marshall asked Ike for his recommendations about officers who should be assigned to serve in the cross-channel invasion— which now bore the codename OVERLORD.

Their deliberations took place in the week after the capture of Messina.[65] They finally settled on Omar Bradley, whom Ike recommended as "the best-rounded combat leader I have met."[66] Marshall ordered Bradley to England to oversee preparations for OVERLORD.

Meanwhile, FDR, Churchill, and the Combined Chiefs of Staff met again to formulate strategy, this time in Quebec.

The conference, which lasted from August 11 to 24, was codenamed QUADRANT. Churchill was beside himself with expectation due to the fall of Mussolini and the chance of getting the Badoglio regime to surrender. Just before the conference, FDR brought Churchill to Hyde Park. He saw that Churchill was still intent on scuttling the cross-channel invasion and replacing it with an all-Mediterranean strategy.

So FDR became tough. In Nigel Hamilton's opinion, he used the following threat to force Churchill into line: if Churchill continued to resist a cross-channel invasion, America would refuse to share the MANHATTAN project research—the United States would reserve to itself the right to develop and use nuclear weapons. FDR also insisted on an American commander for OVERLORD.[67]

Whatever leverage he used, he got his way.

Churchill continued to hope that he could use the exigencies of combat in Italy as leverage for his alternate strategic scenario: to make the so-called "soft underbelly" of the Axis the main focus of the action. He would insist for the rest of his life that if only the Italian operation had been given the resources it deserved, the Allies could have pushed their way into central Europe, perhaps getting through the Alps via the Brenner Pass or else through the Ljubljana Gap.

The behind-the-scenes discussions at the QUADRANT conference were stormier than the sessions at TRIDENT. Brooke insisted that the Italian invasion should go as far north as Milan. He argued that the seven divisions reserved for OVERLORD should be available as needed in Italy.

It was in these chaotic circumstances that Ike was obliged to plan the Italian campaign. As Carlo D'Este has written, "Eisenhower was directed to fight a war in Italy with no identifiable or stated strategic goal, rapidly diminishing assets, and only the vaguest prior planning." He "was further handicapped by the requirement to use only assets already available to him, a great many of which were due to be sent to England by the end of 1943."[68]

Thus began a campaign that was ill-conceived from the beginning—ill-planned, ill-thought-out, opportunistic. The politics between FDR, Churchill, and the Combined Chiefs created this situation, and disagreements between Marshall, Ike, Alexander, Montgomery, Clark, and the British sea and air commanders made what D'Este calls "the committee system imposed on Eisenhower by the British at Casablanca" a planning nightmare.[69]

The hasty deliberations assigned combat command to Montgomery and Mark Clark. Marshall designated Naples as the primary target, and Clark believed that the best landing spot would be at the Bay of Gaetna, north of the city. But British Air Chief Marshal Sir Arthur Tedder said that such a target was beyond the range of his Sicily-based air squadrons. So the Gulf of Salerno was selected, despite Clark's objection that the beaches were surrounded by mountains.

Hitler made the decision to do exactly what he did to the Vichy regime: he poured massive forces into Italy that turned the nation from an Axis ally into an occupied territory. Kesselring was determined to make maximum use of Italy's mountain ranges to force the Allies to fight for every inch and to turn the Italian campaign into a bloody stalemate.

Ike and his team decided to put Montgomery's forces ashore at the "toe" of the Italian boot, in the hope that this landing might draw German forces away from Salerno, the primary target. The timing was also political: the landing of troops might encourage the Italian negotiators in Lisbon to make up their minds.[70] Moving troops across the Strait of Messina would be quick and efficient.

A shortage of landing craft prevented simultaneous landings: Montgomery's forces went ashore on September 3, and the Salerno landings took place a week later on September 9.

The Badoglio regime agreed to surrender to the Allies on September 8. Ike, via Beetle Smith, led the Italians to believe that no fewer than twelve Allied divisions would land in Italy. In fact, Montgomery's landing comprised only two divisions and Clark's encompassed only three. Hitler put fourteen divisions into Italy, plus the four evacuated from Sicily.

Ike, Alexander, and Clark all hoped that the Germans would not oppose the Salerno landings but would establish a line to the north of Rome along the Arno River. Kesselring decided to ignore Montgomery's landings and repel the Allies at Salerno. Clark's forces encountered heavy German artillery and mortar fire when they landed, so Allied naval forces shelled the Germans' positions and the Germans pulled back.

But Kesselring had five divisions ready to counterattack, and on September 13, an immense German onslaught began. Clark had to fall back to the beachhead, and he began to consider evacuating his forces.

Ike swung into action, telling Butcher that "if the Salerno battle ended in disaster, he would probably be out."[71] So he ordered Tedder to deploy all his bombers, and he ordered Cunningham to rush his main battle fleet to Salerno. And he ordered Montgomery to hasten his advance northward to help relieve Clark.

The battle lasted for four days.

Cunningham's naval forces poured eleven thousand tons of shells upon the Germans, and Tedder's bombers dropped about a thousand tons of bombs per square mile. This firepower was overwhelming, and its purpose was achieved. On September 16, Kesselring pulled back to the north of Naples, which was occupied by the Allies on October 1.

It had been a very close call for Ike.

He and Clark had badly underestimated the capacity and the will of the Germans to resist, and Salerno came close to being a disaster.

Marshall criticized Ike for having landed Montgomery's forces so far away from the Salerno beachhead. "You gave the enemy too much time to prepare and eventually found yourself up against very stiff resistance," he wrote.[72]

Ike was chastened, and he sank into a mood of foreboding. He could see what the Italian campaign would be like: a bloody and miserable fight against heavy German resistance and with ever-shrinking resources. If he stayed in command of the Mediterranean theater, that would be his fate.

The most likely alternative was a return to Washington to take Marshall's place as chief of staff. A great many people presumed that Marshall would be the commander of OVERLORD. Stimson called Marshall "the strongest man there is in America."[73]

Kay Summersby recalled that "rumors had been flying, rumors that struck panic into my heart—rumors to the effect that Ike would be recalled to Washington to serve as Chief of Staff and General Marshall would come to Europe to take over the Allied command of Overlord." She reflected that "if Ike was recalled to Washington, there was not a chance in the world that I would ever see him again."[74]

There were other possibilities for Ike. Despite the close call at Salerno, his role as theater commander had put him on the cover of *Time* magazine. After the September 13, issue of *Time* hit the newsstands, Kansas

Republicans began talking about the possibility of getting Ike to run for the Republican presidential nomination in 1944.[75]

The fact of the matter is that war heroes had figured prominently in presidential politics ever since George Washington. Jackson, William Henry Harrison, Zachary Taylor, and Grant won the presidency, and Teddy Roosevelt's status as war hero was integral to his subsequent political ascent.

Political kingmakers had their eyes on Ike by 1943.

So all through the autumn, celebrities and dignitaries came to visit Ike in Algiers. Kay remembered the never-ending dinner parties as congressmen, cabinet members, even movie stars came to pay their respects.

And whenever Winston Churchill came to call, he asked for Kay to be seated at his side.[76]

FDR's Decision

The first meeting of the "Big Three"—FDR, Churchill, and Stalin—was scheduled for November 28 in Teheran. Before this summit, the Combined Chiefs would meet with FDR and Churchill in Cairo for a strategy session.

On November 17, Churchill, on his way to Cairo, met with Ike in Malta. While expressing his misgivings about OVERLORD, he also said that "we British will be glad to accept either you or Marshall" as commander.[77]

This was the first intimation that Ike might be considered for the command of OVERLORD.

Two days later, Ike flew to Oran to await the arrival of FDR, Hopkins, and the Joint Chiefs, who were travelling aboard the USS *Iowa*. Ike waited in the company of Roosevelt's sons Elliott and Franklin Jr., both of whom were serving in uniform.

FDR planned a one-day stop in Tunis before proceeding to Cairo the next morning. Ike asked him to stay another day and take a night flight to Cairo for security reasons. FDR agreed—if Ike would take him on a tour of the battlefields, ancient and modern, around Carthage.

The two men hit it off enormously. FDR asked to meet Kay, who was assigned to be his driver. She was seated next to FDR at dinner that night. Like Churchill, FDR found Kay Summersby fascinating.

Ike and President Franklin Delano Roosevelt review the troops in Algiers, 1943.

The following day, they all took the battlefield tour, and they brought along Telek. They packed a picnic lunch, and at noon they stopped at a eucalyptus grove. After everyone was settled, FDR asked Kay, "Won't you come back here, Child, and have lunch with a dull old man?" Kay recalled that she "soon got over my awe of him and was chatting away as if I had known him all my life."[78]

FDR asked Kay if she would be interested in joining the WAACs (Women's Army Auxiliary Corps). She said she would love to, but she would have to become an American citizen. "Well, who knows," Roosevelt replied; "stranger things have happened."[79]

At the airport, before boarding his plane for Cairo, FDR told Ike that George Marshall deserved to be given the command of OVERLORD. "I hate to think that 50 years from now practically nobody will know who George Marshall was," the president said. "That is one of the reasons why I want George to have the Big Command—he is entitled to establish his place in history as a great general."[80]

In truth, however, FDR had not made up his mind.

He believed that if Marshall remained chief of staff, he could continue to fight for American interests among the Combined Chiefs. He could also keep MacArthur under some semblance of control. Furthermore, Marshall had tremendous credibility on Capitol Hill. Leahy, King, and Arnold all wanted him to remain the chief of staff.

So FDR was taking Ike's measure again in the course of their meeting in Tunis.

He ordered Ike to join the conference at Cairo and present a report about the Mediterranean situation, so Ike instructed Kay to get ready to travel with him again.

The Cairo conference, codenamed SEXTANT, took place between November 22 and 26. The policy disputes were more acrimonious than ever. When Churchill insisted on a campaign to take the island of Rhodes, George Marshall retorted that "not one American soldier is going to die on that goddamned beach."[81]

FDR told his son Elliott that "I think Winston is beginning not to like George Marshall very much," adding that "one man deserves a medal for being able to get along with Winston. And that's Eisenhower."[82]

Ike's presentation to the Combined Chiefs was realistic, and it went over well. Afterward, Marshall told him to take a break from his duties because he was showing obvious signs of fatigue.

So Ike, Kay, Tex Lee, and some others took a tour of the ancient Egyptian monuments. Then they flew to Palestine and stayed at the King David Hotel. Ike and Kay took a stroll through the Garden of Gethsemane. He gave her a souvenir postcard, jotting down the following message on the back of its envelope: "Good night! There are lots of things I could wish to say—you know them. Good night."

Kay kept this item until she died, and it is reproduced as an illustration in her book *Past Forgetting*.[83]

At the meeting with Stalin, Churchill kept up his usual campaign for expanded Mediterranean operations. Neither Stalin nor FDR showed any interest. Stalin was focused single-mindedly on OVERLORD: When would the invasion occur and who would command it? FDR told him it was scheduled for May 1944, but he had still not made up his mind about the commander. Stalin was firm: he should make that decision right away. The conference broke up on December 2.

Back in Cairo, FDR sent for Marshall and told him the OVERLORD command would be his if he wanted it, but his services as chief of staff were also invaluable. Then FDR asked Marshall to state his own preference.

Marshall's reply was the quintessence of duty: he would accept whatever decision the president made. "Then it will be Eisenhower," Roosevelt said. "I don't think I could sleep at night with you out of the country."[84]

According to James Roosevelt, his father explained that he had chosen Eisenhower because he was "the best politician among the military men," a "natural leader who can convince other men to follow him."[85]

Overlord

Ike was ordered to wrap up his affairs in the Mediterranean and be in London by January. His successor in the Mediterranean would be General Sir Henry Maitland Wilson, to whom both Harold Alexander and Mark Clark would report.

Ike began selecting the members of his OVERLORD team right away. When his choices were questioned—by the British or by George Marshall—he stuck to his guns.

He did not always get what he wanted, but his wishes generally prevailed. He got Air Chief Marshall Tedder, who advocated close air–ground coordination, as his deputy. He got Beetle Smith as chief of staff.

Per the Casablanca arrangement, his subordinate commanders were mostly British. As his naval commander, the British gave him Admiral Sir Bertram Ramsay, who had masterminded the Dunkirk evacuation. The air arm would be commanded by Sir Trafford Leigh-Mallory.

Ike wanted Harold Alexander as the ground commander for the OVERLORD landings, but Churchill—who wished to retain Alexander as commander of the Italian campaign—assigned him Montgomery.

After Ike had moved his headquarters to France, he would take over the direct command of the ground operations.

Ike put an American officer in charge of logistics: John C. H. Lee, whose performance would be key to victory.

He also picked commanders for the American invasion forces after engaging in some tug-of-war with Marshall: Omar Bradley for the army, Tooey Spaatz for the air forces, Harold Stark as commander for the navy.

Despite the great fear of a cross-channel invasion that had pervaded British military thinking, contingency planning for such an invasion had begun as early as 1941 with the creation of "Combined Operations," the "Commandos," under the leadership of Lord Mountbatten. Churchill, still imbued with the defiance of Hitler that sustained both him and the British people through the Blitz, ordered Mountbatten to begin conceptualizing the basis for an invasion of Europe.

The British contribution to the cross-channel invasion would therefore be fundamental—and enormous.

Mountbatten foresaw the need to get fuel across the channel, so tankers and even a submerged fuel pipeline were in the cards when Ike took charge of OVERLORD. British planners foresaw the need for artificial harbors, so designs for gigantic prefabricated harbors codenamed Mulberries were in the works. Major General Sir Percy Hobart had been designing unconventional vehicles to assist the landings by destroying German obstacles on the beaches.

In March 1943, the British had commissioned an invasion contingency plan supervised by General Frederick E. Morgan, whose command was designated COSSAC—which stood for chief of staff, supreme Allied commander-designate. This plan was based around a bold deception: the Germans would be led to believe that the invasion would cross the channel at the narrowest point and land at Pas-de-Calais, whereas the real invasion force would head for Normandy.

In order to deceive the Germans, a fictitious army would be created: fake radio traffic and physical props (designed to be viewed at a distance by German spies) would create the illusion that an army commanded by Patton was being assembled to invade at Pas-de-Calais. If the Germans took the bait, they would keep enough forces at Pas-de-Calais to leave the beaches at Normandy less well-defended than they would have been.

To fool the Germans even more, a second deception was created—a deception to create the impression that the Allies were sending an invasion force to Norway. But the Pas-de-Calais deception was the one that was the most important.

The "ULTRA secret"—the British intelligence breakthrough that cracked the Germans' ENIGMA code—would be used to ascertain whether or not the Germans were falling for the ruse.

In the hope that the deception would work, the COSSAC scheme proposed landing only three divisions on the beaches of Normandy—a case of best-case planning, since no one knew if the deception would succeed. The size of the invasion force was also based upon the projections of available landing craft.

As soon as Ike and Montgomery took a look at the scheme in December, they saw its weakness: the invasion force was too small.

Just a month earlier, a landing by marines on the Pacific island of Tarawa had resulted in terrible casualties. Ike had learned from the experience of Salerno: his experience included expertise in the challenge of amphibious landings.

So as soon as he looked at the COSSAC plan, he said, "Not enough wallop in the initial attack."[86] Monty came to the same conclusion: he told Churchill that the plan "will never do." Instead of three divisions in the first assault wave, Monty wanted five. These five divisions would be followed up by nine others.

Monty also said that "the air battle must be won before the operation is launched," and Ike agreed with that as well.[87]

Despite the nasty features of his personality, Montgomery *at his best* could be an excellent combat commander and a good planner. Like Patton, he had a charismatic side that could rally his troops.

He made invaluable contributions to OVERLORD. As he and Ike worked together on the early phases of invasion planning, they overcame their mutual aversion. This would be a high point in their relationship.

They could both see that the COSSAC plan had been drawn up by military planners with no experience of combat.

On December 28, Marshall ordered Ike to return to the United States to meet with War Department officials, visit his family, and get some relaxation before going to London to command OVERLORD. Marshall made it very clear that this was an order.

Kay Summersby drove him to the airport on New Year's Eve.

At the plane, Ike reached into his pocket, pulled out a note, and gave it to Kay, saying, "Take care of this for me."

His note to her read, "Think of me. You know what I will be thinking." This note was auctioned off at Sotheby's on June 13, 1991.[88]

On the way to Washington, Ike flew to Morocco to consult with Montgomery and Churchill, who was recuperating there from an illness. He also seized the opportunity to meet with Charles de Gaulle, who he correctly sensed might be the future leader of France. Ike and de Gaulle hit it off, and over time they became good friends.

When Ike got to Washington, his interactions with Mamie were just what could have been expected: distant.

He visited the Pentagon, where the War Department had relocated its offices, and he consulted with Marshall, especially about the necessity of gaining control over the strategic bombers based in Britain.

He also went to the White House to confer with FDR, and one of the issues they discussed was what to do about de Gaulle.

De Gaulle had emerged as the undisputed leader of the French Committee of National Liberation (FCNL), which had been taking on many of the functions of a French government in exile.

FDR's aversion to de Gaulle was undisguised. In light of the way that FDR had lost face so badly in the Darlan/Vichy episode, de Gaulle was a living reminder of that embarrassment. Ike could see that de Gaulle would have to play a role in the OVERLORD invasion and its aftermath, so he would need to figure out a method for bringing him aboard. Churchill, of course, would play a useful role in that process.

Ike and Mamie visited John at West Point, and the reunion was not entirely pleasant. Years later, John reminisced that his father was tense at the time, and he was acting abrupt. When Mamie called this to Ike's attention, he snapped, "Hell, I'm going back to my theater where I can do what I want."[89]

Then Ike and Mamie went to the Greenbrier resort in West Virginia—on Marshall's orders. After that, they flew to Kansas for a family reunion. Ike's mother was eighty-one years old. Milton had become the president of Kansas State University.

Back in Washington, Ike paid another call upon FDR, and the president gave him a signed photograph to be given to Kay Summersby.

Before leaving for London, Ike had made arrangements to have Kay pick him up at the station.

On January 15, 1944, Ike returned to London and was greeted by Kay, who was in the company of a Colonel James Gault—an officer whom the British had assigned to serve Ike as a military aide. Gault had found a townhouse for Ike near Berkeley Square, which was close to the London headquarters of SHAEF (Supreme Headquarters, Allied Expeditionary Force).

Kay and Ike went in and looked around.

They were joined by Harry Butcher and Mickey McKeogh. After drinks, Ike told McKeogh that nothing further would be needed for the evening, and Butch went upstairs to bed. Then, according to Kay, she and Ike found themselves alone—completely alone.

What happened was entirely predictable: they undressed and began to get intimate. But Ike was too nervous to perform.[90]

It didn't take Ike long to make a big decision: he would move back to Telegraph Cottage, relocating SHAEF and its staff to a small group of buildings nearby.

In the weeks ahead, Ike and Monty created the preliminary plan for the Normandy landings. Five landing beaches were designated, three for the British and two for the Americans. The British zones were codenamed Juno, Sword, and Gold. The American beaches were Utah and Omaha.

The specific command structure was arranged. Within the high command, Monty was in charge of all the ground forces, but Bradley would command the American landing forces, and General Sir Miles Dempsey would command the British forces.

Every individual beach would be invaded by a separate corps; the American VII Corps under Major General J. Lawton "Lightning Joe" Collins (who had fought at Guadalcanal in the Pacific) would land at Utah, and the U.S. V Corps—under the command of none other than Gee Gerow—would land at Omaha.

Massive bombardments would precede the landings, and three paratrooper divisions would be dropped behind enemy lines.

The U.S. VII Corps under Collins would cut across the Cotentin Peninsula and capture Cherbourg. Until Cherbourg was secured, supplies would be brought in via two massive prefabricated Mulberries.

As the invasion forces moved inland, more troops—including the American Third Army under Patton—would arrive at Normandy.

Before the invasion, Patton would pretend to be the commander of the make-believe army whose bogus operations were intended to convince the Germans that the Normandy landing was a feint. This massive deception, which was scheduled to commence in March 1944, was codenamed FORTITUDE.

For months, Allied planners had included a second invasion force from the Mediterranean that would land in southern France. This secondary invasion—codenamed ANVIL—was created to pull German forces away from Normandy.

But the British kept trying to cancel the operation, while Marshall and Ike would insist on it. The controversy over ANVIL centered on British desires to divert the operation's landing craft and use them elsewhere. Monty wanted to use the ANVIL resources for OVERLORD, and Churchill wanted them for Italy.

Ike had to deal with this issue when he got to London, and he had to get control of the strategic bombing forces. Moreover, he needed to figure out ways to promote the involvement of de Gaulle, for the troops in ANVIL would include French troops from North Africa.

As soon as he arrived in London, Ike received a telegram from the State Department directing him to have nothing to do with de Gaulle or the FCNL.

He asked Marshall to intervene, and Marshall turned the problem over to Assistant Secretary of War John J. McCloy, who got along extremely well with Roosevelt.

All through February, Ike worked with Marshall on the interrelated ANVIL and landing craft issues. Marshall found ways to have some landing craft sent over from the Pacific, and for this and other reasons, Ike postponed the Normandy invasion until June.

He also decided to postpone the ANVIL invasion until August. ANVIL and OVERLORD had been designed to happen simultaneously. But the Normandy invasion was all-important, so Ike decided to divert landing craft from the Mediterranean to support it. Then the vessels would be sent back to the Mediterranean for use in ANVIL.

On the issue of strategic bombing, Ike had to resort to a threat: a threat to resign.

Tooey Spaatz, who commanded the U.S. Army Air Forces, and Air Chief Marshal Sir Arthur "Bomber" Harris, who commanded the RAF Bomber Command, believed that bombardment of German cities and military targets would end the war, making OVERLORD unnecessary. So they refused to divert aircraft to OVERLORD. They also refused to put themselves under the authority of OVERLORD's air commander, Leigh-Mallory.

By March, Ike told Churchill that he would resign and go home if he could not get sufficient air support for the invasion.[91]

Churchill gave in: he placed Spaatz, Harris, and Leigh-Mallory under the direct command of Air Chief Marshal Tedder, Ike's deputy. Through Tedder, Ike would have authority to give direct orders to Spaatz and to Harris.

Before D-Day, Ike's strategic bombers would drop seventy-six thousand tons of bombs on French rail lines, bridges, and tunnels, in the effort to seal off Normandy from German reinforcements.

Ike was now a global figure.

From a colonel he had risen to become a man who consulted with national leaders, a man on the cover of *Time*, a man in command of huge armies, a man whose strategic decisions would affect the fate of millions.

But would he be a success?

OVERLORD was the most gigantic armada in recorded history: over six thousand ships—twelve hundred warships and over four thousand landing craft—more than eleven thousand aircraft, and more than one hundred fifty thousand men from the United States, Britain, and Canada would be hitting the beaches.

"As the big day approaches," Ike wrote in April, "tension grows and everybody gets more and more on edge."[92]

He wrote letters to Mamie that were obviously responses to her expressions of suspicion and discontent. "I know that people at home always think of an army in the field as living a life of night clubs, gayety and loose

153

morals," he wrote to her on May 12. "But so far as I can see," he continued, "the American forces here are living cleaner and more nearly normal lives than they did in Louisiana—California—etc."[93]

An interesting thing to say: the American forces in England were living "more normal" lives than at home.

Ike had moved the advance headquarters of SHAEF to Southwick House, a mansion near Portsmouth, the main embarkation point for the invasion. From there, Kay drove him to the various troop encampments, where his presence and grin could help to lift the morale of his men. "Eisenhower is just the right man for the job," wrote Montgomery on June 2. "He is really a big man and is in every way an Allied commander. I like him immensely."[94]

The success of OVERLORD would depend upon exactly the right combination of factors. The moon, the tides, the weather all had to be perfect, and so many things could go wrong. It was essential for the Germans to believe that the invasion was headed toward Pas-de-Calais. ULTRA intercepts implied that the Germans were swallowing the deception. But ULTRA intercepts had also proven misleading in the days leading up to Kasserine Pass.

What if Allied intelligence in the days preceding OVERLORD should prove unreliable?

And even if the landings succeeded, no one could tell whether Hitler would continue to hold back panzer divisions at Pas-de-Calais.

A week before D-Day, Air Chief Marshal Leigh-Mallory told Ike to cancel the airborne operation. Reconnaissance photos, he said, showed that German antiaircraft fire would slaughter the paratroopers.

Ike told Leigh-Mallory to write down his views in a memo. "I took it to my tent alone," Ike recalled, "and sat down to think. I took the problem to no one else. I realized that if I disregarded the advice of my technical expert and his predictions should prove accurate, I would carry to my grave...the stupid, blind sacrifice" of lives.

But he decided to go ahead, because "our experience in Sicily and Italy did not support his degree of pessimism."[95]

D-Day was set for June 5.

The moon, the tides, and the weather would be in the proper alignment for only three days: from the fifth to the seventh. The next opportunity would not arrive until June 18. A moonlit night was needed for the benefit of the airborne troops, and a low tide was needed to reveal the offshore mines and obstacles.

On June 3, the weather turned bad.

Ike was told that air support would be impossible by D-Day, that the naval bombardment would fail, and that landing craft would founder in the high surf. The armada was already at sea. What should he do?

Ike consulted Montgomery and his other commanders. They were generally in favor of going ahead—while keeping tabs on the weather. De Gaulle, who had been flown in by Churchill, thought that Ike should go ahead.

Ike postponed the invasion for a day—until June 6.

By the fourth, the winds had begun to reach gale force.

But the head of SHAEF's meteorological team reported that the speed of the storm was increasing and that a brief break in the weather would occur from the evening of the fifth through the morning of the sixth. Then conditions would worsen again.

Ike polled his commanders. Admiral Ramsay was in favor of going ahead, but Leigh-Mallory and Tedder were doubtful. Montgomery said to go ahead. A postponement would have shoved the invasion off to the 18.

Beetle Smith remembered that Ike sat in silence for about five minutes. "I never realized before," he remembered, "the loneliness and isolation of a commander at the time when such a momentous decision has to be taken, with the full knowledge that failure or success rests on his judgment alone."[96]

Ike looked up and said, "OK, we'll go."[97]

On June 5, Ike composed this message to be broadcast in the event of failure:

Our landings in the Cherbourg-Havre area have failed to gain a satisfactory foothold and I have withdrawn the troops. My decision to attack at this time and place was based upon the best information

Ike greets the men of the 101st Airborne on the eve of D-Day.

available. The troops, the air, and the Navy did all that bravery and devotion to duty could do. If any blame or fault attaches to the attempt it is mine alone.[98]

On the evening of the fifth, Ike visited the troops of the 101st Airborne division. He "got out and just started walking among the men," Kay recalled. "When they realized who it was, the word went from group to group like the wind blowing across a meadow, and then everyone went crazy. The roar was unbelievable. They cheered and whistled and shouted, 'Good old Ike!'"

Slowly, Ike "went from group to group and shook hands with as many men as he could. He spoke a few words to every man and he looked the man in the eye as he wished him success."

As the air operation began, Ike and Kay went over to the headquarters building and climbed up on the roof. "There were hundreds of planes circling above us," Kay remembered, and "I knew I had never seen anything like it before and never would see anything like it again. We stayed on the roof for a long time watching the planes. Ike stood there with his hands in his pockets, his face tipped toward the sky. The planes kept circling, and then they began tailing off and heading toward Normandy. We sighed. A lot of those men ... were going to their deaths."[99]

Ike and Kay drove back to his command trailer, and they stayed there together through the night.

Ike's eyes were bloodshot, his neck was in knots, and Kay massaged him to ease the tension. Around 4 a.m., he agreed with her suggestion that he needed to try to get some sleep, so they went back to quarters.

On the morning of June 6, the weather was clear.

CHAPTER FIVE

War Hero

*Almighty God: our sons, pride of our nation, this day have set upon
a mighty endeavor, a struggle to preserve our Republic, our religion,
and our civilization, and to set free a suffering humanity....
Success may not come with rushing speed, but we shall return
again and again; and we know that by Thy grace,
and by the righteousness of our cause, our sons will triumph.*

—Franklin Delano Roosevelt,
D-Day prayer, broadcast by radio to the American people

Ike had been extremely lucky in gaining the support of successful men down the years.

It began with Bob Davis, who taught him poker and some other basic skills, and then the mentors followed one another in a rapid succession: Conner, Pershing, MacArthur, Marshall, and FDR became his sponsors.

No wonder Eric Larrabee mused that Ike gravitated upward as naturally as a sunflower seeks the sun.

He was *propelled*.

But there was more than mere luck in this: Ike had been a brilliant staff officer down the years. He made himself *invaluable* to one superior officer after another. As word of his achievements circulated, the opportunities followed—some of them *lucky*. Hard work is sometimes rewarded if the circumstances are right, and Ike's accomplishments triggered opportunities.

George Patton created a new nickname for Ike during World War II—"Divine Destiny" (a play upon his first two initials, "D. D.")—and this nickname was fraught with resentment, for Patton was jealous. He saw Ike as a lucky politician who had been in the right places at the right times and whose skills as a commander could not compare with his own.

But Ike's skills were distinctive, and experiences had been improving them. He surpassed George Marshall by the time that FDR selected him for OVERLORD. He had the direct experience of commanding amphibious landings (Marshall had no such direct experience), and FDR could see in him a charisma that was different from the austere appeal of Marshall. Not only was Ike a savvy politician, he projected a charm that put people at their ease while he pursued his hidden-hand maneuvers.

As Michael Korda has observed, "it was typically astute of that supreme master of politics Franklin Roosevelt to see that quality in Ike at once, and to recognize, however much he admired Marshall, what a formidable weapon it was. And why not? It was one he and Ike shared."[1]

Ike's preeminence by 1944 was a convergence between the opportunities and the man. When his opportunities arrived, Ike's innate shrewdness—the shrewdness that prompted him to avoid overplaying his hand—guided his actions. His ambition was governed by a subtlety of judgment that FDR had perceived.

Nonetheless, he was still very lucky.

Fox Conner might have lived to become a famous general except for the fact that by the time of World War II, he was too old to serve.

Ike was just the right age.

It was a convergence of the man and his times that would generate the following order to Ike from the Combined Chiefs of Staff when he assumed the command of OVERLORD: "You will enter the continent of Europe and…undertake operations aimed at the heart of Germany and the destruction of her armed forces."

It would be Ike's world-historical responsibility to see that German militarism was *crushed*.

Nothing less would suffice.

As supreme commander at D-Day, he was poised to become the greatest hero of the war—with greater things ahead.

And he knew it.

How different things would have been for Ike if he had followed Edgar to the University of Michigan. He might have gone on to become a professor of history, as many of his friends had predicted.

High school contemporaries had toyed with the idea that Edgar Eisenhower might become president. Now it was Ike whose name was being bandied about by the political kingmakers.

Ike was thinking about Edgar in the months before D-Day—thinking of their long-ago rivalry. A month and a half before the Normandy landings, Ike wrote to Edgar as follows: "You could run faster, hit better, field better, tote the football better, and do everything except beat me at shotgun shooting.... I was just the tail to your kite."[2]

So many continuities from Abilene days would abide as Ike rose to his destiny.

He was reading pulp fiction at night to help himself sleep, the sort of fiction he read as a kid—tales of the Wild West that reconciled the pacifism of his mother with the use of violent force to keep the peace.

Ike knew that Ida was continuing to pay close attention to the things that he did, and he could only hope she would approve.

Regardless, he would do what he had to do.

D-Day

The Germans were caught by surprise on the morning of June 6.

They knew an invasion was coming, but they figured the destination would be Pas-de-Calais. Moreover, they believed that they had no reason to presume an invasion was imminent due to the heavy weather that began on June 3.

It seemed a very safe presumption that no one would risk an invasion in weather like that, and so they dropped their guard and made little use of their remaining surveillance assets near the English Channel. Erwin Rommel, in charge of defending Hitler's Atlantic Wall, returned to Germany to celebrate his wife's birthday.

The scale of the OVERLORD operation was staggering. Over a million Americans had been brought to Britain to support it, and over two million servicemen overall would be involved in one way or another.

Over two hundred trainloads of troops would be landed at D-Day on the American beaches alone, and that was just the beginning. So many vehicles of all kinds would be landed in the course of the invasion that a double line of them would have stretched all the way from Pittsburgh to Chicago. Every effort had been made to anticipate the things the soldiers would need and arrange them in a logical sequence to be unloaded from the landing vehicles.

The industrial output and coordination behind all this were America's distinctive contributions to the war.

Despite the preparations, some mistakes were made. American troops were loaded from the ships onto the landing craft too far from the landing zones, and many arrived at the shoreline seasick. Amphibious tanks were launched too early, and they sank. The Americans failed to make use of Percy Hobart's ingenious devices for clearing obstacles on the beachheads. The naval bombardment of the German fortifications was insufficient.

Even so, the landings went relatively well—except for the one at Omaha Beach that came so close to disaster that Omar Bradley considered evacuating the men.

Weather conditions around Omaha Beach remained bad, and the bombers overshot their targets. The Germans had extremely good defensive positions at the top of steep cliffs, and, unbeknownst to Allied intelligence, an excellent German infantry division had been placed there.

Ike's choice for the task force commander was his old friend Gee Gerow, who lacked the combat experience of the other American task force commander, "Lightning Joe" Collins. The choice of Gerow was a sign of some lingering sentimentality in Ike that needed purging.

Slowly, the situation at Omaha stabilized and improved as the veteran 1st Division improvised tactics and fought the battle through, with heavy casualties.

The German commander in chief in the West, Gerd von Rundstedt, remained convinced that the main invasion force would land at Pas-de-Calais, and he could not move troops in any case without Hitler's permission.

As Ike waited for news from the front, he grew irritable, and then depressed. When he received news of the Omaha crisis, he ordered Leigh-Mallory to

Ike aboard the British minelayer Apollo *on June 7, 1944, the day after D-Day.*

bomb the Germans' positions through the cloud cover. The next day, June 7, he got aboard the British minelayer HMS *Apollo* to visit the front. He conferred with Montgomery and Bradley and approved of their plan to consolidate the British and American beachheads.

He continued to visit the front in the weeks ahead, and on one occasion he actually flew over the front lines in a two-seater P-51 Mustang—a dangerous thing to do.

Kay Summersby remembered that "there was a terrible let-down after D-Day," and that "Ike was tired as if he had run out of steam."[3] He travelled back and forth to London for consultations, and he felt disconnected from unfolding events at the front.

On June 6—D-Day—his son John had graduated from West Point, and he flew over to England for a visit. George Marshall made special arrangements for this after Ike had requested it.

After John's arrival on June 13, Kay joined the father and son at Telegraph Cottage. "I was interested to observe that Ike was not a particularly doting father," she remembered. While he "loved John very much," he was constantly scrutinizing him to make sure he was "tough enough."[4]

On June 19, Ike was on the cover of *Time* magazine again.

Politics and Economics

1944 was an election year, and American politics were rife with issues that would intersect Ike's presidency later. In observing the convergence of the man and his times, it is important to track these issues closely.

Millions of Americans had been observing the before-and-after comparison of America's economy in the Depression and conditions during World War II. America was generating superabundance, and the lesson for many was obvious: the suffering during the Great Depression had been needless.

In 1944, FDR called for a new "Economic Bill of Rights" that would take effect after the war; among its other provisions, this bill of rights would guarantee a job for every American who wanted one. Roosevelt's Republican opponent in the 1944 presidential election, Thomas Dewey, said the same thing: the federal government should be responsible for making certain that no one who wanted a job was unemployed.

In 1944, Congress passed the "G.I. Bill," whose intention was to remove American veterans from the job market for a few years—as the economy shifted over from wartime to peacetime production—by paying for their college and grad school tuition.

Here was systems analysis that aimed to prevent a repetition of the economic woes that had plagued America in 1919.

Just after the war, Congress passed the Employment Act of 1946, which established the Council of Economic Advisers and vested the federal government with permanent responsibility for ensuring high levels of employment.

Thomas Dewey was a liberal-to-moderate Republican, a representative of the party's "progressive" wing that adhered to the values promoted by Theodore Roosevelt a generation earlier. All of the Republican presidential candidates who had run against FDR after Hoover—Alf

Landon in 1936, Wendell Willkie in 1940, and Dewey in 1944—had been progressives. Though their rhetoric attacked "big government" and "bureaucracy," they were not averse to the policy presuppositions of the New Deal. They just argued that they would do a better and more efficient job than FDR.

The Republican Party's conservative wing was quite another story. One of the foremost leaders of the Republican right was Senator Robert Taft of Ohio. He had risen to prominence in FDR's second term, and he attacked the New Deal as a harbinger of communism. "If Mr. Roosevelt is not a communist today," he wrote in 1936, "he is bound to become one."[5]

Taft was also an isolationist who declared that in 1941 "war is worse even than a German victory."[6] Moreover, he proclaimed that "the victory of communism in the world would be far more dangerous to the United States than the victory of fascism."[7]

The Democratic Party was every bit as divided as the Republican Party. Southern Democrats defended Jim Crow, and they were shrill as they attacked FDR for providing opportunities for Blacks during World War II. They defeated a bill in 1944 that would have expedited voting for American servicemen in the combat zones. They did not want southern Blacks to have the experience of voting—anywhere.

FDR and Wendell Willkie, his Republican opponent of 1940, grew increasingly close in the war, and they became political allies. It bears noting that Willkie was a passionate supporter of racial equality.

In 1944, he and FDR had secret discussions about a party realignment. Willkie sent a feeler to FDR via Gifford Pinchot, an ally of Theodore Roosevelt. According to FDR's adviser and speechwriter Samuel Rosenman, Roosevelt was ready to join with Willkie to shake up the party structures.

"I think the time has come," Roosevelt said, "for the Democratic Party to get rid of its reactionary elements in the South, and to attract to it the liberals in the Republican Party. Willkie is the leader of those liberals."

Willkie's idea, said FDR, was to create "a coalition of the liberals in both parties, leaving the conservatives in each party to join together as they see fit. I agree with him one hundred percent and the time to do it is now—right after the election."[8]

But it was not to be, for Willkie died in October 1944, and FDR was already dying when he decided to run for a fourth term in 1944. He looked gaunt and he was wasting away—everyone could see it—and so the choice of his 1944 running mate would be critically important. Conservative Democrats managed to remove Vice President Henry Wallace from the ticket—he was "too liberal"—and they replaced him with Senator Harry Truman, who seemed more moderate.

Normandy—and Paris

Ike was impatient with what seemed to be the slow progress of penetrating Normandy after D-Day. Montgomery was still in command of ground forces, and Ike, like others, was inclined to attribute the slow pace to Monty's reputation for slow movement.

The controversies and recriminations over Monty's performance have continued ever since. A new tension was developing between Ike and Monty, and the two of them became outright foes by the end of the year.

Plans for the penetration of France and the campaign against the Germans after D-Day went back to the COSSAC strategy of 1943, which had specified the general arrangement of British and American forces based upon their embarkation points from England: the British would cover the left flank (i.e., the northern end) of the combined operations, and the Americans would cover the right flank, (i.e., the southern flank).

Ultimately, British forces would advance up the channel coast through the low countries, and they would garrison a northern occupation zone in Germany itself. American forces would advance to the South.[9]

In the short run, it was the task of Monty to occupy and control Caen, a key transportation hub, and his critics accused him of causing a stalemate in Normandy by failing to do so. He had pledged to move swiftly, but he also took steps to cover his reputation—to hedge his bets—by saying that regardless of when the town fell, the objective was to *pin down* German forces.

To his credit, he had engaged a total of eight German panzer divisions when the battle for Caen began. But the Germans held out, for which reason he emphasized that his goal was to pin down the Germans so that Collins's advance across the Cotentin Peninsula would encounter lighter resistance.[10]

There were several reasons for the slow progress in Normandy.

For one thing, the worst channel storm in forty years came along on June 19, and supplies were cut off when one of the two Mulberries got destroyed and the other one was damaged. Furthermore, Collins's advance on Cherbourg was delayed because of the "bocage" features of the Normandy terrain: French farmers from medieval times had divided their plots with huge earthen walls that impeded the progress of military forces.

An inventive American sergeant named Curtis Culin came up with an idea that would solve the problem: taking steel blades from the demolished German beach obstacles and welding them to the front of a tank. The result was the "Rhino" tank, which could bulldoze its way through earthen walls.

Ike gave the sergeant credit for this idea in his war memoir, *Crusade in Europe*.[11]

On June 8, Marshall, Ernest King, and Hap Arnold flew over to inspect conditions at the front. It pleased Marshall to see the army that he had created in action against the Germans in France.

By the time Cherbourg fell on June 27, the Germans had wrecked the port, and it would remain unusable for months.

Still, the Allies should have counted their blessings: Hitler kept nineteen divisions north of the Seine in the expectation that the main invasion was still to come at Pas-de-Calais. The Germans had terrible supply problems of their own, due to the effectiveness of Ike's preinvasion bombing of railroads. And the Russians launched a colossal attack on the eastern front: two million men and thousands of tanks were hurled at the Germans, thus making it impossible for Hitler to shift more divisions to France.

Rommel and von Rundstedt understood that their situation was grave, and they said so to Hitler, who came to meet with them at Soissons on June 17. Hitler was rigid: he refused the requests of his commanders to redeploy.

He also told them that the new V-1 jet-propelled "buzz bombs" that he had unleashed against London would cause the British to sue for peace. The more destructive V-2 ballistic missile would supplant it in September.

Hitler also commissioned a V-3 "super-gun," a subterranean multi-charge cannon to lob gigantic shells a hundred miles and pulverize

London. Long guns in five clusters with thirty-two booster charges would hurl the shells across the Channel.

The weapon was built by slave labor in a cavern at Mimoyecques, below Calais in France. Allied reconnaissance planes discovered the project in 1943.

In July 1944, the V-3 would be destroyed by British bombers releasing "Tallboy" bombs, twelve thousand-pound and twenty-one-foot-long projectiles that could generate shockwaves as powerful as earthquakes.

The ruins of this Nazi project in France are preserved as a museum.

By late June, the Germans had committed all of their available forces in France: fourteen divisions at Caen and eleven divisions facing Bradley's American forces. German lines held firm, and Ike complained to Churchill that Monty was dithering.

But Ike's German counterparts could see that it was only a matter of time before Allied forces would overpower them because their reserves were all committed. They could not replace their losses, whereas the Allies could depend upon a steady inflow of reinforcements.

By June 30, Rommel and von Rundstedt were both recommending a withdrawal to the Seine.

Hitler refused. He commanded a counterattack against the British and Canadians at Caen. When von Rundstedt demurred, Hitler ousted him.

On July 20, members of the German high command—with the possible foreknowledge of Rommel—tried a coup by assassinating Hitler. Their attempt did not succeed, and the officers were tried and executed. Rommel was given the option of poisoning himself, which he did, to protect his family from further reprisals.

In June, Churchill tried once again to get the Americans to cancel the ANVIL operation in southern France.

He proposed to use the troops for a landing on the Adriatic coast of Italy, followed by a campaign to capture Trieste and then proceed through the Ljubljana Gap into Austria. Ike said no, and he told Marshall that "to contemplate wandering off overland via Trieste to Ljubljana is to engage in conjecture to an unwarranted degree. We must concentrate our forces to the greatest possible degree and put them into battle in the decisive theater," i.e., "Western Europe."[12]

Churchill took his case for the cancellation of ANVIL—which he began to call Operation DRAGOON, which denoted a chore that he had to perform against his will—to FDR, who replied that the operation was part of the promise they had made to Stalin. Besides, said Roosevelt, if OVERLORD should fail, his political fortunes in election year 1944 would never survive the charge that he diverted forces that were destined for France and sent them off to the Mediterranean instead.

Operation ANVIL/DRAGOON took place as planned on August 15.

If Ike was feeling frustrated, he made up for it through his dealings with de Gaulle. He had been instructed to keep de Gaulle's participation in the French campaign limited to military matters, but he chose to disregard these instructions and—making common cause with the British war cabinet—sent de Gaulle to visit the town of Bayeux, which had been liberated from the Germans. On June 14, de Gaulle strode through the town as cheering crowds hailed his arrival.

On his own initiative, Ike promoted the political fortunes of de Gaulle. He had the backing of Churchill, and he used it to outmaneuver FDR: when necessary, he could justify his actions by pointing out that civil arrangements for France would have to pass muster with the British war cabinet as well as with authorities in Washington.

In truth, his instincts told him that de Gaulle was the very best candidate to unify the French and avert the danger of French infighting (or even civil war) that could hamper his military operations.

But what he did for de Gaulle went far beyond such short-term calculations: it took on a grandeur of its own.

Without making it apparent, Ike was taking some actions that were worthy of a head of state: he was creating new arrangements that would alter the nature of global politics, and he did it because it seemed right to him.

As Michael Korda has observed, after suffering "through the chaos and danger brought about by American policies in North Africa, when he had paid too much attention to Robert Murphy and the wishes of the president, he was not about to let it happen again."[13]

His power and his stature were growing.

In 1940, he had been a lieutenant colonel serving at Fort Lewis in Tacoma, Washington. Four years later, he was taking actions at odds with the manifest wishes of his own commander in chief. He knew that he was rising to global fame and he could get away with such things—if he was careful.

Because D-Day had made him a celebrity.

On the morning of June 6, he had released a prosaic announcement: "Under the command of General Eisenhower, Allied naval forces, supported by strong air forces, began landing Allied armies this morning on the northern coast of France."

The announcement itself was understated, but its impact electrified people. The Liberty Bell rang out in Philadelphia, church bells pealed across America, switchboards were jammed as people called friends and family. The name "Eisenhower"—"Eisenhower"—was repeated again and again.

"Under the command of General Eisenhower."

When John walked up to receive his diploma at West Point, he received a tremendous ovation.

Ike was famous.

Montgomery and Bradley had been planning a breakout offensive, code-named COBRA, to commence on July 25. An enormous air offensive subjected the German lines around Saint-Lô—another transportation hub like Caen—to a carpet bombing.

The air–ground operations were enhanced by the work of Major General Elwood "Pete" Quesada, who got radios installed in American tanks. This allowed the tank commanders to communicate with aircraft and direct their fire where it was needed.

Quesada came to Ike's attention in North Africa, and Ike promoted his career because he thought like Ike about the need to coordinate operations.

After suffering heavy casualties, five American divisions captured Saint-Lô on July 18, and Caen fell on July 20 after another heavy bombing campaign.

On the 26, Collins's VII Corps smashed its way through the Germans' positions, and Montgomery ordered a massive attack through the gap. Patton, who had long since arrived with his forces, was happy to comply. He was now in his element.

He drove his forces through Brittany, and then swept into southern Normandy, advancing one hundred miles and penetrating to the rear of the Germans' positions, thus threatening them with encirclement.

On August 7, Ike established his French headquarters in the bucolic Norman village of Tournières. The Normandy breakout was finally succeeding, and Ike told Marshall on August 11 that "I would expect things to move extremely rapidly."[14]

The new German commander, Günther von Kluge, was inclined to form a new line at the Seine, but Hitler overruled him and ordered a counterattack. Four German panzer divisions attacked with heavy losses, then withdrew. Hitler ordered them to attack again, and the result was a decisive Allied victory. Fifty thousand German troops were nearly encircled and trapped by the Allies at Falaise on August 19.

When Ike toured the battlefield, he encountered "scenes that could only be described by Dante.... It was as if an avenging angel had swept the area bent on destroying all things German."[15]

The battle for Normandy was over, and Allied armies continued their pursuit of the retreating Germans.

The initial plan for the pursuit of the Germans did not involve the liberation of Paris. Ike presumed that street fighting in the French capital might tie the Allies down, so Patton was ordered to sweep around the city to the south and proceed toward the German border. Other Allied forces would proceed toward Belgium, destroying German V-1 launching sites on the French coast.

But resistance to the Germans was increasing in Paris, French communists were active, and de Gaulle requested Ike to liberate the city as quickly as possible. He met with Ike on August 20.

Hitler sent orders to *destroy the city* rather than surrender it. Parisian landmarks were being wired for demolition as de Gaulle made his plea to Ike.

The German officer in command at Paris, General Dietrich von Cholt-itz, sent word through the Swedish consul general that he would surrender the city if the Allies would take swift action.

He would not carry out the führer's orders.

To Ike's everlasting credit, he acted and, accepting the surrender of von Choltitz, diverted Allied troops from the pursuit of the retreating Germans to occupy Paris. The French 2nd Armored Division, under the command of General Jacques-Philippe Leclerc—a special outfit formed for the express purpose of representing France in Operation OVER-LORD—arrived at the outskirts of Paris on August 24, and American troops joined them the next day.

On August 26, two million Parisians watched de Gaulle, Leclerc, and French resistance leaders parade down the Champs-Élysées with their troops.

On August 27, Ike and Bradley paid a call upon de Gaulle at the Palais de l'Élysée, where the president of France had resided. Ike intended to bestow "a kind of de facto recognition of him as the Provisional President of France," and this culmination of Ike's campaign to support de Gaulle delivered benefits later on when Ike was president. He noted that de Gaulle "never forgot it."[16]

When de Gaulle, still president of France, attended Ike's funeral in 1969, he leaned over to John Eisenhower and whispered, "Vous savez que le general était près de mon cœur."[17]

Ike had an underlying predilection for saving Paris—the city Hitler tried to destroy. In OVERLORD, Ike had issued special orders that Amer-ican troops were to do their utmost to safeguard European art, historic sites, and places of cultural significance.

In the summer of 1944, Ike put in a request for Kay Summersby, still a British subject, to become an American WAC, a member of the Women's Army Corps. (The acronym was shortened from WAAC to *WAC* when the adjective "auxiliary" was dropped). It was FDR who had broached this possibility back in North Africa.

Kay wished to become an American citizen, and this was a step in that direction.

Then—when John's visit with his father was over, Ike sent Kay to accompany John when he returned to the United States. They flew off together in the company of Tex Lee and other staff people early in July.

Kay and John got a chance to become much better acquainted, and Kay of course got to meet ... Mamie.

As for Mamie, Ike informed her about Kay's visit in a supremely matter-of-fact letter—a letter that was hand-delivered by John. Their son was being accompanied by several other people, Ike wrote, including "my secretary Mrs. Summersby," who "is going to try to find Mrs. Arnold, mother of her late fiancée [sic]."[18]

Those who doubt the allegation that Ike and Kay were having an affair cite this episode as evidence that the rumors were absurd. Historian Gil Troy wrote in the 1990s that, in addition to other factors that made an affair between Ike and Kay unlikely, "it is even harder to believe that he would be so cruel as to send his son John (then 22) to be his mistress's escort during Kay's visit to the United States and meeting with Mamie later in the war."[19]

Cruel?

There are other ways to view the matter—admittedly conjectural.

When Michael Korda tried to make sense of the episode, he found himself ambivalent. "It seems unlikely that Mamie would have received Kay or that John would have taken her on a trip to New York"—John suggested that they take in a Broadway show, and they got tickets to the Rodgers and Hammerstein musical *Oklahoma*—"if either of them had really believed she was Ike's mistress."

On the other hand, he mused, the very thought of sending an "enlisted, uniformed member of the British Motor Transport Corps" on a sudden "'holiday' in America in wartime on his personal B-17 was not exactly standard operating procedure between a general and his driver, or even his secretary." Possibly, he wrote, Mamie Eisenhower "does not get enough credit for classy behavior and self-restraint—and perhaps a realistic understanding that making a fuss would backfire on her."[20]

After all: What could she have realistically done when Ike confronted her with this fait accompli?

Ike knew perfectly well how suspicious she was, as proven by his constant denials of wrongdoing in the letters he sent her. In light of that, did he really believe that providing Mamie with an opportunity to size up this supposed rival would relieve her mind?

Or was his real purpose to give Kay an opportunity to size up Mamie?

According to Kay, she and Ike had discussed their relationship and its possible future in the months before D-Day. These conversations began at Telegraph Cottage, and they continued in their outings together going horseback riding in nearby Richmond Park.

We have only her word for this, of course.

But he worried, she said, that he was too old to give her the love she needed and deserved. He worried about their age difference, and he worried about whether he had it in him to be a father again if they should have children. Above all, he worried about whether his feelings of love could be sustained.

Kay said that Ike "talked very seriously and at length about his relationship with his wife. There was deep hurt on both sides, hurt so deep that they were never able to recapture their earlier relationship—although it was not for want of trying." According to Kay, Ike said that he was "not the lover you should have. It killed something in me. Not all at once, but little by little. For years I never thought of making love." Just the same, his attraction to Kay had been *commanding* enough to make him go out of his way again and again to keep her in his presence.

She told him that "someday things will be different."[21]

And now she had been given a chance to get to know his son. And John had been given a chance to get used to her.

If there was method in this, it was not exactly "cruel" to send Kay to America with John, thus giving her a chance to *see* the country where she said she wished to settle and to *meet his wife face-to-face*.

These seemed to be the actions of a man who was coming to grips with a situation that was eating away at him, a man who decided to test and explore the different ways in which that situation might be … resolved.

Broad Front

The Allies were unprepared for the swiftness of the German collapse after Normandy. The question was whether they could find a way to exploit the situation fast enough.

This issue would generate one of the most enduring controversies about Ike's military leadership. The finger-pointing and recriminations began in September 1944, and the acrimony has continued. Historians and biographers are divided in their judgments.

Beyond the general provisions of COSSAC, Ike had a strong idea of what ought to be done. He wanted his forces to be mobile, and he wanted their superiority in numbers to *overwhelm* the enemy. The "total war" campaign that Grant had used against Lee's army in Virginia provided a precedent.

The true inspiration for that strategy had come from Lincoln, who told one of his commanders in 1862 that his "general idea of this war" was that Union forces should attack the enemy "with superior forces at *different* positions, at the *same* time, so that we can safely attack, one, or both, if he makes no change, and if he *weakens* one to *strengthen* the other."[22]

The idea was to stretch the enemy's forces so thin that multiple break-throughs could be achieved.

After the Normandy breakout, Ike decided to use that very strategy: to launch simultaneous campaigns of different army groups.

It was his call, because on September 1, he took over the command of ground forces. This had been part of the OVERLORD plan from the beginning: Monty would command the ground troops during the invasion, but then Ike would take over when he moved his headquarters to France.

The politics behind this provision flowed from the same situation that prompted FDR to call for an American to be supreme commander: America's contribution of men and resources would surpass the contributions of the British.

In the first week of September 1944, Allied progress was spectacular. British forces entered Belgium on September 2, then they liberated Brussels on September 3 and took Antwerp on the fourth.

Monty had an inspiration, which he had already explained to Bradley on August 17 and then to Ike on August 23: the way to defeat the Germans quickly, he said, would be to send a "solid mass" of forty divisions through the low countries, cross the Rhine, and penetrate the Ruhr, which was Germany's industrial heartland.

In his postwar memoir, *Normandy to the Baltic*, Monty expressed it thus: "My own view, which I expressed to the Supreme Commander, was that one powerful full-blooded thrust across the Rhine and *into the heart of Germany,* backed by the whole of the resources of the Allied Armies, would be likely to achieve decisive results."[23]

This concept would go down in history as Monty's "narrow front" strategy—as opposed to Ike's "broad front" strategy.

Monty's narrow front proposal was at odds with the original SHAEF plan, which called for a two-pronged penetration of Germany, consisting of a movement through the low countries supplemented by a lateral thrust below the Ardennes.[24] Patton's Third Army was implementing that southern campaign, and the ANVIL/DRAGOON forces moving up from southern France would be merging into it.

Bradley proposed a completely different narrow-front strategy: put everything into the thrust below the Ardennes.

Ike adhered to the original SHAEF strategy.

There was something to be said for Monty's proposal: the retreating Germans were demoralized, and a massive thrust through the low countries that would *crush* the Germans looked plausible to its supporters.

The American Civil War provided the obvious precedent: once Richmond fell, Grant hounded Lee's army, surrounded it, blocked it, cut off its supplies, until Lee had no choice but to surrender. Speed and audacity were used to quickly *crush him.*

Criticism of Ike's decision to pursue the broad-front strategy has continued. Jean Edward Smith held nothing back when he declared in 2013 that "Montgomery's plan...would likely have ended the war sooner.... The most serious defect in Ike's broad front strategy was that Allied momentum was lost and the Germans were given time to recover.... The door to the Reich through Belgium was open [and] the price the Allies paid for their missed opportunity in September was heavy."[25]

The German general Hans Speidel—chief of staff for the latest German commander in the West, General Walther Model—came to the same conclusion after the war. If the Allies "held on grimly to the retreating Germans," he wrote, "they could have harried the breath out of every man...and ended the war half a year earlier."[26]

Montgomery would never stop criticizing Ike for pursuing the broad-front strategy.

He tried to salvage the opportunity to thrust decisively through the low countries by conducting an airborne operation in Holland to seize bridges and hold them until ground troops arrived. But operation MARKET GARDEN, which began on September 17, did not succeed.

Ike has his defenders in the broad-versus-narrow-front debate.

An early defender of his strategy was biographer Stephen Ambrose, who called Ike "more realistic" than Monty, Patton, or the other narrow-front promoters because he was "acutely aware that every step Montgomery's forces took to the northeast, and that Patton's army took toward the east, carried them farther away from the Normandy ports, adding to an already serious supply problem."[27]

On August 20, Ike had told reporters that because of a rapidly emerging logistics problem, "further movement in large parts of the front even against very weak opposition is almost impossible."[28]

Supplies were running low for the Allied armies, with a shortage of fuel the biggest problem. Though fuel was indeed flowing through the English Channel pipeline—it was also being brought to France via tankers—a multitude of trucks had to bring it to the front, and these efforts fell short, not least of all because the number of Allied troops had increased so rapidly and the trucks themselves needed gasoline.

Both Patton and Bradley were complaining that John C. H. Lee, who was in charge of logistics, was botching the job, and they called for his replacement. Ike considered replacing him with Lucius Clay, whom he knew from his days in the Philippines. Clay had been serving as both deputy for war mobilization and as army chief of procurement, and Ike asked Marshall to send him over.

But then Ike decided that the problems had not been entirely the fault of Lee and that it would be unfair to sack him.

Ike did not reject Monty's proposal in an offhand or peremptory way; he had the SHAEF planners take a look at it and they concluded that it *might* work, but only if certain logistical preconditions were met.

And those conditions did not exist.

In order to seize the opportunity in Belgium *quickly*, Monty's forces, supplemented by those of Courtney Hodges's First U.S. Army—which was covering his flank—would do the work, and all the other Allied operations would have to be halted to prioritize the supply-flow for Monty.

Moreover, since the port of Cherbourg was by then far away from the front, fast supplies would have to be brought in through Antwerp.[29]

But that was not a feasible option.

The port could not be put to use until the islands in the Scheldt estuary—which were blocking the way—had been taken. And the Germans had done a very effective job of fortifying them.

The Battle of the Scheldt, which would finally open up the shipping routes to Antwerp, began on October 2, and success would not be achieved until November 8. In other words, the logistical preconditions for Monty's plan—if it were to be executed *quickly*—did not exist when a thrust up the channel looked so tempting.

Even Monty's own chief of staff, Major General Sir Francis de Guingand, believed that the logistical basis for Monty's proposal was inadequate. "My own conclusion," he wrote, "is that Eisenhower was right."[30]

Ike went over these issues in a meeting with Monty in Brussels. According to Major General Miles Graham, Monty's chief administrative officer, Monty brandished a series of cables that he had received from Ike and proclaimed that "they're balls, sheer balls, rubbish."

"Steady, Monty," said Ike. "You can't speak to me like that. I'm your boss."[31]

Stalemate and Crisis

The broad-front strategy did have a price—a price that was inevitable without a realistic alternative—because as soon as the Germans regrouped, they conducted an extremely effective defense of the Rhine frontier. Hitler brought back von Rundstedt, who did a capable job as the German commander in the West.

The Allies had to fight along a 450-mile front, and the weather conditions turned bitter. Attempts to engage the Germans were repulsed with heavy losses, and the fighting near the Hürtgen Forest was savage.

U.S. forces under General Jacob Devers approached the Rhine near Strasbourg in mid-November, but Ike told Devers to wait until Montgomery and Patton had made more progress.

He wanted a coordinated broad-front crossing of the Rhine. No doubt he was mindful of what happened when nine thousand Allied troops were cut off and surrounded at Arnhem in operation MARKET GARDEN. Two thousand escaped, and the rest were either captured or killed.

Supplies were still a problem. Despite the construction of double pipelines from Cherbourg to Paris and from Marseilles to Lyon, the Allies had too many troops in France to be sustained by the fuel that could be brought to the front. Under Ike's direction, a laborious campaign was mounted to rebuild the French rail systems that Ike's strategic bombing campaign had destroyed before D-Day.

On October 6, George Marshall paid Ike another visit, and they reviewed the supply problems in detail. Marshall proceeded to visit the combat zones, taking great care to converse with front-line combat troops, award combat medals, and take notes so he could write to their families.

In his war memoirs, Ike recalled that the campaign by November 1944 was "the dirtiest kind of infantry slugging. Gains were ordinarily measured in terms of yards rather than miles.... Infantry losses were high," not only due to combat but also because of "frostbite, trench foot, and respiratory diseases."[32] "We were mired in a ghastly war of attrition," wrote Omar Bradley.[33]

Alan Brooke and Monty began to demand the removal of Ike as the commander of ground forces. "If we want the war to end within any reasonable period you will have to get Eisenhower's hand taken off the land battle," Monty wrote to Brooke. "He has never commanded anything in his whole career, and ... he does not know how to do it."[34]

Brooke needed no persuasion; he told Churchill on November 28 that "the whole American conception of attacking all along the front ... was sheer madness," adding that the Allies were "reduced to the trench warfare it has always been our object to avoid."[35]

On November 24, Brooke told the British chiefs that Ike was "on the golf links at Reims—entirely detached and taking practically no part in the running of the war."[36]

While that was a simpleminded fiction, Ike was indeed subjected to distractions. Though Reims was his command post, his principal headquarters was the Trianon Palace Hotel, on the outskirts of Versailles, and Kay remembered he was deluged with politicians who wished to have

Eisenhower Presidential Library

Mamie Eisenhower alone during World War II.

their pictures taken with him. He had to make time for all sorts of VIPs, not only politicians but foreign royalty, as he tried to coordinate actions at the front.[37] The Trianon Palace Hotel became a kind of purgatory.

As Brooke created a caricature of Ike idling in luxury, his fatigue and his weariness worsened.

Ike knew perfectly well what was going on behind his back, and he demanded a showdown with Churchill. And since the prime minister knew that Ike retained the support of both Marshall and FDR, Alan Brooke was forced to back down.

On October 14, Kay's commission as a WAC had come through, thanks to FDR's work behind the scenes. When Brooke noticed the fact that Kay was seated next to Churchill in November, he took sarcastic notice of the fact that "she had been promoted to hostess" by Ike, who had produced such "a lot of unnecessary gossip that did him no good."[38]

The gossip on the other side of the Atlantic intensified, and Mamie's expressions of displeasure were enough to prompt Ike to dash off the following explicit response: "It always depresses me when you talk about 'dirty tricks' I've played, and what a beating you've taken, apparently because of me.... I truly love you and I do know that when you blow off steam you don't really think of me as such a black hearted creature as your language implies."[39]

FDR's Secret Love

Franklin Roosevelt, elected to a fourth presidential term and growing weaker every day, was dying, and there was no doubt about it.

Everyone who got a glimpse of him in 1944 could see the condition he was in. He was preparing for the meeting with Churchill and Stalin that was set to take place at Yalta, in Crimea, early in February 1945.

There was much to be discussed at Yalta—not only the postwar zones of occupation in Germany and the fate of the Eastern European countries, but also the participation of Russia in the war against Japan.

Nobody knew at the time if the MAHHATTAN project would succeed. The war in the Pacific might conceivably last until 1947 or longer—with millions of deaths if an invasion of the Japanese home islands needed to be launched. The scope of that invasion would exceed the size of Operation OVERLORD.

FDR was lonely. His wife Eleanor was always on the move, and that had been the way of things for years. She had achieved a political fame that was all her own—she wrote a newspaper column called "My Day," and her work as a humanitarian and activist had made her a force in the Democratic Party.

But there was a deeper reality: their marriage was a sham because she would never forgive him for his extramarital affair. There had been no intimacy between Franklin and Eleanor for a long time.

FDR's daughter Anna saw how lonely he was as his life ebbed away, and so she did something no one else would have been able to do: she gave him the consolation of seeing the love of his life, Lucy Mercer, as he approached the end.

FDR and Eleanor had begun to drift away from one another when FDR was assistant secretary of the navy under Woodrow Wilson, and he fell in love with Eleanor's social secretary, Lucy Mercer.

The two of them exchanged love letters, which Eleanor discovered. She presented her husband with an ultimatum: either divorce her or else stay away from Lucy for the rest of his life.

He had to make a choice: divorce Eleanor and live his life as a New York attorney whose divorce precluded a political career, or else sacrifice his love for Lucy and fulfill his own potential—become a man who could change the future of the world, like the cousin he idolized, Theodore.

FDR made his choice.

And his daughter Anna would gradually discover what had happened.

Doris Kearns Goodwin tells the story of what transpired in the summer of 1944: FDR asked Anna whether she would consider "inviting an old friend of mine to a few dinners at the White House." Anna "knew at once" to whom her father was referring, and, after some initial indignation, she decided that "if seeing Lucy again provided the inspiration he needed to assuage his loneliness and buoy his spirits, then who was she to stand in the way?" After all, "she herself had fallen in love with her second husband before she was divorced from her first."[40]

So FDR began to see Lucy again, and she was with him when he died in Warm Springs. Once the liaisons started, Anna found that she could get along with Lucy just fine, and she liked her very much.

Is it any wonder that FDR looked so kindly upon the relationship of Ike and Kay Summersby?

Battle of the Bulge

On December 15, 1944, FDR promoted Ike to the five-star rank of "general of the army," a permanent rank that would last for the rest of his life. It was equivalent to being a field marshal in the armies of other nations.[41]

On the very next day, a surprise attack by the Germans erupted through the Ardennes, the same attack route that the Wehrmacht had used to catch the French by surprise in 1940. Von Rundstedt deliberately launched the attack in bad weather so that Allied air support would be impossible.

At first the German panzers swept everything before them: the Allied defense gave way. But then, as Jean Edward Smith has acknowledged, "Ike's finest hour as a military commander" began.

Omar Bradley let two days elapse before he began to react to the assault. General Courtney Hodges suffered a nervous breakdown. But Ike swung into action quickly. He met with Bradley, Patton, Tedder, Beetle Smith, and others, including Montgomery's chief of staff, at Verdun on December 19.

"The present situation," Ike said, was "to be regarded as an opportunity, not a disaster."[42] The Germans had emerged from behind their defenses, and the very success of their early attack created vulnerability.

They were out in the open—and exposed.

So Ike began to plan a pincer movement that would hit them from the north and from the south.

The Allies could deliver a smashing counterattack of their own, Ike said, and he told George Patton that he wanted him to spearhead the campaign. He asked Patton how soon he could attack, and Patton gave this immediate reply: "The morning of December twenty-first, with three divisions."[43]

The performance of Patton would become legendary, and his skills in fast attack and maneuver would now set a standard that was worthy of Stonewall Jackson. He and Ike got to act out the fantasy that Patton had dreamed up in 1919, when he had said to Ike, "I'll be Jackson, you'll be Lee."

Patton halted his advance to the East, turned his army ninety degrees to face north, dealt the Germans a devastating blow at Bastogne, and performed the whole thing in three days. Before he had even arrived at the Verdun meeting, he had written up three alternative plans designed to accommodate the different scenarios.

Meanwhile Ike—even though he was smarting from the efforts of Monty and Brooke to remove him as ground commander—placed the American Fifth and Ninth Armies in the North under Montgomery's command.

"By God, Ike," said Bradley, "I cannot be responsible to the American people if you do this. I resign."

"Brad," Ike replied, "I—not you—am responsible to the American people. Your resignation therefore means absolutely nothing."[44]

As Jean Edward Smith has acknowledged, Ike's performance in the Battle of the Bulge "showed a quicker grasp of the situation than any of his subordinates, and he acted decisively to contain the attack."[45] His calmness under pressure was remarkable.

Michael Korda has observed that under the kind of pressure and provocations that would try the patience of anyone, Ike "kept silence, no doubt at great damage to his cardiovascular system, as if he were always conscious that a supreme commander must above all present to the world a picture of confidence, self-control, and courage."[46]

But his calmness broke down when Monty finally pushed him too far.

Monty showed none of the speed that George Patton would display in the Battle of the Bulge. Ike visited Monty on December 28 to urge haste. Monty made another pitch for a single campaign along the channel coast, and Ike of course rejected the idea.

After Ike departed, Monty sent him a cable that was carefully crafted to give the impression that Ike agreed to his plan—which of course was not the truth. Meanwhile, Bradley forwarded copies of British newspaper coverage attributing the turning of the tide in the battle to Montgomery's stalwartness. These articles implied that Ike was at a loss about what to do. Patton was not mentioned at all.

Marshall sent Ike a cable mentioning the British press coverage and telling Ike that he should make no concessions to the British, lest it trigger a dire political reaction in the United States.

That was it: Ike's willingness to overlook Monty's arrogance and make use of him as a soldier came to an end.

Ike prepared a message to the Combined Chiefs declaring that unless Montgomery were relieved of command, both he and his staff would resign. When Monty's chief of staff Freddie de Guingand found out about this, he flew to SHAEF headquarters on December 30, persuaded Ike to hold off, and then warned Montgomery that he was close to getting fired.[47]

Monty apologized, and Churchill went out of his way to hail the American performance in the Battle of the Bulge in a speech before the House of Commons. Even so, on January 7, Monty held a press conference at which he gave the distinct impression that he and the British were saving the day when the Americans had fallen into disarray. Churchill came to France to mend things, and he broached the idea of appointing Harold Alexander as Ike's deputy. But Marshall, when he heard about it, said no.

Notwithstanding all these troubles, Ike was on the cover of *Time* magazine again—as man of the year.

The German retreat would continue through the month of January. When the Russians began a great winter offensive on January 12, Ike sent his deputy Arthur Tedder to confer directly with Stalin in regard to the endgame operations in the European theater.

Once again, Ike was acting like a head of state—going straight to the top and engaging in direct communications with Stalin before FDR and Churchill had met the Soviet leader in Yalta.

Tedder told Stalin that Ike was planning to cross the Rhine at two locations, then rendezvous with Russian forces somewhere around Leipzig.

Victory in Europe

On January 12, 1945, the Russians launched their last offensive in the war against Hitler: four million men and ten thousand tanks set out under the command of Field Marshals Zhukov, Konev, and Rokossovsky. The Germans had no choice but to rush more troops to the East. By February 2, the Russians were thirty miles from Berlin.

With German troop strength dwindling on the western front, Ike prepared his own final offensive: three million American, British, French, and Canadian troops would penetrate the Reich. The Allied buildup had reached flood tide, and it encompassed multiple armies and army groups.

On February 24, Ike held a press conference at the Hotel Scribe in Paris, and over two hundred reporters attended. White House Press Secretary Stephen Early called Ike's performance "the most magnificent...of any man at a press conference that I have ever seen."[48] Merle Miller—the same Merle Miller who would interview Harry Truman in 1961—wrote that "Ike is a master.... The boys and girls of the press acted as if they had heard Einstein explain relativity."[49]

On March 7, General Courtney Hodges's forces captured Cologne—or what was left of it, since most of the city was destroyed in a firestorm created in a thousand-bomber raid that was unleashed by "Bomber" Harris.

On the same day, American troops reached Remagen, south of Bonn, and they discovered that the Ludendorff Bridge across the Rhine had not been destroyed by the Germans. "When Bradley reported that we had a permanent bridge across the Rhine I could scarcely believe my ears," Ike recalled. "This was completely unforeseen."

Bradley requested instructions, since he knew that Ike wanted a simultaneous penetration of Germany.

"How much have you got in that vicinity," Ike asked Bradley, who replied that he had four divisions that could cross the bridge. "Well, Brad," Ike replied, "go ahead and shove over at least five divisions and anything else that is necessary to make certain of our hold."[50]

Within a few weeks, Hodges's troops had constructed six additional pontoon bridges across the Rhine.

With the penetration of Germany underway, Ike accepted the invitation of the wealthy Dillon family to spend a few days at their villa on the Riviera. He departed in the company of Kay, Beetle Smith, Beetle's girlfriend Ethel Westermann, Tex Lee, and two WACS from SHAEF.

Kay Summersby recalled that Ike slept all day at first, and then the two of them would "sit on the terrace all day long, looking out over the Mediterranean, chatting lazily, drinking white wine and sunbathing."[51] The accuracy of her account is borne out by surviving photographs that show Ike sipping wine as he sits on a deck chair as Kay, who is wearing a two-piece bathing suit, applies suntan lotion.

On March 27, Ike reviewed the overall situation with Bradley, and the two of them considered the issue of Berlin. Ike had previously told Stalin that American and Soviet forces would link up near Leipzig, and the Soviets were only thirty miles from Berlin, which was mostly in ruins. The city was within the Soviet occupation zone that had been negotiated at Yalta (though Berlin itself would be divided up for occupation purposes after the war among the four Allied powers).

Ike asked Bradley for an estimate on casualties if a race for Berlin were undertaken. "What would it take," Ike asked, and Bradley answered as follows: "Probably a hundred thousand casualties. A pretty steep price for a prestige objective."[52]

The famous snapshot of Ike and Kay Summersby on the Riviera, 1945.

Ike agreed, and he proceeded to preempt Montgomery, who was poised to make a race for Berlin, by sending a personal letter to Stalin reaffirming his intention to meet the Russians near Leipzig.[53]

Monty was outraged when he got the news that Berlin would be left to the Russians—and so was Churchill, especially in light of the fact that Ike had acted without the knowledge of the Combined Chiefs.

George Marshall was also displeased.

The British chiefs sent a protest to Washington, and Ike told Churchill on March 30 that his decision to stop at the Elbe—his decision not to make a race for Berlin—was based upon military considerations.

On April 1, Churchill took up the matter with FDR, who received the message at Warm Springs, Georgia, the retreat that he had created in the 1920s for the treatment of polio. "I do not get the point," replied Roosevelt, adding that he found it rather strange that "at a moment of great victory for our combined forces we should become involved in such unfortunate reactions."[54]

FDR had no time for this quarrel, since his mind was on other things.

One night he got behind the wheel of the car whose hand controls he had designed himself, and he drove with Lucy Mercer to the top of a nearby mountain so that they could gaze at a beautiful vista as he described to her his hopes and dreams for the postwar world.

On April 12, he died in Lucy's presence from a stroke. "I have a terrific headache," he said, and collapsed.

On April 30, Adolf Hitler blew his brains out in his subterranean Berlin bunker, as Russian troops entered the city.

Thus ended the Nazi empire—the nightmare realm that had been dreamt up, created, and sustained by one of the sickest minds that ever existed, the mind of a man who lusted not only for power but also for the torture and death of all the innocent men, women, and children he could get his hands on. It was a mind that could perpetrate obscenities beyond comprehension.

His *appetite* for turning human beings into corpses would continue right down to the end. Psychiatrist Erich Fromm would later theorize that Hitler was not only a sadist but a closet necrophile.[55]

On April 12, the day when FDR died, Ike was given a tour of Ohrdruf, which was part of the Buchenwald concentration camp, in the company of Patton and Bradley. The men were led past heaps of slaughtered men, and they talked with survivors.

Ike gave orders for his visit to the concentration camp to be filmed. He told Marshall that "the evidence of bestiality and cruelty is so overpowering as to leave me a bit sick. In one room, where there were piled up twenty or thirty naked men, killed by starvation, George Patton would not even enter. He said he would get sick if he did so. I made the visit deliberately, in order to be in a position to give first-hand evidence of these things, if ever, in the future, there develops a tendency to charge these allegations merely to 'propaganda.'" [56]

Ike suggested to Marshall that members of Congress and editors should be flown over to Germany to see the evidence for themselves.

Ike anticipated "Holocaust denial," and he hoped to head it off.

A New American Hero

On May 7, 1945, General Alfred Jodl—chief of staff of the German high command—surrendered to the Allies on behalf of the German armed forces at Ike's Reims headquarters. Ike had the pleasure of cabling the Combined Chiefs as follows: "The mission of this Allied force was fulfilled at 0241, local time, May 7, 1945."[57]

He had been ordered to enter the continent of Europe and commence operations aimed at the heart of Germany and the destruction of her armed forces. That mission had just been achieved.

The surrender ceremony was grim. In a measure of calculated disrespect—such was his association of the Wehrmacht with Nazism—Ike refused to attend the signing, but he had Jodl ushered into his office afterwards. Through an interpreter, Ike asked Jodl if he understood the terms of the surrender, and, after the German answered, "Ja," Ike warned him that he would be held accountable for carrying out the terms, and then dismissed him.

The tension broke as photographers were summoned; Ike grinned and held up the pens that had been used at the signing ceremony. Kay Summersby grinned in the background as the pictures were taken.

After V-E Day—"Victory in Europe Day"—Ike insisted on going to London with his staff to celebrate. John, who was there on a visit, came along, and Kay found him a date. Omar Bradley and Kay Summersby's mother joined them for an evening on the town.

After a buffet dinner, they went to the theater and Kay was photographed sitting next to Ike; her mother and Bradley sat behind them. Then they had another meal at Ciro's restaurant, and Ike and Kay danced together.

President Truman designated Ike as the military governor of the U.S. occupation zone in Germany. His headquarters would be in Frankfurt. General Lucius Clay would be his deputy.

In April, Ike sought permission from the Combined Chiefs for his army group commanders to meet with the Russian commanders to arrange the withdrawal to the occupation zones agreed to at Yalta. Churchill objected; he was reluctant to give up any bargaining leverage with Stalin.

Associated Press

Ike and Kay Summersby at the theater together, celebrating V-E Day. To the left is Ike's son John and his date for the evening. To the right is General Omar Bradley.

President Truman—struggling to take in the vast array of overlapping issues that the death of Roosevelt dumped in his lap—supported Ike. "The only practical thing to do," Truman recalled years later, "was to stick carefully to our own agreement and to try our best to make the Russians carry out their agreements."[58] He sent Harry Hopkins to Moscow to organize another big-three meeting in the summer.

Ike emerged as the greatest hero of the war, and the magnitude of his celebrity status was overwhelming. He received ovations, decorations, and honors from Britain, France, Belgium, the Netherlands, Denmark, Norway, Poland, and Czechoslovakia. Even Latin American nations joined in.

In Paris, he laid a wreath at the tomb of the unknown soldier and received on behalf of the American people a sword that belonged to Napoleon. De Gaulle presented him with a platinum cigarette case embossed with five sapphires.

An early biography was rushed into print: *Soldier of Democracy,* by Kenneth S. Davis.

On the twelfth, in London, he was given the "freedom of the city"— an honor that dated from medieval times—and there, in the presence of Churchill and other dignitaries, he gave an impressive speech at London's Guildhall, which was built in the fifteenth century. "I come from the very heart of America," he said, and as "a Londoner will fight" when his liberties are threatened, "so will a citizen of Abilene." Through the Anglo–American effort on behalf of freedom, "the valley of the Thames draws closer to the farms of Kansas."

"Humility," he proclaimed, "must always be the portion of any man who receives acclaim earned in blood of his followers and sacrifices of his friends."[59]

This speech made a huge impression on the British. Even Ike's detractor Alan Brooke was moved. "Rushed off to the Guildhall for Eisenhower's speech," he wrote in his diary. "Ike made a *wonderful* speech and impressed all hearers in the Guildhall including the Cabinet.... I had never realized that Ike was as big a man until his performance today."[60]

Ike had spent weeks preparing this speech, and at Harry Butcher's suggestion he memorized it so his presentation would seem to be extemporaneous. After the speech he was given a state dinner by Churchill at 10 Downing Street. He had tea with the royal family at Buckingham Palace.

Then he flew back to America to receive a hero's welcome.

On June 16, he arrived at National Airport in Washington, and was greeted by Mamie and George Marshall. "Oh God," he said, "it's swell to be back," and this statement made headline copy in the papers.[61]

Thousands of people lined the route as he was driven in an open limousine with Marshall from the airport to the Pentagon. "Stand up so they can see you," Marshall told him.[62] Ike made some impromptu remarks to a crowd of War Department staff in the Pentagon courtyard. Then the motorcade drove him to Capitol Hill for an address to a joint session of Congress.

"General Ike was standing, waving like a prize fighter," wrote Harry Butcher.[63] As the motorcade passed, Arthur Burns, who was then an economist teaching at George Washington University, turned to his wife and said, "This man is absolutely a natural for the Presidency."[64]

Ike's extemporaneous speech to Congress received the longest standing ovation in the history of Congress. Afterward he was driven to the White House to meet Truman, and later he flew to New York, where his reception was even more tumultuous. Almost two million people turned out to see and hear him at New York's City Hall, where he gave another impromptu speech, which the *New York Times* called "masterful."[65] Harry Butcher summarized its theme: "I'm just a Kansas farmer boy who did his duty."[66]

Ike was driven through the city in a victory parade. He stood up in the car with his hands stretched high as he waved to the crowd and projected the warmth of that dazzling grin that would endear him to so many millions.

The talk about Ike as a presidential candidate had started in 1943.

When a friend sent newspaper clippings about the political speculation with a note asking how it felt "to be a presidential candidate," Ike scrawled down this hasty reply: "Baloney! Why can't a simple soldier be left alone to carry out his duty? And I furiously object to the word 'candidate'—I ain't and I won't."[67]

In the summer of 1945, the political talk became pervasive. Ike's old friend Swede Hazlett told him that "no matter what party you are affiliated with (and I have no idea if you're D. or R.), you could carry the country without even taking to the road."[68]

In the course of the Potsdam summit meeting, Ike told Harry Truman that he had "no ambition except to retire to a quiet home and from there do what little I could to help our people understand...the inescapable responsibilities that would devolve upon us all" in the aftermath of war. He found Truman's reaction stunning: "he suddenly turned to me and said, 'General, there is nothing that you may want that I won't try to help you get. That definitely and specifically includes the presidency in 1948."[69]

Ike treated the suggestion as a joke.

In August when a friend in San Antonio wrote that he was ready and eager to form an "Eisenhower for President Club," Ike retorted that "nothing could be so distasteful to me as to engage in political activity of any kind."[70]

These disclaimers would continue in the years ahead, as both Democrats and Republicans courted him.

George Marshall had a different sort of destiny—different, but in some respects comparable. He was tired of serving as the army chief of staff, and he wanted Ike to succeed him.

He told Truman he was willing to serve as chief of staff until the war with Japan was over, but then he wanted a different assignment.

Truman obliged by converting Marshall into a diplomat: he sent him on a mission to China to see if any rapprochement could be arranged between Chiang Kai-shek and the Chinese communists. Then he took the extraordinary step of making Marshall his secretary of state, the secretary of state who would give the world...the Marshall Plan.

Decisions

Ike and Kay were in love.

There is no reason to doubt what happened to them between 1942 and 1945. The gossip was pervasive for a reason: they acted like a couple.

They acted as if they were dating.

And we don't just have to rely on the narrative of *Past Forgetting*—or the diary entries of gossips. People took pictures.

We can look at the snapshots of them together on deck chairs at the Riviera—sipping wine—pictures of them on horseback as they prepared to go riding in the country, and pictures of them in the theater before they went dancing. These are the sorts of things that men and women do when they are dating.

This was no ordinary relationship of boss and assistant: they were... "going together."

It would have been easy for Ike to keep her at a distance and keep their relationship formal. But the way he behaved got everybody talking—or whispering. The gossip was incessant because the situation was obvious.

He and Mamie had considered a divorce, their relations were distant, and he had flirted with other women—like Marian Huff. His correspondence with Mamie makes it clear that she assumed what other people were assuming about his behavior with Kay.

But this time he was approaching a crossroads in his life.

Ike and Kay were a couple—and the people around them could see it. They made each other happy.

The question was what they were going to do about it.

All through the summer of 1945, Ike and Kay were together—at his Frankfurt headquarters and at other destinations in Europe where his rapidly expanding activities took him: Vienna, Moscow, Salzburg, even Berchtesgaden, Hitler's mountain retreat, which gave Kay the creeps.

John Eisenhower was stationed near Frankfurt, and he often came over to join in a game of bridge. After the photograph of the theater party in London got circulating—the picture showing Kay sitting next to Ike in the very same row where John and his date were sitting, and they certainly looked like two couples—the gossip reached a new level of intensity.

Ike could probably tell that some sort of decision about Kay—a moment of truth—was approaching, and he might have acted quickly.

According to Merle Miller, Harry Truman claimed that "right after the war," Ike "wrote a letter to General Marshall saying that he wanted to be relieved of duty, saying that he wanted to come back to the United States and divorce Mrs. Eisenhower so that he could marry this Englishwoman."

Truman (supposedly) continued as follows: "Well, Marshall wrote him back a letter the like of which I never did see. He said that if he…if Eisenhower even came close to doing such a thing, he'd not only bust him out of the army, he'd see to it that never for the rest of his life would he be able to draw a peaceful breath. He said it wouldn't matter if he was in the army or wasn't. Or even what country he was in. Marshall said that if he ever again even mentioned a thing like that, he'd see to it that the rest of his life was a living hell."

Then Truman (supposedly) said that "one of the last things I did as President, I got those letters from his file in the Pentagon, and I destroyed them."[71]

The response to these allegations among historians and biographers has been generally scathing. Stephen Ambrose wrote that the story was "completely untrue," and that Truman was "approaching senility" when Miller interviewed him.[72]

The most compelling reason for dismissing the allegations, wrote Ambrose, is that Ike wrote a letter to Marshall on June 4 that was completely the reverse in its intentions from the supposed divorce letter: Ike requested permission to bring Mamie over to join him, because he was lonely for her. Ike "did not want to divorce Mamie," Ambrose concluded, "he wanted to live with her." "I just plain miss my family," is what Ike told Marshall on June 4, 1945.[73]

Interestingly, while Ambrose dismissed the Miller/Truman allegations, he was quite prepared to admit that Ike and Kay might have had an affair. "Kay's book, as a whole," he wrote, "was a vivid and moving account of a wartime romance that was both frustrating and exciting. Nowhere did she claim too much for her own role in his life, but she was always around, a keen and sensitive observer who was, for her part, deeply in love with her boss. Whether Eisenhower loved her in turn or not is less certain, although obviously he had strong feelings about her."[74]

The controversy over the Miller/Truman allegations would continue.

As previously noted, Robert Ferrell, who edited Eisenhower's diaries, thought that Miller invented the story of Truman's revelations. Michael Korda sided with Ferrell, calling Miller's account "both mischievous and unlikely."[75]

But Jean Edward Smith, who consulted other sources and who also conducted lengthy interviews with Lucius Clay—Eisenhower's deputy during the occupation of Germany and a man who would play an extremely important role in Ike's quest for the Republican presidential nomination—believed that the story as told by Miller was essentially true.

"I am convinced," Smith wrote, "that Eisenhower wrote to Marshall in the heady aftermath of victory in Europe seeking to divorce Mamie and marry Kay, and that General Marshall stomped on the idea."[76]

How did Smith account for Ike's June 4 letter to Marshall expressing his loneliness for Mamie? Simple: in Smith's opinion, Ike was beating a tactical retreat after Marshall's rebuff; he was "signaling that his affair with Kay had ended" because that was exactly what Marshall wanted to hear.

In Smith's view, the incident offers "tangential corroboration" of the divorce letter, because (and Michael Korda made the same observation) if he had really missed Mamie, he could have brought her over to join him on his own authority. It was not standard practice, but allowances could be made in unusual circumstances.

Douglas MacArthur had his wife living with him at his headquarters in the Pacific. She was with him in the Philippines, and she had left with him when he was evacuated to Australia.

As Korda said, "if Ike had simply told Mamie to pack her bags and join him, it is hard to imagine that anybody would have been shocked or angered."[77] Stephen Ambrose made the same point.

"If Eisenhower was considering divorce he played his cards close to the chest," wrote Smith, and "there is no doubt he could have turned on a dime" when Marshall "replied harshly."[78]

By writing the June 4 letter, he would have accomplished two things: he would have defused the situation and bought himself additional time— time to consider all the options that seemed viable.

If there is anything to be said for this theory—and of course we will probably never know the truth—it would have made a certain kind of sense under the circumstances. If Ike really did write the alleged divorce letter to Marshall, and if Marshall really did react with indignation, then the subsequent letter—the letter asking whether Mamie could join him—would have been an exercise in good psychology: it would have amounted not only to a covert apology but an invitation for Marshall to help save the Eisenhower marriage. George Marshall would have liked that.

The last thing that Ike needed or wanted at that point was Marshall's hostility as he made up his mind about Kay.

All through the war, Marshall visited Mamie to give her the latest news about Ike, and he had *ordered* Ike to come home and spend time with her early in 1944. His own marriage was extremely important to him, and he and his wife were very close. *Family* was important to Marshall, and when his beloved stepson Allen was killed on the Italian front, he made a special trip to see the very spot where Allen had been killed and to talk to the men who were with him when he died.

In any case, the answer to Ike's request to have Mamie join him was no; Truman said that an exception for Eisenhower could not be made, since other men in uniform would also want to bring their wives over, and that would put too great a strain on the system. By calling attention to the issue,

Ike had triggered an objection that would probably not have occurred if he had acted on his own.

In his conversations with Clay, Smith asked about the different options that Ike might have been considering after Germany surrendered. Clay pointed out that "General Eisenhower was under considerable pressure immediately after the war to take up permanent residence in England. A group of leading citizens, led by Jimmy Gault, who was very influential in London financial circles, wanted General Eisenhower to live in Britain and had even selected a residence for him."

Smith asked Clay "if that would have involved Kay Summersby." According to Smith, "Clay blushed and did not answer." Then, "after a significant pause, Clay continued: 'General Eisenhower was a General of the army. That was a lifetime appointment. He would never be required to retire. He could always draw his pay and allowances. So living in England was a real possibility.'"[79]

According to the Miller/Truman story, Marshall said that if Ike ever mentioned divorcing Mamie, his life would be a living hell whether he was in the army or not, and *no matter where he was living.*

Marshall was heavily involved in the planning of the hero's-welcome celebrations for Ike.[80] If the divorce letter—which also included a request *to be relieved of duty*—had also mentioned the possibility of *living in England,* that would certainly have cast a pall over the hero's-welcome plans.

Perhaps Jimmy Gault had broached the prospect of living in England in the rosy afterglow of the London theater party. If so, the emotional force of the situation could have been compelling for Ike. Smith's theory was predicated upon the supposition that Ike wrote the divorce letter in May of 1945.

The timing would have fit.

The most responsible way to address the controversy about Ike and Kay Summersby is to acknowledge that we will never know how far the relationship went. Perhaps it never became sexual, but it was a romance. There is no doubt about it.

There were powerful emotions in play between this man and this woman.

And even if they never crossed the line and became intimate—even if Kay's allegations in her book *Past Forgetting* were untrue—Ike was clearly in the grip of a tremendous attraction toward Kay throughout the war.

The question for him at the end of the war would have been what to *do* about it.

This question would have been an urgent one in the summer of 1945, and he would need to find an answer. It was obvious that he would have to make a fundamental decision because the basis for the wartime romance would evaporate once his tour of duty in Europe came to an end.

If they *were* intimate—if Kay's allegations *were* true—then three different options would in all probability have occurred to Ike in the summer months of 1945: (1) getting a divorce from Mamie, and disregarding the consequences, (2) ending the relationship with Kay, and (3) setting up an arrangement more or less similar to what Douglas MacArthur had with Isabel Rosario Cooper—if Kay would accept that arrangement. Ike had known about the Cooper affair when he worked for MacArthur.

It is entirely possible that Ike would have decided to test the first scenario—divorce—by getting a response from Marshall as an exercise in "intelligence-gathering." He would "test the waters," which would have been in character for him.

If he did write the letter that Miller and others have alleged, he would in all likelihood have known that Marshall, the devout family man, would have reacted in a moralistic and indignant manner—unless he decided to mind his own business and avoid sitting in judgment on the private circumstances of others.

But even though the reaction of Marshall would have been largely a foregone conclusion—not least of all because of the institutional culture of the army itself—Ike might have decided to go ahead because it would help him to determine the broader implications of what he was considering. It would have been an exercise in worst-case planning and risk assessment. How harsh would the reaction be?

If the Miller story is true, then he got his answer.

Turning to another of the options that he might have been considering, Ike was clearly in a position to maintain an ongoing liaison with Kay—i.e., a continuing extramarital affair. At FDR's suggestion, Kay had become an American WAC, and she had made it very clear that she would love to become an American citizen. If and when Ike succeeded Marshall as army chief of staff, it would be easy to bring his wartime staff with him to the Pentagon, and that would include Kay—presuming that her citizenship application could be expedited. Maintaining an affair when prying eyes might have tried to intrude would of course have constituted a challenge, but Kay made it clear in *Past Forgetting* that she would have been willing to try it.

Ike decided against that option.

He decided to cast her away—to break off the relationship and take the emotional consequences.

In October, Kay left for the United States to take out citizenship papers. When she returned, Ike told her that he would soon be taking George Marshall's place as army chief of staff.

He would have to go to Washington for several weeks, he told her, and then, when he returned, they could make plans to move to Washington early in 1946, and she would join his staff at the Pentagon.

But it never happened.

"The last entry in my office diary for 1945," she wrote in *Past Forgetting*, "was on Saturday, November 10. It read: 1:30. E leaves for Paris en route to U.S. After that, the pages are blank. Ike never came back."[81]

She was stunned as the meaning of this situation began to sink in.

After a while, "we were notified that the General's personal staff should be ready to leave for the States in ten days. Almost immediately after that, a Telex came in from Washington saying that Lieutenant Summersby was dropped from the roster of those scheduled to leave for Washington."[82]

Lucius Clay contacted her and said that a job was waiting for her in Berlin. She was not interested—although she took the job later on.

At the end of November, she received a letter from Ike—a typewritten letter—on War Department stationery. "Dear Kay," the letter read, "I am terribly distressed, first because it has become impossible longer to keep you as a member of my personal official family, and secondly because I cannot come back and give you a detailed account of the reasons." He added that those reasons amounted to things "over which I have no control."

Below his signature he wrote, "Take care of yourself—and retain your optimism."[83]

We will never know exactly the way that Ike's feelings and decisions played out in the summer and autumn of 1945, but the gist of it is clear enough: he turned Kay loose, put an end to their relationship, and he did it with a tough-as-nails decisiveness.

He did it abruptly.

The impersonal nature of the way that he did it drew forth the condemnation of Jean Edward Smith, who called his action "cold-blooded and ruthless."[84]

But Kay was far more understanding. "The General was a very ambitious man," she wrote in *Past Forgetting*, "and while I think he might have been happy if somehow we could have found a way to spend the rest of our lives together, I do not think he would have been able to respect himself if he felt that he had gained a measure of personal happiness by giving up the privilege of serving his country."[85]

He would not have been able to "respect himself," she wrote, if he sacrificed his future for her.

And that was probably the essential truth: that was probably the key to his decision.

Though he outwardly dismissed the political talk about him that was circulating in 1945, he could sense within himself the capacity to give the world leadership, the kind of leadership that would guarantee *peace*.

"Peace is an absolute necessity in this world," he proclaimed in a speech at the Waldorf-Astoria during his triumphal visit to New York.[86] In the presence of Mayor Fiorello La Guardia, he said that his generation had a duty to protect the nation's children from the horrors of war.

The advent of nuclear weapons made that duty particularly urgent.

At Potsdam, he learned about the recent success of the atomic bomb test at Los Alamos. Henry Stimson revealed to him that the bomb would be used against the Japanese if they did not surrender.

Ike was reportedly appalled.

More than ever, the values of his mother began to surge forward in his mind, and the impetus to give the world leadership grew apace. Something would have to be done to protect the world—to protect the world's children—from the horror of World War III. Ike saw in an instant the implications of the bomb, and he probably felt that all other decisions he was making in 1945 would have to be made against the background of his calling—his responsibility to the world.

Even the most personal decisions.

In August, he accepted the invitation of Stalin to come to Moscow. He flew from Berlin in the company of Zhukov, and the men enjoyed one another's company immensely. In Moscow he stood next to Stalin as they watched parades in Red Square and they conferred about the postwar world. Ike told a *New York Times* reporter that he found Stalin "benign and fatherly," and at a press conference in Moscow he declared that he "could see nothing in the future that would prevent Russia and the United States from being the closest possible friends."[87]

Except the bomb.

It is easy to make allowance for Ike's *apparent* ignorance at the time regarding the evil side of Stalin's nature—his sadism, his paranoia, his delusions, and the murderousness that made his rule in Russia such a nightmare. The point is that Ike the soldier was *the son of Ida Stover,* and the wishful thinking that he was expressing in regard to the Soviets' intentions was rife with the theme that would infuse his presidency: he would bring the world security and *peace.* This was terribly important to him.

It would be his abiding mission to bring the world peace, using all the shrewd gifts at his disposal. That was the way he had reconciled his mother's pacifism with the shooting skills he learned from Mr. Dudley and Henny Engle back in Abilene: the highest and best calling of a fighter, he told himself, was to *keep the peace.*

He had proven his skill as a warrior. Could he prove that he could keep the peace?

Ike probably made the decision in 1945 that FDR had been forced to make so many years before: he would sacrifice romantic fulfillment for a different form of personal fulfillment. As of 1945, no president had been divorced, and divorce was widely viewed as inimical to presidential aspirations.

Adlai Stevenson was divorced in 1949, and though he won the Democratic nomination twice, he was not elected. A more glaring example of the divorce handicap would be the case of Nelson Rockefeller, whose quest for the presidency was hampered as late as 1964 by the fact that he was divorced.

The taboo would last until Ronald Reagan's time. Reagan—whose marriage to his wife Nancy was his second, since he had divorced his first wife, Jane Wyman—broke the taboo.

If FDR had not given up his love for Lucy Mercer, the New Deal would never have been. His partnership against Hitler with Winston Churchill would never have occurred. If FDR divorced Eleanor because of his deep love for Lucy Mercer, he would probably have become an obscure and frustrated New York lawyer.

Notwithstanding the fact that sophisticated mores had infiltrated popular culture—as previously noted—there remained within mainstream values a censoriousness that the probity of George Marshall exemplified. If Ike wished to fulfill his destiny at the highest level of American power—the presidency—then his personal life would have to be above reproach.

Strange as it may seem by today's standards, many people at the time viewed divorces as just as scandalous as extramarital affairs—if not *more so*. Marriage was *for life*, as the wedding vows said.

Harry Butcher would divorce his wife, Ruth—Mamie's best friend among the military wives—so he could marry his girlfriend. Such a thing was out of the question for Ike if he wished to get anywhere in *politics*.

Douglas MacArthur's affair with Isabel Rosario Cooper made him vulnerable to blackmail. He had to buy back his love letters. Ike had been careful to keep the few notes that he wrote to Kay rather bland. Nothing was made overt; he expressed his feelings in statements like this: "you know what I will be thinking."

But if he wrote the much-disputed divorce letter to Marshall, it would add an element of great uncertainty to his future. The letter would remain within his Pentagon file, and there was nothing that he would be able to do about it. The motivation to write such a letter would have flowed from a combination of calculation and impulse.

If he really wrote it, it would constitute an *impulse* that he would later regret.

After Merle Miller's book appeared, Major General Harry Vaughan—who was Truman's military aide—claimed that the Ike–Marshall divorce correspondence had been quite real. He made this claim in an interview with the Associated Press.

He said that operatives of Senator Robert Taft tried to get copies of the letters in 1952 and that when Truman heard about it, he had Vaughan bring the letters to him. Vaughan did so, without having read them. Then Truman allegedly sent the letters off to George Marshall, stating that the documents belonged in his personal files, and should not remain items that could be used for "dirty politics."[88]

Two decades later, additional corroboration was provided by John R. Steelman, a special assistant to Truman who would begin to serve as Truman's presidential chief of staff in 1946 (his title became "*the* assistant to the president").

According to Steelman, Marshall brought the divorce letter to Truman's attention *immediately* in 1945. In an oral history interview conducted in 1996 for the Truman Presidential Library by Niel M. Johnson, Steelman said that Marshall was so upset by the divorce letter that he brought it to Truman in the Oval Office. He called Steelman before coming to the White House and asked him to sit in on the meeting.

According to Steelman, "Marshall wanted to criticize Eisenhower and he was afraid that Truman was too prejudiced in favor of Eisenhower and so he wanted me as a witness." Marshall said that he was going to "burn Eisenhower up" because of the divorce letter, and he wanted Truman to know about it.

Steelman: "Eisenhower had said he was going to divorce Mamie and marry Kay, and Marshall told him, 'If you do that, I'll bust you out of the army, so help me. Don't you dare do that.'"

Truman told Marshall to destroy the divorce letter, but Marshall filed it instead. He said that "he wasn't going to do it, he was going to put it in the files, because Marshall didn't trust Eisenhower as much as Truman did."

An extended excerpt from this interview at the Truman Library can be read in the corresponding endnote at the end of the book.[89]

The point bears emphasizing: both Truman's military aide and his chief of staff confirmed that Ike sent Marshall the divorce letter and that Marshall answered it, thus supporting the Miller allegations.

The circumstantial evidence for corroboration of the divorce issue keeps expanding: from Garrett Mattingly to Merle Miller to Harry Vaughan to John Steelman, and Jean Edward Smith was convinced by 2013. Further evidence may very well emerge in the future.

Which would have been the better choice for Ike: continued happiness with Kay at the cost of frittering away his potential, or the sacrifice of such romantic love to achieve his *political* potential? Could he make the sacrifice?

Could it be that his wartime romance had met a need that was no longer urgent for him? Could he let it go and... move on?

When Ike met Kay, he was able to recover what he lost when he let Gladys Harding slip away. It appears that he found his way to the "absolute naked adoration" that Mamie never gave him. For three years, he had regained his lost youth in the joyous company of Kay.

Wasn't that enough?

How much more of that kind of fulfillment did he really have to have at the cost of other kinds of fulfillment? Was it not time for him to..."act his age?"

He had been given the chance by Marshall and FDR to be a commander—to make tough calls under pressure—to exercise powerful authority. He had gotten used to the challenge and he liked it—even at the cost of the stress.

Because it was heroic.

He went ahead with the invasion of Normandy when the weather threatened disaster. He mastered the situation when the Germans broke through the Ardennes. He had trusted his judgment and acted on his own authority to make de Gaulle president of France. He cultivated Stalin and talked with him about the nature of the postwar world. He was proud of being able to do such things, and he did not wish to give up the chance to continue.

He had tasted *greatness*—and he liked it.

He had gotten used to the experience of shaping world events—and he was good at it. Anything less in the future would have constituted a let-down for him, a come-down, an anticlimax, a disappointment—a surrender.

He had become a great global figure. Would he settle for anything less as he planned the next chapter of his life? He was still a comparatively young man—still in his fifties. If he spurned his destiny, what would he think of himself in the future, looking back at the things that he had not tried to do? Could he live with that?

He could not, and Kay Summersby knew it.

She understood the man very well. Mamie, on the other hand, did not: when Ike died, she told her granddaughter Susan that no one had probably understood her late husband, least of all herself.

We will probably never know exactly when Ike made the decision in 1945—the decision to sacrifice Kay. But he made it, and the joy that she had been giving him went out of his life forever.

Perhaps he reflected again upon the difference between their ages. Perhaps he reflected on their private frustrations as well. In *Past Forgetting*, Kay said that they tried to get intimate again when the privacy of Ike's Frankfurt residence gave them the chance.

It didn't work. "Wait," she said to him, "you're too excited. It will be all right." "No," he supposedly replied. "It won't. It's too late. I can't."[90]

Best to give it up, he might have told himself at that moment, when the timing was right—just as he would give up cigarette smoking a few years later by going cold turkey.

He would do it suddenly—and never turn back.

Ike would never be the man of pure icy intelligence that he would *strive* to be. He remained full of passion at the height of his powers.

But he would *make* himself a man of cold judgment to the best of his ability. The anger within him was far too keen—and the need for the vicarious release that mischief could provide was too great—for him to achieve comprehensive success in his quest to become a man of steel.

His health and his emotional composure would be strained to the limit by the challenge.

Even so, he would practice self-control—the fine art that his mother had taught him. He would bring to the work of *self*-governance the same rationality that he would seek to bring to politics. He would be brilliantly careful—boldly calculating—*guardedly* audacious as the circumstances might require in order to give the world *guardianship*.

As for Kay—she came to America and earned her living as a fashion and set design consultant for television and stage productions. Eventually she did become an American citizen.[91]

She wrote a first memoir that was published in 1948—*Eisenhower Was My Boss*—a book that said nothing about the wartime romance, and the book was so successful that it led to a whirlwind lecture tour that made so much money for her that she would have no financial worries. She lived on Park Avenue and became a regular at all the swanky destinations: the Stork Club, El Morocco, the Copacabana.

She dated—and eventually she married a stockbroker named Reginald H. Morgan. The marriage was not a success, and it ended in divorce.

According to Kay, she and Telek visited Ike at the Pentagon several times after the war—probing to see if anything could be salvaged. But the encounters were extremely awkward.

One summer she was visiting her mother in England, and she read that General and Mrs. Eisenhower were in London for a visit, so she dashed off a note, but there was no reply. Then one day a young major appeared at her door and said that General Eisenhower had asked him to take her out for a drink.

She figured that he was a messenger, and she was right. He said, "Kay, it's impossible. The General is really on a tight leash. He is not his own master." He was "always surrounded by political people who dictated his every move."[92]

She had no regrets, looking back upon her life, and she cherished her memories of Ike. "I do not believe that anyone today will construe our relationship as shameful," she wrote in *Past Forgetting*, for she was in love, and she was always convinced that the love she felt was fully mutual.[93] She was writing after all in the 1970s, when attitudes about such things had become more tolerant—for a while.

She said that her experience with Ike had been "perfect."[94]

She was given three wonderful years with a man who exemplified everything she wanted in a man. And that was enough for her, though it naturally took her some time to work her way through the disappointment when it ended.

She had cried her eyes out at first when he left her, but she pulled herself together and became a socialite. She was given three years with a man she adored, and the memory of that sustained her.

It was enough.

She had lived her emotions to the full, she had not held anything back, and whatever happened afterward, nothing could spoil what had been— and even the memory of what *might* have been seemed beautiful to her as she was dying. She had experienced the kind of love that many other people never find.

At least that was what she told herself at the end.

As for Ike—he made a very strange entry in his diary on December 2, 1947.

He had heard, he wrote, "through a mutual friend, that my wartime secretary... is in rather dire straits. A clear case of a fine person going to pieces over the death of a loved one, in this instance the man she was all set to marry. Will do what I can to help, but it would seem hopeless.... Makes one wonder whether any human ever dares become so wrapped up in another that all happiness and desire to live is determined by the actions, desires—or life—of the second. I trust she pulls herself together, but she is Irish and tragic."[95]

Irish and tragic.

Kay mentioned nothing of this loss—a loss akin to the death of Dick Arnold, her fiancé in North Africa—in the pages of *Past Forgetting*.

There is much that we will never really know about the private lives of Kay Summersby and Dwight Eisenhower.

But his diary entry makes us wonder.

"Irish and tragic" he had called the insouciant Kay, and perhaps she did experience a tragedy that never found its way into the pages of her second memoir. If so, she recovered and went on to find other forms of happiness.

Ike never recovered the kind of happiness that she had given him.

In that sense, he was the one who was tragic in the end since the sacrifice that he made when he abandoned Kay was permanent.

The gap that it left in his emotional life would never be filled. In a sense, he became a different man.

He would start life over with Mamie, but what was the chance that they would ever have the kind of joyous and carefree existence that had made him feel so young again when he was with Kay?

The chance was nil.

He had to brace himself for new forms of stress that her gaiety and warmth would never ease. He would find some diversion with casual friends and with golf, but the radiance he felt in her presence was gone.

He would deal with that.

"Activity helps," he had told Kay when her fiancé died, and there was plenty to do as he became the new army chief of staff. After that, he and Mamie would have to decide what to do with the rest of their lives—if a political future was not in the cards.

One way or another, he would prevail with the life he chose to live.

That is certainly one way of being a hero—a tragic hero—and the sadness of his choice gives a special dimension to his life.

He made a sacrifice, the dimensions of which only he would be able to appreciate fully as he sat within his fortress of solitude.

Would it be worth it to him as he changed the world for the better in his presidential years?

CHAPTER SIX

Destiny

Dwight D. Eisenhower was not a happy man in the years right after the war.

He savored the experience of shaping world events, and he knew he had an aptitude for it. His destiny was clear.

But instead of plunging into politics, he plunged into an undertow. He denounced suggestions that he run for the presidency, and he found himself so exasperated by people who nagged him about his future that he dashed off complaints about them in his diary entries and letters. Here are some examples:

- March 8, 1947: "By this time I thought that a soldier (unless he deliberately sought public notice) would be forgotten and left alone to do his job."[1]

- August 27, 1947 (to Swede Hazlett): "Frankly, if Mamie and I could have our way we would, without the slightest hesitation, retire to the quietest and least publicized neighborhood in the United States."[2]

- December 31, 1947: "The irritating insistence of certain columnists and commentators that I take a partisan political stand [is] based upon the erroneous assumption that I would like a high political office."[3]

- January 15, 1948: "The tossing about of my name in the political whirlwind is becoming embarrassing."[4]

- November 25, 1949: "After all these years of nagging at me, pro and con, Democratic and Republican, I still do not want any political office, even if it could be handed to me without effort on my part."[5]
- January 1, 1950: "I am not on any fence with respect to my attitude toward a possible nomination for a political office. I want none of it."[6]

Fair enough, one is tempted to say: Ike had earned the right to be left alone if that is what he wanted.

But one look at the famous photograph of Ike at the rostrum accepting the Republican nomination in 1952 is enough to make us wonder what was going on in his mind as he jotted down the scribblings quoted above. His gesture in that photograph was almost the same as it was in the 1945 victory parades: hands held high in a posture of triumph and a smile that is beaming with radiance.

He looked euphoric.

In the 1952 picture, the radiance has taken on another dimension: he looks like a *master*.

He is grinning in a way that pulls us out of our seats and commands us to see…*what he is!*

He stands revealed as a *master* of politics, a man who was *born* to enjoy the political game, a sly operator who cannot keep from grinning to himself as he contemplates the secret plans that he has up his sleeve.

So what *did* account for Ike's reluctance to plunge into politics after the war? Why did he have to be dragged kicking and screaming to his destiny?

"Throughout his whole career," Michael Korda has said, Ike "had always been fiercely ambitious, but he had just as fiercely never wanted to be seen as ambitious. It had never been Ike's way to reach for promotion; he let promotion reach out for him."[7]

True—though he did learn the art of networking from Fox Conner, and he used Conner's help to get better assignments. But as for promotion as such—yes, he let promotions come to him.

And one could certainly argue there was *method* in Ike's reactions to the presidential talk. To play the political game, he would have to be courted—unless he wished to emulate the fatuous MacArthur.

Eisenhower Presidential Library

CAN NATIONAL CONVENTION

Ike accepting the Republican presidential nomination in 1952.

Allowing himself to be courted would constitute good politics for a military man in Ike's position. It would add to his luster.

But his diary notes suggest that the aversion to politics that he kept expressing was genuine. It was different from the pose of a man who plays hard to get to advance his ambitions.

His statements suggest that however heady the prospect of advancing to the presidency might be, a "still small voice" kept telling him that it would be wrong—for *him*. There was something powerful holding him back.

Even so, he was tempted.

He turned his thoughts to public policy issues in 1946, and he began to familiarize himself with ideology. He took some time to examine the controversies of the day, and he began to figure out where he stood.

But before very long, he reverted to the old disclaimer: he had no interest in politics. And it appears that he made himself believe it.

There were reasons for his attitude that are easy enough to comprehend. His wartime labors were exhausting, and his duties as army chief of staff were both grueling and thankless. He was pestered by admirers and well-wishers, deluged with invitations to give speeches that became increasingly repetitious.

But there was something else going on.

Here was a man who had shaped the course of history and experienced greatness. He possessed excellent leadership skills—he knew it—and he reveled in the arts that could change and manipulate events.

In the aftermath of such achievements, anyone possessing Ike's gifts would confront the possibility that the rest of his life might constitute an anticlimax. But there was an obvious antidote: the presidency would be the perfect next step for him, and it would constitute the culmination of his life. Why not embrace the prospect?

He did no such thing: he constantly proclaimed to himself—and to others—that the prospect repelled him.

Why?

Only a man who was *alienated* would give the impression—and this theme resounds over and over—of being *hunted* in a world that refused to leave him alone.

He sounded like a cranky old man whose opportunities for satisfaction were blighted. His feeling that a welter of scheming politicians, pesky bureaucrats, and parasites of every description were *stalking* him would get worse in the years leading up to his presidency. His mind was agitated—off-balance.

He felt hounded to death by people and forces that were totally inimical to what he wanted, people and forces that were hell-bent on making him do things that he did not want to do, *make sacrifices he did not want to make.*

Are these the feelings that a *happy* man would express?

Obviously not.

Ike told himself that his residual dreams of happiness should be minimalistic: all he wanted was a place of peace and quiet in which to eke out his dwindling days and try to educate his fellow citizens.

It is easy to conclude that such feelings are salutary for people at the brink of old age. But there are plenty of people who keep on living adventurous lives no matter how old they are. And Ike wasn't really that old.

No, there was something else going on.

The feelings that Ike was expressing suggest a man who senses that his life has taken a wrong turning, that he made a bad bargain, that a well-rounded feeling of satisfaction would never be his. Aggravation would be his lot, and the world would vindictively *deny* him the relief that he needed in a simple life of peace and quiet.

He would have to suffer.

Dare we suggest that he was in the throes of some dark emotions? The exercise of asking such questions is conjectural. But the questions are still worth asking.

Ike's resentment toward people who suggested a political future for him seems excessive—reactions arising from a deeper state of discontent. What might have been the causes of such discontent?

The historian Perry Miller once wrote that we sometimes come across statements that demand to be "read for meanings far below the surface, for meanings of which, we may be so rash as to surmise, the authors were not fully conscious, but by which they were troubled and goaded."[8]

According to Kay Summersby, Ike's reticence in confronting his emotions was a problem he admitted. Once, when they were riding on horseback, she teased him by saying, "I know more about the Belle Springs Creamery Company in Abilene than I do about how you feel about me."

Then, according to Kay,

Ike hit his horse with his crop and they went tearing over the rocky fields as if ghosts were chasing them. He was back in minutes, coming around in a wide circle and slowly gentling his horse down to a sedate walk. "I'm sorry," he said.... "It's hard for me to talk about things... about people...that mean something to me.... I have always kept my feelings in check. Not talked about them. Not even thought much about them."[9]

This account rings true because of what Ike would acknowledge later on about the power of his mother's teachings—the teachings about controlling one's emotions.

Kay shared another reminiscence about a conversation they had—an extremely emotional conversation—that was more painful.

Ike opened up about the way in which his marital problems had changed his whole outlook on life.

He said that "he had thrown himself so completely into his work that there was room for nothing else." Then, after pondering this observation for a moment or two, he turned to Kay and said, "I'm a damn fool. But you know that. God, I don't know what's the matter with me."

"Nothing," she replied, "nothing at all." "Somehow I just lost the way," he continued, and she consoled him: "Someday things will be different."[10]

It would be easy—for reasons already set forth—to say that Ike failed to follow the promptings of his heart when he made the decision to throw away Kay Summersby, and he was paying the price. But the truth was messier. His desires had been contradictory. At last, he made the choice that he thought was most appropriate.

It was not an easy choice to live with.

No matter what decision he had made, a feeling of bitterness and self-recrimination would have followed. But he had chosen the worst of all possible options if the goal was to maximize the satisfactions of life.

Shall we spell things out?

He had behaved in a manner that his wife considered a betrayal, he had dumped a woman who was dear to him without any warning at all, and in the process of *making two women unhappy,* he had sold himself short when it came to the sheer joy of living.

A miserable outcome.

Almost anyone would be depressed by an outcome like that—a no-win outcome. All the more reason for plunging ahead toward the deep satisfactions that the presidency might confer: the satisfactions of creating a better world.

But could it be that Ike was deeply in doubt about the kind of personal destiny that he...deserved?

After the war, Kay remembered, "I was in and out of the Pentagon a lot seeing old friends," and she decided "it would have been ridiculous not to say hello to the General." This was not a spur-of-the-moment thought.

She brought Telek along.

Her meeting with Ike was a very "strange experience." "The General stood up to greet me as I came into the office," she recalled. "I stooped and let Telek off his leash, and he ran straight to Ike after all those months and rolled over on his back, paws in the air, to have his stomach scratched. I could tell that Ike was very much affected. He got all red."

She made small talk by telling him about her plans to find work in New York. "'Good, good,' he said briskly. 'That sounds sensible.'"[11]

They parted on extremely awkward terms.

She returned to visit him a few other times—and the results were never any different. She always brought Telek.

If this visit occurred—and it probably did—it would have happened in 1947, for that was when Kay arrived in Washington.[12] The implication of the visit was perfectly clear: an invitation to resume their relationship.

Michael Korda was convincing when he argued that the prospect from Ike's point of view would have seemed hopeless: as army chief of staff, he was "a major figure in Washington," a resident of Quarters 1 at Fort Myer, "surrounded by his army staff and servants," and "constantly in the eye of the press." He was "living in a fishbowl," and continued relations between them, "given the amount of speculation that had already gone on...was a pipe dream."

He would have to put her out of his mind—or reconsider the idea of divorce, and, as Korda has said, "nobody was more familiar with the unbreakable dos and don'ts of army life than Ike was, unless it was Mamie."[13]

He was living with Mamie—he had to face her every day and every night—and she watched him.

Kay's visit—and she would return to the Pentagon a number of times—must have been torture.

Here is a very simple force that could have been the one that was holding Ike back: the force of conscience.

Though tough-minded, he could sometimes be conscientious to a fault. And if he pondered the mess he had created—if he paused now and then to reflect upon the lingering sadness—what kind of a future would he seek? Would he feel inspired to seek new forms of self-glorification? Or would he wince?

Did he think very much about such things? Was he really in the mood for further glory? How could he be?

When Kay appeared at the Pentagon—and he knew that she would probably drop in again—everything froze. What would happen to his sense of self-respect when she appeared? What would he feel?

And when he sensed a disapproving gaze from Mamie, he would face the unavoidable question: How should he feel?

Best to hide himself away in some remote location with her and attempt to start over. Like Thoreau, he would simplify. He would teach his fellow citizens about civic virtue. By teaching others, he would heal. He would get back to basics in a place that reminded him of childhood.

He would shun the world stage until *others* could persuade him that the people of the world were in peril.

Only then would he allow himself to make full use of his powers and shake off the spell.

Only then would the process of blaming himself—if that was indeed what was happening—die away.

But one thing is certain: he was *restless*.

He remained extremely ambitious, extremely analytical, extremely challenged by the prospect of shaping the world. Amid his angry denials of interest in the presidency, his destiny continued to intrigue him. As he fled from the prospect of presidential power, he was steadily, carefully, sedulously preparing for it.

The evidence for this assertion is legion.

His diary entries from 1946 are rife with the calculations of a man who knew that he *ought* to prepare for the White House. In 1947 he lurched in the other direction and rejected a series of overtures that could have made him president by 1948. But the kingmakers would be back—and this fitful drama would continue playing out until the springtime of 1952.

Ike was playing hide-and-seek with himself.

A Tutorial in Politics

Ike's ruminations of 1946 reveal a growing interest in politics. He paid attention to controversies, and he strove to formulate well-considered points of view. His reflections in 1946 make interesting reading.

He pondered the looming Cold War, notwithstanding all his oft-expressed hopes for peace with the Soviets. Dark realism pervaded his thoughts, and he began to see communism for what it was, a ruthless threat to free people everywhere.

On November 15, 1945, he had claimed in congressional testimony that "Russia has not the slightest thing to gain by a struggle with the United States."[14] But he felt differently when he proclaimed in his diary on May 16, 1946, that "our form of government is under deadly, persistent, and constant attack." He made it clear that he was speaking about the Russians.

Looking back years later in his diary, he recalled that James Forrestal—who became secretary of the navy upon the death of Frank Knox—gave him pointed advice about the Russians during the war: "Be courteous and friendly in the effort to develop a satisfactory modus vivendi, but never believe we have changed their basic purpose, which is to destroy representative government."[15]

After World War II, Ike was firmly convinced that Forrestal had been right.

"Russia," he wrote, was "completely statist": it was a totalitarian behemoth that stifled liberty. Moreover, the Russians were "so anxious to spread communism" that they would use naked force to "see that communism gets in the saddle."[16]

America, he said, must ensure that its democratic system exemplified "individualism rather than statism."

He was not at that point prepared to embrace the creed of minimal government—and he never fully embraced it. Though he began to denounce the ways of "bureaucracy" with increasing fervor, he believed that limited forms of governmental supervision and regulation were justified. The key was his aversion to *excess*.

To "maintain free enterprise," he wrote in 1946, "we must police...but not destroy, either by legislation or by class conflict."[17]

He admitted to himself that he was still uncertain about where he stood on particular issues.

"Class conflict" was a potent theme that carried over from the Great Depression. After the war, it was implicit in a wave of crippling strikes—the most serious of them being a coal strike that started in April 1946. By December, Ike was wondering whether the army would be ordered to intervene. He wondered "what we are to do about the coal strike if called upon by the president to preserve order in the face of cold and privation."[18]

He was candid as he pondered the power of labor unions. "I know nothing of the long, tedious process whereby certain labor leaders have become dictators," he wrote, and "yet all my sympathies are with the workers (my youth was one of such hard work, and my memories of my father's life so clear that I could do nothing else)."[19]

What he wanted was a politics of unification, and the *principles* were easy to articulate: "We must produce a healthy economy, raise living standards for all, and preserve individual liberties." But the "practical application" was difficult, since "no one is ready to abandon immediate advantage or position in practicing cooperation."[20]

He jotted down notes for further study as he pondered the issues of corporate regulation and labor-management relations.

He made lists of alternative policy prescriptions and arranged them against each other. "These must be studied," he wrote: "closed-shop, check-off, industry-wide unions, responsible, corporate organization of trade unions (one side). Effective antitrust laws, lockouts, control of raw materials, sound financing—private and government—limiting bureaucratic rule (other side)." "All laws affecting the above subjects," he wrote, "should be evenhanded."[21]

Ike was putting himself through a cram course on matters ideological and policy-related: he was finding his way along the spectrum of left-and-right opinion.

He was not at all sure that he wished to participate in presidential politics. "I'm suspicious of anyone who believes he could take over the presidency successfully in these days and times," he wrote on November 12, 1946.[22]

But supporters and admirers were creating a nonprofit Eisenhower Foundation to purchase his boyhood home in Abilene and establish a museum in his honor. After Ida passed away in 1946, the Foundation purchased the home, which was opened to the public in 1947. The cornerstone for the museum would be laid in 1952.

Anticommunism

By 1947, Ike began to associate his feelings about Russia with increasing hatred of communism.

"Russia is definitely out to communize the world," he wrote in his diary, either by conquest or by creating "starvation, unrest, anarchy, in the certainty that these are breeding grounds for the growth of their damnable philosophy." Russia was "the great exponent of dictatorship [that] has announced its fundamental antagonism to all sorts of capitalism (essential to democracy)."[23]

It is important to recognize that such feelings were not exclusively the property of conservatives. Many liberals were expressing them in the 1940s.

Communism was—and remains, in places where it still exists, like North Korea—a monstrous corruption of left-of-center ideals, much as fascism represented a perversion of conservative ideals. After the creation of the Soviet Union, naïve liberals in the West often looked to Russia as a kind of egalitarian utopia. A comparable impulse on the right led the poet Ezra Pound to view Mussolini as a latter-day Caesar Augustus.

It was predictable that militant conservatives would begin to attack the New Deal in the 1930s as communist-tending. They reasoned that the government activism of FDR was leading toward a sinister "statist collectivism."

But what such conservatives did not understand at the time—as a point of historical fact—was that the "welfare state" had conservative as well as liberal antecedents.

The idea of a social security system, for instance—old-age pensions and unemployment compensation—was created under Otto von Bismarck in imperial Germany as a *conservative* reform. Its whole thrust was counterrevolutionary.

The idea was to *undercut* Marxist agitators by demonstrating that the monarchy and the aristocracy would protect the working class from poverty. So there would be no need for workers to go chasing after radical remedies.

In 1910, in a visit to Germany, Theodore Roosevelt listened as Kaiser Wilhelm explained this principle. The two of them were sitting together on horseback watching war-games exercises as the Kaiser talked. It was "the business of those who believe in monarchical government," said Wilhelm II, "to draw the teeth of the Socialists by remedying all real abuses."[24]

The elder Roosevelt was impressed enough by the principle to recommend a social security system for the United States in 1912. And that system would be created by the younger Roosevelt in 1935.

"Socialism"—as such—spanned an ideological range that extended from the radical, Marxist, and revolutionary version to the peaceful, democratic, and moderate creed known as "Fabian" Socialism, as propounded in England by Sidney and Beatrice Webb. The British Labour Party exemplified this socialism. Its politics were democratic, and its program advocated the nationalization of certain basic industries.

This could be compatible with capitalism depending upon the specifics.

Right after World War II, for example, the Labour government nationalized the Bank of England by purchasing its bank stock. The Bank of England remained the fount of Britain's free enterprise system—it was integral to capitalism—but the Labour Party turned it into a publicly owned utility whose lending practices would be guided by Parliament.

Great Britain was hardly a totalitarian police state like Russia under the influence of this kind of socialism. Neither were the Scandinavian countries, whose welfare states, developed in the 1930s by social democrats, were consistent with free elections and individual liberties.

But communism as such—like fascism—was totalitarian, and it was George Orwell, *an English socialist,* who alerted the left in the 1940s to what Stalinism had created in his nightmarish novels *Animal Farm* and *1984.*

The point is this: people on the left could be as fervently anticommunist as people on the right.

And so it was that an American liberal anticommunist organization was founded in 1947 by Eleanor Roosevelt, Hubert Humphrey, John Kenneth Galbraith, and others. The group was called the "Americans for Democratic Action" (ADA), and its views were extremely influential in the Truman administration. Truman started an internal security program designed to weed out communist spies, and in 1947 his administration announced the goal of "containing" Soviet expansionism.

These ideological cross-currents were playing out as Ike's anticommunist convictions took shape after World War II.

The Truman Era's Challenges

Truman had never sought the presidency, and he was not at all sure that he liked the job. He was a man of duty, and his duties after Roosevelt's death were clear: finishing the war with Japan and making America's postwar transition a seemly and successful one.

He was an internationalist, and he aimed to prevent a relapse of the United States into isolationism. Moreover, he aimed to protect the economy from sliding back into depression. Like many Democrats—and like many progressive Republicans—he believed that the federal government had a duty to institute necessary social reforms.

The postwar moods of America did not make his experience in the presidency a happy one.

There was a huge psychological letdown after the war, very similar in some respects to the letdown after World War I. Much of the victory rhetoric in World War II had been prompting utopian expectations: expectations that America—and/or the new United Nations—would fix what was wrong with the world, and fix it *permanently.*

This time, the slogans proclaimed, would be the *last time* that Americans would be called upon to fix the world.

After the euphoria began to wear off, disillusionment set in. The Cold War turned this to bitterness. A neo-isolationist backlash was inevitable under the circumstances, and the old isolationists (sunk in disgrace for a while after Pearl Harbor) began to regroup.

Short-term economic dislocations after World War II were also inevitable. The G.I. Bill helped prevent a new depression, but a surge of inflation took off in 1946—notwithstanding the fact that wartime wage and price controls remained in place.

Contentious strikes and labor-management conflicts added to the economic uncertainties, just as they had done in 1919.

As the Cold War began to shape up, Americans had to make fundamental decisions about national security.

One of the major questions was how much military power the United States should have. What was to be the nation's long-term security posture in the decades ahead? How could the postwar *demobilization* be reconciled with the nation's ongoing security challenges? America had emerged as a superpower at the end of World War II—but should it remain one? And what was to be done about atomic weapons?

In July 1946, two atomic explosions were triggered at Bikini Atoll in the Pacific—explosions to test the effects of these bombs against ships. One of the bombs was exploded in midair and the other was detonated underwater. The sheer size of the explosions was grotesque, and the radioactive pollution at Bikini Atoll remains dangerously high to this day.

Plans were underway to design a strategic bomber to succeed the B-29 Super Fortress. The B-47 "Stratojet" would be introduced in 1951, and the B-52 "Stratofortress" emerged from the drawing boards in 1948. German rocket scientists were being recruited to help the United States develop missiles more powerful than Hitler's V-2.

One of the major structural reforms to be given priority in the field of national security was the unification of the armed forces. Truman began to advocate this reform in 1944, and Ike was an enthusiastic supporter. Just after he returned from Germany in November 1945, he testified on Capitol Hill in support of the measure—the bill that would result in the creation of the new Defense Department.

For America to take its place in the world as a permanent superpower, certain preconditions would have to be met, and the National Security Act of 1947 would help to meet those preconditions.

The act transformed the War Department into the Department of the Army and merged it with the navy and a newly independent air force to form the Department of Defense. The act also created the Central Intelligence Agency and the National Security Council.

Ike believed wholeheartedly in these reforms, and his foremost job as army chief of staff would be to diminish interservice rivalries in the interest of military unification.

He would also have to oversee the army's postwar demobilization and craft an army budget that was realistic in light of congressional politics.

On May 9, 1946, Ike flew to China as a special emissary of Truman, who was hoping to get George Marshall to consider the post of secretary of state. When Ike put the proposition to Marshall, the response was immediate. "Eisenhower," he said, "I would do almost anything to get out of this place. I'd even enlist in the army."[25]

Marshall played a key role in the development of Cold War policy because the State Department took the lead in anticipating and responding to aggressive actions by Stalin.

In 1946, Russian expert George F. Kennan sent a highly pessimistic view of Stalin's intentions to the State Department. The establishment by the Soviets of totalitarian police states in eastern Europe fulfilled his predictions. In February 1947, Undersecretary of State Dean Acheson joined with State, War, and Navy officials in preparing a working paper for Truman in response to these events.

The paper recommended assistance—primarily economic assistance—to "support free peoples who are resisting attempted subjugation by armed minorities or by outside pressures." On March 12, 1947, Truman asked Congress to grant such assistance to the governments of Greece and Turkey.

Thus began the Truman Doctrine and its policy of containment.

It was in this context that Secretary of State Marshall proposed *comprehensive* economic assistance to European nations in an address that he delivered at Harvard University in June 1947. Lucius Clay—Ike's deputy for the German occupation as well as his successor in that post—played a role.

Through 1946, United States policy had called for the deindustrialization of Germany—the object being to prevent a resurgence of German militarism. FDR's treasury secretary Henry Morgenthau Jr.—who bristled with indignation over the anti-Semitic aspects of State Department policy under Cordell Hull—convinced Roosevelt that German power had to be *destroyed*, that Germany as a nation should be broken up, and that the German people should be reduced to an agricultural subsistence.

This policy became known as the Morgenthau Plan.

But Lucius Clay was in charge of feeding and supporting an impoverished German population, and he saw the suffering—and the potential for communist exploitation of it—that mandated a rethinking of the Morgenthau Plan.

In light of Soviet aggression—and with the economies of western European nations in a shambles—Kennan, Acheson, Marshall, and Truman agreed that a policy of economic assistance to *all* European democracies, including West Germany, would have to be created.

Chief of Staff

When Ike was army chief of staff, he and Mamie were given a chance to begin the slow process of salvaging their marriage.

After the death of Icky, a chill had come over their relationship, and Mamie's suffering in the Panama episode led her to consider divorce.

The marriage recovered some vitality during their years in Washington: they had fun with their friends in Club Eisenhower days, and then the trip to Paris had made things even better.

But the Philippines episode plunged the marriage back into crisis. Ike was the one to consider divorce, and his flirtation with Marian Huff was a pointed gesture of rebellion toward Mamie.

Then the Summersby romance made the Eisenhowers virtually estranged—notwithstanding Ike's professions of devotion.

What kind of a married life could be crafted in the aftermath of such damage?

One joyous event would help them in 1947: their son John would get married to Barbara Jean Thompson, whom he met when he was stationed in Vienna. She, too, was an "army brat," and they were married in the chapel at Fort Monroe, Virginia. Their first child—Ike's grandson, David—would be born in 1948.

Ike's position as chief of staff gave Mamie a luxurious home in Quarters 1 at Fort Myer: they were waited upon by servants, and Mamie brought her favorite things out of storage, though she did feel pangs of separation when she left the Wardman Park.

Moreover, Ike's new duties gave them opportunities to travel together, and perhaps this created pleasant times.

In his two-year term as army chief of staff, Ike visited every state of the union, plus Hawaii and Guam. In his first year he made forty-six speeches and travelled to thirteen foreign countries. Mamie got the chance to come along.

Ike's perks as army chief of staff surely must have pleased the belle of the Douds: they rode in a limousine, and their home was managed by a devoted and hardworking staff.

One sobering issue confronted them: the perks would vanish when Ike retired, and his pension would become the new basis for their subsistence.

Under the circumstances, he and Mamie discussed the idea that he might become the president of a small college. They had no particular destination in mind.

But a bigger and more significant possibility was arriving.

On April 2, 1946, Ike gave a speech in New York City at the Metropolitan Museum of Art, and his host was Thomas J. Watson, the chairman of the Met's board and also a trustee of Columbia University. Watson asked Ike if he would consider being president of the university.

The university's illustrious president, Nicholas Murray Butler, was in ill health, and a search committee would have to choose his successor when the time was right. Watson wanted to know if Ike would consider becoming a candidate. He said that this famous Ivy League university deserved a president with international prestige. Ike recommended his brother Milton, who was the president of Kansas State University.

No, said Watson, he wanted Ike—who replied that he could not consider the possibility until his services as chief of staff were concluded in 1948.

That was good enough for Watson.

Ike had a magnificent staff at his disposal in the Pentagon, but his duties were laborious: he had to struggle with the army budget and the politics of interservice unification, which the navy was resisting.

His old friend Swede Hazlett—a navy man, as he had gone to Annapolis when Ike went off to West Point—took the navy point of view in their correspondence, and Ike honed his arguments for unification by trying them out on Swede.

He put his friend at ease when it came to the predictable fears: each service would maintain its own uniform, service academy, and traditions. The Marine Corps would not be taken away from the navy and given to the army.

But he pressed the point that there was no way for any of the services to get the proper level of support from Congress "*unless the broad yearly program for all three services is presented ... as a unit* [original emphasis]."

Behind the scenes, he was fighting for the army's share of the budgetary pie, and he had to control the army's demands. His duty to supervise the budget led to swift applications of the thrifty habits he had learned from his mother.

In the course of his duties, he flew to Japan to visit MacArthur, who was in command of the occupation. They discussed the budget—but they also discussed politics: MacArthur asked Ike if he intended to run for the presidency in 1948.

Thirteen months after Watson approached Ike about the possibility of becoming Columbia's president, the search committee for the university reached an impasse, and so Watson approached Ike again.

Ike thought about the offer long and hard. At first, he saw nothing but tiresome responsibilities—like fundraising—and he had no experience in academic administration or faculty politics.

He consulted Milton, who urged him to accept since his duties would be largely ceremonial and being president of an Ivy League university would afford him a wonderful platform for addressing national issues.

Ike found the choice extremely difficult. "I had to struggle against every instinct I had," he wrote to Beetle Smith, adding that his "real dream was to get a small college of an undergraduate character somewhere in the Virginia or Pennsylvania area or possibly even in the Northwest and live quietly with Mamie in that kind of an atmosphere."[26]

He was pining for obscurity—pining to *retreat*. This was a moment of truth for him, and he held back in indecision. But at last, he made the decision to *advance*.

Columbia would be a platform—a stage in his continuing ascent.

On June 2, 1947, Ike was the commencement speaker at West Point, and Watson drove up from New York City with another Columbia board member to tender Ike the university's formal offer of the presidency.

Watson gave him the right assurances: he would not be given burdensome duties, and he could use his visibility to speak about urgent issues confronting American democracy.

The university let him assume his new duties at the end of the next academic year, which meant that he would have time—after he stepped down as chief of staff on February 7, 1948—to take advantage of another handsome offer: the offer of a book contract for his military memoirs, to be supplemented by newspaper serialization.

Still another offer came his way in 1947: Harry Truman offered Ike his support for the 1948 Democratic presidential nomination. Associates of Truman's later confirmed (in interviews with the journalist Robert J. Donovan) that Truman made this offer—men such as John Steelman, Truman's chief of staff, and John Snyder, a friend of Truman's who was serving as secretary of the treasury. The offer was also confirmed by Milton Eisenhower.[27]

Ike turned it down.

1948

But other Democrats revived the idea because they were worried that Truman, if he ran for reelection, would lose. FDR's son James Roosevelt, a congressman from California, teamed up with party leaders like New York mayor William O'Dwyer to float the idea of drafting Ike as the Democrats' candidate. By summer, this idea would have widespread support among Democrats.

Meanwhile, on January 9, a group of Republicans who wished to draft Ike put together a slate of Eisenhower delegates for the New Hampshire primary. Leonard Finder, publisher of the Manchester *Union-Leader*, wrote an editorial endorsing the action, and he sent Ike a letter urging him to toss his hat in the ring.

Ike declined.

By that time, of course, he had other plans. He would be the new president of Columbia, and he would write his memoirs.

Ike had made plans for writing his memoirs during the war, and he instructed Harry Butcher and Kay to keep diaries for him to consult when the moment arrived to start writing. After the war, he read the memoirs of Ulysses S. Grant as a literary model.

Both Simon & Schuster and Harper & Brothers approached him— Richard Simon of Simon & Schuster had discussions with Ike as early as July 1946—but he eventually made a deal with Doubleday in conjunction with the New York *Herald Tribune*, which would serialize the book, and he signed the contract in December 1947. The deal made him rich.

Instead of the usual payment in the form of an advance against royalties, Doubleday offered him a lump-sum payment of $635,000 when he completed the manuscript. That was the equivalent of over $6 million in today's values, and the tax implications for Ike were outstanding because of federal policies in 1948.

IRS policy permitted one-time authors who received this kind of a lump-sum payment to treat it for tax purposes as a capital gain instead of income. That meant that Ike would give only 25 percent of his earnings to the government—instead of the 82.13 percent that he would otherwise have paid.

For the first time in his life, he would be financially independent.

Ike began writing on February 8, 1948, with the help of three stenographers, and he finished the book in three months, working sixteen hours a day. When the manuscript was finished, William Robinson, publisher of the *Herald Tribune,* presented Ike with two checks totaling $635,000. Then he treated Ike and Mamie to a vacation at the exclusive Augusta National Golf Club in Georgia.

Bill Robinson would become an enormously influential figure in Ike's career, not least of all in politics.

While they were in Georgia, Robinson introduced Ike to a group of very wealthy—and Republican—businessmen, all of whom were destined to play important roles in his future. Ike would call them "the gang."

The principal members of the gang were Robinson, Clifford Roberts (an investment banker), Robert Woodruff (chairman of the board of Coca-Cola, whom Robinson would later succeed in that post), W. Alton "Pete" Jones (president of the Cities Service petroleum company), Ellis Slater (president of Frankfort Distilleries), and George Allen, a wealthy attorney and political activist. Allen was the only Democratic member of the group.

The gang made Ike a member of the exclusive Augusta National Golf Club and built a cottage for him with a fishing pond near the tenth tee.

Meanwhile, *Crusade in Europe,* Ike's memoir, became a bestseller and reviewers loved it. The book is still in print.

On May 2, 1948, Ike and Mamie moved to New York City and settled into the official mansion of Columbia's president.

This mansion, in Morningside Heights, had been the residence of the legendary Nicholas Murray Butler, a celebrated educator, philosopher, diplomat, and sometime politician. President Theodore Roosevelt attended Butler's investiture as president of Columbia, and Butler's Republican credentials were considerable.

He had been a delegate to every single Republican convention from 1888 to 1936. The elder Roosevelt called him "Nicholas Miraculous." He was a close friend of Elihu Root, one of TR's most important associates.

Under Butler's leadership, the culture of Columbia University's board of trustees became heavily Republican.

Butler's celebrity status in America grew apace. He masterminded a major expansion of the university's campus. He persuaded Andrew Carnegie to donate $10 million that launched the Carnegie Endowment for International Peace.

This was the man whom Ike would be succeeding as president of Columbia.

Ike's duties as president of Columbia would commence on June 7, 1948. His formal investiture would occur in the autumn.

The magnificent mansion where Ike and Mamie would live was designed by the celebrated architectural firm of McKim, Mead, and White. Built in 1912, it was a four-story Italianate creation, with the lower floors reserved for entertaining. The house was lavish.

Butler's guests had included the king and queen of England, heads of state, and Nobel prize winners. Almost two thousand guests had come to the house every year for receptions and dinners. The interior designer Dorothy Draper was hired to renovate the décor in anticipation of the Eisenhowers' arrival.

The family quarters were on the third floor, with the servants' quarters up above. Draper created a rooftop solarium for Ike, which he used to host bridge parties for members of the gang when they were in town. He also used it as an art studio.

At Winston Churchill's suggestion, Ike had taken up the hobby of painting.

Thomas Dewey, whom the Republicans ran for the presidency in 1944, was competing with Robert Taft for the Republican nomination in 1948.

Bill Robinson talked at great length with Ike about the situation. Robinson's *Herald Tribune* was the editorial voice of the Eastern internationalist wing of the Republican Party. Robinson did not want Taft to be nominated. So he tried to get Ike to run as an alternative to Dewey for the purpose of stopping Taft.

Robinson warned Ike that the Republican right might turn to MacArthur to prevent the nomination of Dewey. "My God, anything would be better than that," replied Ike, but he was absolutely unwilling to get involved.[28]

Dewey won the nomination.

Thomas Dewey was a liberal-to-moderate Republican. As governor of New York, he supported public housing, slum clearance, expanded mental health treatment, and reforestation. He was friendly to business, and he created programs to help small businessmen navigate federal regulations. Dewey was a pragmatist. He was a man of the Republican "Eastern Establishment," and Taft, the midwestern isolationist and antigovernment zealot, was his enemy.

Pollsters predicted a Republican year, and the Democrats were justifiably worried. Truman, who had not planned to seek a second term, was so incensed by the efforts to dump him that he fought back and sought reelection.

In May, two of FDR's sons, Elliott Roosevelt and Franklin Jr., issued statements calling on the Democrats to draft Ike. On July 3, a select group of Democratic leaders sent telegrams to over a thousand Democratic convention delegates inviting them to attend a caucus on July 10. Everyone knew that the purpose of the caucus was to call for an Eisenhower draft.

Ike ordered the director of public information at Columbia to issue a strong disavowal on July 5. With prompting from Truman, he issued an even stronger disavowal on July 8.

Truman's victory over Dewey and the "Give 'em Hell, Harry" campaign that had brought it about became the stuff of legend.

The Democratic Party suffered schisms in 1948, and two breakaway candidacies revealed the fault lines. Former vice president Henry Wallace broke away and ran as a "progressive" candidate. He represented the segment of liberal opinion that viewed the Cold War liberalism of Truman as warlike. Governor Strom Thurmond of South Carolina broke away and ran as a "Dixiecrat." He represented the Jim Crow southern Democrats who hated the fact that Truman's "Fair Deal" was starting to encompass civil rights reform.

But the Republicans were also divided. For years the party had run progressive or liberal candidates for the presidency and the conservative Republicans who held positions of dominance in Congress were angry about that.

Truman turned the situation to humorous advantage: he called the Republican Congress into special session and dared the Republicans to write their own party's progressive presidential platform into law.

Few Republicans laughed at the joke, which did wonders to lift the morale of the Democrats.

When did Ike become a Republican?

There is good reason to believe that events in election year 1948 played a fundamental role in his choice. And *conservative* tendencies in the Republican Party were attractive to him by the end of the year.

Ike had been glad when FDR beat Hoover in 1932, and he had supported Roosevelt's leadership during the Great Depression. He had also been drawn toward the politics of Democrats when he graduated high school.

On the other hand, he supported decentralized government when he discussed politics with Milton in 1927. The Douds were conservative, and the army high command, as previously noted, was often conservative.

So how did Ike's political and ideological thinking evolve?

The evidence is scanty until the autumn of 1948—when he began to make strongly conservative statements.

On October 12, in his inaugural address at Columbia, he warned that "a paternalistic government can gradually destroy...the will of a people to maintain a high degree of individual responsibility. And the abdication of individual responsibility is inevitably followed by further concentration of power in the state." He warned against "government ownership or control of property."[29]

On January 14, 1949, he wrote that "the trend toward governmental centralization continues, alarmingly. In the name of 'social security,' we are placing more and more responsibility upon the central government, and this means that an ever-growing bureaucracy is taking an ever-greater power over our daily lives. Already the agents of this bureaucracy cover the land [and] they nag, irritate, and hound every businessman in the United States."[30]

A month later, he told Columbia students in a "Forum on Democracy" that if "we allow this constant drift toward centralized bureaucratic government to continue," the "ownership of property will gradually drift into that central government."[31]

On September 27, 1949, he wrote that he would "fight for what I believe in, which is decentralization of both responsibility and authority in government."[32] On January 1, 1950, he declared his support for "competitive enterprise" as opposed to "the welfare state"—or the "handout state," as he put it.[33]

On April 5, 1950, he proclaimed that "we must have a Republican victory in 1952."[34] In 1951, he wrote that "four years more of Democratic, uninterrupted government in our country will put us so far down the road to socialism that there will be no return to free enterprise," adding that under the Democrats "we would follow the example of Britain until we become fully socialized, which means, of course, fully regimented."[35]

He was clearly a Republican by then—a Republican with definite conservative leanings.

But he had never before expressed these sorts of opinions with this kind of fervor. What made the difference?

Some of his new rightward tilt can be explained by the influence of others.

When he joined "the gang," he began fraternizing with businessmen who were, with one exception, Republicans. The resentment of "big government" within corporate culture was and is pervasive. One encounters it to this day in the rhetoric of the Chamber of Commerce.

Furthermore, when Ike arrived at Columbia, he joined an institution whose board was rife with Republican associations.

And there are good reasons to believe that his own state of mind was more receptive to conservative attitudes.

When people feel imposed upon, they may tend to view large and impersonal forces with suspicion. "Government" may appear to them a pervasive and meddlesome presence whose sole purpose is to hinder, thwart, and take away.

They forget about its positive functions.

Ike did feel harassed after World War II—as previously noted. So when he heard complaints about bureaucrats from friendly businessmen in the course of bridge games, he was in a receptive state of mind to identify with their complaints and to merge them with his own.

But there were doubts—whether Ike chose to acknowledge them or not. Consider this diary entry from 1950:

> The last thing that an office seeker seems to think of is just plain honesty. If he can be devious, he thinks he is smart; he'd rather be evasive than direct. He wants to give pat answers—he will never, for

a second, admit that *the true course, usually, is a middle one, between extremes*. He hasn't the guts to be "middle of the road" [emphasis added].[36]

Here was a statement that foretold the "Middle Way" of Ike's presidential years.

One of the interesting things about Ike's conservatism is the way that it gradually diminished. After complaining about the welfare state in such strident terms, he did not choose to roll it back much when he attained the presidential power to do so. In certain ways, he chose to extend it.

Why?

By the middle of Ike's presidential years, conservatives started calling him a socialist.

There is something rather odd about the mood swings—if it is fair to use such a term—in Ike's ideological development.

In June 1948, Bill Robinson wrote a letter to Helen Rogers Reid, the owner of the *Herald Tribune*, in which he described Ike's political tendencies as centrist. "He says," wrote Robinson, "that actually the middle of the road in America is no narrow white line; it is a broad highway that reaches over to a fanatical fringe on the left and a benighted strip on the right."[37]

Ike's generalizations about the threat of centralized government were exercises in hyperbole. When he complained about bureaucrats who "nag, irritate, and hound *every businessman in the United States*," he was speaking carelessly.

He was *not* expressing a well-considered view that could pass the test that he had always insisted upon as a commander and would insist upon again in his presidency: the test of dispassionate analysis.

As supreme commander, he was merciless on subordinates who made exaggerated statements. He insisted on empirical facts that were based upon data and very close reasoning. He subjected the shrill bluster of Montgomery to scrutiny by the planners at SHAEF. "Steady, Monty," he had told his gung ho associate.

So consider this: When Ike wrote in his diary that federal bureaucrats were hounding *every single businessman in the United States*, did he mean this generalization to be taken literally?

Of course he didn't. He was...venting.

And when he worried that "ownership of private property" would "drift" into the hands of government, did he really believe that a movement to *abolish private property* in America could succeed through nothing more than *stealth*?

He was talking about a process so slow and so insidious that it would never be detected in time to cut it off. He said that Americans would be "regimented" by the Democrats and that there would be "no return to free enterprise."

In other words, capitalism would... *vanish.*

Did he really believe that?

If not, we are justified in asking ourselves why he chose to engage in such oversimplifications—such hyperbole—that defied the close *analysis* in which he could excel.

Why?

It is easy to understand such attitudes among people who have had bad experiences with government. Consider the experiences of Stanley Rumbough Jr. and Charles Willis, who in 1951 created the "Citizens for Eisenhower" movement. They had heard from reliable sources that Ike disliked "big government."

He would do something about "the mess in Washington."

Rumbough and Willis had been pilots during World War II, and they created a small airline after the war. They encountered so much obstruction in their dealings with the federal government's Civil Aeronautics Board (CAB) that it ruined their business.

It is easy to understand why they would become conservative Republicans.

But a true systems analyst would look at the other side of the question: Should commercial aviation have been unregulated?

Herbert Hoover had forced the regulation of airlines when he was secretary of commerce. At his prompting, Congress passed the Air Commerce Act of 1926, which set standards for aircraft safety, airport safety, and coordination of routes, not least of all to prevent midair collisions.

Rumbough and Willis had encountered certain tendencies in human nature—stupidity, mendacity, procrastination—that appear in almost any organization: government, business, labor, and even...the military. But to take such experiences and extract from them enormous negative generalizations—i.e., government as such is *bad,* business is *bad,* labor is *bad,* and the military is *bad*—is childish. It is not the kind of thinking that does much credit to anyone whose experience of life has been rich and complex.

It was only a matter of time before Ike's stated aversion to "centralization" would collide with his view that society needs *coordination.*

He was still a master of systems analysis.

He still understood that there are times when the ethos of super-individualism must yield to broader patterns.

Truth be told, his new friends in the business community were also practitioners of systems analysis. They were proud of their entrepreneurial individualism, but their enterprises consisted of vast and far-flung organizations.

Their business models were grounded in the patterns of integrated mass society—not the world of yeoman farmers, small shopkeepers, and "every man for himself." Moreover, Ike's business friends were *internationalists.* They abhorred the isolationism that was still so influential within the Republican far right.

As an intellectual, Ike himself could be supremely flexible—at his best.

"I just read an article by Bertrand Russell, philosopher," he wrote in his diary on May 15, 1951. "Very good indeed as a mode or code of living today."[38]

Ike's talk about "centralized government" impinging upon the lives of individuals was *symbolic.* It was talk from a man whose own private life had indeed been imposed upon—but not by "government."

By 1948, the government was leaving him alone.

He was getting rich, and not a soul in the government was stopping it. His tax situation was enviable.

His new friends were all rich and happy. They complained about taxes, but they still lived luxurious lives, and they enjoyed themselves as they basked in their country clubs, their palatial homes, their expensive vacations.

Ike himself was in the lap of luxury. So why wasn't he happy?

His generalizations about the influence of government were all *negative*—not a single word about government's power to create such things as…interstate highways. And so again we ask the question—why?

Something else was oppressing Dwight Eisenhower, something else from which his sour mood sprang. "Government" can serve as a convenient punching bag if people are angry at the world—or at life.

Much easier to vent your anger on a vast and impersonal force than take a look at your own bad choices. Much easier to say to yourself that you are up against…"the system."

Poor you.

But there is something more specific about "government" that would have been obnoxious to Ike by 1948: *the presidency* is the capstone of our government, and it was *presidential ambition* that had eaten away his happiness.

He was resisting the call *to the presidency* when he condemned the evils of "government." Why seek the highest office in the land if there were nothing to be done in Washington that is *positive*?

Why *preside* over…"bureaucratic government?"

Ike was pushing from his mind any thoughts about the great potentiality of the presidency for *glory*.

And we know the reason—do we not? "Government" was not the real issue for him—it was his happiness.

And since he didn't wish to acknowledge that fact, he vented his anger on scapegoats.

He had thrown away a wonderful chance to be happy because of the bitch goddess of ambition. And now—what he wanted was for people to *leave him alone*, except for bridge sessions with the gang.

But there was someone who would not leave him alone.

"One day I picked up the paper," wrote Kay Summersby, "and saw that General Eisenhower had been appointed president of Columbia University and would be moving to New York." She explained what happened next in *Past Forgetting*:

The famous studio portrait of Kay Summersby, late 1940s.

I had thought I was completely over the affair. I was having a good time and I had two quite attentive men friends, one of whom I was to marry a couple of years later. But that newspaper story—well, my hands were shaking when I finished reading it. I started thinking and dreaming about Ike all over again, lovesick as a young girl. There was nothing I wanted more than to see him…. I was obsessed with the idea. I missed him bitterly. I started haunting Columbia University. I would take the subway up to 116th Street, go through the iron gates and walk around the university. I soon learned where his office was in the Low Library and where his house was…. Only a few weeks after he had been installed at Columbia, I ran into the General as he walked though one of the gates leading onto the campus. He was very much surprised to see me. And I acted surprised too. I had a story ready. I told him I was there to look up the sister of an English friend of mine…. He looked very much bothered, and after a few minutes, he said, "Kay, it's impossible. There's nothing I can do."… There were tears in my eyes, but I tried to smile. "I understand," I told him.[39]

Months before Ike was inaugurated as president of Columbia on October 12, 1948, the Cold War escalated.

The leaders of western Europe feared Soviet aggression, and Britain, France, Belgium, the Netherlands, and Luxembourg began discussions about mutual assistance. Communists with Soviet backing had overthrown the democratically elected government of Czechoslovakia. Would the same thing happen elsewhere?

Concurrently, Truman called for a peacetime draft, more military spending, and an alliance with the nations of western Europe. In May, Republican senator Arthur Vandenberg proposed a resolution for such an alliance, and it passed.

Thus negotiations began to create the North Atlantic Treaty Organization: NATO.

On June 24, 1948, Stalin's aggressiveness was displayed again: he cut off access to the Allied occupation zones in West Berlin. Lucius Clay recommended swift action, not least of all for the sake of maintaining the prestige of western democracies.

Truman agreed, and on June 26 he approved the Berlin airlift, a round-the-clock mission to supply West Berlin. As a power gesture, Truman also sent B-29 Superfortress bombers—capable of delivering nuclear weapons—to Britain.

On August 25, 1948, in hearings before the House Un-American Activities Committee (HUAC), Whittaker Chambers, a confessed former communist, accused Alger Hiss, a high official at the State Department, of having been for years an undercover Soviet agent.

Thus began a drama that would continue through 1950, when Hiss was convicted of perjury and sentenced to prison.

Richard Nixon, a young Republican congressman from California, made it his business to seek definitive proof of Hiss's guilt. Nixon in time became a hero to members of the Republican right, and so did Whittaker Chambers.

By 1950, ultraconservative Republicans were saying that Hiss was merely a specimen of the treachery in FDR's New Deal, with its "creeping socialism."

"All of the New Dealers I had known were Communists or near-Communists," Chambers proclaimed in his book, *Witness*. "None of them took the New Deal seriously as an end in itself. They regarded it as an instrument for gaining their own revolutionary ends."[40]

Columbia

Eisenhower was pleased at first with the life he had chosen at Columbia. And the faculty and students seemed pleased with him in return.

On November 7, 1948, the *New York Times* proclaimed that "General Eisenhower has taken Columbia the way he took Normandy beach. The entire university population of 35,000—students, professors, officers, trustees, and janitors—has happily surrendered and adores its conqueror."[41]

Not the least of the reasons for this state of affairs is that Ike used his clout to get 116th Street closed between Broadway and Amsterdam Avenue. This unified the Columbia campus, which for years had been broken up by the busy thoroughfare. Everyone at Columbia was grateful to Ike for having solved this problem.

Ike enjoyed himself by attending home football games at Baker Field. He gave a guest lecture to a class on historiography. Columbia historian Allan Nevins went out of his way to praise *Crusade in Europe*, and the stellar reviews of Ike's book were contributing to the university's prestige.

In *Harper's*, Richard Rovere called the book "a document that sometimes comes close to splendor."[42]

At a black-tie dinner for Columbia history faculty, Ike stole the show. According to historian Jacques Barzun, he reacted quickly when a member of the department cited Churchill's fixation with the "soft underbelly of Europe." According to Barzun, Ike

> got quite huffy, and said, "That is one of the most ignorant remarks made by anybody," and he proceeded to give us, without prompting, a history of the campaigns, beginning with Thucydides and the Peloponnesian War, that had taken place in the south of Europe which, as we all know, is a mass of mountains, and he went right on to the Austrian War of 1866, the German-Austrian War. It was a masterly performance and with hardly a hesitation for words.[43]

Ike settled into his new academic life with satisfaction—at first. Morningside Heights was not the quaint location that he and Mamie had been looking for, but his first months at Columbia were pleasant.

He enjoyed the solarium in the president's mansion, which he used as an art studio. He developed a new routine of creating oil paintings in the evening. "I simply get a bang out of working with colors," he told Swede Hazlett.[44]

He was a vigorous defender of freedom of speech in his days at Columbia. In response to some protests over the appearance of a communist speaker on campus, he replied that "the virtues of our system will never be fully appreciated...unless we also understand the essentials of opposing ideologies.... I deem it not only unobjectionable but very wise to allow opposing systems to be presented by their proponents."[45]

The presidency of Columbia opened doors for Ike. Henry Wriston, president of Brown, introduced him to scores of people who were influential in the world of public policy. Wriston chaired the prestigious Council on Foreign Relations, established in 1921 as an internationalist think tank.

He appointed Ike to direct one of the Council's study groups. Through this work, Ike interacted with many senior political figures in Washington.

He also joined the board of the Carnegie Endowment for International Peace, whose chairman was John Foster Dulles.

And his circle of powerful and wealthy friends in corporate America kept expanding. Before long, his new friends would include Philip Reed, the board chairman of General Electric; Edward Bermingham, an investment banker at Lehman Brothers and Dillon, Read & Co., who served as a trustee of Columbia as well as serving on the Republican National Committee; and Sid Richardson, an oil tycoon from Texas.

In the years ahead, Ike would travel to a great many fundraising events around the country that were hosted by these men. They admired him. But they were also cultivating him, guiding him...grooming him.

Then things changed at Columbia—for the worse.

Ike was informed—to his chagrin—that the university was in financial trouble. Its endowment was dwindling, and so he had to organize a $210 million fund drive and set up an organization to receive private gifts.

Once again, he had budgetary worries—not exactly the kind that he had faced as army chief of staff, but just as aggravating.

He told Columbia's dean that "in a moment of weakness I listened to the blandishments of a couple of your Trustees and here I find myself with a gigantic organization on my hands, and I don't know a goddamn thing about it."[46]

It is hard to know when Kay Summersby crossed his path as he walked across Columbia's campus. She recalled that the encounter had taken place "one fine spring morning, only a few weeks after he had been installed at Columbia." So perhaps she had surprised him with her presence in May or June of 1948, when the Eisenhowers moved to New York and he took up his duties. Or perhaps it occurred in the weeks right after his October investiture—in which case her recollection of a springtime encounter would be mistaken.

No matter—the effect would have been the same as it was when she appeared at the Pentagon. He knew he might encounter her again.

She was persistent.

"A few months after that encounter," she wrote, "I learned that the General was going to speak to the Fellowship of the United States-British Comrades. I made up my mind to attend the meeting. It was at the Seventh Regiment Armory on Fifth Avenue."

She discovered next day that "the gossip about us was still as virulent and wildfire contagious as ever. Even the very proper *New York Times* in its report on the General's speech made a point of noting that I had been in the armory and had left without speaking to the General. I wondered what Ike would think when he read it in his copy of the *Times*."[47]

Ike was playing bridge on election night 1948 with members of the gang as they listened to the election results. When it became apparent that Truman was winning, Ike was "just as disappointed" as everyone else, recalled Cliff Roberts. [48]

A few days after the election, Ike wrote to Defense Secretary James Forrestal offering his services on budgetary matters: he was ready to come back to Washington. "I can scarcely think of any chore that I would refuse to do whenever people in responsible positions feel that I might be able to help," he explained.[49]

This was only a month after his investiture as president of Columbia and only five months after he had taken up his duties as its president.

Forrestal suggested to Truman that they ask Ike to chair the Joint Chiefs of Staff. He agreed, and he assured the Columbia trustees that he could do both jobs.

He seemed to want to get out of New York as often as possible.

Within a few months, the rat race of commuting back and forth between Columbia and the Pentagon affected Ike's health. The health of Forrestal was also at risk. Both of them were trying to cope with the interservice war between the navy and the air force over naval aviation and rival service budgets.

Ike requested a three-month leave from Columbia to try to resolve this crisis in military politics. He had to work on it full-time.

Columbia's chairman decided to let him have his way. So Ike's duties were turned over to the university's provost.

Mamie continued to live in the university's mansion, Ike lived in Washington at the Statler Hotel, and he commuted back and forth between Washington and New York once a month.

On February 4, 1949, Ike jotted down thoughts about the hubris of navy personnel. The navy men, he wrote, could insist with straight faces that "their maintenance system is the biggest and the best, their organizational system is superior to anyone else's, their carriers can carry on an air war much better than can a land-based air force, their planes are faster, cheaper, longer-ranged, etc., their personnel systems are the best, every vessel they have, active and inactive, is vitally important to the security of the United States, [and] the navy is not getting enough money."

"Something has to snap," he continued, "and so far as I'm concerned it will have to be the patience of the president and secretary of defense."[50]

Something snapped: Forrestal suffered a mental breakdown, and he died by suicide on May 22, 1949.

On March 21, Ike came down with severe gastroenteritis, and Truman had him flown to Key West naval base, which was near his own presidential retreat in the Florida Keys. After two weeks of care, Ike was flown to the Augusta National Golf Club for recuperation. Mamie joined him there. He decided to give up smoking.

When Ike returned to Columbia, he was less than enthusiastic about resuming his duties. He declined to host the traditional reception for honorary degree recipients at commencement. The provost held the reception, while Ike had dinner with Lucius Clay and his wife.

Ike took a long summer vacation in Wisconsin and Colorado. In May he told Milton that if he could not maintain a schedule of ten weeks' leave from Columbia every year, he would "quit all my jobs except helping out in Washington."[51] Faculty and student resentment toward Columbia's absentee president festered.

In July, when he returned to the mansion at Morningside Heights, he was visited by Thomas Dewey. The Republicans' 1948 nominee made a strong political pitch—a conservative pitch.

And since Dewey's own politics remained quite progressive, his conservative pitch to Ike was in all probability a ploy. No doubt he had kept his ear to the ground and was familiar with Ike's latest thinking.

Ike recorded in his diary that Dewey told him that he and only he—Ike—could "save the country from going to hades in the handbasket of paternalism, socialism, dictatorship." He urged Ike to declare himself as a Republican, run for governor of New York in 1950, and then accept the Republican nomination in 1952.

Ike said no: he told Dewey he would "never want to enter politics."[52]

By the autumn of 1949, Ike's honeymoon at Columbia was over. His absences had damaged his standing. Liberal faculty members had come to predictable conclusions about his steadily expanding circle of wealthy friends, and they didn't like the way he kept attacking the legacy of the New Deal.

Ike loathed the experience of sitting in on faculty meetings, where discussions meandered for hours.[53] Committee meetings were even worse, and before long he stopped attending them. He and Mamie discontinued the dinners and receptions for faculty members at the presidential mansion. Instead, they played bridge with members of the gang or with army friends.

By the spring of 1950, Richard Rovere reported an "intense hostility" toward Eisenhower had developed "on the part of both faculty and the student body."[54]

*Thomas Dewey,
Republican presidential
candidate in 1948 and
one of the architects of
Ike's nomination four
years later.*

Ike was also growing tired of Washington.

"The bitter fight still goes on in Washington," he wrote on October 14, 1949, "with the navy cursing the other services. The whole performance is humiliating—I've seriously considered resigning my commission."[55] In November, Thomas Dewey came visiting again, urging Ike to make the jump into politics.

For once, Ike wavered.

He admitted in his diary that "the whole matter cannot be lightly dismissed," but he was convinced he would "be more influential (over the long term) by promoting respect for American institutions by following my present course than by entering politics."[56]

On New Year's Day 1950, he wrote out a soul-searching essay in his diary as to whether or not he should become a politician. He admitted to himself that the issue about what to do with the rest of his life was a "confusing problem." But he could still not believe that a political career would be a good idea.[57]

So he decided to double down on one of his favorite Columbia projects: "the American Assembly," a discussion forum where business leaders and academicians could discuss public policy issues. In raising money for the Assembly, he took a conservative line. "The Columbia conference plan," he wrote, was designed to address concerns about politicians who were leading America "down a primrose path whose end could be...a socialized form of economy."

"Bureaucratic controls, deficit spending, subsidies, and just plain hand-outs," he wrote, could produce "dictatorship."[58]

Before the end of 1949, the Cold War escalated again. The communists took over in China, and the Russians gained nuclear weapons. Communist spies had stolen atomic secrets from America and Britain.

The "loss" of China prompted far-right attacks upon Truman and the people who served him. Marshall and Acheson had given up on the anticommunist government of Chiang Kai-shek because it did not command the support of the Chinese people.

Their arguments were valid, not least of all because they foreshadowed the later futility of the war in Vietnam—and the recent war in Afghanistan.

1950

On February 9, 1950, Senator Joseph McCarthy of Wisconsin proclaimed in a speech in West Virginia that the State Department was infested with communists, and that he and the secretary of state both knew who they were. Dean Acheson was secretary of state, since George Marshall had retired in 1949.

A Senate committee was formed to look into McCarthy's allegations, and his name was known to millions in weeks.

Thus emerged one of the foulest demagogues in American history, a man who hid behind Senate immunity—immunity from libel suits—to call people communists without any evidence, thus costing them their jobs.

Only hysteria could have sustained the power of such a slanderer. But the loss of atomic secrets to Russia—and the Cold War's tensions generally—created hysteria.

It was all a game to McCarthy, who enjoyed creating chaos and who reveled in the glare of publicity as he hurt people. He was a hero to the far right because his charges were part of a broader campaign to slander Democrats.

"The Democratic label," sneered McCarthy, "is now the property of men and women who have...bent to the whispered pleas from the lips of traitors, men and women who wear the political label stitched with the idiocy of a Truman [and] rotted by the deceit of an Acheson."[59]

He called the Truman administration an assortment of "Communists and queers," a collection of "egg-sucking phony liberals" who "sold China into atheistic slavery."[60]

There was no language too crude for McCarthy, no slander from which he would shrink. He was a creature of the gutter, and his methods degraded American life with shocking speed.

Despite the fact that he was vile, he developed a tremendous following among Americans from all walks of life.

Nothing like this would ever happen again in American politics until 2016 and its aftermath.

On March 8, 1950, McCarthy accused ambassador-at-large Philip C. Jessup, who was also a professor at Columbia, of having "an unusual affinity for Communist causes." Ike sent a letter in Jessup's defense when he was called upon to give congressional testimony.[61]

In 1950, Ike finally took action on his notion of retiring to a distant location. He bought a farm to the west of the Gettysburg battlefield and made plans with Mamie to renovate it and turn it into their retirement home.

On June 25, 1950, North Korea invaded South Korea.

In the aftermath of World War II, the United States and the Soviets established northern and southern occupation zones in the Korean peninsula. These zones in time became sovereign states, with North Korea ruled by the brutal communist dictator Kim Il-Sung. South Korea was ruled by the autocratic Syngman Rhee. Each government claimed to be the legitimate government of all Korea.

After the North Koreans invaded, the United Nations Security Council denounced the invasion, and created a U.N. command to repel it. Truman sent forces under the command of Douglas MacArthur to South Korea.

Ike supported Truman's decision. On June 30, he wrote that "we'll have a dozen Koreas soon if we don't take a firm stand."[62]

The early months of the war went badly for the U.N. command: its forces were pushed back to a small defensive line known as the Pusan Perimeter. In September, MacArthur launched an amphibious counterattack behind enemy lines at Inchon, and the North Koreans retreated. By October, MacArthur crossed over into North Korea and his forces rushed toward the Yalu River, the border with China.

Then the Chinese communists intervened with massive force and the South Koreans and their U.N. defenders were overwhelmed. The result was a long and bitter winter retreat.

America was once again at war, and the mood of the American people grew darker. World War I had been hailed a generation earlier as the "war to end wars," and it turned out to be no such thing. World War II was supposed to be the one that would "finish the job," and of course it did nothing of the kind.

Only five years after the defeat of the Axis, American men were back in action in a murderous war.

Is it any wonder that millions of Americans began to feel that there must have been some kind of *betrayal* for this to happen?

Several months before the Korean War started, Truman *militarized* his Cold War strategy. A top-secret memorandum from the National Security Council (NSC 68) called for a huge defense buildup. The memo was largely the work of Paul Nitze, who headed the State Department's Policy Planning Staff, and it led to a vast expansion of "containment." NSC 68 had been presented to Truman in April 1950, and he implemented its recommendations.

Defense appropriations skyrocketed above the cost of the Korean War. Truman authorized the development of the thermonuclear "hydrogen bomb," and he called George Marshall back from retirement to become secretary of defense.

As this vigorous response to communist aggression unfolded, McCarthyism—a phrase coined by newspaper cartoonist Herbert Block—grew apace. McCarthy and his allies insisted that communist aggression overseas would never have occurred if the federal government had not been subverted by "Reds."

Consequently, when Marshall was being confirmed as defense secretary, Senator William Jenner of Indiana—a McCarthy henchman—went on the attack. He called Marshall a "front man for traitors," adding that "this is no new role for him, for Gen. George C. Marshall is a living lie…. This government of ours has been turned into a military dictatorship, run by a Communist-appeasing, Communist-protecting betrayer of America."[63]

Jenner blamed Marshall for a great many things: for Pearl Harbor, for "tricking" the American people into war, for abetting the Yalta "sell-out," and for "losing" China.

Jenner was a vicious simpleton who reveled in the chance to spread desecration. Calling Marshall a "traitor" appealed to his lust for indecency. But Jenner was merely an understudy: he was taking his cues from McCarthy, and that master of indecency had already surpassed the pupil in vilifying Marshall.

McCarthy called Marshall "part of a conspiracy so immense as to dwarf any previous such venture in the history of man, a conspiracy of infamy so black that when it is finally exposed, its principals shall be forever deserving of the maledictions of all honest men."[64]

McCarthyism loomed as a threat that would turn these sorts of thugs into formidable powers in America. McCarthy and Jenner were also close to being isolationists, for they brushed aside Truman's anticommunist actions abroad as *distractions* when the real problem was communist subversion *at home*.

On October 13, 1950, Thomas Dewey told Ike that he was going to endorse him for the 1952 Republican nomination. Ike issued another disavowal. After thanking Dewey for his "compliment," he stated that the best service he was capable of providing would be to remain at Columbia and continue his work there.[65]

But a few weeks later, Ike received a call from Truman asking him to come to Washington and discuss a new assignment: Truman wanted to call him back to active duty and appoint him commander of the European security force that was meant to deter the Russians from invading western Europe.

Truman wanted Ike to command NATO.

NATO

Ike was interested.

He met with Truman on October 27, and they discussed the tasks of getting troop commitments from European nations and resolving the issue of German rearmament.

Ike wrote in his diary that "the chances are about nine out of ten that I will be back in uniform in a short time."[66] He would have to step down as president of Columbia or request an indefinite leave of absence.

Several things concerned him: "Mamie's heart condition deteriorates a bit year by year and I hate to contemplate the extra burden thrown upon her by attempting to set up housekeeping in Europe."[67] Moreover, NATO was still just a paper organization, and the scope of American participation remained vague.

He was somewhat ambivalent. He believed in collective security, but he wondered "whether I do not exaggerate in my own mind the seriousness of the world situation."[68]

By December, his doubts were resolved—"everyone is in a blue funk over the tragic news from Korea," he wrote—and he told his study group at the Council on Foreign Relations that America should send no less than twenty divisions to Europe.[69] At his behest, the group wrote a letter to Truman recommending "powerful military forces" for NATO. Allen Dulles—the brother of John Foster Dulles—offered to call upon Averell Harriman and set up a meeting with Truman for the presentation of the letter.[70]

The vagueness of the planning for NATO troubled Ike, and he could "obtain no satisfactory answers to such questions as how many divisions, groups, and ships are involved in America's building programs. Vagueness seems to be no crime or fault—the answer is 'In Europe Eisenhower can solve all the problems.' Sweet, but valuable only as opiate. Goddamnit, is there no desire to know where we are going?" He criticized "poor HST [Truman], a fine man who, in the middle of a stormy lake, knows nothing of swimming."[71]

Ike's NATO appointment could not be confirmed until the North Atlantic Council in Europe requested him. The Council met on December 18, 1950, and the vote was unanimous. Truman called Ike with the news.

Columbia's board of trustees granted him an indefinite leave of absence. Vice President Grayson Kirk would run the university until such time as Ike returned.

Ike prepared to leave for Europe on January 6, 1951, to conduct a preliminary inspection. But before he left, he decided to have a secret meeting with Senator Robert Taft, the front-runner for the Republican presidential nomination in 1952.

Taft had voted against the NATO treaty, and he also endorsed former president Herbert Hoover's call for America to retreat into isolation and guard itself with nuclear weapons. Ike paraphrased Hoover's notion as follows: "Arm to the teeth and stay home."[72]

In the face of all the bad news from Korea, that sounded like a tempting proposition to many people.

Ike's new assignment in Europe would be meaningless if Taft were elected and withdrew America from NATO.

Taft's stature among conservative members of his party was such that he had been dubbed "Mr. Republican." In the great scheme of things, he did not deserve the nickname, because his isolationism tarnished the legacy of former president William Howard Taft—his own father—as well as the Republican legacy of Theodore Roosevelt.

The elder Taft had supported the League of Nations. As early as 1915, he led a group called the "League to Enforce Peace (LEP)," which championed the concept of collective security.

Robert Taft wanted none of that.

In 1940, when Hitler's armies were devouring western Europe and Britain was preparing to fight for its life, Taft proclaimed that war would be worse for America than a German victory.

That was why internationalists mounted a fervent campaign to stop him from getting the 1940 Republican nomination. The campaign in 1940 to stop Robert Taft foreshadowed the campaign that would lead to the nomination of Ike in 1952.

As early as February 1939, columnist Arthur Krock began a campaign to promote the fortunes of Wendell Willkie, an internationalist who had made a name for himself by opposing some of FDR's domestic policies.

In April 1940, Henry Luce ran an article by Willkie in *Fortune* magazine. A New York lawyer named Oren Root was so impressed by Willkie's article that he drafted a "Declaration" calling for his presidential nomination and mailed it to people whom he knew in the Princeton class of 1924 and the Yale class of 1925. They were invited to sign the Declaration and return it to him.

The response was overwhelming, so Root forwarded copies to the *New York Times* and the *New York Herald Tribune*.

The campaign to draft Willkie for the Republican nomination caught on, even though Willkie had only recently changed his party affiliation from Democratic to Republican. Two weeks before the Republican convention, Willkie agreed to run.

The Republican convention was overwhelmed by chants of "We want Willkie" from the floor. Taft tried to get a recess in order to reorganize his supporters, but the convention chairman refused. On June 28, 1940, a week after France had surrendered to Hitler, Wendell Willkie, a lifelong Democrat who had never before run for public office, won the Republican nomination for president.[73]

Thomas Dewey, who had also been a presidential hopeful in 1940, remembered these events as he stepped up the pressure on Ike to get into politics.

Taft had been quirky and unpredictable in his policy stances between 1940 and 1951. He became less conservative on some domestic issues, supporting a public housing bill in 1949 and telling fellow Republicans that they should support a "minimum standard floor under subsistence, education, medical care, and housing."[74]

Ike would come around to this position himself.

Taft's foreign policy preferences veered back and forth between isolationism and aggressive militarism. In the aftermath of the reverse in Korea, MacArthur called for war with China and the use of nuclear weapons. Taft wavered between support for MacArthur's position and the isolationism of Hoover.

As historian Alonzo Hamby observed, Taft found it hard to make up his mind about a great many things as the Korean War unfolded; "he was powerfully attracted to intervention across the Pacific," but he remained "a conservative repelled by the means that a total offensive against Communism would require—expensive foreign aid programs, heavy military spending, big government."[75]

Taft did not favor American commitments in Europe. As Michael Korda has observed, there was a division in conservative culture when it came to foreign policy: a division between "those who looked eastward toward Europe and viewed America as an 'Atlantic power' and those who looked westward to the Pacific."[76] There was a religious dimension in this, since the "loss" of China to communism blighted the hopes of evangelical Christians who for generations had sent missionaries to China and had not given up on Chiang Kai-shek.

Taft accepted Ike's invitation to meet him at the Pentagon—in secret.

Ike's agenda was straightforward: if Taft would support Ike's NATO mission, he would pledge to stay out of politics and let Taft have the Republican nomination.

Ike wrote out the following statement and showed it to Taft: "Having been called back to military duty, I want to announce that my name may not be used by anyone as a candidate for president—and if they do I will repudiate such efforts."[77]

Ike had drafted this statement with the help of two staff assistants, and they knew about his plan. Years later, he wrote that he intended to issue the statement "that evening, on the assumption that Taft would agree that collective security should be adopted as a definite feature of our foreign policy."

When Taft arrived "at one of the less obvious entrances to the Pentagon, a staff officer met him and whisked him to an elevator and into my office," Ike recalled. Ike put the proposition to Taft, and the conversation played out as follows:

> I used all the persuasion I could but Senator Taft refused to commit himself. He said several times, "I do not know whether I shall vote for four divisions or six divisions or two divisions." I assured him...that I had no interest in that detail at the moment. I only wanted to know whether he would support the concept of collective security for the North Atlantic community. Our conversation was friendly but I had no success.

After Taft departed, Ike tore up the statement that he and his assistants had drafted. He told them, "It would be silly for me to throw away whatever political influence I might possess to help keep us on the right track."[78]

Days later, Ike told Cyrus Sulzberger of the *New York Times* that he had found Taft "a very stupid man. He has no intellectual ability, nor any comprehension of the world."[79]

Ike left for Europe on January 6 and returned to the United States at the end of the month. Truman met him at the airport, and they drove to the White House for a briefing. Then Ike addressed a joint session of Congress and delivered a radio and television broadcast to the nation.

By accepting the NATO assignment and by issuing his ultimatum to Taft, Ike was finally reaching toward his destiny.

He was once again a player on the world stage, and he was breaking the power of the spell that had been holding him back.

But the transition would be slow.

On February 8, 1951, Ike met with the Columbia trustees and told them they should open up a search for a new president if they wished because he had no idea of how long his NATO assignment would last. At a farewell reception at the faculty club, he said that he would "always have a warm spot in my heart for Columbia," adding that he "hoped to return some day."[80]

He and Mamie left for Europe on February 15 aboard the *Queen Elizabeth*, and they arrived in Cherbourg a week later.

Assuming his duties as Allied supreme commander in Europe on April 1, Ike was driven to Marnes-la-Coquette, a village ten miles outside of Paris. It was here that the emperor Napoleon III had maintained a complex of four mansions, and he and Mamie set up housekeeping in one of them: Villa-Saint-Pierre.

The office facilities for NATO were located in the village of Rocquencourt. Ike was given a staff of 250, including some familiar faces: General Alfred Gruenther, Jimmy Gault, and none other than Bernard Law Montgomery (now Viscount Montgomery of Alamein). Ike and Monty discovered that they got along fine: the old enmity of 1945 had disappeared.

Ike travelled back and forth between the eleven NATO capitals seeking troop commitments. The Soviets had a huge preponderance of power in the form of available ground troops: over seventy-five divisions. The Allies had less than a handful. Ike knew that it was nuclear force that stood behind the power of NATO, but ground forces were necessary as a buffer against World War III.

Ike told Swede Hazlett that "each country must provide the heart and soul of its own defense.... In the long run, it is not possible—and most certainly not desirable—that Europe should be an occupied territory defended by legions brought in from abroad, somewhat in the fashion that Rome's territory vainly sought security many hundreds of years ago."[81]

French military force was being heavily diverted from Europe to oppose a communist insurrection in Indochina. Ike feared that if "Indochina falls to the Commies, it is easily possible that the entire Southeast Asia and Indonesia will go, soon to be followed by India." But he also believed that "no military victory is possible in that kind of theater."[82]

He listened to reports that "the position of the West, specifically Britain, is deteriorating rapidly in Iran.... Lord knows what we'd do without Iranian oil."[83]

And he kept a vigilant eye on American politics. He noted in his diary on March 13, 1951, that "Drew Pearson reports Senator McCarthy is digging up alleged dirt with which to smear me if I run for president."[84]

Decades ago, historian Blanche Wiesen Cook concluded that Ike had been "a presidential contender" since 1948. "If he did not admit it to himself, if he denied it to his closest associates, including his brother Milton and his childhood friend Swede Hazlett, he refused no public appearance, no fund-raising party, no opportunity to meet the affluent and the influential. The truth was that Eisenhower was surrounded by a political team of financiers and friends who conducted a masterful campaign."[85]

He listened to political advice throughout 1951, and even took a few steps to position himself in Republican politics. But he denied to himself that he was doing these things at the very moment when he did them. He filled his diary with sincere-sounding statements about his disdain for a political career.

The canniest of his political coaches understood this psychological process, so they fine-tuned the tactics they used to nudge Ike in a political direction.

The foremost among them was Lucius Clay, who by 1951 had surpassed Bill Robinson as the architect of Ike's coming victory. Clay's strategy was subtle. He began by feeding Ike *information* about political developments back home. Then he let the power of suggestion do most of the work, for he knew that this information was fraught with potential excitement. Slowly, "advice" would begin to insinuate itself into the information.

In this manner Clay was prompting Ike to think about politics without pushing him too hard. He used the power of suggestion—and he let Ike's mind do the rest, whether consciously or not.

Clay and Ike went all the way back to the Philippines together, and their work in the German occupation drew them closer. Clay was the son of a United States senator from Georgia, and he had known his way around Washington since the time his father introduced him to Theodore Roosevelt.

After Clay retired from the army, he entered the business world and became the CEO of Continental Can Company. He was at ease with the members of the "gang" who had been grooming Ike for the presidency.

In 1950, Clay took charge of the "Crusade for Freedom," an organization set up to help fund and support "Radio Free Europe." Clay recruited Ike to give a speech in Denver supporting the "Crusade" on Labor Day, 1950. They corresponded regularly.

In April 1951, Truman fired Douglas MacArthur.

A huge backlash erupted, and congressional hearings gave MacArthur a chance to sound off. He had called for nuclear attacks against Chinese cities. He had lobbied members of Congress in support of his position.

His charisma cast a spell upon hardened isolationists, and one by one they called for war—in the Pacific.

Taft and Hoover did a quick about-face: Hoover, who had called for an American Gibraltar, called MacArthur "the reincarnation of St. Paul." Taft, who had voted against NATO, called for bombing China and said that the United States must "use the same methods which communism has adopted or be swept away."[86]

In congressional testimony, MacArthur proclaimed that "Asia is where the Communist conspirators have elected to make their play for global conquest.... There is no substitute for victory."[87]

In 1951, negotiations began for a Korean cease-fire, but these discussions continued interminably. The war was devolving into a bloody stalemate.

On April 15, Clay phoned Ike in France to discuss the situation and followed up with a letter of advice: Ike should *avoid* saying anything about MacArthur because the Taft forces were trying to "maneuver you into taking a position on the MacArthur issue, thus aligning you with the President and indirectly with his party and its inept conduct of government."

In this manner, Clay began his pitch by advising Ike to *do nothing*.

But then he switched to a strategy of cautious encouragement: he wrote that "we cannot let the true isolationists gain control of government if we are to endure as a free people over the years. This may depend on you and, whether you like it or not, you must be prepared to meet that challenge."[88]

That was as far as Clay was willing to go—in April.

By June, Ike's mission for NATO was causing him to think even more expansively about the challenge of communism.

Swede Hazlett wrote to Ike deploring the election of a leftist government in Iran.[89] Ike replied that people he knew attached "as much blame to Western stupidity as to Iranian fanaticism and Communist intrigue." He added that the situation in Iran might stand "at the same place that China did only a very few years ago," adding that "now we have completely lost China—no matter how we explain it ... we FAILED."

But Ike made it clear that he could not support MacArthur's call for nuclear attacks on China: "Unless you can get at Mao and the small group of advisers he has around him, I do not believe we would be punishing the aggressor merely by bombing Canton, Shanghai, or any other place where we would certainly be killing a number of our friends."

"The average United States citizen is confused, if not fearful and afraid," he wrote in his diary.[90] Strong leadership was needed to put things right in America.

Against this background, he met with a delegation of congressmen on June 19, and he talked about the world situation. He did it in a way that made no direct references to Truman or MacArthur.

He worried about the prospect of coordinated and continuing communist aggression against democracy. There was a "relationship between the time that the Marshall Plan was really reaching fruition in Europe and the starting of the Korean War," he said. The attack in Korea was "a diversion" to weaken Europe by creating an emergency elsewhere. And the insurgency in Indochina was serving the same purpose.

Ike was using his position as NATO commander to speak about more than just the European challenge. He was speaking about the global situation.

He added another comment that was fraught with political significance: he called "the loss of China to the Communists the greatest diplomatic defeat in the nation's history."[91]

In Blanche Wiesen Cook's opinion, this provocative comment was "a carefully timed, well aimed announcement of his long obscured political presence."[92]

It is interesting that just a few months before he made this politically charged comment, he jotted these thoughts in his diary: "How tragic that, at this critical stage in world history, we should be torn apart by human selfishness.... There is much room for instructive discussion and argument, but we have not a minute to waste, nor any right to weaken ourselves, in the wicked business of attempting to satisfy personal ambition."

He continued as follows: "For my family and for America, the only real passions of my life, I shall continue to work."[93]

In June 1951, Stanley Rumbough and Charles Willis created the "Citizens for Eisenhower" group. They set up a national organization in which, as Rumbough explained it years later, "state-by-state coordinators" would "appoint county chairmen who would recruit city chairmen who would be given the task of establishing local clubs." And they developed "a handbook, a manual, to guide the efforts of all."

The *Citizens for Eisenhower Handbook* was modeled on the *General Foods Sales Manual*: "pure marketing and public relations." Instructions told organizers "how to hold a meeting, how to organize a petition drive (and to what purpose), how to arrange a public roundtable discussion, how to stage a rally or organize a parade, how to work with local media."

A starter kit of "We Like Ike" banners, campaign buttons, and photographs of Ike was offered to members.[94]

Meanwhile, Bill Robinson came over to Paris, and he urged Ike to make serious plans for a political career.

Thomas Dewey joined forces with Clay in September 1951. They met for dinner and talked about the way to get Ike off the fence and into politics.

Clay wrote to Ike on September 24 about the meeting. He began to use the term "Our Friend" in reference to Dewey, and Ike replied as follows: "You and I think so much alike on so many problems connected with public service...that I think it would do me good just to have a long talk with you one of these days.... My warm regards to Our Friend and to any others of our common friends that you may encounter."[95]

Ike was watching the polls.

On September 29, Clay told him that Truman "will not run if you run. He has made this statement to two separate and reliable persons." But Truman would run if the Republicans nominated Taft.[96]

A diary entry in October makes it clear that Ike was thinking about a presidential run, but only if a groundswell of public opinion—a draft— were to happen.

"The only way I could leave this duty [NATO]," he said, "is to believe that a great section of the United States want me to undertake a higher one. This could be a real draft, something that all agree cannot happen."[97] A day later, he marveled at the idea "that anyone would want to be president. Not me."[98]

He returned to Washington in November and had breakfast with Clay. Then he met with Truman, who renewed the offer he had made back in 1945, 1947, and 1948: he would bow out and retire if Ike would agree to accept the Democratic nomination.[99]

On November 10, Dewey and Clay got together and decided to set up a formal Eisenhower-for-president campaign. Other like-minded Republicans joined them: Herbert Brownell, who had run Dewey's previous campaigns; Senator Henry Cabot Lodge Jr. of Massachusetts; Harold Talbott of Chrysler, who had been Dewey's fundraiser; Russell Sprague, Republican National Committee member from New York; and Harry Darby, a participant in a Kansas-based "Eisenhower for President" group.

The group decided that Lodge should be the campaign chairman. Lodge recalled that "I was there because they needed a front man.... Herb Brownell was the planner and thinker. And it was Lucius who called the shots. In those early stages Clay was the key figure."[100]

On December 11, Ike wrote in his diary that he would write to Lodge "saying that he and his friends must stop the whole thing, now."[101] But then he lurched in the other direction.

On December 19, he asked Clay to tell "Our Friend" that "my own convictions align me fairly closely with what I call the progressive branch of the Republican party."[102]

In light of the conservative rhetoric that he had been using since 1948, this embrace of "progressive" Republicanism—in a message to be aimed at Dewey—was interesting.

On December 28, Ike received a handwritten letter from Truman. "As I told you in 1948 and at our luncheon in 1951," the president wrote, "do what you think is best for the country. If I do what I want to do, I'll go back to Missouri and *maybe* run for the Senate. If you decide to finish the European job (and I don't know who else can) I must keep the isolationists out of the White House. I wish you would let me know what you intend to do."[103]

Beating Taft

Nudged by Dewey and Clay, Ike took preliminary steps in December 1951 to make a run for the presidency.

Army regulations permitted officers on active duty to accept nominations for elective office, but only if they did nothing to seek the nominations. On December 27, Ike gave Clay indirect approval to act as his agent. "Only yesterday," he wrote, "I was asked to name the personality in the United States who was best acquainted with me and my methods.... Without hesitation I gave your name."[104]

On December 29, he told Lodge that "my confidence in General Clay is such, his accuracy in interpretation is so great, and his personal loyalty to me is so complete, that nothing he could ever say about me could be contrary to his belief as to what I would want him to say."[105]

The signal was obvious: Clay was empowered to act on Ike's behalf in matters that related to his presidential candidacy.

On January 4, 1952, Clay authorized Lodge to enter Ike's name in the New Hampshire primary as a *Republican*. Lodge notified New Hampshire's governor, Sherman Adams, and then he called a news conference.

It is a commentary on Ike's state of mind that he was furious when he heard about this—or he *claimed* to be furious.[106] Clay was tired of this never-ending game, and so he told Ike to stop fooling around and get serious if he wished to beat Taft. Ike reiterated the point that he had a military duty to fulfill.

On January 7, he issued an announcement confirming that Lodge gave "an accurate account of my political convictions," but cautioned that "under no circumstances will I ask for relief from this assignment in order to seek nomination for political office."[107]

A wealthy businessman named George Sloan asked Ike to explain his views about the proper role of government in times of economic emergency. Sloan was a director of United States Steel, and he was active in the Chamber of Commerce. Ike's answer to Sloan on January 3, 1952, was a defining moment in his ideological evolution.

"When people are out of work, bewildered, and see their families enduring privation," Ike wrote, "they instinctively turn to the greatest temporal force of which they know—the government—for relief. In doing so, it is easy enough to forget that all powers of government must always be carefully and intelligently limited or it is certain to become the master of the people who have set it up."

Then he got down to business.

"These things could be thought about in advance," Ike affirmed, "they could be studied and the intellectual climate so developed that, in time of emergency, *the individual would get all the help he needed* but without permanent damage to the essentials of representative government."[108]

Ike was moving toward the Middle Way.

When Lodge's appointment as campaign chairman was made public, the leaders of Citizens for Eisenhower asked for a meeting and the organizations were blended.

Consequently, "Citizens" played an important role in a major event of election year 1952: a gigantic rally for Eisenhower in Madison Square Garden.

The idea came from the husband-wife team of John "Tex" McCrary and Eugenia "Jinx" Falkenburg. He was a public relations man, and she was an actress and tennis star. They had a radio show called *Tex and Jinx*. They had sponsored events in the Garden, and the planning for the rally began in December 1951.

Investor and financier John Hay "Jock" Whitney raised the money and co-chaired the event. The other co-chair was Jacqueline Cochran, a famous aviatrix whose husband was a financier.

A galaxy of celebrities from show business were recruited to "serenade" Ike on February 9, 1952—at midnight.

Upwards of twenty thousand people jammed Madison Square Garden, while ten thousand listened outside. Loudspeakers filled the streets with music.

As the guests chanted, "We Like Ike," Ethel Merman sang "There's No Business like Show Business," and Mary Martin, via shortwave radio from London, sang "I'm in Love with a Wonderful Guy." Richard Rodgers, who had composed the song for *South Pacific*, accompanied her on the piano. Clark Gable introduced composer Irving Berlin, who sang a song about Ike that he had written for a Broadway musical.

The whole event was filmed, and Cochran flew straight to Paris to show the film to Ike and Mamie.

The result was one of the emotional turning points in Eisenhower's life. "As the film went on," he recalled, it "impressed me more than had all the arguments presented by the individuals who had been plaguing me... for many months."[109]

In his diary he wrote that "our times are tumultuous—people are returning to instinct, emotion, and sentiment. Responsibility is becoming again something real." It brought home the "mass longing in America for some kind of reasonable solution for her nagging, persistent, and almost terrifying problems. It's a real experience to realize that one could become a symbol for many thousands of the hope they have."[110]

Millions of Americans *wanted* to believe that Ike would bring them good times. They simply... *liked* him.

And he symbolized *strength*.

As Lucius Clay affirmed, "the American people took him for what they wanted Americans to be; I don't think they really cared much about what he stood for."[111]

All the more reason to protect his reputation, as the operatives of Taft began looking for "dirt" about Ike and Kay. On January 30, Walter Winchell reported that they were actually approaching Kay directly. Harry Butcher warned Ike that some of Taft's people might try to put a wiretap on Kay's telephone.[112] When Citizens for Eisenhower opened up a New York office, Kay strolled in to volunteer. Stanley Rumbough told her that "the most helpful activity you could undertake would be to stay out of sight."[113]

After Ike finished watching the film, he told Jackie Cochran to tell Clay to "come over for a talk. And tell Bill Robinson that I am going to run."[114]

Ike and Clay met in England at Jimmy Gault's estate (Ike was attending the funeral of King George VI). Ike said he would run, and Clay urged him to declare his candidacy quickly. Ike would have to resign from the army to do that, and they agreed that he would do so by June 1 at the latest. Taft had a tremendous lead in delegates, and it was entirely possible that Ike would lose the nomination to Taft.

On March 11, Ike swept the field in the New Hampshire primary. Citizens for Eisenhower held well-funded rallies with performances by popular entertainers.

A week later, Ike won an impressive number of votes in Minnesota without even being on the ballot. Citizens for Eisenhower had organized a write-in campaign.

Truman wanted to retire, and his popularity was plummeting. He was beaten in New Hampshire by Senator Estes Kefauver of Tennessee. Embittered, Truman decided he would not stand for reelection. His displeasure with Kefauver prompted him to push the party bosses to find someone else to run in 1952.

On March 30, Dewey sent Ike a warning: if the race with Taft became close, Republicans might turn to MacArthur. On April 1, Taft won the Illinois, Wisconsin, and Nebraska primaries. He was far ahead in delegates.

On the following day, Ike wrote to Truman asking to be relieved of duty as NATO's supreme commander on June 1. Brownell flew to Paris to keep Ike briefed about plans for the convention floor fight.[115]

Ike began consulting on foreign policy issues with John Foster Dulles, whom he knew from the Carnegie Endowment. Dulles had been Dewey's foreign policy adviser, and his views gave Ike an alternative to Truman's containment policy that would prove to be extremely useful in the months ahead.

On June 1, 1952, Ike resigned from the army and called upon the president to pay his respects. He told Truman that the dirty tactics that were being used against him by Taft's supporters were appalling.[116]

That summer, John Eisenhower volunteered for combat duty in Korea. He vowed that the enemy would never capture him alive. John was by then the father of three children: David, born in 1948, Anne, born in 1949, and Susan, born in 1951.

On June 4, Ike kicked off his campaign in Abilene. The rally was timed to coincide with the laying of the cornerstone for the Eisenhower Museum.

Everything went wrong. As viewers watched on television, Ike addressed a crowd in a howling rainstorm. He was bundled in a raincoat and rainhat, and as he read aloud from a prepared speech, he lost his place.

The speech, which was written by Kevin McCann—a Pentagon aide who accompanied Ike to Columbia—was mediocre.

Dewey, Clay, and Brownell brought Ike to New York for a postmortem. They all agreed that he should no longer read aloud from prepared speeches.

Ike began meeting with state delegations and with special-interest groups. Citizens for Eisenhower sent him briefing books with information about individual delegates, so that he could establish rapport.

Ike made Denver his campaign headquarters. One hundred thousand people greeted him when he arrived, and June 26 was designated "Eisenhower Day." He met with throngs of delegates and representatives of many different groups. Then he left for ten days of speechmaking on the way to Chicago—and the Republican convention.

In the preconvention jousting, Taft supporters engaged in rhetorical charges like these: "REDS, NEW DEALERS USE IKE IN PLOT TO HOLD POWER" and "IKE CODDLED COMMUNISTS WHILE PRESIDENT OF COLUMBIA UNIVERSITY."[117]

Taft had 530 delegates going into the Republican convention, and Ike had between 400 and 500. He needed 604 to win.

Citizens for Eisenhower used tricks to help their candidate catch up. Taft men controlled the admission to the convention floor, but "Citizens" found a friendly security man who let the Ike supporters in. They yelled themselves hoarse with the "We Like Ike" battle cry, and they paraded with banners.

Thousands of Ike supporters came from all over the country to Chicago. Ten thousand of them met Ike when he stepped off the train. "Citizens" organized street-corner rallies and sent well-organized teams to greet delegates as they arrived. Eisenhower clubs around the country sent thousands of telegrams to their state delegations.

An industrialist named Langhorne Washburne purchased war-surplus helium barrage balloons—they looked like small dirigibles—painted "Ike" on every one of them, and then floated them around the city from support trucks. At night he used antiaircraft searchlights to illuminate them.

Lodge made overtures to Richard Nixon, now a California senator: he might be considered for the vice presidential slot if he proved himself helpful at the convention.[118]

When the convention opened on July 6, Ike's managers organized a challenge to great numbers of Taft delegates from states without primaries. A party rule adopted in 1912 allowed contested delegates to vote on the issue of seating other contested delegates. Ike supporters had challenged the credentials of Taft delegates from Louisiana, Georgia, and Texas.

Herbert Brownell, who was Ike's convention strategist, forced a fight by introducing a new "Fair Play Amendment" that would bar contested delegates from voting on the question of seating other contested delegates. Ike supporters carried banners emblazoned with the slogan "Thou Shalt Not Steal"—the very same slogan that supporters of Theodore Roosevelt had used back in 1912 when they challenged *William Howard* Taft. Governor Sherman Adams of New Hampshire was Ike's floor manager. He took his orders from Brownell.

One of Ike's public relations consultants arranged for television coverage of the floor fight. After a very bitter struggle, the Fair Play Amendment was adopted.

The convention opened with a labored keynote oration by Douglas MacArthur followed by a rant from Joe McCarthy. Ike watched the proceedings on television in the company of Clay, Brownell, and his brother Milton. When the balloting began, Brownell's intention was to use a modest strategy: contain Taft's success on the first ballot, then push delegates to switch to Ike on the second ballot.

But Dewey was so successful at holding the New York delegation together for Ike—"wait until you see my steamroller operate," he bragged—and Nixon's work with the California delegation was so effective that Brownell told Sherman Adams to abandon caution and push for a first-ballot victory.[119]

It worked.

Ike decided to reach out to Taft immediately: in an unprecedented action, he called Taft and asked if he could come over—their hotels were right across the street from each other—and pay a courtesy call.

Taft was taken completely by surprise, and Ike's graciousness elicited graciousness in return. After they talked, Taft told reporters he wanted to "congratulate General Eisenhower. I shall do everything possible in the campaign to secure his election and to help in his administration."[120]

Three weeks later, the Democrats nominated Illinois Governor Adlai Stevenson for the presidency.

Beating Stevenson

As Ike celebrated with Clay and Brownell after their victory, they discussed the selection of Ike's running mate. According to Brownell, Ike recommended businessmen whose executive abilities he respected.

Brownell and Clay exchanged bemused glances. Then they explained the basics of creating an electoral ticket. Brownell told Ike that they needed "a name that would be recognizable to the average delegate on the floor." They needed a younger man, a man from the West, a man with political experience.[121] They recommended Richard Nixon.

He had performed good service with the California delegation at the convention. His reputation would go a long way toward reconciling diehard Taft supporters to Ike's nomination. Lodge had already made the overture. "We needed a counter to Taft in California," Lodge recalled, "and Nixon was it. I approached him on the Senate floor, well before the Convention, and asked him if he would be interested in the vice presidency. 'Who wouldn't?' he said. Not very elegant, but that's what he said."[122]

Lodge reported this to Clay, who reported it to Dewey, who invited Nixon to speak at a fundraising dinner in New York. Then Dewey, Clay, Brownell, and Nixon sealed the deal. It was only a matter of selling the deal to Ike.

When Brownell suggested Nixon to Ike, the new Republican presidential candidate told Clay and Brownell that he "would be guided by our advice."[123]

It was as simple as that: the fateful association of Dwight Eisenhower and Richard Nixon began just as simply as that.

In August, after the convention, Dewey, Clay, and Brownell dropped out of the picture due to other obligations.

Ike took a brief vacation in Colorado at the ranch of Aksel Nielsen, a friend of the Douds. He selected a new team for the fall campaign: Sherman Adams would become his chief of staff; Arthur Summerfield, the new chairman of the Republican National Committee, would be his campaign manager; James Hagerty, Dewey's press secretary, agreed to perform the same service for Ike; Emmet John Hughes, a senior editor at *Life*, became Ike's principal speechwriter; and Robert Cutler, a Boston banker, became Sherman Adams's deputy.

Ike began to listen closely to the advice of John Foster Dulles, who drafted the Republican platform plank on foreign policy. Dulles had called for the repudiation of "all commitments contained in secret understandings such as those of Yalta which aid Communist enslavement." Republicans, he said, looked "happily forward to the genuine independence" of "captive peoples" in Eastern Europe, whom Democrats had "abandoned."[124]

On August 13, Ike held a joint press conference with Congressman Charles Kersten, a proponent of "liberating" Eastern Europe. Ike endorsed the proposition, with the stipulation that it would not lead to war. There was no explanation as to how Eastern Europe could be liberated from Soviet domination without war.

Adlai Stevenson never stood a chance against Ike in 1952; the national mood was swinging in a pendulum, and the Korean War alone would have led to an Eisenhower landslide. Ike could have done it by just being *Ike*— the boy next door who became a world hero.

Or so it can be argued. We will never know because he chose a very different path and behaved in a very different manner. He behaved like the kid from the wrong side of the railroad tracks: the pugilist who swings the first punch.

It would have been easy for Ike to act like a unifier in 1952 because he had the friendly image and the sunny smile to pull it off. Besides, all the circumstances were on his side: the Democrats were weak, the independents were up for grabs, and the Taftites would have to snap out of their funk and climb aboard.

But what if they refused to climb aboard?

In Jean Edward Smith's opinion, "the Democrats were less of a worry to Eisenhower in September 1952 than the cohesion of his own party."[125] If the Taftites decided to sit out the election, could Stevenson win?

Smith believed this concern was the primary reason why Ike behaved the way he did: instead of acting as a unifier, he conducted a divisive, partisan, and no-holds-barred campaign to pulverize the Democrats.

That is not the way that Ike's many admirers wish to remember him. But that was how it was in September 1952.

Perhaps he was pulling off a power demonstration as well—proving toughness to the seasoned politicians. He was new to the ways of civilian politics, and he had to show the regulars that he was not to be trifled with.

And so his military instincts took over: he fought to dominate and never ease up. After *victory* would come the peace. Politicians must be able to threaten sometimes, and to do it they must show how mean they can be in a fight.

Ike had certainly made that demonstration by October 1952, and some examples of this will be provided.

But perhaps there was another reason for his manifest aggressiveness, a reason that was more fundamental—more primitive.

He had broken the spell—the spell that had been holding him back for the better part of half a decade. He had overcome the ambivalence—he had freed himself from the tendency to live on the run because he didn't know his own mind.

Now he *did*.

So one senses something else in his behavior that fall: catharsis. After all the fluctuations he made the decision, and the years of frustration were *over*.

And the pent-up anger was *released*. His displays of aggression were a way to show something to himself.

He had taken command of his future.

He was master.

It was not a pretty spectacle, nor was it meant to be.

It meant further polarizing the ideological climate, and it meant picking fights with Harry Truman. Ike made himself do it.

We can only guess about the feelings that were swirling in his mind. He may have told himself that collateral damage would be justified later by the good that he intended to do—once he had the *power*.

He had the potential to be a brilliant centrist.

But it would require *power*—the power of the presidency—to unleash the full dimensions of his gifts. Only power would make him the guardian of peace and the bringer of an age of serenity. Only power would bring... the Middle Way.

A fight with Truman broke out in August. Truman had invited Stevenson to the White House for a foreign policy briefing. Ike was invited as well, and the invitation was supposed to be extended via Omar Bradley, who was serving as chairman of the Joint Chiefs of Staff. But there was a slipup. Bradley was distracted and the invitation was neglected.

Ike pounced.

He accused Truman of playing politics with national security. Truman explained the situation, apologized, and invited Ike to come for a briefing.

Ike refused.

He proclaimed himself the "standard bearer of... Americans who want to bring a change in the national government," and he said that Americans were called upon to choose between "the Republican nominee and the candidate you and your cabinet are supporting and with whom you conferred before sending your message."[126]

Between the lines of this pompous proclamation was a clear accusation that Truman had slighted him deliberately.

Ike was picking a fight. His competitive instinct to *win* was the dominant instinct.

But Truman had always treated him with kindness, respect, even deference—he had asked him to be his own successor and viewed him with something close to awe. "Poor HST," Ike had written, "a fine man who, in the middle of a stormy lake, knows nothing of swimming."

Truman was a fighter, and he rolled with this particular punch: he said he was sorry that Ike "allowed a bunch of screwballs to come between us."[127]

But this was the beginning of the icy new feelings that would ruin their relationship.

Ike needed to establish himself as the Republican Party's leader. If he won in November, he would have to maintain enough party cohesion to prevail. And he would have to figure out how to roll back the influence of McCarthy and McCarthyism.

In August he held his first postconvention press conference in Denver. By prearrangement with Jim Hagerty, reporter Murray Kempton asked Ike what he thought about the people who had called George Marshall a "living lie."

By prearrangement, Ike got livid, and he shouted with indignation, "How dare anyone say such a thing about Marshall, who was a perfect example of patriotism?"[128]

Ike kicked off his campaign on September 2 in Atlanta, and he proceeded in a swing through the South. This was bold strategy for a Republican, since the Democrats had kept their control of the "Solid South" for generations.

Then he went to Indianapolis to give a speech in the Butler University fieldhouse on September 9. He would be on the same stage with William Jenner, who had called George Marshall a "living lie." Ike wanted to avoid this event, and he asked Lucius Clay for advice. Clay told him that, distasteful as it was, he needed to go through with it.

So Ike appeared with Jenner, whom he never mentioned by name. He urged Indiana voters to support the whole Republican ticket. He gave them some low-brow partisan invective, saying he was sick of America being "the prey of fear-mongers, quacks, and bare-faced looters."[129]

He called his campaign a "crusade" against the "mess in Washington," and he promised to root out corruption. Jenner grabbed his arm and held it high after every partisan sally.

After the event Ike told Emmet Hughes that "I felt dirty at the touch of the man."[130]

On the twelfth, Ike went to New York to meet with Taft. They met over breakfast, and Taft presented Ike with a document outlining his policy preferences. They agreed to disagree about foreign policy, but the meeting was friendly.

When reporters were ushered in, one of them asked Ike what he thought about McCarthy. Ike looked at Taft, shook his head, and left. He let Taft be the one to do the talking.

On September 18, the Eisenhower campaign was confronted by a crisis of great magnitude. "SECRET NIXON FUND," blared the headline of the *New York Post*: "SECRET RICH MAN'S TRUST FUND KEEPS NIXON IN STYLE FAR BEYOND HIS SALARY."[131]

Nixon supporters had raised a fund of $16,000 to help him pay for office expenses, and this was not illegal. There had been no bribery: no favors had been sought or paid for.

But it sounded bad.

When Nixon was accosted by reporters, he dodged their questions and dismissed the story as a communist smear. Before long, the Nixon story was dominating the news, and Ike had to do something about it.

He told Sherman Adams to investigate, and Adams commissioned an accounting firm to audit the fund. He had a Los Angeles law firm review the legal implications. Meanwhile, Ike sent a message to Nixon telling him that he needed to make everything public. Ike said that the two of them had to confer as soon as possible.[132]

He began to distance himself from Nixon: he told reporters it was up to Nixon to prove that his ethics were above reproach.

Ike's advisers wished to make short work of the matter and get Nixon off the ticket. Dewey, Clay, and Brownell went into a huddle. They decided that Nixon should go on national television, explain himself, and then offer to step down. Clay got in touch with Ike in Jefferson City, Missouri, and told him that Brownell was on his way to explain the strategy.[133]

Ike and Brownell had a long conversation, and Ike approved. But he made it clear that Nixon's speech should conclude with a resignation offer. Brownell told Summerfield to get $75,000 from the Republican National Committee to pay for the speech.[134]

Then Ike placed a telephone call to Nixon, who was campaigning in Portland, Oregon.

The conversation was cool, and Ike told Nixon that he had to make a television speech that was effective. He also said that no decision had been made regarding Nixon's status on the ticket.[135]

Three hours before Nixon's speech, Ike told Dewey through an intermediary that Nixon should resign. Dewey telephoned Nixon, and they spoke just an hour before the speech. Nixon was resentful and defiant.[136]

On the evening of September 23, Nixon made his speech to an audience of over sixty million. Ike watched in the manager's office of the Cleveland Public Auditorium. Down below, fifteen thousand people were waiting for an Eisenhower rally.

As they waited for Ike to address them, they were given a chance to watch Nixon's speech on a large screen.

The speech that would go down in history as Nixon's "Checkers speech" was a lengthy self-justification. Nixon said that he had done nothing wrong. He talked about his struggle to rise from humble origins, about the obstacles that he and his family had overcome, about how hard it was to make ends meet. "Pat doesn't have a mink coat," he said, "but she does have a respectable Republican cloth coat. And I always tell her that she looks good in anything."

Then he talked about a cocker spaniel that a well-wisher had given to his family. "Our little girl," he related—"Tricia, the six-year-old—named it Checkers. And you know the kids love the dog and I just want to say right now, that regardless of what they say about it, we're going to keep it."

Then he went on the offensive. He called for all the other candidates—Stevenson, his running mate John Sparkman, and even Ike—to make their finances public.

And instead of offering to step down, Nixon put the decision about his status on the ticket in the hands of the Republican National Committee—not Ike.

He told viewers to "wire or write the Republican National Committee whether you think I should stay or whether I should get off. And whatever their decision is, I will abide by it."[137]

Ike was enraged. He would not let Nixon get away with this, and the way to strike back at him was obvious. But he had to make allowance for the possibility that Nixon's speech would prove effective.

And it was.

Though sophisticates smirked, Nixon managed to elicit the sympathy of millions. In the Cleveland auditorium, the crowd chanted, "We want Nixon!" Clay recalled that he "thought the speech was so corny that it would be an immediate flop. I went downstairs to get a newspaper. I found the elevator man crying and the doorman was crying, and I knew then that I was wrong."[138]

Ike went to the auditorium and spoke to the crowd.

He positioned himself carefully. "I have seen many brave men in tough situations," he said, "but I have never seen anyone come through in better fashion than Senator Nixon did tonight." Then he turned the tables on Nixon and put himself back in command.

He made it clear that he alone would decide whether Nixon remained on the ticket. And he would make Nixon crawl: Nixon would be forced break off his own campaign and make a pilgrimage to Ike.

He read the audience a telegram that he was about to send off to Nixon, a telegram in which he made it clear that (1) he alone would decide whether Nixon stayed on the ticket, and (2) Nixon would have to fly to Wheeling, West Virginia, immediately. And Ike would be waiting for him.

Ike would show Richard Nixon who was boss.

"Your presentation was magnificent," Ike wired Nixon, but "in view of your comprehensive presentation, my personal decision is going to be based on a personal conclusion.... I would be most appreciative if you could fly to see me at once. Tomorrow evening I shall be in Wheeling, West Virginia."[139]

Nixon had no choice: Ike had revealed his command to the public. He had showed this upstart who was boss.

Meanwhile, Ike would find out how well the Checkers speech had gone over. He discovered it had gone over well.

In Wheeling, he met Nixon at the plane and proclaimed, "You're my boy."

But from that point on, Ike and Nixon would be on very formal terms—they would never be close—though Ike did try to make limited use of Nixon as a political operative. The distant relations between them would last right down to Ike's death.

On October 3, Ike gave a speech in Wisconsin—McCarthy's state.

He decided to defend George Marshall and to do it "right in McCarthy's backyard."[140] He wrote a defense of Marshall and sent advance copies of his speech to the press. Everyone knew what Ike planned to say.

But McCarthy jumped aboard the campaign train, and Ike listened to advice from Sherman Adams, who urged him to delete the statement praising Marshall. Wisconsin's Republican governor had pushed for the deletion for the sake of party harmony. Ike went along.

And he regretted this decision for the rest of his life.

He may also have regretted the shrillness of the speech that he gave in Milwaukee. He condemned the "surrender of whole nations" in Eastern Europe to communism, condemned the way that communism "insinuated itself into our schools, our public forums, some of our news channels, and—most terrifyingly—into our Government itself," and he called communism in government "treason itself."[141]

McCarthy reached over and shook his hand.

Edward Mead Earle—a scholar of international relations and an Ike supporter—complained to Ike about the "mental pain" that such speeches were creating. Ike defended himself in his reply. He cited the case of Alger Hiss, and he avowed that "I sincerely believe that some years ago, subversion and communism had succeeded in penetrating dangerously into important regions of our government and our economic life."

In the opinion of Stephen Ambrose, Earle's letter had probably "touched a sore nerve, perhaps even some guilt."[142]

Because Ike sounded like McCarthy.

Ike had written in his very own diary that "four years more of Democratic, uninterrupted government in our country will put us so far down the road to socialism that there will be no return to free enterprise." And that was close to saying that four more years of Democratic policies would institute communism—or something like it.

Ike would have to atone for this oversimplification in the things he had been telling himself. He would have to make amends because of something else that he wrote in his diary: "*the true course, usually, is a middle one, between extremes.*"

He would have to find his way to a defensible position in light of that principle.

As Blanche Wiesen Cook pointed out many years ago, Ike's statements on these matters were "entirely contradictory."[143]

In August, Ike had gone public with his Middle Way motto. Against those who demanded "an all-powerful government" and those who tended to "deny the obligation of government to intervene on behalf of the people even when the complexities of modern life demand it," Ike said, Americans were obliged to "proceed along the middle way."[144]

Ike had decided to become a politician and politicians say demagogic things. Ike's political decisions in the autumn of 1952 were strategic. But they were also highly emotional. Collateral damage may be frequently justified in war. Did Ike feel any guilt?

Perhaps. But the secret knowledge of the new dispensation he would bring to America sustained him. He had a crystal-clear vision of the wholesome and rational governance his leadership would bring.

But the campaign would turn even uglier.

Truman, incensed by the way that Ike pandered to McCarthy, said that such "moral blindness brands the Republican candidate as unfit to be president." Ike swore that he would "never ride down Pennsylvania Avenue" with Truman.[145]

And then the director of the FBI—J. Edgar Hoover—leaked rumors that Adlai Stevenson was gay. Hoover had for years been abusing his power as FBI director.

He kept files on the sex lives of all sorts of people, ostensibly for the purpose of determining whether they were "security risks." But his darker purpose was the fine art of blackmail—and sabotage.

McCarthy made it known that he would attack the Stevenson campaign for being populated by "pinks, punks, and pansies." Word about McCarthy's intentions found its way to the Truman White House.[146]

And then, according to Jean Edward Smith, "White House aides let it be known that if McCarthy attacked Stevenson on the basis of sexual orientation, they would leak General Marshall's 1945 letter to Eisenhower."[147]

McCarthy backed down and there were no repercussions for Ike. But Ike apparently found out. He found out about this threat to himself.

He could have been ruined.

And Smith was convinced that the hostility between Ike and Truman during the presidential transition was linked to this affair.

The ugliness of the campaign would fade away.

Ike was headed toward the landslide victory that many foresaw and that events would deliver on schedule. Millions were determined to put their favorite war hero in the White House. They wanted him.

Eisenhower Presidential Library

Ike in the Inauguration Day parade, waving to the crowds in Washington.

They were confident that he would end the Korean War on decent terms and bring the boys home.

On October 24, in a televised speech from Detroit, Ike proclaimed that his responsibility as president-elect would necessitate a trip to Korea: "I shall make that trip. Only in that way could I learn how best to serve the American people in the cause of peace. I shall go to Korea."[148]

Ike made this pledge in the most dramatic way possible—on television.

His entire campaign had made effective use of television. His advertising men created thirty-second ads that filled the airwaves. Well before that, his name had become a "brand"—"IKE" was the name on the illuminated barrage balloons that made people look skyward in Chicago. "IKE" was the name that people chanted as he waved to them in 1945. "IKE" was the name on people's lips when the troops stormed ashore on D-Day.

The consummation of the Eisenhower boom had arrived, and he would no longer hide from his fortune.

He was master.

CHAPTER SEVEN

Self-Command

"Know Thyself"
"Nothing in Excess"

—Inscriptions on the Temple of Apollo at Delphi

After he left the presidency, Ike consented to a series of televised interviews with Walter Cronkite.

When asked to name the most important thing he did in his White House years—the very best thing—he said it was giving the American people a sense of "serenity," and to do it he started with himself.

He developed a routine that was a regular feature of life at the White House for him and for everybody else.

His presidential aides, he explained, understood they might be called at any time into the Oval Office. Everyone knew what to expect: They would listen in silence as he cursed a blue streak, and they would leave when the tantrum was over. He would always thank them later.

Only by venting his anger to a listener could he restore within himself the equilibrium he knew he had to have. This was a very different method from *suppressing* his anger, which his mother had taught him to do.

As he explained these things, a dazzling smile spread over his face.

It took a transformation in Ike to create this mastery, and the presidency was what caused it. It gave him the motivation that he needed to confront his emotions and learn the fine art of *understanding* them.

He had to pass through a long dark night of the soul after World War II to emerge into the light. Catharsis—purgation of the poison that was blighting his world-historical potential—did not come easily. It appears from the evidence that his problems had reached such a crisis by 1948 that he found himself miserable most of the time. He was a bitter man—so bitter he was fit to be tied. If you read his diary, you will feel the rage.

He was not at his best in the years that followed World War II. He could not put his mind to best use. The anger and frustration that consumed him were far too powerful, and his thought process suffered.

The feelings he committed to his diary and letters were often simplistic. Petulant, angry at the world, he was in no condition yet to assume the presidency, and this would remain the case through 1952. Only the actions of others—Bill Robinson, Thomas Dewey, Lucius Clay—and the *wish* of all the millions who were looking for a hero worked the magic.

But—with the power at last in his possession, he wrought the great change within himself that he needed. He achieved the emotional command that would make his Middle Way possible. The tension within him would always remain a problem—its sources were too fundamental and too deep to eradicate—and the tantrums would remain a necessity. His moods in the first year of his presidency continued to be volatile. But by 1954, his self-transformation was sufficient. His mind was working right side up after years of angry confusion.

As for happiness—who can say?

Kay Summersby married someone else.

Her marriage was destined to fail, but she developed the outlook that gave her such grace at the end. In *Past Forgetting*, she shared the knowledge that sustained her: she *succeeded in finding the love of her life and she had not missed out* on that experience. *That* was her triumph—and she found the wisdom to know it.

Perhaps Ike found his way to the very same wisdom when he visited his hometown in 1953 and saw the woman run out to the motorcade—the woman who was so eager to throw her arms around him. Perhaps in the eyes of Gladys Harding he could see what he needed to see to put his own life achievement in perspective.

He had *not missed out*: through the miracle of Kay, he found his way to complete adoration. Nothing could take that away from him.

Poor Gladys missed out, but Ike and Kay would always have the memory of what they attained. Kay knew this.

And we can hope that Ike knew it too.

He loved to listen to a song by Rodgers and Hammerstein in the years before he died: "Climb Every Mountain."[1]

He had not missed out on the fullest experience of love, and he would not miss out on the presidency. He did it all.

But was he happy?

The anger within him never seemed to abate, no matter what that dazzling smile of his might imply.

Transition

The combative moods of the 1952 campaign would linger.

Mastery would come gradually for Ike, and the wisdom he attained would be cumulative. There would be missteps—bad actions for which historians would criticize him later, especially some CIA operations that he approved. Some of his errors were clear to him in hindsight, but others, alas, never were.

When Ike met with Truman and his staff for a briefing on November 18, toxicity filled the room. Dean Acheson remembered that Ike's "good nature and easy manner tending toward loquacity were gone. He seemed embarrassed and reluctant to be with us. Sunk back in a chair facing the President...he chewed the earpiece of his spectacles."[2] He did not seem to be paying attention.

But he did pay attention to Lucius Clay and Herbert Brownell when they discussed cabinet appointments. Brownell had come calling on election day, and Ike offered to make him chief of staff. But Brownell was a Lincoln Republican, and he had a special agenda: Black civil rights. He said he wished to work as a lawyer.

Ike offered to make him attorney general, and Brownell agreed at once.[3] They would do extremely important work together on the civil rights front.

Ike had been thinking of asking California governor Earl Warren—Dewey's 1948 running mate—to be attorney general, but Brownell suggested a different destination for Warren: the Supreme Court. Ike

Library of Congress

Herbert Brownell,
Ike's attorney general.

phoned Warren and told him that he could have the first Supreme Court vacancy if he wanted it.

The process of making cabinet selections would continue for several weeks. Ike delegated the preliminaries to Clay and Brownell, and the first position they considered when they met on the day after the election was secretary of state. They made the problematical selection of John Foster Dulles.

Clay had favored John J. McCloy. A partner in a New York law firm, he was an internationalist Republican who came to Washington in 1940 with Henry Stimson. He was easy to get along with. Ike favored him—until Brownell weighed in.

Brownell pointed out that Dulles served as Dewey's foreign policy adviser and his credentials in fighting isolationism were considerable. Ike knew Dulles from his work with the Carnegie Endowment, and he had also used Dulles as a foreign policy adviser—during the 1952 campaign.

Dulles's grandfather John W. Foster and his uncle Robert Lansing had both served as secretary of state, and Dulles himself had diplomatic experience.

Truman used him as a delegate to the U.N. General Assembly and as a negotiator in creating the postwar security treaty with Japan. Like McCloy, he was a partner in a big New York law firm.

These were valid credentials, but Dulles could also be a troublemaker.

He hated communism—like Ike—but he had no great urge to keep the peace. He was bellicose. His religious convictions came close to being fundamentalist, and he was always preaching to people. He conveyed false certitude—he had no sense of the ironic—and this made sophisticates loathe him.

The British found him insufferable. "Dull, duller, Dulles" was the joke that made the rounds among the British diplomatic corps, and Churchill deliberately mispronounced his name to annoy him, calling him "Dullith."

Ike was one of the few people who actually came to like "Foster," as he called him, and the reasons can only be inferred.

Like Nixon, Dulles was obviously useful as a symbol to placate the Republican right—without appeasing isolationists. His call to "roll back" Soviet power came in handy when Ike was running for the presidency: it made Truman's containment look defeatist.

During Ike's presidency, Foster Dulles would come to symbolize toughness—the hard line. This could lead to orchestrations when Ike decided to distance himself, and he often used Dulles as a front man—or a fall-guy.

The urge to roll back communist power could of course lead to World War III, and a man like Ike—especially with his deep dedication to peace—was aware of this. Dulles could be dangerous if left to himself.

And yet—in a profound sort of way—his posturing on strategic issues helped to stimulate Ike's thinking on the gravest conundrum that he faced: the nuclear peril. Ike's "New Look" for defense would be grounded in "deterrence." The idea was painfully simple: the Soviets would hesitate before attacking the United States because mutual annihilation would result when America retaliated.

Ike's nuclear policy was one of the most profound legacies of his presidency—a legacy that has haunted Americans, whether conservative (like Ronald Reagan) or liberal. It was of course impossible to put the nuclear "genie back in the bottle," so humanity would have to live with this hideous new reality.

Ike took the aggressiveness of Dulles and turned it against itself for its deterrent effect: He kept the Soviets wondering. Would America *really* resort to the use of nuclear weapons?

The very horror of the threat would help to ensure the safety of humanity—unless a madman came to power.

The "New Look" in defense was a term that would be used by Admiral Arthur Radford (the term was borrowed from a name of the first design collection from the newly founded House of Dior). It was highly unpopular among the Joint Chiefs of Staff, and Foster Dulles became one of Ike's most important allies in advancing it. Cutbacks in conventional war-fighting capability in exchange for nuclear deterrence was the issue that united them. Dulles became Ike's spokesman for the policy.

By 1954, Dulles put the matter this way: instead of being ready to fight anywhere, the new strategy was to "depend primarily upon a capacity to retaliate instantly, by means and at places of our choosing."[4]

The press quickly dubbed this formulation "massive retaliation."

Ike's close relationship with Dulles went beyond this important alliance on policy; it encompassed a very strange personal dynamic that drew out the qualities in Dulles that others found aggravating.

Ike enjoyed using Dulles as a foil.

They would spar in top-secret planning sessions, and Ike always found ways to talk him down. Abrasive and domineering as Dulles could be, he would usually behave himself at the command of…the *master*. And so a master-apprentice relationship developed that took on a life of its own.

Consider the following interaction in 1953. Dulles sent Ike a draft for a U.N. speech attacking the Soviets. Ike told him to tone it down. "I have no quarrel with indicting and condemning them," Ike wrote, but he told Dulles to "be positive and clear, without giving the impression we are merely concerned with showing that we have been very nice people, while the others have been very wicked indeed."[5]

Dulles's reply: "I see on rereading that my language can be much improved and I shall do this along the lines of your suggestion, which certainly has validity."[6]

Ike was teaching Dulles to detach himself from his irate feelings and learn some self-discipline. But wasn't this *the very same thing that Ike was doing for himself* as he sought to find the equilibrium he needed?

Perhaps working on Dulles made it easier to work on himself, and maybe *that* was the reason Ike became so fond of him. He was more than just a foil: he was something of an alter ego.

But the roles could also be reversed: Ike sometimes allowed Foster Dulles to chide him for being "soft."

Stephen Ambrose marveled at the way that Ike overpraised Dulles. Ike credited him with "a wisdom and experience and knowledge that I think is possessed by no other man in the world." This was obvious nonsense: as Ambrose put it, "too much an exaggeration, and said too often, to be believable."[7]

Dulles knew that he could aggravate Ike, and he became almost touchingly eager to make up for it. He could be a useful work horse, and in the early days he was especially useful as a counterpoise to Joe McCarthy.

But the fact remains that he did some very bad things that will be covered at length in due course.

There was something else problematical about Dulles: his brother, Allen Dulles. As "Foster" developed his career niche in diplomacy, Allen ensconced himself in the espionage establishment. He served in the OSS during World War II, and his rise within the newly created CIA was meteoric. The agency got off to a shaky start, and its failure to predict the attack of the North Koreans in 1950 and the subsequent intervention by the Chinese was seen by many as tantamount to another Pearl Harbor.

Truman brought in "Beetle" Smith to sort out the agency after its early miscues, and Allen Dulles headed up an internal study group. So he appeared to have the right credentials for the job when Ike made him CIA director.

But the tenure of Allen Dulles at the CIA would be as bad in some ways as the tenure of J. Edgar Hoover at the FBI because, like Hoover, his arrogance led to abuses of power, the full dimensions of which would only come to light decades later. Consider, for instance, the "MK-ULTRA" program, which Dulles approved right away—in 1953. Its purpose was to test the effects of hallucinogenic drugs like LSD for the interrogation of enemy agents. But CIA operatives gave the drug to some innocent people in hospitals without their knowledge or consent. Some of these people took their own lives because they believed that they were going mad.

Allen Dulles would prove to be a dangerous man, and in light of the primacy that Ike would give to CIA operations in his "New Look" defense policy, this problem was serious. It led to covert operations that continue to tarnish the reputation of Ike.

When Joe McCarthy threatened to investigate the CIA, Ike appointed his own team to take a look at the agency. General James Doolittle headed the investigative team, and he reported to Ike that Allen Dulles was "too emotional" and that his "emotionalism was far worse than it appeared on the surface."

Ike's reply: "Here is one of the most peculiar types of operation any government can have, and it probably takes a strange kind of genius to run it."[8]

The Doolittle report also charged that the CIA was behind the times in technological know-how. Ike gave Allen Dulles a copy of the report with the admonition to make changes. Ike decided to give the CIA a paramount role in the new initiatives in aerial reconnaissance that air force planners were developing. Ike liked the way the CIA could act quickly, outside of the usual channels. So Ike cultivated Allen Dulles.

But he also set up a panel of advisers to keep watch on the agency.

It would have been simpler by far to replace him with someone he knew better and trusted more. But Ike as a presidential boss seemed temperamentally averse to replacing almost anybody in his entourage. He would rather override his impatience and exasperation and work with them.

After he had sacked Lloyd Fredendall in North Africa, he vowed to make himself ruthless in weeding out subordinates. He never was.

And this would prove to be one of his greatest weaknesses as president.

In his first presidential term, his inclination to maintain the solidarity of his team was reinforced by the siege psychology spawned by the incessant attacks of McCarthy, whose tactics led to a circle-the-wagons mentality. In one confidential meeting, Ike shared with his staff a slogan that he attributed to the influence of a West Point boxing instructor:

"Don't see, don't feel, don't admit, and don't answer; just ignore your attacker and keep smiling."[9]

Ike would brazen out attacks through the subterfuge of hidden-hand methods.

There was something else about the Dulles brothers that probably clicked with Ike, because he was a rebel: he had always been eager to assert his own individuality, to challenge the ossified "system." He behaved that way at school and at West Point.

He had a healthy respect for fellow officers who dared to challenge the military norms they regarded as stale.

The Dulles brothers—for all their Ivy League background—also flouted rules and defied the genteel norms. They reveled in their reputations for being…"bad boys" who could get away with things that other people couldn't. They maintained their chosen facades—in Foster's case, the piety of a church deacon and in Allen's case the hearty demeanor of a prep school principal.

That did not fool Ike.

And this fact appealed to him—it appealed to him a lot—for he enjoyed that sort of thing himself. He could be mischievous.

He enjoyed being "bad," notwithstanding—or secretly because of—his respect for his mother's code of life.

He adored her, yes, but he could never let himself become a mama's boy. He had to rebel as he acted out her ideals.

After the cabinet selections of John Foster Dulles and Brownell, Ike flew to Augusta for a golf break, and Brownell came along. Lucius Clay flew to Sea Island, Georgia, for a meeting of the Business Advisory Council. He used the occasion to float the names of other cabinet possibilities. Not surprisingly, corporate executives predominated.

Among the people whom Clay recommended to Ike were Charles E. Wilson, the head of GM, to be defense secretary, and George M. Humphrey, president of a conglomerate with heavy investments in iron and steel, to be treasury secretary.

Wilson's appointment struck Ike as a good move because his experience in running the biggest business in America might help him to ride herd on the top brass at the Pentagon. As it happened, Ike and Wilson were not destined to get along, whereas Humphrey would become one of Ike's close personal friends.

Humphrey was a hard-boiled advocate of frugality in government and balanced budgets. This suited Ike, since it matched his own convictions.

But as Ike found himself confronting new complexities in economic policy, his thinking became more flexible. And just as he would have to tone down the more dogmatic proclivities of Foster Dulles, he would have to do the same thing with George Humphrey.

He faced a similar problem with Sinclair Weeks, a conservative banker whom he chose to be secretary of commerce. Ike confided in his diary that Weeks "seems so completely conservative in his views that at times he seems to be illogical. I hope that I am mistaken or if not that he will become a little more aware of the world as it is today."[10]

Most of Ike's cabinet appointments were conservatives. One of the most ultraconservative was Ezra Taft Benson, whom his cousin Robert Taft recommended as secretary of agriculture. An elder of the Mormon Church, Benson insisted that cabinet meetings should begin with a silent prayer.

Though Ike, at the suggestion of Cliff Roberts, would join a church for the sake of appearances, he admitted that "my brothers and I have always been a little bit 'non-conformist.'"[11] His propensity to be a free thinker was too strong to be denied, even though he had grown up in a home of intense religiosity. "I have always sort of treasured my independence," he told Roberts.[12]

"Oh goddamnit," he remarked at one cabinet meeting, "we forgot the silent prayer."[13]

But he began to use piety as a theme that would powerfully resonate with the American people, and he began to do it in his first inaugural address.

Like FDR, Ike appointed a female cabinet member.

Her name was Oveta Culp Hobby, and Ike met her during World War II, when she commanded the Women's Army Corps. She was the publisher of the *Houston Post* as well as the leader of a Texas "Democrats for Eisenhower" group.

Ike named her to head the Federal Security Agency, established in 1939 to coordinate health and education programs. This agency would be superseded by the new Department of Health, Education, and Welfare (HEW), that Ike created in 1953, and Hobby's leadership role carried over: she became the first secretary of HEW.

The creation of this department was a major programmatic extension of the welfare state. And Ike would work with Hobby to extend the welfare state even further.

On November 29, Ike flew to Korea, bringing along with him Omar Bradley, Charles Wilson, and Herbert Brownell. At Iwo Jima, they were joined by Admiral Arthur Radford, the navy's commander in chief of the Pacific.

Ike spent three days in Korea, during the course of which he visited the front and spent time with his son. He could see at a glance that this was no terrain in which to fight. In bitter cold and wearing heavy winter gear, he was taken to the craggy mountainous terrain from which he could see the positions where the Chinese and North Koreans were dug in. He had made up his mind that Korea's strategic value did not justify any further loss of life.

MacArthur's replacement in Korea was Mark Clark, who regaled Ike with a MacArthur-style plan for an all-out assault on China using nuclear weapons. But Ike wouldn't buy it. "I know just how you feel, militarily," he told his old West Point friend, "but I have a mandate from the people to stop the fighting. That's my decision."[14]

In his first presidential memoir, *Mandate for Change*, Ike put the matter this way: "We could not stand forever on a static front and continue to accept casualties without any visible results. Small attacks on small hills would not end this war."[15]

He left Korea on December 3, and flew immediately to Guam, where he would go aboard the cruiser *Helena*, en route to Hawaii. He would be joined there by Foster Dulles, Humphrey, Clay, and others for deliberations on strategic and policy issues.

On the day that Ike left Korea, MacArthur announced that he had a new proposal for ending the war that he would only share with the president-elect.

This of course enraged Truman, who declared that MacArthur had a duty to propose the plan to *him*.

When Ike announced that he would meet with MacArthur, Truman called the Korea trip a "piece of demagoguery." And this of course enraged Ike, who was already furious with Truman.

The stage was being set for the bitterest transfer of power on Inauguration Day since 1933, when Herbert Hoover refused to say anything at all to FDR as the two of them rode together in the limousine to the Capitol.

Aboard the *Helena*—in conversations with the members of his new inner circle—Ike hammered out the fundamentals of his first-term policies. He agreed with Humphrey that the federal budget should be balanced and that federal expenditures—including military expenditures—should be cut. With Foster Dulles he agreed that the threat of massive retaliation with nuclear weapons should become the new linchpin of American global strategy and that conventional war-fighting capability should be cut back.[16]

Here was the New Look, as it was developed in embryonic form on the high seas during the voyage from Guam.

Here, too, was the Middle Way—for Ike made it clear that he would not attempt to roll back Social Security or any other program that was central to the New Deal/Fair Deal legacy.

Notwithstanding the conservative rhetoric he used in the 1952 campaign—and notwithstanding the tone of his own diary entries as recently as 1951—he was emerging as a centrist, just as Bill Robinson had predicted in 1948.

When the *Helena* reached Hawaii, Ike issued a statement on Korea with a vivid warning between the lines for the North Koreans and Chinese: "We face an enemy," Ike said, "whom we cannot hope to impress by words, however eloquent, but only by deeds—executed under circumstances of our own choosing."[17] Some took this to be an implied nuclear threat.

When Ike met MacArthur in New York, he came face to face with a man who wished to act out the nuclear threat. Here was the gist of MacArthur's suggestion: demand a summit with Stalin and propose that Germany and Korea be united through free elections to be followed by (1) a joint U.S.-Soviet guarantee of the neutrality of both nations, and (2) a joint U.S.-Soviet promise to outlaw war as an instrument of policy. Thus spoke Douglas MacArthur—career soldier turned would-be utopian pacifist.

But if Stalin refused to cooperate, MacArthur told Ike, then the United States should wage all-out nuclear war against North Korea and China.

According to Stephen Ambrose, Ike stated in an interview years later that he "was appalled at MacArthur's willingness ... to advocate the use of atomic weapons against Asian people only seven years after Hiroshima."[18] He told MacArthur that "if we're going to bomb bases on the other side of the Yalu ... we have to make sure we're not offending the whole world."[19]

MacArthur remarked to some friends in the aftermath of this meeting that Ike "never did have the guts and never will."[20]

Ike had not ruled out the possibility of using nuclear force against the North Koreans—but only if they refused to negotiate an armistice. It was peace that he wanted, not the "rollback" of communist power.

And it was *peace* that he meant to guarantee by making the nuclear threat so vividly real—so plausible—that it would never be acted out if the world's leaders could be kept sane.

Inauguration Day 1953 was not the shining moment that it could have been. Two weeks earlier, Truman ordered John Eisenhower back from Korea so he could see his father sworn in as president. The tradition on Inauguration Day was for the president-elect to come into the White House and greet his predecessor before the motorcade departed down Pennsylvania Avenue for the Capitol.

Bess Truman prepared coffee for the Eisenhowers, but Ike refused to come in. He just waited in the car for Harry Truman.

Three days later, Ike sent Truman a letter to thank him for bringing John to Washington. That was the only note of mitigation to appear in this unhappy drama: two of our best presidents parted company in churlish animosity.

In his interviews with Cronkite, Ike related that he wrote himself a note on his first day in office as a reminder: never under any circumstances mention the name of Joe McCarthy in public.

Since he knew that McCarthy craved attention, he would *deny* it to him. He hoped that this would goad him into such a frenzy that he would lose control of himself in ways that might lead to his downfall.

A great many people wanted Ike to be aggressive and blow McCarthy away. He chose the hidden-hand method instead. He told Cronkite his reason for this decision: he did not want to poison the public's mood any further. He told others he had no intention of getting into a "pissing match with a skunk."[21]

It was vital to maintain the demeanor he established for himself: serene, in charge, with no outward displays of temper except within the White House for the edification of people who would keep their mouths shut.

Nothing could be allowed to interfere with this new modus operandi for maintaining self-control—*nothing*.

And this imperative prompted him to adopt the hidden-hand method as his standard procedure. Except for some carefully timed and carefully calibrated speeches, everything he did was low-key—even a public-works project so epochal that even FDR would have envied it, the Interstate Highway System.

Ike told civil rights supporters that he would advance their cause "without fanfare but with determination."[22] Though he paid a price for his hidden-hand method—reformers often failed to appreciate the work that he did behind the scenes—it was vital to his new state of mind and his political objective for America.

On Ike's second day in office, he sent a list of subcabinet nominations to the Senate. He nominated Beetle Smith to be undersecretary of state, and McCarthy put a hold on the nomination, saying that Walter Bedell Smith was a likely communist sympathizer, a charge that was of course ludicrous.

Smith's politics were deeply conservative. Ike called Robert Taft and told him to get McCarthy back in line, which he did, but the battle lines between McCarthy and Ike had been drawn.

Their next clash was the nomination of James B. Conant, president of Harvard, to be American high commissioner in Germany. Ike sent Nixon over to talk McCarthy down. On February 4, Ike called McCarthy himself, and this telephone call did the trick.[23] But when Ike nominated Charles E.

"Chip" Bohlen, a career Foreign Service officer, to be ambassador to the Soviet Union, McCarthy proclaimed that he was a traitor, and this time McCarthy would not back down.

Bohlen's "treason" consisted of the fact that he served as FDR's interpreter at Teheran and Yalta. The fight over the Bohlen nomination would be bitter.

As Senate majority leader, Taft had the power to assign committee chairmanships. In a huge disservice to America, Taft decided to put McCarthy in charge of the Government Operations Committee, which in turn put him in charge of its Permanent Subcommittee on Investigations.

Soon McCarthy would be holding one-man hearings and unilaterally setting committee and subcommittee policies. The Democrats on the subcommittee refused to participate in its workings.

Ike made the strategic decision to adopt a defensive and reactive position for the time being. He had far too much to sort out first—especially on the national security front—to launch a hidden operation against McCarthy.

Ike settled into his presidential routine right away.

He took it in stride because he anticipated its demands, and he was used to such things. On his first day in office, he wrote that there were "plenty of difficult problems," but "such has been my portion for a long time." [24]

He established a regular schedule, rising early in the morning and reading the papers, then going to his office. Mamie was a night owl, and a late riser. Their opposite schedules led them to sleep sometimes in different bedrooms when it suited them. But Mamie let it be known that she had had a king-size bed installed so that "I can reach over and pat Ike on his old bald head anytime I want to." [25]

Mamie liked to watch TV, and she played canasta in the afternoons with friends. Ike liked to watch western movies, and he also continued to paint. He converted a spare White House bedroom into a studio. He also used the upstairs solarium for painting.

As first lady, Mamie recovered the joie de vivre that she had known as a young woman. She was a trendsetter, and her brand of femininity become very popular and influential.

President and Mrs. Dwight D. Eisenhower.

The Gettysburg farm that the Eisenhowers bought was being renovated, and they hired Dorothy Draper to handle the interiors. Mamie renovated FDR's presidential retreat in the Catoctin Mountains, "Shangri-La," which Ike decided to rename "Camp David" for his grandson.

On February 1, Ike chose to be baptized in the Presbyterian church, which was Mamie's church. Though he understood the political necessity of the symbolism, he chafed at it. When Dr. Edward Elson, the pastor of the National Presbyterian Church who performed the ceremony, publicized the event, Ike growled that "I feel like changing at once to another church of the same denomination. I shall if he breaks out again."[26] The event made front-page newspaper copy.

But he soon began to cultivate clergymen—especially the evangelist Billy Graham—and he would use the theme of piety as he sought to enhance his position as an inspirational figure in American culture.

For relaxation, he tried to play golf as often as he could, and he brought in members of the gang for marathon bridge games. He often held "stag dinners," male-only events allowing off-the-record conversations with other men of influence.

But there remained an underlying tension. The golf and the card games certainly helped, but they could also bring forth in Ike an unbecoming and compulsive perfectionism.

An angry and aggressive perfectionism.

And according to many accounts, the stag dinners were outlets for less than admirable feelings.

The first cabinet meeting was held on January 23, and Ike made several things clear: he would delegate, and he did not want to be bothered with petty details. He preferred to keep his eye on the big picture. For that reason, he demanded transparency; "there is no use in trying to conceal any error," he said, so "advertise your blunders, then forget them."[27]

He discussed the upgrading of Truman-era policies for weeding out "security risks" in government, and he said that he wanted maximum publicity when serious cases were discovered.

Sherman Adams agreed to serve as Ike's chief of staff, and he would bear the brunt of the delegation that Ike's methods entailed. Eisenhower's secretary was Ann Whitman, whom he recruited from the New York office of the Crusade for Freedom. She moved to Washington, while her husband remained in New York. She was passionately devoted to her boss.

Mamie was so angry at the thought that Ike might flirt with her that she tried to get her fired.[28]

Robert Cutler, a Boston banker who had been Ike's deputy chief of staff in the 1952 campaign (and who had risen to be a brigadier general in World War II), became Ike's special assistant for national security affairs.

Jim Hagerty agreed to continue as Ike's press secretary, and C. D. Jackson—a former publisher of *Fortune* magazine who had worked with Lucius Clay on the Crusade for Freedom and Radio Free Europe projects—became a presidential assistant with a broad sweep of duties. He had been a "psychological warfare" expert in World War II, and he took a keen interest in reigning in Joe McCarthy. But he was also a vigorous Cold Warrior.

A year later, General Andrew Goodpaster became Ike's staff secretary. He became a member of the inner circle because Ike trusted his judgment. Goodpaster had received a PhD in politics from Princeton.

The National Security Council (NSC) was more important in Ike's view than the cabinet. The statutory NSC members were the secretaries of State and Defense, the chairman of the Joint Chiefs of Staff, the director of the CIA, the director of defense mobilization, and the vice president. Ike often asked the attorney general and treasury secretary sit in on the NSC meetings, which were held every Thursday morning.

He presided in a way that made his own decision-making powers clear to all. Gordon Gray, who would eventually succeed Robert Cutler, remembered that "his grasp of complex issues was profound, and his exposition of his own views forceful and clear."[29]

New Look

In the first months of his presidency, Ike seemed to flirt with the possibility of using nuclear weapons to end the Korean War.

Eisenhower scholars are deeply divided on the issue of whether or not he was bluffing. Journalist Evan Thomas, who has studied this issue in great detail, has observed that "with Ike, it was sometimes hard to know if he really meant what he said." He was "cagey, and he could be a provocateur, jumping into discussions to stimulate debate."[30]

He was also a strategist who remained committed to the use of overwhelming force in military matters. So he ordered the military to develop a contingency plan for using nuclear weapons to force an end to the war. That plan was completed by May 20, 1953.[31]

In March, Foster Dulles flew to India to confer with Prime Minister Jawaharlal Nehru regarding terms for a Korean armistice. There was controversy—and the controversy continues—as to whether Dulles told

Nehru that America might use nuclear weapons in the expectation that Nehru would convey this information to the Chinese and Soviets.

The minutes of an NSC meeting on March 31 contain the following account: "The president then raised the question of the use of atomic weapons in the Korean War. Admittedly, he said, there were not many good tactical targets, but he felt it would be worth the cost if, through use of atomic weapons, we could...achieve a substantial victory." He added that "somehow or other the tabu [sic] which surrounds the use of atomic weapons would have to be destroyed."[32]

In the opinion of historian William I. Hitchcock, "Eisenhower was deadly serious" when he said this.[33] In Evan Thomas's opinion, the question of whether or not Ike was bluffing must remain unanswerable.

"Even if Eisenhower had ruled out nuclear weapons," Thomas wrote, "he never would have revealed it for one simple, if profound, reason:"

> To be credible about using the bomb as a deterrent to war or as a prod to diplomacy, he had to show a willingness to use nuclear weapons—not just in his public statements but *in his most private deliberations*. If he ever let on, even to his most intimate friends, that he had no intention of using nuclear weapons, he risked undercutting his entire strategy—in the slip of a tongue by a self-important staffer at a Georgetown cocktail party, or just because there is, over time, no such thing as a secret policy in Washington. The essence of effective deterrence is to never let on that you are not willing to use your ultimate weapon—*to tell no one*.[34]

In his memoirs, Ike affirmed that he had used the nuclear threat in Korea: "We dropped the word, discreetly, of our intentions," he wrote, and "we felt quite sure it would reach Soviet and Chinese ears."[35]

On March 4, 1953, Joseph Stalin died.

After making fast inquiries, Ike was chagrined to discover that no one had been thinking very much about the possibilities for change that might emerge in a post-Stalin Soviet Union.

He sent out an empathetic public announcement that day expressing the hope that "the Almighty will watch over the people of that vast country," Russia, in a world that was at peace.

On March 15, Georgy Malenkov, Stalin's immediate successor, declared in a speech that the Soviet Union and the United States could settle their differences peacefully. Shortly thereafter, on March 28, the North Koreans and Chinese called for an intensification of Korean armistice talks.

These events were connected, though Americans would only learn later that on March 19, the Soviet Council of Ministers directed Mao and Kim to negotiate an armistice or else run the risk of diminished Soviet support.[36] The Soviets needed time to get their own political house in order, and they wanted no distractions. This development of course was a windfall for Ike.

In a conversation with speechwriter Emmet Hughes, Ike found out that Foster Dulles was expressing the hope that no peace in Korea would be negotiated until the communist enemy had been given "one hell of a licking."

Ike was livid.

"All right," he replied, "if Mr. Dulles and all his sophisticated advisers really mean that they cannot talk peace seriously, then I am in the wrong pew. For if it's *war* we should be talking about, I know the people who should give me advice on that—and they're not in the State Department."[37]

Ike told Hughes that he wanted to make a speech about peace and the reduction of armaments.

At an NSC meeting on April 9, Foster Dulles and Charles Wilson openly urged Ike to reject the Korean peace overtures. Ike cut them off abruptly: "the American people will never stand for such a move."[38] Then he silenced any further debate: continued discussion of the subject would not be entertained, he announced, and that was that.

On April 16, Ike gave one of his most important speeches at the annual meeting of the American Society of Newspaper Editors. Even though he was suffering from an intestinal attack that was extremely painful, he made himself deliver this speech because it was so important to him.

"Every gun that is made, every warship launched, every rocket fired," he declared, was "a theft from those who hunger and are not fed, those who are cold and are not clothed." He continued: "This is not a way of life at all, in any true sense.... It is humanity hanging from a cross of iron."

He called for armaments reductions, for the international control of nuclear energy, and for its restriction to peaceful uses.[39]

This speech was, without a doubt, idealistic and sincere. The *New York Times* called it "magnificent," and so it was.

But it was also a move on the gameboard by a strategic who already had plans for the buildup of military strength. And there was no inconsistency about this because Ike was conducting a test.

It seemed to be a test of the best-case future: if the new leaders of the Soviet Union were interested in arms control, Ike wanted to know it. He would follow up vigorously, and he would not let the opportunity pass. He was eager to explore the possibilities for mutual and verified reductions in nuclear weapons.

If not, then his alternative was ready.

Only time would reveal the way that Stalin's successors would behave. And it was best to take nothing for granted.

Just the day before, a secret report began circulating in Washington among people with security clearances, and this report was alarming in the extreme. It asserted that a Soviet nuclear surprise attack on America's Strategic Air Command (SAC) bases would be spectacularly successful.

The report had been produced by the RAND Corporation, a research and development think tank created after World War II by the Douglas Aircraft Company in affiliation with the air force.[40]

This report was the latest in a series of secret worst-case strategic inquiries that had people in Washington frightened. Right after his Inauguration, Ike formed a subcommittee of the NSC to "evaluate the net capabilities of the Soviet Union to inflict direct injury on the United States, up to July 1, 1955." On May 18, the subcommittee delivered its report. The finding: the United States was indeed vulnerable to nuclear surprise attack.[41]

From 1945 onward, worst-case strategists and technological innovators had pushed for the development of advanced reconnaissance systems to prevent another Pearl Harbor—aircraft that could fly so high that the Soviets could never shoot them down, and satellites that could spy on Russia from hundreds of miles out in space. The RAND Corporation championed the latter idea.

Key figures in the air force, particularly General Bernard Schriever, became very interested in developing a reconnaissance satellite. In August

1953, the air force launched a project: it was known as Weapon System-117L.[42] Eventually all of the armed services would develop satellite projects, but the air force effort was the one that was destined to pay big reconnaissance dividends.

Meanwhile, research and development of missile and rocket technology was proceeding. The Americans and Soviets had spirited out German rocket scientists and V-2 missiles after the war, and the army developed an antiaircraft rocket called the "Nike." As early as 1946, the army air forces began to study the concept of an intercontinental ballistic missile (ICBM). In 1951, the air force launched the program that would lead to the development of the "Atlas," which would be tested in 1957 and deployed in 1959.[43]

In 1950, a group of American and British scientists called for the launching of a civilian research satellite.[44] Their target date was 1957, a year of projected high solar activity. 1957 would be designated "International Geophysical Year," and the navy would be tasked with developing the satellite, to be launched with its "Vanguard" missile.

Ike's "New Look" in defense comprised three essential elements, all of which overlapped: enhanced nuclear strike capabilities, reductions in conventional military spending, and CIA covert operations that would be less expensive—and hopefully less risky—than military operations. A common theme bound these elements: fiscal discipline and balancing the budget.

Hopefully, a slimmed-down defense posture would reduce the chances of war and give "more bang for the buck." The Pentagon economizing that Ike had tried to force as army chief of staff and as chairman of the Joint Chiefs of Staff would now be commanded from the top down. The top brass resisted, but Ike took his case to the country. In a televised address on May 19, he told a national audience that he was determined to prevent the United States from becoming a "garrison state." That was not the right way to defend America.[45]

Balancing the budget was a fundamental concept for Ike. It is now time to ask some hard questions about this doctrine, Ike's dedication to it, and the economic policies associated with it.

There is nothing necessarily wrong with the wish to save money, so long as one's goals are achieved.

Ike's insistence on balancing the budget derived—or so it could be argued—from emotion as much as calculation. He imbibed an aversion toward debt from the teachings of his father, who developed, Ike recalled, "an obsession against ever owing anyone a nickel."[46]

The maxims of thrift had been hammered into him throughout his childhood—"the Indian on our penny would have screamed if we could possibly have held it tighter," he reminisced—and his duties as army chief of staff reinforced these maxims.

Moreover, there is *symbolism* in the vision of "balance"—any kind of balance—for a person who is seeking moderation.

Ike surely was.

But economic forces in general and financial needs in particular do not exist in a state of equilibrium. Emergencies demand surges of investment, and enterprises demand to be launched with dynamism. When necessities cannot be supported out of steady income, then borrowing can be quite normal: car loans and home mortgages bear witness to this. State governments often maintain *two* separate budgets: an "operating budget" for normal expenditures and a "capital budget" for projects so large they can only be financed via bond sales, i.e., deficit spending. Budgeting is an accountant's convention: its procedures can be modified to suit as long as necessary things get *paid for.*

All of this is standard procedure—except for people who regard a "balanced budget" obsessively because of its *symbolism.*

Consider a comparison: Lewis Douglas, a former congressman who served FDR as budget director, wrote the following message to Roosevelt when he resigned in protest over New Deal public-works spending:

> I hope, and hope most fervently, that you will evidence a real determination to bring the budget into actual balance, for upon this, I think, hangs not only your place in history but conceivably the immediate fate of western civilization.[47]

The fate of western civilization.

Western civilization would indeed be jeopardized in the age of FDR, but not for budgetary reasons. It was *Nazi barbarism* that would threaten the fate of western civilization, and to avert that threat—to win the Second World War—federal budgeting would be thrown so far out of balance that the national debt of the United States ($258.7 billion) would be so great at the end of the war that it was greater than America's gross national product ($213.4 billion).[48] These are historical facts, so look them up if you doubt them.

Think about it: America's national debt was so great by 1945 that it surpassed the gross national product. And yet the economy did not collapse. Far from it.

And remember that the money supply of the United States would be doubled in World War II to create the monetary base that was necessary for such a huge increase in national debt—debt that took the form of *war bonds*. An expanded money supply was a necessity if banks were to have the funds to *buy* the war bonds.

Economic historians Gary M. Walton and Hugh Rockoff present this comparison: "The stock of money in 1939 was only slightly higher than that of 1929, but by 1944 it had more than doubled." Once again, the point bears emphasis: it was "fractional reserve" money creation by banks that made it all possible.[49]

Ike often spoke of "bankruptcy" and "insolvency" as threats to America. What do these terms mean? They mean something very specific: the inability to pay one's debts.

Let's consider that for just a moment from the standpoints of monetary practice and law.

Ike was uninformed about the history of money and banking, and his fear of national bankruptcy was also uninformed. The government can *always* pay its debts because the government is *sovereign*.

An abstruse point? Not in light of the following: in the Civil War, the Republican Congress created new money and *spent it right into circulation*. Just like that. And the Supreme Court upheld this practice. In the 1871 case of *Knox v. Lee*, Justice William Strong confirmed that Congress may create a "currency," and then "give to that currency few, many, or all of the faculties of money."[50]

Just like that.

"Confederate money"—as everybody knows—became worthless, but the "greenbacks," or United States notes that were created by Lincoln and the Civil War Republican Congress, did *not* become worthless.

The Civil War could not have been won without them.

But these facts didn't matter very much when it came to Ike's concern about "bankruptcy." Why? Because his pragmatism, his common sense, and his big-picture thinking saw him though. There is nothing illusory about the way that economies can go wrong when the underlying forces of production and consumption go awry.

And the instincts that Ike developed in the course of the Great Depression served him well.

When economist Arthur Burns reported at a cabinet meeting on September 25, 1953, that an economic downturn was coming, Ike's response was immediate: there would not be "another 1929," and the "full power of government" would be used to prevent it.[51] Suddenly the issue of "bankruptcy" was forgotten. Balanced budgets were forgotten as well.

Ike was flexible enough to take effective action when economic problems arose, and he had little patience with people whose common sense was weak.

Consider his encounter with Robert Taft on May 1, 1953, when Republican leaders attended a cabinet meeting at which budget reductions were presented. Ike set forth the following account in his diary:

> In spite of the apparent satisfaction of most of those present, Senator Taft broke out in a violent objection to everything that had been done. He accused the National Security Council of merely adopting a Truman strategy... and classed the savings as "puny." I think everyone present was astonished at the demagogic nature of his tirade, because not once did he mention the security of the United States. He simply wanted expenditures reduced, regardless.... I do not see how he can maintain any reputation for considered judgment when he attempts to discuss weighty, serious, and even critical matters in such an ill-tempered and violent fashion.[52]

So much for balancing the budget as an end in itself: it would *never* be an end in itself for Ike because his vision was global.

And so much for people losing their tempers when serious issues were at stake. Ike would keep his temper tantrums harmless, and he would carefully protect his own ever-developing power to *think*.

Taft had only a few more weeks to live. Unbeknownst to all, he had stomach cancer, and he passed away on July 31, 1953.

Ike had cultivated him and made effective use of him while he was alive, and this had been wise, because Ike's problems with the members of his own party were just beginning. After Taft's death, Ike reflected in his diary that, compared with other Republican conservatives, Taft could be at times "extraordinarily 'leftish.'"[53]

Taft's successor as Senate majority leader was Senator William Knowland of California, whom Ike regarded as a doctrinaire thinker. McCarthy would get further and further out of control once Taft was gone.

Ike had forced the Bohlen nomination through the Senate on March 26, but McCarthy found new games to play. He sent two of his henchmen, staffers Roy Cohn (who would later be a mentor to Donald Trump) and G. David Schine, on a rampage in Europe, purging Voice of America libraries of books they didn't like.

On June 14, Ike was commencement speaker at Dartmouth. John McCloy, who was seated right next to him on the platform, made conversation by talking about the books in the VOA libraries that were being burned. "Oh, they're not burning books," said Ike.

"I'm afraid they are, Mr. President," replied McCloy, and "I have the evidence."[54]

So Ike extemporized in his commencement address, and he told the graduates, "Don't join the book burners. Don't think you are going to conceal faults by concealing evidence that they ever existed. Don't be afraid to go to your library and read every book, as long as that document does not offend your sense of decency.... How will we defeat communism unless we know what it is?"[55]

Meanwhile, another conservative Republican was causing headaches for Ike: Senator John Bricker of Ohio, who proposed a constitutional amendment to give Congress the power to cut back presidential authority in negotiating and implementing agreements with other nations. That amendment would make it impossible for Ike to formulate Cold War policy if Congress should pass it and if the states should ratify it.

On July 27, the Korean War came to an end: an armistice was signed at Panmunjom, and Ike turned away from the challenges of hot war to the ongoing issues of the Cold War. President Syngman Rhee of South Korea had tried to sabotage the armistice because he was still intent on victory. Ike forced him into line.

He announced the end of the Korean War in a speech to the nation: "At long last the carnage of war is to cease and the negotiations at the conference table to begin. On this Sabbath evening each of us devoutly prays that all nations may come to see the wisdom of composing their differences in this fashion."[56]

With the war ending, Ike held an important exercise that began in the White House between June 10 and July 15: PROJECT SOLARIUM, a study of long-term Cold War strategy options for America. The idea was developed in discussions among Robert Cutler, Foster Dulles, and Beetle Smith, but as Evan Thomas has argued, Ike "quickly highjacked" the exercise—he made it his own, and the results would undercut Foster Dulles by discrediting his demand for the "rollback" of Soviet power.[57]

SOLARIUM led to a covert reaffirmation of the Truman-era containment policy that had started with the recommendations of George F. Kennan. So Ike brought Kennan back to the White House to participate.

Though the initial proceedings took place in the solarium room that Ike sometimes used for painting, the deliberations would continue in extended sessions at the National War College.

Three task forces were given the job of taking a specific strategic scenario and making the best possible case for it. Team A, chaired by Kennan, was to study the containment policy as developed under Truman, with an emphasis on cooperation between America and its allies. Team B was told to look at a modified containment stance that relied on the unilateral nuclear deterrent power of the United States. Team C was told to look at the rollback option. But Ike was careful in choosing the people who would serve on Team C.

Whereas he brought Kennan back for a repeat performance, he did *not* invite Paul Nitze—principal author of NSC 68, with its bold assertion that the Soviet Union "must and can be shaken apart"—to be a member of Team C.

He stacked the deck.

And then he made his general Cold War preferences clear at the end of the exercise: "Rollback" was abandoned.[58]

The SOLARIUM teams submitted their analyses to the National Security Council. The result was NSC 162/2, a directive that gave Ike everything he wanted in the formulation of Cold War strategy. Ike signed this directive on October 30, 1953. By eliminating "rollback," he had out-maneuvered Foster Dulles.

In William Hitchcock's opinion, NSC 162/2 was "a blueprint for the warfare state—an official plan to mobilize the nation and put it on a per-manent war footing."[59] The document did call for a "mobilization base... adequate to ensure victory in a general war," and for "superiority in quan-tity and quality of weapons systems." It provided that "in the event of hostilities, the United States will consider nuclear weapons to be as avail-able for use as other munitions."

On the other hand, the document stated that "as a general war becomes more devastating for both sides the threat to resort to it becomes less available as a sanction against local aggression." It called for America to "keep open the possibility of settlements with the USSR," and to "promptly determine what it would accept as an adequate system of arma-ment control."[60]

Ike's worries about the nuclear peril kept him agitated. On August 12, 1953, the Soviets exploded their first thermonuclear weapon, and Ike pondered the growing nuclear threat. The United States had tested its first "hydrogen bomb" on November 1, 1952, just a few days before Ike won the presidency.

The shocking results of the test were conveyed to him in a top-secret memorandum from Gordon Dean, the chairman of the Atomic Energy Commission, which was created in 1946 to supervise the development of nuclear weapons. The thermonuclear explosion on November 1 had destroyed an entire atoll in the Pacific—blown it off the face of the earth. The power of the bomb was almost five hundred times greater than the bombs that were dropped on Hiroshima and Nagasaki.

In the aftermath of the Soviet thermonuclear test, Ike found himself haunted. Robert Cutler told Emmet Hughes that he had "never seen the president so concerned." Ike reportedly muttered, "My God, ten of these things and..."[61]

He left the sentence uncompleted.

He began to entertain apocalyptic visions.

And then—he began in a tone of devil's advocacy to discuss *a preemptive strike against the Soviets.*

In a letter to Foster Dulles on September 8, he wondered "whether or not our duty to future generations did not require us to initiate war at the most propitious moment we could designate."[62] In a meeting of the National Security Council on September 24, he asked whether, in light of the danger of a nuclear surprise attack, it might be necessary for the United States to conduct a preemptive surprise attack of its own—"to throw everything at once against the enemy."

Did he really mean it?

He said that he had "raised the terrible question because there was no sense in merely shuddering at the enemy's capacity. We must indeed determine our own course of action in light of this capacity."[63]

Here is where Evan Thomas's thesis about "Ike's bluff" becomes central to his legacy.

What were Ike's true intentions?

In December, he flew to Bermuda to meet Winston Churchill, and he said that he intended to be very tough with the Soviets. He added and that "atomic weapons were now coming to be regarded as a proper part of conventional armament."

Churchill had been hoping to sponsor a summit that might end the Cold War. According to the British, Ike was so defiant—he spoke in off-color terms and called Russia a "woman of the streets"—that Churchill was offended.[64]

What was really going on in Ike's mind as he behaved this way?

Was his mood reverting to the angry condition that his diary entries in the late 1940s recorded—or was it shaped by some off-the-record conversations with hawkish characters in stag dinners at the White House?

Was his mind off-balance again? Was he *faking it*—creating an "impression?"

Was he weaving back and forth to keep the minds of *other* people off-balance—keep them wondering?

He flew to New York and gave a speech at the United Nations on December 8 espousing the cause of "Atoms for Peace." He pledged that the United States would "devote its entire heart and mind to find the way by which the miraculous inventiveness of man shall not be dedicated to his death, but consecrated to his life."[65]

Just a few weeks later, Foster Dulles delivered a speech at the Council on Foreign Relations setting forth his soon-to-be famous doctrine of "massive retaliation"—the doctrine that the United States would "depend primarily on a great capacity to retaliate, instantly, by means and at places of our own choosing."

The strange dynamic that evolved between Ike and Foster Dulles in the dangerous bluff game of "brinksmanship" would continue to evolve.

If it really *was* a game of bluff.

As Thomas has noted, the doctrine of massive retaliation led many to ask the inevitable question: "Did the Eisenhower administration intend to treat every border incident as a nuclear showdown?"[66]

Ike's willingness to use nuclear weapons would be put to the test within just a few months—in Vietnam. It would be tested again a year later in the Formosa Strait crisis. And every time his advisers recommended using nuclear weapons, Ike overruled them.

And then he turned about-face again—he dared them to consider the benefits of starting a world war.

He was extremely adept at keeping other people off-balance.

"The President Wants Peace," wrote Foster Dulles as he doodled on a piece of scrap paper at a foreign minister's meeting in London. Someone saved the paper and released it to the press; it was soon front-page copy in the *New York Times*.

Critics of the New Look would complain that by reducing America's conventional fighting capabilities, it left the United States confronting aggression with nothing but the nuclear option. But Ike had every intention of developing and using intermediate options. He would use the CIA's capacity for covert operations as a low-cost surrogate for conventional military force. And he would give its intelligence-gathering functions the most up-to-date technology available.

The New Look required extremely accurate knowledge of enemy capabilities. And Ike insisted on assessing the likelihood of a Soviet surprise attack.

The need for information was underscored in the summer of 1953 when Americans discovered that the Soviets had produced a new jet-powered heavy bomber, the Myasishchev M-4, that was capable of bombing American cities with nuclear weapons. Americans nicknamed this new Soviet bomber the "Bison."

The plane was the strategic equivalent of America's new B-52 Stratofortress, which was just going into production.

A week after Ike signed NSC 162/2, he issued a secret directive establishing a "Sensitive Intelligence" (SENSINT) program for coordinating aerial reconnaissance efforts. A highly restricted group including the Dulles brothers would oversee the enterprise. The program would eventually encompass an air force–CIA partnership that would make use of sophisticated aircraft and (later) satellites to monitor Cold War adversaries.

This was a "black program."

It was "compartmented," which meant that the vast majority of the participants would be kept in the dark as to where their piece of the overall puzzle fit in. And the funds to pay for it would come from a "black budget."

Decades later, historian R. Cargill Hall teased out some details of the program's inception via oral history interviews. SENSINT, he wrote, "was far more than a 'hidden hand'; SENSINT was entirely off the political table."[67] It never appeared on the agenda of the National Security Council.

It would be decades before the preliminary histories of these classified programs could be written.

Over time, the compartmented nature of SENSINT led to the emergence of codenamed "compartments"—TALENT, KEYHOLE, RUFF, ELINT, GRAB, and a myriad of others. Some of them accompanied the creation of the U-2 spy plane, and others accompanied the creation of the CORONA reconnaissance satellite.

They were all top secret.

Guilty Men

Ike once told Senate Majority Leader Knowland that "in the conduct of foreign affairs, we do many things that we can't explain.... There is a very great aggressiveness on our side that you have not known about." He said that "there are a great many risky decisions on my part constantly," adding that he "knew so many things that I am almost afraid to speak to my wife."[68]

In 1953 and 1954, he approved some covert actions by the CIA that are blots upon his record.

He approved the overturning of two democratically elected governments—the governments of Iran and Guatemala. These were left-of-center governments, so the rationale for toppling them was the preemption of Soviet influence.

It was an all-too-easy rationale.

The case can be made that these interventions were unnecessary, counterproductive, and wrong. Though successful, they put the United States on the wrong side of history. Ike was responsible. But he was hoodwinked by the Dulles brothers, who played upon the vestiges of his prepresidential thinking.

He would know better in just a few years, when he partially atoned for what happened in 1953 by standing up for Third-World interests in the case of Egypt.

In 1933, the shah of Iran had granted the Anglo-Iranian Oil Company (the ancestor of BP) a sixty-year concession. It was a sweetheart deal, and a corrupt one: Iran got only 16 percent of the proceeds.

There were demands in Iran to renegotiate the deal after World War II, especially since other oil-exporting nations were getting better bargains from the oil companies. But the British refused to negotiate.

In 1951, Mohammad Mosaddegh became prime minister of Iran—the shah remained a figurehead monarch—and he demanded the nationalization of Iran's oil. The British Labour government under Clement Attlee moved toward a compromise. After all, Britain's own socialist government was nationalizing industries, as Foreign Secretary Ernest Bevin admitted. "We are doing the same thing here in coal, electricity, railways, transport, and steel," he wrote.[69]

In 1951, *Time* magazine featured Mosaddegh on the cover as "Man of the Year." He symbolized anticolonialism and the demand of third-world nations for economic justice.

The Truman administration pressured the British to negotiate. Dean Acheson told the British ambassador that Mosaddegh represented "a very deep revolution, national in character, which was sweeping not only Iran but the entire Middle East."[70]

Winston Churchill defeated Attlee at the polls in October 1951, and then the British position hardened. Churchill remained an ardent imperialist, and he was openly contemptuous of Third-World nationalism. "We tried to get the blockheaded British to make a fair deal with Iran," wrote Truman, but "no, no, they couldn't do that."[71]

After Ike's election, British MI6 intelligence officials flew to Washington and conferred with CIA Director Walter Bedell Smith and his deputy Allen Dulles. They proposed a coup to topple Mosaddegh, and the CIA signed on. Beetle Smith was extremely enthusiastic about the idea.

Ike had been contemptuous of Mosaddegh back in 1951 when he wrote to Swede Hazlett about Iran. But as president-elect, he became more reflective. He discussed Iran with Churchill when the latter came to New York in January 1953. Churchill was stubborn, and Ike began to sympathize with the Iranian point of view.

"Winston is trying to relive the days of World War II," Ike wrote, but "the free world's hope of defeating the Communist aims does not include objecting to national aspirations."[72]

Unfortunately, Allen Dulles was making plans of his own. He instructed his Middle East operations chief Kermit Roosevelt Jr.—a grandson of Theodore Roosevelt—to cause disorder in Tehran as the pretext for covert intervention by the United States.

On March 1, 1953, the CIA warned that a communist takeover in Iran was becoming possible. On March 4, Foster Dulles asserted at an NSC meeting that Iran could slip into the orbit of the Soviets. British foreign secretary Anthony Eden flew to Washington to make the case against Mosaddegh.

Ike pushed back, calling Mosaddegh "the only hope for the West in Iran," adding that "I would like to give the guy ten million bucks" to build up his country.[73] But Eden persevered.

Little by little, Ike slipped back into his earlier stance on Iran. As he did so, the CIA subversion continued, and the spectacle of Iranian disorder increased. Mosaddegh appealed to Ike for economic assistance in May.

But it was too late. The Dulles brothers, Beetle Smith, Charles Wilson, and other officials agreed to support an Iranian coup, to be codenamed operation AJAX. And Ike went along. Stephen Ambrose explained that while Ike "kept his distance and left no documents behind that could implicate the President in any projected coup," he "was kept informed by Foster Dulles."[74]

Allen Dulles came to the White House on June 14 to brief Ike in more detail.[75]

By summer, the pretext was established: the streets of Tehran were rife with CIA-fomented violence. Ambrose confirmed that the plot involved "using CIA money...to bribe Iranian army officials and to hire a mob in Tehran in order to turn out Mosaddegh and bring back the shah."[76]

In late July, Foster Dulles called his brother at the CIA to egg him on and make certain that the coup would be launched.[77] On August 15, Mosaddegh was arrested and the shah of Iran put firmly in power.

So a democratically elected secularist was replaced by an autocrat whose misrule would trigger the Islamist revolution of Khomeini a generation later. This was an episode of Cold War excess for which the United States and the world are continuing to pay.

Ike never looked back and questioned what had happened, but Mosaddegh had plenty of time to look back: he would be under house arrest for the rest of his life.

A comparable CIA intervention began to shape up in Guatemala. A decade earlier, Guatemalans overthrew a brutal dictator, Jorge Ubico, who permitted an American corporation, the United Fruit Company, to own 42 percent of the land in Guatemala while paying no taxes. Most of the land was kept idle to prop up the price of bananas.

In 1951, Jacobo Arbenz Guzmán was elected president of Guatemala, and he promised land reform. In May 1952, the Guatemalan government established a policy of redistributing idle lands held by large landowners, who were to be compensated with government bonds. In March 1953, 234 thousand acres of United Fruit lands on the Pacific slope were taken, with more expropriations to come on the Caribbean coast.

The *New York Times* editorialized that these land reforms were "long overdue" and that "fair distribution of the land" was a matter of "social justice."[78]

But the president of the United Fruit Company called the seizures communistic, and the company called in all of its influence in Washington, which was enormous. Foster Dulles and Allen Dulles had represented the company when they worked at the law firm of Sullivan & Cromwell. Robert Cutler was the company's banker in Boston. Beetle Smith would go to work for United Fruit after retiring from government. Ann Whitman's husband was a corporate executive at United Fruit.

It is a commentary on the times that no one even thought to raise the issue of conflict of interest or to question the limits beyond which American business interests should not be allowed to interfere with foreign policy.

The ideological issue in Iran and Guatemala was democratic socialism—not communism. And the tragedy was that Ike was becoming more broad-minded as an intellectual when it came to this question. Even as NATO commander in 1951, he foresaw the day when a "socialist Sweden could live alongside a capitalist Germany."[79] And when George Humphrey opposed foreign aid to India on the ground that the nation appeared to be "going socialist," Ike had this to say:

> George, you don't understand the Indian problem. Their situation isn't like our situation. We can operate a free-enterprise economy, but it depends on a whole lot of underpinnings that the Indians simply don't have. If I were the prime minister of India, I would have to resort to many measures which you would call socialistic.[80]

On October 27, 1953, the socialist Norman Thomas called upon Ike at the White House. Ike noted in his diary that "the name socialist covers such a wide range of political thinking...that a so-called rightist-socialist is as much a middle-of-the-roader as is a liberal-conservative."[81]

But the die was already cast for Guatemala: in September 1953, another CIA coup was set in motion. The coup would be carried out in 1954, and one of the CIA operatives was E. Howard Hunt, the same malefactor who would serve Richard Nixon later on in the Watergate scandal—and then go to prison.

Why mince words about these CIA operations?

Ike should have known better, and he *would* know better by 1956 when he redeemed himself in Suez. His reactions to Churchill when they had discussed the Iran situation in January 1953 show that he understood anticolonial, anti-imperial, and nationalistic movements. He also understood the insidious power of concentrated wealth, notwithstanding his immersion in corporate culture via "the gang."

In light of the United Fruit Company's pillage of Guatemala, it is poignant to read what Ike said to one of his economic advisers and speechwriters, Dr. Gabriel Hauge, when the two of them were discussing the issue of corporate influence in 1956. "Our political and economic life are so intertwined, that we cannot separate them," Ike said, and that "can be very dangerous." He would say the same thing about the military-industrial complex when he left the presidency.

When Hauge pointed out that "business must have an honorable place" in society, Ike's reply was immediate: "I want to give businessmen an honorable place, but they make crooks out of themselves."[82]

He was reacting to a brand-new lobbying and bribery scandal that Congress was beginning to investigate.

Ike's anticolonial sympathies would merge with his dedication to peace when he refused in 1954 to pull France's colonial chestnuts out of the fire at the cost of American lives in Indochina—i.e., Vietnam.

The blame for Ike's failure in Iran and Guatemala should rest primarily where it belongs: with the Dulles brothers. But Ike should never have taken their word at face value when they asserted that Mosaddegh and Arbenz were pawns of Soviet influence.

There were others who were equally guilty: Ike's ambassador to Guatemala told him that Arbenz "thought like a communist and talked like a communist, and if not actually one, would do until one came along."[83] CIA officials *presumed* that Arbenz was directed from Moscow. And Ike's zeal to stop communism remained strong; "just think what it would mean to us," he exclaimed at a cabinet meeting, "if Mexico went to the communists!"[84]

Beetle Smith should also bear some blame.

But Arbenz had done nothing to the United States that could justify what Eisenhower did. True, Arbenz was a leftist—that was perfectly clear—and he had purchased some arms from Czechoslovakia. But so what? Gamal Abdel Nasser would do much the same thing just a few years later, and that wouldn't trouble Ike in the slightest.

That being the case, it is time for some very tough talk.

If the CIA possessed actual proof that Mosaddegh and Arbenz were Soviet agents, *it is time for that information to be declassified—now.*

Otherwise, we can only conclude that the Dulles brothers—and Ike—committed acts of war against democratic nations whose leaders were exercising a power that our own law recognizes as fundamental: eminent domain.

Assistant Secretary of State for Latin American Affairs Henry Holland protested to Ike about the overthrow of a democratically elected government. He was right to protest, and Ike was wrong to do what he did.

The whole thing was disgraceful.

Fortunately for Ike, the many excellent things that he did as president tip the balance in the right direction for his place in history.

Race Equality

To his credit, Ike had always been a supporter of racial equality, and race discrimination repelled him. And his methods of advancing Black civil rights would put him overwhelmingly on the right side of history.

Ike had some African American friends—among them Sergeant John Alton Moaney, his wartime valet who continued to serve him in the White House. The two were so close that Ike gave Moaney a picture of Telegraph Cottage that he had painted from memory to commemorate the time they spent together in World War II.

On his own initiative in World War II, Ike had pushed back against army segregation policies, and he tried to give Black soldiers a chance to earn glory in combat. He was glad to pledge cooperation to civil rights leaders when they sought him out in the 1952 campaign, and he was pleased when an African American, E. Frederic Morrow, was assigned to him by the Republican National Committee. Ike would later make Morrow the first Black presidential assistant.

Ike was also pleased when Herbert Brownell declared his interest in advancing the cause of civil rights. He and Ike would make their own distinctive contribution to the heritage of Lincoln Republicanism.

Because his civil rights work was carried out in part through hidden-hand methods, Ike was given insufficient credit by many observers in the

Eisenhower Presidential Library

Ike and Frederic Morrow, the first African American presidential adviser.

1950s—even though the reportage of journalists like Robert J. Donovan revealed what he did.[85] It would take the path-breaking scholarship of historian David A. Nichols to give Ike the long-overdue credit he deserves in the field of civil rights.

Ike pledged in the 1952 campaign to eliminate discrimination wherever the federal government had the jurisdiction—and that included the District of Columbia, the nation's capital, which was still governed under federal authority. In the springtime of 1953, Ike followed up, not only by invoking that authority but also through behind-the-scenes discussions with the owners of local businesses and even with the owners of Hollywood film studios, who put pressure on the owners of local movie theatres.

African American leaders in Washington were jubilant in 1953 as the old Jim Crow barriers melted all over the city.[86] They knew that it was Ike who was making it happen.

Ike also went to work to enforce a Truman-era ban on discrimination in the armed forces. He issued orders as commander in chief and overruled subordinates. On October 24, 1954, Defense Secretary Wilson reported that all segregated units in the armed forces had been abolished. Ike went further and forced the desegregation of schools on military posts as well as hospitals run by the Veterans Administration. The last holdouts were navy yards in the South, and Ike integrated them too.

In Nichols's opinion, "Eisenhower accomplished the racial transformation of the nation's combat forces with breathtaking speed," and he was able to do it "despite the military's legendary resistance to change."[87]

Moreover, Ike worked with Brownell to support litigation that was destined to overturn school segregation throughout the United States in 1954.

At the heart of the matter was the 1896 Supreme Court decision in the case of *Plessy v. Ferguson,* which declared "separate but equal" schools constitutional by standards of the Fourteenth Amendment. The NAACP had been challenging that doctrine, and litigation that began in 1951 had reached the Supreme Court by 1952.

In 1953, the Supreme Court invited Brownell as attorney general to present a brief on the matter. In August, while on vacation in Denver, Ike talked to Brownell about the controversy, and he asked for Brownell's opinion. The attorney general told him that "in my professional opinion public school segregation was unconstitutional and that the old *Plessy* case had been wrongly decided."[88] Ike told Brownell to submit that opinion to the court.

On September 8, Chief Justice Fred Vinson passed away from a stroke. His death was unexpected. Ike had promised Earl Warren that he could have the first vacancy on the Supreme Court, but that did not preclude the promotion of one of the court's sitting justices to replace Vinson with the subsequent nomination of Warren to the newly vacated seat.

Ike made Warren chief justice.

And the administration's brief was filed on November 27, 1953.

As Nichols has affirmed, "Eisenhower and Brownell knew Warren's political views. Brownell had managed Dewey's 1948 campaign"— Warren had been Dewey's running mate—"and he and Warren were friends and frequently socialized. Eisenhower knew that Warren was in favor of civil rights."[89]

Ike's appointment of Warren smoothed the way for the *Brown v. Board of Education* decision in 1954. Congress was out of session, so this was a "recess appointment" that would have to be confirmed when Congress returned.

The battle to confirm Earl Warren would be one of the pivotal events in Ike's ideological migration from right to left.

Congressman Adam Clayton Powell, who represented Harlem, declared on February 28, 1954, that "the Honorable Dwight D. Eisenhower has done more to eliminate discrimination and to restore the Negro to the status of first-class citizenship than any President since Abraham Lincoln."[90]

1954

As far as most Americans could tell, the big event of Ike's first year in office was the armistice in Korea. The far-reaching measures that he put in place to transform American governance were mostly invisible. And this would continue to a limited extent in 1954, when Ike implemented the SENSINT program for aerial reconnaissance. This would be the year when the U-2 spy plane was developed.

Ike's aerial reconnaissance program would reconfigure the architecture of American foreign and military policy.

Ike would also set in motion a program that would reconfigure the architecture of American domestic and economic policy. This was the Interstate Highway System, the largest public-works project in American history. It would transform our economy, the physical dimensions of the continent, and the American way of life.

And in creating this program, Ike tipped his "hidden hand" and took actions that everyone could see.

1954 would be a year of visible and momentous developments: the Army–McCarthy hearings, the *Brown v. Board of Education* decision, the crisis in French Indochina, and the showdowns in Congress that would infuriate Ike and push his ideological development steadily leftward.

Ike proposed a legislative agenda: expanding social security benefits, improving the system of agricultural price supports, and the sharing of nuclear technology through an "Atoms for Peace" program.

Fights in Congress

Earl Warren had been sworn in as chief justice on October 5, 1953, but this "recess appointment" would have to be confirmed. The Senate Judiciary Committee held hearings in January 1954, and conservative Republicans resisted. Senator Barry Goldwater of Arizona complained that Warren "hadn't practiced law in twenty-five years" and was a "socialist."[91] Senator William Langer of North Dakota, chair of the Judiciary Committee, opposed the nomination.

Ike's brothers Edgar and Milton, the former an ultrareactionary and the latter an avowed liberal (and now president of Pennsylvania State University), opposed it for opposite reasons. Edgar called the nomination a "tragedy," and Milton believed that Warren was not liberal enough. Ike's responses were centrist; he told Edgar that Warren was a man "of middle-of-the-road views," and he told Milton that Warren "has been very definitely a liberal-conservative."[92]

Warren's nomination was confirmed on March 1, but the attacks from the right had inflamed Ike, who wrote in his diary that "if the Republicans should try to repudiate him, I shall leave the Republican Party and try to organize an intelligent group of Independents."[93]

This was not a new thought: as early as April 1953, Ike had toyed with the idea of forming a new political party whose creed would be…"the Middle Way."[94]

The Bricker Amendment—the proposed constitutional amendment that would reduce presidential authority in foreign policy—had great support in Congress among conservatives. It would give Congress the power to review and even change treaties after they had been signed.

Ike quietly opposed it in 1953, but the alarm bells were ringing in internationalist circles by the end of the year. The danger was that other nations would hesitate to sign treaties with the United States if Congress had the power to tinker with them from year to year.

Constitutional law scholars John W. Davis and Edward S. Corwin organized a group to oppose the amendment. They recruited Lucius Clay to approach Ike and to encourage him to fight it tooth and nail. They succeeded, and Ike declared his categorical opposition on January 23, 1954.

The Bricker Amendment was defeated on February 26, but that was only because of some arcane maneuvers by Senate Minority Leader Lyndon Johnson.

Ike would find himself reaching out to Democrats more often.

He had been encouraged by Henry Cabot Lodge to embrace bipartisanship in the midterm elections. McCarthy had been making incendiary speeches charging that Democrats had committed "twenty years of treason." Lodge warned Ike that it would be "out of character for bitterly partisan remarks to be associated with you." Lodge's advice: "talk *pro-Eisenhower* and not anti-Democrat."[95] Ike took this advice.

Vietnam

During World War II, a communist-led movement for national independence took shape in Vietnam, which was a part of French Indochina. The Truman administration sent billions of dollars to assist the French, but to no avail. Ho Chi Minh, the communist leader, and Vo Nguyen Giap, his commander, had the French bogged down in guerrilla warfare.

In September 1953, a new French commander, Henri Navarre, tried a different strategy: he created a base on the Laotian border from which his forces could conduct raids. The location of the base was Dien Bien Phu.

This base became a trap: Dien Bien Phu was at the bottom of a valley, and Giap surrounded it with artillery, which hammered the French day and night. The siege began on March 13, 1954, and the French called for American intervention.

Ike had no intention of a unilateral intervention on the Asian mainland.

But he covered his bases. He affirmed the importance of supporting the French in a news conference on April 7. He did not want to let Joe McCarthy make the claim that he had "lost" Indochina the way Truman allegedly "lost" China.

Yet Ike set conditions for American intervention that could never be fulfilled: the French would have to grant independence to Indochina, the United States would have to be part of an international coalition (including the British, Australians, and New Zealanders), American forces would not fight under French command, and the entire operation would have to be authorized by Congress.

All four of these conditions were nonnegotiable, and they had to be worked out simultaneously.

Ike used Foster Dulles to do some heavy lifting. He told him to ask top congressional leaders if they wanted American troops to be sent back into combat on the Asian mainland. The answer of course was no—there should be "no more Koreas." The news of this meeting was leaked to the *Washington Post*, which ran a story under the headline "The Day We Didn't Go to War."

The congressional leaders told Dulles that they *might* be willing to back intervention if some other nations joined in. Ike sent Foster Dulles to sound out the British. Churchill remained rather angry at Ike because of the way he had behaved in Bermuda. So the British answer was no, and that answer was leaked to the press.

As the French position eroded, Ike was put under pressure by the members of the National Security Council to intervene. Foster Dulles cabled from Geneva pleading with Ike to send troops: he refused. Admiral Radford, now chairman of the Joint Chiefs—as well as a nuclear saber-rattler—and Vice President Nixon added their voices, and Ike stood firm against them.

"We would," he avowed, "in the eyes of many Asian peoples merely replace French colonialism with American colonialism." Furthermore, "to go in unilaterally in Indochina...amounted to an attempt to police the entire world." America "could never survive if we frittered away our resources in local engagements."[96]

Robert Cutler supported a proposal from the Joint Chiefs to carpet-bomb the communist positions and employ nuclear weapons. "You boys must be crazy," Ike supposedly replied. "We can't use those awful things against Asians for the second time in less than ten years. My God."[97]

Ike related the exchange years later in an interview with Stephen Ambrose. Cutler denied it, and some other historians have questioned it.

But the records of the National Security Council revealed that Ike said something much more interesting about the nuclear option. He decided to play devil's advocate again. In light of proposals for using nuclear weapons in a local theater of operations, he asked the members of the council whether it might not be better to go all the way—to *start a new world war* by attacking the Soviet Union directly and by doing so immediately. The president asked

> whether the right decision was not rather to launch a world war. If
> our allies were going to fall away in any case, it might be better for the
> United States to leap over the smaller obstacles and hit the biggest
> one with all the power we had. Otherwise we seemed to be playing
> the enemy's game—getting ourselves involved in the brushfire wars
> in Burma, Afghanistan, and God knows where.[98]

The members of the National Security Council had no answer whatsoever to a suggestion that was so unexpected—and so brazen.

How could they? Ike had shut their mouths to perfection with a bluff that puts his earlier ruminations about the prospects of a preemptive strike in a better—and in this case a darkly hilarious—perspective.

As Evan Thomas has observed, it was sometimes hard to know if Ike meant what he said, but in this case, it seems very easy.

Of course he didn't.

Before it was over, two military colleagues came to Ike's defense. Alfred Gruenther, now commander of NATO, confirmed that the French could never win. And Ike's new army chief of staff, Matthew Ridgway, estimated that America would have to send upwards of a million men to Vietnam once intervention started. Draft calls would exceed the Korean War.

On May 7, Dien Bien Phu capitulated, and talks at Geneva worked out a settlement to partition Vietnam into northern and southern states. Ike had kept the United States out of war.

He sent Foster Dulles back to Capitol Hill for the purpose of mollifying the Republican right. Senator Knowland wailed that the French had agreed to a "Far Eastern Munich," and the U.S. was guilty of appeasement. Dulles replied that the position was "not as black as it might appear on the surface," and the end of French colonialism would give the United States a chance to turn the southern part of Vietnam into an anticommunist bulwark.

Moreover, a new Southeast Asia Treaty Organization—SEATO— could be formed as a counterpart to NATO. Eisenhower had discussed this idea with his aides in the early part of the year.

On July 21, Foster Dulles released a statement saying that the important thing was "not to mourn the past but to seize the future."[99] He had the anticommunist credentials to pull this off, and he was proving his usefulness to Ike.

Breaking Joe McCarthy

Joe McCarthy was a psychopath.

He was a creature of opportunism, with no clear strategy for rising above his senatorial status. Some suspected that he intended to pursue the presidency, but no one knew for sure. In any case, he was restless.

He craved sensationalistic publicity, and he craved the satisfaction of hurting people. And he had to play the game for escalating stakes.

It made no difference that his own party had taken possession of the White House. McCarthy lusted to pick a fight with Ike, so he began to look for communists in Ike's own institutional backyard: the United States Army.

In late summer, 1953, he began interrogating low-level army employees who had been associated with left-of-center causes. Then he alleged that members of the army Signal Corps at Fort Monmouth, New Jersey, gave American secrets to the communists. Scores of people were unjustly suspended from their jobs.

Discontent with Ike's self-restraint became pervasive in the White House, and staffers were demoralized. So was Ike.[100] McCarthy had been making some mistakes—like a ridiculous claim that the Protestant clergy was infested with communists—but his public approval ratings stayed high. Ike temporized. He dodged questions and issued disavowals couched in rambling language at press conferences. He had not yet made up his mind about the best strategy for neutralizing McCarthy beyond the principle of "refusing to get into a pissing match."

David Nichols has advanced an interesting theory as to why Ike resisted mounting an open attack against McCarthy: he might have been afraid that McCarthy would dredge up Ike's earlier praise of Stalin and the Soviets in 1945. He had stood at Lenin's tomb with Stalin and called that dictator "fatherly and benign."[101] Swede Hazlett warned Ike that McCarthy "will attack you directly. He'll paint you redder than red (I

321

understand he is stocking ammo from that Russian 'good will era' when you were in Berlin)."[102]

We must also remember Ike's diary entry of March 13, 1951: McCarthy was "digging up alleged dirt" with which to smear him.

McCarthy's attacks upon the army continued.

One of his nameless informants—he fomented vigilantism throughout the executive branch—told him that an army dentist at Camp Kilmer, New Jersey, named Irving Peress had refused to sign a loyalty oath and was in fact a member of a Trotskyite group. The army was preparing to discharge him.

He had been drafted per the terms of a Korean War "doctor draft law," and due to a grade-adjustment law that had been passed by Congress, he was promoted from captain to major before his discharge.

That was enough for McCarthy.

"Who promoted Peress," he raved—as if the actions of a dentist could have threatened the security of the United States in the first place. But McCarthy's antics did not have to make sense to his gullible followers.

McCarthy dragged the commanding officer of Camp Kilmer, Brigadier General Ralph Zwicker, before his committee and browbeat him. When Zwicker explained that the promotion of Peress was required by statute, McCarthy said, "You are a disgrace to the uniform you wear."

At last McCarthy had crossed the line in a way that played definitively into Ike's hands.

Besides, Ike had been warned by Henry Cabot Lodge that McCarthy's vendetta against the army was "actually a part of an attempt to destroy you politically."[103] Lucius Clay called Ike with the same warning: McCarthy had become "too powerful."[104] Ike could feel it now: the threat to his renomination chances.

So he set in motion the process that would destroy McCarthy. The preliminaries of the strategy were put in place in a meeting at the Justice Department that was chaired by Attorney General Brownell on January 21, 1954.[105]

The American Legion and the Veterans of Foreign Wars had rebuked McCarthy for his treatment of Zwicker, and Ike swung into action on two fronts. First, he arranged for the secretary of the army to prevent any further testimony in hearings before McCarthy's subcommittee without guarantees of fair treatment. In May, he prohibited members of the executive branch from giving testimony about confidential discussions. This was a bold application of the constitutional theory of "executive privilege." Brownell had prepared the constitutional arguments.

Second, Ike had the army release to selected members of Congress— and then to the press—a report on a separate but tangentially related matter that was too good to resist. McCarthy's demagogic legal counsel Roy Cohn had been subjecting the army to improper demands. This report became the basis for a formal set of charges against McCarthy.

Cohn was on *intimate* terms with his fellow McCarthy staff member G. David Schine, and after Schine was drafted, Cohn demanded that the army give him special treatment—or else, Cohn said, he would "wreck the army."

Congressional leaders forced the Senate's Permanent Investigations Subcommittee (which McCarthy chaired) to hold hearings. McCarthy was forced to step down as chair. And the hearings were televised—live.

This was "must-see TV" in the early days of television, and millions were glued to their sets as the drama began on April 22.

Since 1950, most Americans had known about McCarthy via newspaper headlines. Now they could see him and hear him in action for the first time—and they were sickened. He was everyone's worst nightmare of a back-alley thug.

He was disgusting.

The army was represented by a charming and elderly Boston lawyer named Joseph Welch, who stole the show with his gentlemanly repartee and droll humor. Welch had been recruited to play this role by Thomas Dewey.

At last McCarthy made the mistake of trying to smear one of Welch's young legal associates. Welch seized the opportunity, and the result was riveting telegenic drama. Speaking slowly—his dulcet voice heavy with sadness—Welch turned years of courtroom virtuosity to maximum advantage as he lectured his opponent like this:

> Until this moment, senator, I think I never really gauged your cruelty
> or your recklessness. Little did I dream you could be so reckless or
> cruel as to do an injury to that lad. I fear that he will always bear a scar

needlessly inflicted by you…. If it were within my power to forgive you for your reckless cruelty, I would do so. I like to think that I am a gentle man. But, Senator McCarthy, your… forgiveness… must come from someone… other… than me.

McCarthy, caught flat-footed, tried to stammer out something or other, and Welch silenced him by telling him that he had done enough damage already. One could have heard a pin drop in that committee room as the elderly lawyer looked at the swarthy and heavyset demagogue and asked, "Have you no sense of decency, sir, at long last? Have you left no sense of decency?"[106]

It was straight downhill for McCarthy after that, and he would never recover.

On December 2, 1954, he was censured for conduct unbecoming a senator, and he would die of alcoholism in 1957.

Toward Interstate Highways—and Dynamic Centrism

Eisenhower meant it when he said there would be "no more 1929s," and he pondered the issue in 1953. He was warned in September that a major recession might be coming. This directed his thoughts to the nature of the business cycle, the mutuality of private enterprise and government, and a dream that he had been nurturing since 1919.

On January 4, he announced a new activist program in a televised address. "No American," he said, "can truly prosper unless all Americans prosper." It was therefore time to spend money on all sorts of things: to eliminate "the slum, the outdated highway, the poor school system, deficiencies in health protection, the loss of a job, and the fear of poverty in old age."[107] It sounded like he had become a full-fledged disciple of FDR.

According to journalist Robert J. Donovan, Ike told his cabinet to get ready in a meeting on February 5. He said that he had asked economist Arthur Burns to

co-ordinate reports from the various departments and agencies on their plans for public works projects. It would be essential, he said, to have planning advanced sufficiently to ensure that men would be put to work quickly. Too often, he added, preliminary planning, testing and surveys delay start on work.... Projects actually under way, he noted, gave the government flexibility in speeding them up or stretching them out, as conditions required.[108]

"An interesting aspect" of the ensuing discussion, wrote Donovan, was "a muting of emphasis on balancing the budget.... With the fate of the economy in the balance, it was submerged under the determination of the President and Cabinet generally to undertake an expensive public works program if necessary and to prevent a serious depression at any cost."[109]

The discussion began with a review of public-power projects, but Ike quickly changed the subject to...road-building. He "suggested building new toll roads with the government guaranteeing the bonds."[110]

Here was the inception of the Interstate Highway System.

Ever since the cross-country motor tour of 1919, Ike had dreamed about bringing modern superhighways to America, and when he saw the Autobahn system of Germany after World War II, he dreamed of it again.

In 1944—even in the midst of World War II—Congress laid the groundwork for an interstate system by passing the Federal Aid Highway Act. And yet the funding was completely insufficient.

Ten years later, in 1954, Ike would start to make it happen.

The interstate system would revolutionize American life. It was integral to 1950s iconography and culture: high-powered cars with exuberant tail fins, streamlined gasoline stations, neon-clad drive-in restaurants, and brand-new motels. All of these things became signature items in the nascent "Eisenhower prosperity."

On April 8, Ike wrote in his diary that an economic stimulus would have to be *sustained*: "I am convinced that the dangers of doing nothing are far greater than those of doing too much.... Everything that the government can now do to increase the spending power of the country, both by the individual and by the government, will, at least until there is a decided upturn in economic activity, be a good thing."[111]

In May he got Congress to authorize $2 billion for road construction, a very significant sum in 1954 values. On April 2, he told the cabinet to "be ready to *act every day*." According to Stephen Ambrose, "he wanted the departments, especially such big spenders as Defense and Agriculture, to hurry up with their purchases, and he made it clear that he wanted it done well before the fall elections."[112]

He appointed Lucius Clay to chair a blue-ribbon task force charged with examining alternatives for the Interstate Highways project. Clay's committee delivered its report on January 12, 1955. It recommended spending $101 billion over ten years to construct forty-one thousand miles of highways.

The legislation that launched the system—the Federal Aid Highway Act of 1956—established a gasoline tax whose proceeds would be channeled into a federal Highway Trust Fund.

It was significant that Ike wanted to design projects that could be "speeded up or slowed down" to fine-tune the economy. This was the legacy of John Maynard Keynes in action, whether Ike was aware of it or not: the vision of "contra-cyclical" interventions to smooth out the ups and downs of the business cycle. In 1955, Ike would say that he wanted the Commerce Department to "use the Interstate System for managing the economy."[113] Here was the culmination of years of reflection that had started so long ago for Ike at the Industrial College.

The Employment Act of 1946 had vested the federal government with permanent responsibility for guaranteeing high levels of employment. In 1957, economist Arthur Hansen reported that the Eisenhower administration "leaned heavily upon the machinery set up under the Employment Act" in responding to threats of recession: "The main significance of the 1954 Economic Report [of the president]," he wrote, "was the firm declaration…that the government would use its 'vast powers' to help maintain employment and purchasing power."[114]

In addition to launching the interstate project, Ike forced through a measure that had languished for almost half a century: the creation of the St. Lawrence Seaway, whose construction would open the Great Lakes to interoceanic commerce. The measure cleared Congress in May 1954, and Ike's support was crucial.

In all, Ike was aligning himself definitively with the legacy of the New Deal. He declared in October 1954, that "so long as any citizen wants work and cannot find it, we have a pressing problem to solve. This administration is working vigorously to bring about a lasting solution."[115]

He had been receiving a steady flow of letters from his brother Edgar protesting his indulgence of the New Deal legacy. In November 1954, he answered back:

> Should any political party attempt to abolish social security, unemployment insurance, and eliminate labor laws and farm programs, you would not hear of that party again in our political history. There is a tiny splinter group, of course, that believes you can do these things. Among them are H.L. Hunt...a few other Texas oil millionaires, and an occasional political or business man from other areas. Their number is small, and they are stupid.[116]

Even in the heat of the 1952 campaign, Ike had advocated constructing a "floor over the pit of personal disaster in our complex modern society."[117] He reiterated the point when he was in the White House: "It is a proper function of government to help build a sturdy floor over the pit of personal disaster."[118]

So he worked with Oveta Culp Hobby to expand the sweep of social security coverage in 1954. He proposed to add ten million people to the program—people who worked in professions that had not been covered by the original Social Security Act.

In contrast to his pre-presidential condemnations of the "hand-out state," he emphasized that social security recipients *worked*, and they made contributions to the system. Furthermore, since the economic well-being of the American people mattered to everyone, the United States government should work in partnership with hard-working people.

He prevailed: Congress did what he requested, and he signed the Social Security Amendments of 1954 on September 1.

Meanwhile, he suggested to Oveta Culp Hobby that a national health care system should be established, one that would be comparable to what enlisted men received in the army.[119]

When he had courted Republican donors for his American Assembly project, he vowed to oppose "socialized medicine." Now, as president, he began to explore the possibility. In March he sent Congress a proposal to set up a $25 million fund that would guarantee medical insurance to low-income and high-risk citizens. Over sixty million uninsured people would have been covered.

But in this case, Congress said no.

The more he turned his mind to the presidential legacy that he wanted to leave, the more liberal he seemed to become.

And it happened very quickly.

Even so, he felt twinges of ambivalence. In a diary entry on February 26, 1954, he declared that his administration remained dedicated to "maximum decentralization."[120] In light of this ambivalence, he redoubled his quest for ideological balance.

His stance on federal aid to education would be indicative. In 1955, he sponsored a White House conference on education. He acknowledged that many states and localities were in need of financial assistance to build schools in response to population growth. So here is the balance that he struck:

> In the last ten years, our population has increased by 26 million souls. But during that great increase a similar increase in the number of schoolrooms and qualified teachers available for teaching our youth has not come about. Many facilities are lacking—many things have to be done.... But there are two points, I think, on which we all agree. The first thing is that the education of our young should be free. [And] it should not be controlled by any central authority. We know that education, centrally controlled, finally would lead to a kind of control in other fields which we don't want and will never have. So we are dedicated to the proposition that the responsibility for educating our young is primarily local. At the same time we know that everybody must have a good education if they are properly to discharge their functions as citizens of America.[121]

Ike was laying down precepts that are useful today as parents, teachers, and students resist the burdensome federal mandates of the No Child Left Behind law and the Common Core standards. We can learn a lot from the concerns that Ike was expressing.

On February 8, 1955, Ike proposed to Congress a three-year, $7-billion school construction program for America.

The Formosa Strait Crisis

Early in 1955, the United States confronted the sudden possibility of war—off the coast of China. When the Chinese communists took over in 1949, Chiang Kai-shek's nationalists withdrew to Formosa (Taiwan) and both sides vowed that they would eventually renew hostilities and unify China.

Chiang kept garrisons of troops on several island archipelagos in the Formosa Strait: the Pescadores islands (close to Taiwan), the Tachen islands (to the north), and the Quemoy and Matsu island groups, both of which were close to the Chinese mainland.

In the autumn of 1954, the communists began shelling Quemoy, and the prospect of invasion loomed. By the end of the year, a full-scale war scare with China was in progress. Most of the Joint Chiefs of Staff recommended nuclear air strikes against mainland China. Senator Knowland called for preemptive war against both China and the Soviet Union.

On January 29, 1955, Congress at Ike's request passed a resolution authorizing him to use force to defend both Taiwan and the Pescadores. The resolution also authorized him to defend "such related positions and territories of that area now in friendly hands … as he judges to be required or appropriate." This language was designed to leave the communists guessing as to whether or not Ike would defend Quemoy and Matsu and the lengths to which he might go in order to defend them.

Ike played his cards.

He quietly sent General Goodpaster to confer with the admiral in command of the Pacific fleet regarding the communist threat. The answer: Quemoy and Matsu could defend themselves without U.S. assistance unless a massive amphibious invasion were attempted. And there were no signs that the Red Chinese were preparing to do such a thing.

But Foster Dulles, Admiral Radford, and others kept ringing the alarms and calling for the use of nuclear weapons. Dulles told the Senate Foreign Relations Committee that the United States should prepare for the possibility of war. He travelled to Formosa, and then made a televised speech on March 8 that hinted at the use of nuclear weapons.

Ike approved of this brinksmanship: it was integral to his strategy of deterrence. And he was privately convinced that a conflict with China was "entirely possible." He wrote in his diary on March 26 that the Chinese communists "appear to be completely reckless, arrogant, possibly over-confident, and completely indifferent as to human loss."[122]

But should Americans also be indifferent to human loss?

Robert Bowie, director of policy planning at the State Department, elicited a chilling estimate in consultations with the CIA and the Atomic Energy Commission: a U.S. nuclear strike at Chinese airfields across the Formosa Strait would probably kill more than ten million people, given the proximity of those airfields to population centers.[123]

Ike continued to play his cards, and he bided his time. He deliberately sent mixed signals.

In a press conference on March 16, he gave a reporter this answer when asked whether he would authorize the use of nuclear weapons in an Asian war: "I see no reason why they shouldn't be used just exactly as you would a bullet or anything else." But then he qualified this answer in the following manner: "The great question about these things comes when you begin to get into those areas where you cannot make sure you are operating merely against military targets."[124]

He proceeded to negotiate a deal with Chiang: if he would evacuate the Tachen islands, the United States would guarantee the security of Taiwan and the Pescadores. Chiang agreed. So that left the issue of Quemoy.

The furor and the public concern about the possible use of nuclear weapons increased.

As a press conference on March 23 was approaching, Jim Hagerty told Ike that perhaps "the Formosa Strait situation is so delicate that no matter what question you get on it, you shouldn't say anything at all."

"Don't worry, Jim," Ike replied, "I'll just confuse them."[125]

At the press conference, the *Christian Science Monitor*'s Joseph C. Harsch asked Ike if he would use nuclear weapons to defend Quemoy and Matsu. Ike's answer was a masterpiece of comic circumlocution:

Well, Mr. Harsch, I must confess I cannot answer that question in advance. The only thing I know about war are two things: the most changeable factor in war is human nature in its day-by-day manifes-tation; but the only unchanging factor in war is human nature. And the next thing is that every war is going to astonish you in the way it occurred, and in the way it is carried out. So that for a man to predict, particularly if he has the responsibility for making the decision, to predict what he is going to use, how he is going to do it, would I think exhibit his ignorance of war; that is what I believe.[126]

Ike's detractors down the years—especially liberals who never caught on to his hidden-hand methods—delighted to portray him as a befuddled old duffer whose tangled syntax betrayed the workings of a feeble mind.

Only a man who was supremely sure of himself—supremely in command—would be willing to play the fool, to pretend to be confused in order to confuse other people, and to get his own secret form of amusement from such antics. This man whose angry eyes could pin you to the wall when he was vexed could entertain himself with clowning and self-satire.

The prankster of West Point days was back in action.

But this was very dark comedy indeed.

So Ike moved more decisively to calm things down. When Chief of Naval Operations Admiral Robert Carney predicted war by April 15, Ike summoned him to the White House for a reprimand. And then he told Jim Hagerty to put out the word to the press that while "there is always danger in the Far East ... we are not looking for war."[127]

Would Ike have really used nuclear weapons?

In the opinion of Evan Thomas, we will never know: "if Red China had invaded Formosa, he probably would have" made the decision to authorize the use of nuclear force, but in the case of *Quemoy*, we can only guess.[128]

In the end, Ike was lucky: the crisis began to diminish. The breakthrough occurred at a conference in Indonesia, where the delegates from nations that were former colonial possessions urged China to reduce the danger of nuclear war. One of the issues in play was concern about the radioactive fallout that American thermonuclear tests in the Pacific atolls had been spreading throughout the region.

Chinese foreign minister Zhou Enlai seized the opportunity for diplomatic one-upmanship: he announced that Chinese authorities were willing to sit down with American diplomats in the interest of relaxing international tensions.

Ike was happy to oblige.

Taking Stock

The Democrats gained control of Congress in the midterm elections of 1954, but Ike was content to work with them because their victory eased the burden of having to deal with his own party's ultraconservative fringe. The new Democratic speaker of the house, Sam Rayburn, and the new Senate majority leader, Lyndon Johnson, enjoyed working with Ike, and they said so.

The age of good feelings that Ike had hoped to bring about was well underway.

He had not yet decided to seek a second term, though his ambitions were leading him in that direction. Not least of all, he wished to put the finishing touches on the long-term structural guidelines for American development that he had been so busily and successfully creating behind the scenes.

On May 17, 1954, the Supreme Court had issued its decision in the landmark case of *Brown v. Board of Education*. The Warren court struck down the bigoted *Plessy* decision of 1896 and ruled that segregated schools are unconstitutional. The justices knew that they were unleashing a social revolution that might lead to violence, and they were nervous about it.

So after handing down their reversal of *Plessy*, they deferred the issue of enforcement.

Their eventual enforcement decree arrived in the 1955 "*Brown II*" decision, which called for gradualism: the process would be carried out "with all deliberate speed" by local school boards, supervised by United States District Courts.

Ike proceeded to pack the courts with integrationists to make certain that school desegregation would happen.

When Supreme Court Justice Robert Jackson died, Ike replaced him with Judge John Marshall Harlan II, an appointment fraught with symbolism, since Harlan's grandfather was the sole dissenting justice in *Plessy*. Two more of Ike's nominees would be opponents of segregation: Justices William Brennan and Potter Stewart.

Of equal or greater importance, Ike appointed federal judges in the Fifth Circuit—which encompassed Alabama, Florida, Georgia, Louisiana,

Mississippi, and Texas—who were staunch integrationists, and he did the same thing in the Fourth Circuit, which encompassed Virginia, Maryland, West Virginia, and North and South Carolina.

As David Nichols has said, Ike "consciously made appointments that would entrench *Brown* in the judiciary."[129]

As Ike developed the foundation for the Interstate Highway System—intended not only to modernize America's infrastructure but to manage its economy—he fought to institutionalize the New Look in defense. He believed that defense cuts were necessary, not only to minimize the chance that America would get sucked into needless wars but also to maintain the necessary funding for civilian-sector projects.

In 1955, he faced pushback from military colleagues during congressional hearings. Testifying as army chief of staff, Matthew Ridgway complained that the New Look was forcing an "all-or-nothing" posture on the military.

Ike met with congressional leaders and he told them that Ridgway was just "talking theory—I'm trying to talk sound sense.... The only thing we have to fear is an atomic attack delivered by air on our cities. Goddamnit, it would be perfect rot to talk about shipping troops abroad when fifteen of our cities were in ruins."[130]

In 1954, Ike had asked Dr. James R. Killian, president of MIT, to chair a task force on defense technology. It was known as the Technological Capabilities Panel (TCP), and a special subcommittee on intelligence (known as "Project Three") was chaired by Edwin Land, the founder and CEO of the Polaroid Corporation. In its February 1955 report, the TCP recommended the rapid development of reconnaissance satellites.[131]

General Bernard Schriever accelerated work on the air force's WS-117L satellite project. The initial idea was to launch a heavy satellite that would beam electronic images back to Earth.[132]

A "sleeper" issue of international law was involved in such clandestine efforts: "freedom of space." If established as a precedent, freedom of space could be taken to imply that a nation's sovereign air space stopped at the upper edge of the atmosphere. The "Project Three" group emphasized this.[133]

Consequently, the proposal of civilian scientists to put a research satellite in orbit for "International Geophysical Year," 1957, took on a secret significance. Ike pushed the project as a public-relations cover for the clandestine military presence in space that he was planning.

At a meeting of the National Security Council on May 26, 1955, Ike approved the effort to put a civilian satellite in orbit by 1957, and this decision was announced to the public on July 26. The navy would use its "Vanguard" missile to do the job.[134]

Ike had been placing more emphasis on missile development, both for air defense and to augment his nuclear deterrent. The Nike antiaircraft missile, developed in the Truman years, was deployed in 1953, and a ring of Nike bases was built around Washington, D.C. Some of these bases still exist—as historic sites.

Meanwhile, the air force's Atlas intercontinental ballistic missile was progressing, and a second project was added: the "Titan" ICBM. The army and air force were working on some intermediate-range missiles that could be deployed in Europe: the "Thor" and "Jupiter" missiles. In an "eyes-only" supplement, the Killian report recommended that a submarine-based nuclear missile should be developed by the navy to supplement land-based missile forces.[135] This would be the "Polaris" program.

So a new strategic "triad"—land-based missiles, sea-based missiles, and long-range manned bombers—was shaping up, and by the time that John F. Kennedy succeeded Ike as president, it was in place.

In 1954, the first "SENSINT" aerial reconnaissance overflights of the Soviet Union began. Using the B-57 tactical bomber that was introduced in 1953, the missions were risky because the planes could be shot down. The Soviets knew about these overflights, and they tracked them.

Ike created a coordinating board with the mission of secretly vetting requests from executive agencies for the reconnaissance overflights. He reserved to himself to the right to grant final approval.[136]

In 1954, a brilliant Lockheed designer named Clarence "Kelly" Johnson perfected the design of a light-weight reconnaissance aircraft with sail-like wings that could fly so high that the Soviets could not shoot it down.

This would be the U-2, and the plane would be prepared for a test flight in 1955.[137]

The report of Killian's TCP converged with the Doolittle study of the CIA, which was delivered to Ike on October 19, 1954. The intelligence agency was faulted by Doolittle for slipping behind in state-of-the-art technology. Accordingly, on November 24, Ike put the CIA in charge of the U-2 project with the air force playing a supporting role.[138] He decided to use the aerial reconnaissance mission to force Allen Dulles and his agency to get up to speed. He also did it because the CIA was less hampered by bureaucratic constraints.

The best designers of optical systems, including Edwin Land and James D. Baker of Harvard, were hired under classified contracts to produce lenses capable of producing photographic images from seventy thousand feet in the atmosphere. These lenses would produce photographic images of astonishing clarity.

The U-2 would be put into action in 1956.

Ike was approaching sixty-five, and he had a great deal to make him happy. His presidency was a triumph, and one of the most remarkable things about it was that he was achieving such great things without fanfare. The public loved him because he was fulfilling their hopes and expectations. He was the hero who had promised to bring good times, and the mood of relaxation in America was palpable by 1955. The American people wanted peace, and Ike was the man to deliver it.

It was a commentary on his own state of mind that he preferred to savor the full magnitude of what he was achieving in secret. It was almost a matter of principle with him: *only he* would know the full extent of his victory.

Visionary efforts—to guarantee equal rights, to promote full employment, to build state-of-the-art highways, and to create high-altitude sentinel systems to keep the American people safe—were being quietly, steadily, and expertly put into place by Dwight D. Eisenhower.

As he approached old age, it was time for him to wonder: Had it been enough?

Proud as he was, he was subject to sudden aggravation, and the challenge of anger management was constant. And—successful as he was—there were undertones of sadness that would limit the elation he could feel.

He was tired.

And his regular golf outings at Burning Tree Country Club in Bethesda, Maryland, vacations in Augusta, Georgia, and bridge sessions at the White House with members of the gang were probably reminders that time was closing in.

Could he begin to look toward retirement?

Work on the Gettysburg farm was completed in 1955. Designed by Penn State architecture professor Milton Osborne, the new farmhouse contained fifteen rooms, including eight bathrooms, a handsome living room, and an oak-beamed study. At Mamie's suggestion, it included a glassed-in porch.

Ike wanted the place to be a working farm, and a colleague from SHAEF, Brigadier General Arthur Nevins, agreed to manage it. "Gang" member W. Alton "Pete" Jones acquired three adjoining farms, and he planted the land with trees to ensure the Eisenhowers' privacy.

Geneva Summit

In the springtime of 1955, the Cold War began to thaw. New Soviet leaders—head of state Nikolai Bulganin and Communist Party first secretary Nikita Khrushchev—made an overture: they proposed a meeting in Vienna to discuss the withdrawal of the Allied occupation forces that were placed in Austria after World War II. Accordingly, a treaty was negotiated and signed on May 15. Austria became a neutral nation.

A new modus vivendi—a commitment to maintain the status quo in Europe—was at hand, and an international call arose for a summit meeting in Geneva that would ease Cold War tensions even further.

This suited Ike's purposes, and he prepared a proposal for public presentation that was custom-designed for his own special secret agenda: an "Open Skies" proposal that would give the United States and the Soviet Union permission to conduct reconnaissance overflights of one another's territory. There would be no concealment—and no apology. The idea was to relieve both nations from the fear of surprise attack.

What could be more reasonable or mutually beneficial?

Even if the Russians said no, Ike could go ahead with his secret plans in the happy knowledge that he shared his thinking with the Russians and he did it in a manner that was empathetic and persuasive. No one wanted to be caught by surprise—so why not confess it and try to work together? Even if the Russians rejected the Open Skies proposal, they might find themselves smiling to one another in private as they thought about the chance for a modus vivendi with a sane and steady leader like Ike.

It was worth a try—and it was good psychology for everyone.

Ike entrusted the development of this proposal to Nelson Rockefeller, a grandson of the Standard Oil tycoon and an up-and-coming figure in progressive Republican circles. The proposal was vetted and approved by the National Security Council, even though Foster Dulles was not at all happy about it.

On May 15, the governments of the United States, Britain, and France proposed to Russia that a summit meeting should be held "to remove sources of conflict between us." Republican conservatives accused Ike of opening the door to appeasement. Foster Dulles—again—was disapproving. He recommended a meeting of foreign ministers instead of a gathering of heads of state.

Ike overruled him.

The congressional hard-liners had no conception of how popular the summit proposal would be. Ike assured them that no agreements would be made without congressional approval. The date for the Geneva summit was set for July 18.

The summit lasted for five days, and Ike met with his old friend Marshal Zhukov, the new Soviet defense minister. In the Palais des Nations (former headquarters of the League of Nations), Ike presented his proposal: both sides would give one another "a complete blueprint of our military establishments" with the absolute right to conduct verification overflights.[139]

Though Bulganin supported the proposal at first, Khrushchev shot it down, thus revealing who was boss in Russia. Even so, the very fact that Ike had made the proposal helped to ease international tensions. And the response from the American public was euphoric—the feeling of relief was near-universal. Ike's approval rating soared to 79 percent, and James Reston of the *New York Times* wrote that "the popularity of President

Eisenhower has got beyond the bounds of reasonable calculation." It was a "national love affair."[140]

Ike had used the rhetoric of spirituality to give the Geneva Summit epochal importance. Before he departed, he called it "the greatest step toward peace...that has ever been taken in the history of mankind." And he summoned the nation to prayer:

> Suppose, on the next Sabbath day observed by each of our religions, Americans, 165 million of us, went to our accustomed places of worship and, crowding those places, asked for help, and by doing so, demonstrated to all the world the sincerity and depth of our aspirations for peace. This would be a mighty force.[141]

Was it any wonder that the New York Times said Ike "represented what is best in this nation?"[142] Or that two thousand people met him at the airport when he returned from Geneva? Or that people all over the world hailed his Open Skies proposal as visionary? Or that Billy Graham would declare that "I believe God is really on the side of that man"?[143]

He was a shoo-in for re-election if he chose to seek a second term. He welcomed the chance to institutionalize his policies and revitalize the Republican Party.

He had become a liberal Republican in all but name; as early as November 1954, he wrote in his diary that "the Republican Party must be known as a progressive organization or it is sunk. I believe this so emphatically that I think that far from appeasing or reasoning with the dyed-in-the-wool reactionary fringe, we should completely ignore it and when necessary repudiate it.... They are the most ignorant people now living in the United States."[144]

Lucius Clay decided to reprise the role he had played in 1951 and 1952 as presidential kingmaker: he told Ike that he should seek a second term to transform the Republican Party into "an Eisenhower Republican Party."

Others were thinking the very same thing: in 1955, an Eisenhower speechwriter named Arthur Larsen called for a "New Republicanism" modeled on Ike's politics in his book A Republican Looks at His Party.[145] Larsen would be the principal author of Ike's acceptance speech at the 1956 Republican convention.

Stricken

On July 11, before he left Geneva, fifty-four Republican congressmen issued a statement urging Ike to run for a second term. Upon his return, a group of Ohio Republicans calling themselves the Bull Elephants called upon him at the White House and begged him to run. Henry Cabot Lodge had been advising Ike about the politics of seeking reelection since 1954.

He had not made up his mind—not least of all because of his age and concerns about his health. And those concerns would be proven to be well-grounded.

Three days after he returned from Geneva, Ike was ushered into a secret meeting that placed him under severe emotional strain.

The issue on the table was authorizing the development of thermonuclear warheads—devices to sit atop the new intercontinental ballistic missile ("Atlas") that was well along in development. On July 28, Ike was briefed by air force general Bernard Schriever, assistant air force secretary for research and development Trevor Gardner, and John von Neumann, a world-famous physicist.

Gardner explained that thermonuclear warheads with devastating destructive power would soon be feasible. It was vital, he declared, for the United States to develop them first—to prevent the Soviets from conducting "nuclear blackmail."

He told a startled Eisenhower that "it is now possible to send a ballistic missile armed with a nuclear warhead from the continental United States to Soviet Russia—or vice versa—in roughly thirty minutes."

According to Neil Sheehan, biographer of Bernard Schriever, "the room was absolutely silent. There was no clearing of throats or shuffling of feet or shifting of chairs. Everyone in the room, including the president, had his eyes fixed on Gardner."

Von Neumann hastened to add that the warning time for an ICBM attack would be *less* than half an hour, since radar would not detect the incoming missiles until they had reached the top of their trajectory arcs. Americans would in truth have less than fifteen minutes of warning before they were incinerated.[146]

On August 5, Ike received another briefing from Dr. Willard Libby of the Atomic Energy Commission. Ike asked if there was any limit to the

339

possible size of a thermonuclear bomb. The answer was no. Then he asked how many thermonuclear megatons it would take to make the whole planet radioactive, and he asked whether thousands of nuclear explosions could knock the earth off its axis.[147] The answers were speculative.

On September 13, Ike went ahead and ordered the development of thermonuclear warheads.

Evan Thomas has wondered whether these secret deliberations might have contributed to the stress that would cause Ike's heart attack just ten days later.

On August 14, Ike left for a vacation in Colorado; he visited the Aksel Nielsen ranch, and he stayed in Denver at the home of the Douds. He played golf at the Cherry Hills Country Club with "Rip" Arnold, the club pro.

On September 23, he was interrupted on the golf course by telephone calls from Foster Dulles—calls that he regarded as excessive. His aggravation kept increasing, and after the third interruption, his doctor Howard Snyder, who was a member of the golf party, noted that "the veins stood out on his forehead like whipcords."[148]

At 1:30 a.m., he was awakened by chest pain. Snyder paid a visit, and he diagnosed the problem as indigestion.

He was wrong: Ike had suffered a moderate heart attack.

When Snyder realized his mistake, he called in a heart specialist, and Ike was given an electrocardiogram and sent to the hospital, where he was placed in an oxygen tent. Back in Washington, Vice President Nixon began to preside at meetings of the cabinet and the National Security Council.

All through October Ike recuperated, and at last he returned to Washington on November 11. Five thousand people met him at the airport. Then he and Mamie drove up to Gettysburg.

Would he run again?

He considered his possible Republican successors: Earl Warren, Herbert Brownell, Henry Cabot Lodge, his brother Milton. And what about Nixon? He didn't like that idea one bit.

He decided to be foxy.

Leonard Hall, the new chairman of the Republican Party, drove to Gettysburg. He told Ike that "if I go out of here and say I haven't talked politics with you, they'll call me a damned liar." "Len," Ike replied, "you go out and say what you think you should say."

So Hall issued an announcement: it would be "Ike and Dick" in 1956. "Dammit," Ike announced, "I didn't tell Len to say that."[149]

Clay drove up and told Ike that he intended to set the re-nomination process in motion. "I gave him the opportunity to call me off," Clay recalled, "but he didn't."[150]

Ike was coming to his decision: he would run if the doctors gave him their approval. The strain of another four-year term in the presidency would tax his health, but so would the strain of sitting around in frustration if he gave up the power.

He continued to talk it over with people: on January 13, he hosted a confidential dinner with Brownell, Foster Dulles, Hagerty, and others to discuss the issue.

On February 25, 1956, he returned to the White House. Three days later, he invited Clay and his wife to dinner. In their presence, he asked Mamie whether or not he ought to run. She replied, "It is your decision. If you don't do it and are unhappy because you didn't do it, it's got to be your unhappiness. If you do it and it breaks your health down, that has to be your decision too."

Ike replied, "OK. I have to do it."[151]

CHAPTER EIGHT

Commander In Chief

On February 26, 1956, Ike announced at a press conference that he would seek a second term.

He did not wish to give up the power to protect the world, and he was not impressed by other candidates.

Tensions in the Middle East had been increasing—especially between Egypt and Israel—and the Soviets worsened things by selling arms to the Egyptians. The "spirit of Geneva" had come and gone; the Russians were being provocative.

Ike was increasingly worried about the danger of nuclear war; in a meeting with Foster Dulles on January 10, he said, "The world is on the verge of an abyss." Dulles told him that he was the only man wise enough to lead.

This was of course flattery—effective, too, since Ike reciprocated in his diary by praising Dulles's "great intellectual capacity and moral courage"— but there was a good deal of truth in the notion.[1]

Ike was extraordinarily effective at keeping the peace. It was a role toward which he had been working for most of his life.

Paradoxically, his skill as a peacekeeper derived in part from his aggressive competitiveness. "I am a competitor, a fighter," he told Swede Hazlett in 1956, and his urge to run for a second term flowed in part from his "reluctance to ever accept defeat."[2]

He acknowledged that election-year battles might lead to the sort of hyperactive behavior that his cardiologists warned against, but he chose to risk it.

Early in 1956, he found himself preoccupied with the danger of nuclear war. In an interview with *Life* magazine that appeared on January 16, Foster Dulles bragged that he and Ike had used nuclear threats for the purpose of deterrence: they had taken the nation to "the brink of a new war."[3] This led to a predictable furor: Adlai Stevenson said that Dulles ought to be fired.

But the truth was that Ike, though he vetoed suggestions for the use of nuclear weapons—and though he often toned down the potentially dangerous rhetoric of Dulles—was indeed a party to ventures in nuclear "brinksmanship."

And this could lead to restless nights.

Ike was a brilliant poker player, and he knew how to bluff, but Charles de Gaulle—after he came to power again—said something to Ike about nuclear war that was terribly direct: he said France should have its own nuclear arsenal because "you, Eisenhower, would go to nuclear war for Europe," but other presidents might not.[4]

This of course makes us wonder, as Ike himself must have wondered: Would he *really* push the button and unleash the nuclear horror? Could he bring himself to do it?

That will always remain his secret, but he surely must have been haunted by the question—as we are.

He was deeply immersed in the contemplation of the nuclear peril in 1956. At a January 12 meeting of the National Security Council, he found himself appalled at how little the participants grasped the enormity of what nuclear weapons could do. He told them that "no one would be the winner" in a nuclear war, and that "the destruction might be such that we might have ultimately to go back to bows and arrows."[5]

In his acceptance speech at the 1956 Republican convention, Ike would proclaim that in the nuclear age "war has become, not just tragic, but preposterous. With such weapons, there can be no victory for anyone."[6]

And yet—the threat of using them could keep the peace, and bluffs, as everybody knows, may be called.

And what do you do when that happens?

On January 23, Ike received a report from General Harold Lee George, who chaired a "Net Evaluation Subcommittee" of the National Security

Council charged with conceptualizing the role of the armed forces after a nuclear attack—at a time when they would have to keep order and maybe even improvise a government. The report projected that America would lose roughly sixty-five percent of its population when its cities were devoured by firestorms.[7]

On April 19, Ike convened a secret meeting of cabinet officers and agency heads, and he tasked them with participating in civil defense—specifically a seven-day mobilization exercise called Operation Alert.

This was an annual exercise sponsored by the Federal Civil Defense Administration (created in 1950): a multicity exercise designed to simulate the conditions of a nuclear attack. By 1956, it included plans for evacuating government officials and bringing them to underground shelters. One of them was constructed in the mountains of North Carolina. Another one would be built in West Virginia.

The premise: a hypothetical attack upon America in which ninety-seven nuclear weapons were exploded over sixty-three cities. This, we must remember, was a time when the memory of World War II remained vivid, and people still remembered the bombings that destroyed much of Warsaw, Rotterdam, London, Coventry, Hamburg, Dresden, Berlin, Tokyo—Hiroshima. The bombing of civilian population centers had become a *normal* part of modern war.

Or had it?

There was something *abnormal*—obscene—in the principle of *one* bomb destroying a city. And the new thermonuclear bombs were roughly five hundred times more powerful than the ones that devastated Hiroshima and Nagasaki. Bombs of the earlier class were being relegated to the status of "tactical" nuclear weapons—for use on the battlefield.

The premise of Operation Alert was the vision of America with no more cities, with survivors in the hinterland doing... what?

Was there any point in developing "plans" for conditions of apocalypse? Was the exercise insane? Ike forced himself to believe that he and his officials simply had to do it—because it could happen.

How, he inquired, would "our economy" survive? The point of the exercise, he said, was to "do the normal thing when everybody else is going nuts." "Plans," he continued, were "unimportant but planning is everything."[8]

344

As Ike thought about such things—and his diary entries show that he thought about them constantly—he had to keep his nuclear strike force credible. He had to go on practicing brinksmanship.

How could a man stay sane as he dealt with such pressure?

One way to reduce the odds of nuclear war was to challenge the Soviets *peacefully*—through foreign assistance. Ike convinced Foster Dulles to embrace that strategy and use it as part of his diplomacy. The trick was getting Congress to appropriate the money.

And to make more money available, Ike pushed for ever-greater reductions in military spending.

"Someday," he told Swede Hazlett in 1956, "there is going to be a man sitting in my present chair who has not been raised in the military services and who will have little understanding of where slashes in estimates can be made with little or no damage.... I shudder to think of what could happen to this country."[9]

Here was a precursor to Ike's farewell warning about the danger of the military-industrial complex. And in his second term, the pressure from the military, from its profit-seeking contractors, and from the Atomic Energy Commission to keep escalating the arms race, became overpowering—especially by 1957.

Things were getting out of control, and Ike resented it.

In his 1956 State of the Union address, he proclaimed he was committed to one single thing: "the waging of peace, with as much resourcefulness, with as great a sense of dedication and urgency, as we have ever mustered in defense of our country in time of war."[10]

On April 21, he expressed the hope in a speech before the American Society of Newspaper Editors that "a peaceful era for mankind can emerge from a haunted decade."[11]

The practical politics of running again made him think long and hard about...Nixon. Should he be dumped?

Ever since Nixon had behaved insubordinately in the "Checkers" episode, the men had looked at one another with suspicion. Ike had tried to make use of Nixon in the fight against McCarthy, and he used him in other ways too. They got along in a detached sort of way, but Ike was more than slightly uncomfortable viewing Nixon as a possible successor.

So he tried to get Nixon off the ticket by suggesting that he move to a cabinet position, by serving as secretary of defense, which would add to his administrative experience.

But Nixon was not fooled: the suggestion to him was insulting. To leave the vice presidency would have been a demotion.

Sherman Adams and Jim Hagerty both urged Ike to dump Nixon. Ike thought about it. He told Emmet Hughes that "I've watched Dick Nixon for a long time, and he just hasn't grown. So I just haven't honestly been able to believe that he is presidential timber."[12]

But he could not bring himself to tell Richard Nixon that he wanted someone else on the ticket—someone whose politics were different.

At a press conference on April 25, he said that the situation was still in play, and Nixon could chart his own course. This gave Nixon an opening to take the initiative and approach Ike directly, so he did: he said he would be honored to continue serving as vice president. Ike agreed against his better judgment.

Why?

It was one of the strangest things about Ike's presidency that this tough-as-nails leader kept retaining the services of men whose judgment he questioned. It wasn't just Nixon; it was an assortment of rough-edged characters who might easily have been replaced with better people. This was especially true of Allen Dulles, whose incompetence would be revealed in ever-more painful terms.

Ike shuffled the deck with his military chiefs of staff, but when it came to *firing* someone, he was...hesitant.

This went beyond "politics," though politics can never be dismissed with politicians. One senses something else, however: an aversion to getting rid of people that was framed as a matter of *loyalty* to members of his team.

Was he averse to breaking off relationships?

He had certainly been decisive enough in breaking off his relationship with Kay Summersby in 1945, and perhaps this gets us to the point.

For the flip side of that proposition was the fact that he had forced himself to stay loyal to...someone else.

Consider the following metaphor—with its obvious emotional *symbolism*—that Ike used in discussing a foreign policy situation in 1956.

He was talking about a leader in the Third World whom he continued to cultivate, despite his volatile behavior. "It's just like your family," Ike said at a press conference; "every difference or spat doesn't mean that you're going to the divorce courts."[13]

A slip of the tongue?

The Suez and Hungary Crises

Election year 1956 would be a dangerous year, the most dangerous of Ike's presidency. The lull in the Cold War was over; Khrushchev repeated the old Marxist boast that world victory for communism was inevitable: "We will bury you," he proclaimed.

The Middle East was in turmoil, and Ike—severely ill for several months—would have to turn against America's own allies in World War II to keep World War III from breaking out. He was a natural for re-election—the Democrats made the hopeless gesture of nominating Adlai Stevenson again—but Ike's fortitude as commander in chief would be taxed to the utmost.

The epicenter of crisis was Egypt, and the crisis unfolded in three simultaneous dimensions: the Arab–Israeli conflict, the Third-World rebellion against the vestiges of European colonialism, and the Cold War struggle between the communist bloc and the West.

Gamal Abdel Nasser was the leader of Egypt, and he was a rising figure in Middle Eastern politics. He was anti-Israeli—no surprise—but he was a secularist and a modernizer. He was a politician who sought to play the Russians and the West against each other: to get them into a bidding war to see which side could exert the greater influence.

Meanwhile, the Israelis and Egyptians were competing for military assistance.

The British and the French saw Israel as an ally against Arab nationalism, and they provided weapons accordingly. Fighting broke out between Israel and Egypt in and around the Gaza strip in 1955, and Nasser appealed to the United States for weapons. Failing to secure assistance, he turned to the Soviets, who jumped at the opportunity.

This happened as Ike was recuperating from his heart attack.

Pivoting skillfully, Nasser gave the U.S. an opportunity to compete with the Soviets for influence. Late in 1955, he asked for American help—with supplemental assistance from Britain and the World Bank—in building the Aswan High Dam, a huge irrigation and hydroelectricity project. Foster Dulles was initially receptive, and so was Ike.

The issue was discussed at a National Security Council meeting on December 1, 1955. George Humphrey predictably objected that the U.S. would be helping Egypt down the path to socialism, and Ike calmly reminded him that Hoover Dam could be regarded as socialism. Humphrey backed down, and a financial package for the dam was approved on December 16.

But then opposition to the deal began to surface—first among supporters of Israel in Congress and then among Cold Warriors who resented Nasser's flirtation with the Soviets. Nasser was emerging more and more as a Cold War neutralist, and he recognized the government of communist China on May 16, 1956.

The rigidity of Foster Dulles took over: there could be no middle ground for him in the Manichean struggle against communism—though experience within a few months would teach him a bitter lesson about that—so Dulles began to sabotage the Aswan Dam assistance package.

Ike was at his flexible best: at a press conference on June 6, he said that "if you are waging peace, you can't be too particular about the special attitudes that different countries take. We were a young country once, and our whole policy for the first 150 years was, we were neutral."[14]

But then—two days later Ike suffered a severe attack of ileitis that would put him in the hospital and sidetrack him for months as he recovered from surgery. For weeks on end, he was distracted and depressed, and the price that he paid for keeping John Foster Dulles as his secretary of state was reflected in events.

As David Nichols put it, "Foster Dulles was left to his own devices."[15] And he began to usurp authority. On his own initiative, he took steps to cancel American assistance for Aswan Dam. Eugene Black, the president of the World Bank, warned him on June 25 that "all hell will break loose" if Dulles cancelled the assistance.[16] Arrogant, full of himself, Dulles paid no attention. The loss of American influence on Egypt did not seem to

John Foster Dulles

trouble him. He was quite content to let it go—and he had no authority to do so.

But he took steps to gain that authority—through treachery.

He visited Ike at Gettysburg and reported briefly on Aswan and Nasser. The view of the State Department on the matter, he said, was somewhat altered, and he left it at that. This was deception, for the American ambassador to Egypt did not share his views.

As Nichols has said, Ike was so distracted at the time that "this discussion of Aswan must have sounded like something happening on another planet. He had no up-to-date information and did not seek any."[17]

On July 19, when Ike was back at the White House, Dulles reported at an NSC meeting that relations with Nasser were deteriorating and support for the Aswan Dam should be withdrawn. He said that support in Congress was lacking, not mentioning the fact that he had bad-mouthed the project in talks with congressional leaders.

Ike was not yet fully compos mentis, and he made no objection, so Dulles informed the Egyptian ambassador that the dam deal was off.

A week later, Nasser announced that he was nationalizing the Suez Canal, and he would use the proceeds from the tolls to build the Aswan Dam. This announcement was made on July 26, 1956. The CIA had provided no warning that such a thing might happen.

The Canal had been operated ever since its creation by a Suez Canal Company, in which the British and the French had come to hold the majority of shares.

This crisis would never have occurred in the first place had it not been for the folly of Foster Dulles, but his bond with Ike—and Ike's reluctance to blame subordinates—prompted Ike to keep him on. He gave Foster Dulles a principal role in implementing the decisions that he handed down in the months ahead.

Dulles was chastened and obedient after overreaching—a pattern in his master–apprentice relationship with Ike that was long established.

The bond between the men grew closer.

The British and the French—outraged—made plans to seize the Suez Canal, and the British viewed the nationalization as an existential crisis: the latest in a series of humiliating demonstrations that the British Empire was declining.

Meanwhile, Foster Dulles went shuffling off to Latin America, so Ike turned to a different cabinet member for advice.

He asked Herbert Brownell whether Nasser had legitimate authority to nationalize the Canal. Yes, said Brownell, it was the power of eminent domain, the power of governments to take possession of territory within their own limits.

That was the question that Ike should have asked in 1953 before he let Allen Dulles overturn the governments of Iran and Guatemala when they exercised the very same power.

Brownell's response in 1956 was in accord with Ike's instinctive sympathy for Third-World nationalism—a sympathy that he had shown toward Mosaddegh before the Dulles brothers led him astray.

It is a commentary that CIA operatives attempted on several occasions to circumvent Ike's authority in the Suez crisis. Nichols has observed that "the men in the [CIA] ranks erroneously assumed that the Dulles brothers were running American foreign policy," and they had no understanding of "Eisenhower's grip on decision making."[18]

Ike should have listened when Doolittle pointed out the grievous weaknesses of Allen Dulles. He would receive other warnings in the years ahead.

When Ike became aware of the fact that the British and the French planned to challenge Nasser's action, he wrote to British prime minister Anthony Eden about "the unwisdom *even of contemplating* the use of military force at the moment [original emphasis]."[19]

When Foster Dulles, upon returning to town, suggested an international consortium to run the Suez Canal, Ike squelched him, asking, "How would we like an international consortium running the Panama Canal?" Ike continued: "Nasser embodies the emotional demands of the people of the area for independence and for 'slapping the White Man down.'" Opposing his action could "array the world from Dakar to the Philippine Islands against us."[20]

The Joint Chiefs of Staff recommended a coup against Nasser. Ike resolutely said no.

He himself was displeased with Nasser, but he kept his response to the situation analytical. There were many factors to consider: anticolonialism, Arab-Israeli hostilities, the Soviets, the perils of a crisis that could lead to nuclear war, long-term access to oil for the United States and Europe, and the vital importance of the Suez Canal for international logistics.

He decided that the vital issue was whether or not the Egyptians would operate the Canal efficiently and fairly. The Suez Canal Company had been bound by the terms of an 1888 convention to provide access to signatory nations, and the question was whether Nasser would provide fair access. Since the user nations paid tolls, it was surely in his interest to do so—especially since he intended to finance the Aswan Dam from the proceeds. Compensation for the shareholders of the Suez Canal Company would also have to be arranged.

In October, the Israeli prime minister, David Ben-Gurion, reached a secret deal with the British and the French: they would mount a joint military operation to topple Nasser and seize the Canal. The Israelis would furnish the pretext by invading Sinai on October 29, just a few days before the American presidential election. The British and the French would then issue a bogus ultimatum to the Israelis and Egyptians: stop fighting or else the British and French would intervene and establish Anglo–French administration of the Canal.

In 1950, the United States, Britain, and France had signed a "Tripartite Declaration" pledging to support victims of aggression in the Middle East. The British and the French would use this promise as part of their intervention pretext.

In what Nichols has called "a remarkable failure of intelligence analysis," the CIA reported that the possibility of military action by the British and the French was very slight. [21] Allen Dulles would continue to reveal his incompetence with other ill-informed predictions in 1956.

Meanwhile, crises multiplied. On October 23, an uprising in Hungary was repressed by communist authorities. The Soviets sent in troops, and then withdrew them. The rebels had heard about Khrushchev's "secret speech"—the speech he had given months earlier to the 20th Congress of the Soviet Communist Party, the speech in which he denounced the excesses of Stalin to his fellow Soviet communists. The speech hinted at the possibility for sweeping liberalization. So a new Hungarian government began to initiate sweeping reforms.

Allen Dulles predicted that the turning point in the Cold War had arrived. As usual, he did not know what he was talking about: his intelligence (such as it was) was pitiful. He had no information to provide.

A political crisis in the Kremlin developed: the Hungarians were going too far. And so the Soviets invaded again on November 4 with massive force. Here was communism at its most brutal, and defenders of democracy were outraged. Clare Boothe Luce—Republican activist, socialite, celebrity, and United States ambassador to Italy—implored Ike to prevent "freedom's holy light" from "being extinguished in blood and iron over there."[22]

But what could Ike do?

What could anyone do when the Soviets had nuclear weapons? Besides, Hungary was in Ike's opinion "as inaccessible as Tibet" when it came to American military operations.[23] He sent a sharp note to Bulganin demanding the withdrawal of the Soviet troops and self-determination for Hungary, but beyond that, his hands were tied.

The Israeli operation commenced on October 29.

When Ike learned about it, he suspected at once that the British and the French were behind it. He summoned Foster Dulles and ordered him to send a message to Israel. "Foster, you tell them, Goddamnit, that we're going to apply sanctions, we're going to the United Nations, we're going to do everything that there is so that we can stop this thing."[24]

He felt double-crossed, and he prepared for an open rift with his allies from World War II. He also decided that the crisis transcended the presidential election. "I don't care whether I'm re-elected or not," he declared.[25]

He had a resolution introduced in the U.N. Security Council calling for Israeli withdrawal and a cease-fire. The Soviets supported it, and the British and French vetoed it. They issued their own demand for a cease-fire, to be followed by an Anglo–French occupation of the Canal zone. Nasser indignantly refused. So the British and French began bombing.

Nasser sank a freighter full of cement to block the Suez Canal. Before long, he sank a whole series of ships. His political allies in Syria destroyed oil pipelines that the British depended upon.

Ike moved at once to put even more pressure on the British and the French—especially the British. He sent the United States Sixth Fleet in the Mediterranean toward Egypt. He turned to George Humphrey for advice about economic sanctions. He had Foster Dulles appeal the vetoed Security Council resolution to the U.N. General Assembly, where it passed.

On November 2, Foster Dulles was rushed to the hospital with severe abdominal pain. It turned out to be the colon cancer that would kill him several years later.

Ike continued on his own: he reached out to U.N. Secretary General Dag Hammarskjöld to organize a U.N. peacekeeping force that would preempt the British and the French. On November 4, the peacekeeping force was authorized by the General Assembly.

At a Republican rally in Philadelphia, Ike proclaimed, "We cannot and will not condone armed aggression—no matter who the attacker," adding that "the only way to win World War III is to prevent it."[26]

On November 5, the Anglo–French invasion of Egypt began. Ike cabled Anthony Eden and made it clear that he wanted a reversal. He put the matter diplomatically: "if your troops did nothing but land," he wrote, "we might much more swiftly develop a solution that would be acceptable to both sides and to the world."[27] But the iron fist behind the velvet glove began clenching. Ike wrote privately that while "Britain must continue to be our best friend," the British had been "stupid;" they had "allowed their distrust and hatred of Nasser to blind their judgment and they have used the wrong vehicle for carrying on their fight to deflate him."[28]

And he would show them who was boss.

He would have to bend the British to his will. Even more than the French, the British were susceptible to pressure brought to bear behind the scenes.

The point of maximum leverage was economic, so Ike, with advice from George Humphrey, put the squeeze on the British by destabilizing the new international monetary order that was crafted during World War II.

Here is a sketch of how he did it—beginning with some background.

In the Great Depression, many nations including the United States began to modify "the gold standard." Under the terms of the Gold Reserve Act of 1934, Americans had to surrender any gold in their possession (with limited exceptions for jewelers, dentists, coin collectors, and so forth) in exchange for paper currency. The exchanges took place at local banks under the coordination of the Federal Reserve System.

The gold was melted and shipped to Fort Knox, where it was placed in storage. No more solid gold dollars would be minted. Moreover, paper dollars could no longer be exchanged at banks for solid gold coins. The Gold Reserve Act gave the president power to set a "gold weight" for the dollar, i.e., declare what percentage of an ounce of gold was equivalent to a dollar.

In World War II, the system was modified again when the 1944 "Bretton Woods" monetary pact was negotiated. This was the system that Ike would briefly sabotage in 1956 to put pressure on the British. No doubt George Humphrey instructed him.

The goal of the Bretton Woods system was to stabilize currency values by "pegging" them to the dollar. The dollar was accordingly given the status of an international "reserve currency," and participating nations had "dollar accounts" at the new International Monetary Fund (IMF), set up to help member nations keep the exchange values of their nations' currencies stable.

The value of the pound had been pegged in U.S. dollars at $2.78.

To maintain this value, the British government, in partnership with the Bank of England (which it owned), had to buy its own currency from time to time in U.S. dollars (i.e., convert dollars to pounds) on the international exchange, with IMF help. The point of this procedure was to prop up "demand" for the pound, thus maintaining its value.

In the midst of the Suez crisis, the value of the pound began to drop, and the British—especially Harold Macmillan, who was chancellor of the exchequer—sensed the hidden hand of Ike.

The U.S. Federal Reserve System started selling pounds from its various accounts to drive down their value. In his memoirs, Macmillan noted that the "run on the pound" had been centered in New York, with the Federal Reserve System spearheading the effort.[29]

The British were forced to use dollars from their various dollar accounts around the world to purchase pounds. These dollar accounts were running short, so the deputy prime minister placed a call to George Humphrey asking for a loan. Humphrey's answer: yes, of course, just as soon as the British withdrew from Suez.

Then the British requested to withdraw the funds (in U.S. dollars) that they had on deposit with the International Monetary Fund. Under IMF rules, the U.S. Treasury could block the request, and Humphrey did.

Macmillan told Anthony Eden that a cease-fire in Suez was imperative for the sake of British finances. Moreover, the British were beginning to run desperately short of oil.

Meanwhile, the situation became more dangerous when the Soviets threatened to intervene. Bulganin proposed to Ike that the Americans and Soviets intervene *jointly* against the British, French, and Israelis. Ike was worried about this. He suspected that this proposal was setting the stage for *unilateral* Soviet action.

And he may have been right. On November 5, Bulganin sent messages to Israel, Britain, and France warning that their attack on Egypt would be countered by states "possessing all types of weapons of destruction," and that "we are full of determination to crush the aggressor and re-establish peace ... using force."[30]

It was obvious that the Soviets were trying to deflect attention from their ugly intervention in Hungary by posing as defenders of Egypt. What if they tried to intervene by putting Soviet troops into Egypt?

Ike told some aides that "we may be dealing here with the opening gambit of an ultimatum. We have to be positive ... in our every word, every step. And if those fellows [the Soviets] start something, we may have to hit them—and, if necessary with everything in the bucket."[31]

He did not intend to allow the Russians to put ground troops into the Middle East. But was he prepared to threaten nuclear war if they tried it?

All of this was happening on the eve of Election Day 1956.

The path ahead became clear to Ike: the U.N. peacekeeping force was the key, and *none* of the great powers should be allowed to contribute any troops to it: not America, not Britain, not France, and, most of all, not Russia. America's role—*Ike's* role—was to back up U.N. authority by threatening other powers (i.e., Russia) if they tried to preempt the U.N.

By threatening them how?

With war.

He put American forces in the Mediterranean on full alert, and he refused to reply to Bulganin's message on joint intervention. That refusal *in and of itself* sent a message, but Ike supplemented it with a *public* statement proclaiming that "neither Soviet nor any other military forces should now enter the Middle East except under United Nations mandate." To do otherwise, he said, "would violate the United Nations Charter," and all U.N. members, including the United States, would have to "oppose any such effort."[32]

The strain on Ike was so great that his health began to give way, and Dr. Snyder was called in. According to Snyder, Ike told him that "if he were a dictator, he would tell Russia that if they moved a finger, he would drop our entire stock of atomic weapons on them."[33]

A Soviet attack on the British and the French would trigger the NATO alliance, and America would have to act. Ike believed that a congressional declaration of war would not be necessary. The NATO pact was sufficient.

The fighting in Egypt intensified, and Ike told Sherman Adams and Allen Dulles that "if the Soviets attack the French and British directly, we would be in war, and we would be justified in taking military action even if Congress were not in session."[34]

Ike tried to *force* himself to relax. Members of the gang were flown into town for bridge games, and Dr. Snyder prescribed tranquilizers to help the president sleep.

Anthony Eden was under severe pressure—not only on the financial front but on the political front. His foreign policy in the Middle East was becoming extremely unpopular, and the opposition Labour Party was demanding his scalp. So he finally agreed to a cease-fire, and Ike called him up to offer thanks.

Eden tried to explore the possibility of British participation in the effort to clear the Suez Canal. He said that British troops had the necessary expertise, but Ike said no. British meddling, he asserted, would increase the chance that the Soviets would try to barge in: "I am afraid the Red boy is going to demand the lion's share" of participation if the great powers were involved. Eden kept probing, so Ike let him have it, saying "If you don't get out of Port Said tomorrow, I'll cause a run on the pound and drive it down to zero."[35]

Ike won the election of 1956 in another landslide.

He tried not to get too excited. He told Emmet Hughes that "*emotions are the thing you gotta watch out for.*"[36]

The threat of Soviet intervention in the Middle East would continue for several weeks, and so Ike kept American military forces on alert. The process of getting the British and the French to withdraw from Egypt took some time.

Meanwhile, Ike looked to the future. He decided that the Suez crisis was a sign that America had to play a greater role in the Middle East indefinitely. He told the National Security Council on November 8 that America should "take any kind of action that ... will exclude from the area Soviet influence."[37]

In 1957, Ike asked Congress to give him statutory power to intervene with conventional forces in the Middle East as needed. It was the kind of authorization that he had received in the Quemoy–Matsu crisis of 1955: discretionary authority to deploy U.S. force as necessary in response to provocations. "The existing vacuum in the Middle East must be filled by the United States before it is filled by Russia," Ike told Congress.[38] This became known as the Eisenhower Doctrine.

Congress granted that authority on March 5, 1957, along with authority to offer economic assistance.

Interventions with conventional forces would of course entail a significant modification of the New Look. Ike was forced to embrace the doctrine of "flexible response"—at least to some extent.

On November 19, Anthony Eden began to succumb to a physical breakdown. Macmillan took over. He told the American ambassador that he could get the cabinet to withdraw British troops from Egypt if America would agree to give the British financial assistance—and help to restore the flow of oil.

Ike replied that assistance would be forthcoming once British troops began their withdrawal from Egypt. On November 29, the British cabinet agreed to begin the process on December 3. The last of the British troops departed from Egypt on December 22. In January 1957, Macmillan succeeded Eden as prime minister.

Ike had kept the peace again, and he had forced his will upon everyone. He had no regrets, despite the damage that his policies had inflicted on the British and the French. He held out the olive branch to them in 1957, and the bad feelings faded away.

Ike's prestige in the Third World—and around the world—soared. "Never has there been such a tremendous acclaim for the President's policy," reported Henry Cabot Lodge.[39]

As William Hitchcock has said, Ike "demonstrated uncanny discipline, steadfast leadership, and cool judgment."[40]

Little Rock

Ike's first presidential achievements on behalf of civil rights were comparatively easy. He worked behind the scenes, using hidden-hand methods to preserve the peace of mind of all concerned. Moreover, he had the unquestionable authority—federal authority—to desegregate the District of Columbia and the armed forces.

So he did.

After *Brown*, however, things changed: he was caught between belligerent racists invoking "states' rights" and Black leaders who wanted an *oracular* style of presidential leadership—presidential fervor that would give the white racists the condemnation they deserved, and then follow up with condign punishment.

That was not the way of doing things that Ike preferred when he became president. It was not his particular…"skill set."

As we have seen—and for reasons already explored—the method Ike preferred was to create calm, establish a mood of equilibrium for the American people, and then take effective action out of sight.

He no longer had the luxury of doing things that way by the end of 1955 when it came to civil rights. The sickening murder of a Black teenager named Emmett Till by Mississippi racists prompted calls for Ike to take action like an angel of vengeance and condemn the whole culture of southern white racism in scathing terms.

His inability to do so—his failure to do so—was a measure not only of his temperamental limitations but his mission to pacify America. And these things were interrelated.

Brownell convinced him to endorse a proposition that would have been unthinkable a few years earlier—sending an administration-backed civil rights bill to Congress.

Moreover, he convinced Ike to make preparations for sending troops to southern states if white violence and statutory authority gave him grounds for doing so. The army developed a secret plan to give riot-control instruction to selected units like the 101st Airborne.

Ike did send a civil rights bill to Congress in 1956, while making it clear that its passage was unlikely in an election year. The House of Representatives approved it, and it would be introduced again in 1957.

The bill as drafted by Brownell created a new civil rights commission and a new civil rights division in the Justice Department. It would empower the attorney general to file suits against people who interfered with civils rights, and this would include both the right to vote and (since *Brown*) the right to attend an integrated school.

Ike would try to sell this as a voting rights bill, but its significance extended much further, as the southern bigots could see.

The civil-suit provision was important for two reasons: (1) Civil suits would come before a judge instead of a jury. All-white juries in the South were notorious for their sleazy and farcical decisions. For example, the murderers of Emmett Till had been acquitted by an all-white jury, *after which they confessed.* (2) Defiance of rulings from the bench would constitute contempt of court, and this might very well justify using the enforcement power of the federal government, depending on circumstances.

This draft legislation caused angry disagreements among members of the cabinet as well as agency heads. FBI Director J. Edgar Hoover claimed that most civil rights leaders were incited by communists. He would go on using this for years as a pretext for wiretapping and persecuting people like Martin Luther King.

John Foster Dulles said the administration should "go slow," and he warned that the Brownell's bill, if passed, could "send a large portion of white southerners to jail. Just can't do that."[41] He went on to say that one half of the country could not impose its conscience on the other half of the country.

Meanwhile, southerners like South Carolina governor Jimmy Byrnes warned that the *Brown* decision might prompt southern states to simply eliminate their public school systems. Ike took that threat seriously.

At a news conference on March 14, 1956, Ike said that when it came to progress in civil rights, "we can only believe that the good sense, the common sense, of Americans will bring this thing along."[42] On more than one occasion, he confessed he was "at sea" as he pondered how to lead a nation that might be torn apart by racial hatred, mob violence, and collisions of federal and state power.[43]

White resistance in the South began to get worse, as white racists bombed the homes of activists who led the Montgomery bus boycott. They bombed Black churches, and they beat Black women and children. A white supremacist reign of terror had begun.

"White Citizens Councils" were created to threaten and intimidate Blacks. Senators Strom Thurmond of South Carolina and Richard Russell of Georgia wrote a "Southern Manifesto" signed by 101 members of Congress pledging to overturn *Brown* and defend the "reserved rights of the States." This manifesto was announced in the House of Representatives on March 12, 1956, by Representative Howard Smith of Virginia.

Journalist James J. Kilpatrick started touting a constitutional doctrine of state "interposition"—a resurrection of John C. Calhoun's doctrine of "nullification." Southern politicians by the scores rushed to embrace it.

There were cross-burnings, not only in the South, but in Washington, D.C.—in the yards of Supreme Court justices.

Ike hoped to reduce white supremacist violence by urging patience and calm—and by enlisting the clergy. He asked the evangelist Billy Graham to support integration, knowing that his voice would be heeded in the Bible Belt.

In one southern city after another in 1956, attempts at school integration were met by violence. Civil rights leaders began to turn upon Ike: they demanded that he institute federal action. But his strategy was to wait until the 1956 election was over and the power of the presidency would be his for another four years.

The Republican Party platform in 1956 did not endorse the *Brown* decision. Ike and Brownell had a quarrel about this, but Ike was adamant.

No less than on the global scene, Ike meant to keep the peace—if he could. He declared that when it came to enforcing the *Brown* decision, he was sworn to defend "the Constitution," and he meant to do so.

His composure began to break down—his calm demeanor began to crack—when he expressed his frustration in private with the position in which he found himself. As Nichols has observed, "the conflicts over school desegregation were relentless and maddening for a president who prided himself on orderly planning and efficient execution of those plans."[44]

So there were times in 1956, as Ike recovered from intestinal surgery and faced the ever-changing challenges of Suez, when he sounded a note of despair about *Brown* and civil rights. Emmet Hughes recalled that on one occasion Ike said that the *Brown* decision "set back progress in the

South at least 15 years." He also said that "we can't demand *perfection* in these moral questions—it's not going to come—all we can do is keep working toward a goal and keep it high. And the guy who tries to tell me that you can do these things by *force* is just plain nuts."[45]

But he *would* use force in 1957 to enforce the *Brown* decision, and his action was one of the defining moments in the nation's civil rights revolution.

As he got the Suez situation under better control, Ike found his confidence returning on civil rights. In the spring of 1957, he and Brownell decided they would get a civil rights bill from Congress—the strongest bill they could finesse.

Die-hard southern racists like Senator Richard Russell of Georgia and James Eastland of Mississippi branded Ike's civil rights bill a new federal tyranny, and they launched a hue and cry about the right to a jury trial.

Russell complained—quite accurately—that the legislation as drafted by Brownell was not limited to voting rights. It provided the attorney general with power to prosecute civil rights issues across the board.

Russell warned that the launching of civil suits by the attorney general could lead to "invasions" of the South by federal troops, and he raised the specter of a brand-new Reconstruction.

Civil rights leaders like Martin Luther King demanded action in response to the terrorism and murder by southern racists.

Ike employed his standard Middle Way techniques: he distanced himself from both sides, and he called the legislation innocuous.

As theatrics, he put himself on record as an *advocate* of states' rights—he condemned the evils of "centralized government"—*except*, he explained, in cases where state inaction or perfidy created a "vacuum of power" that demanded a constitutional remedy.

When Martin Luther King and other civil rights leaders asked to meet with him, he asked them to delay their requests until after a civil rights bill had passed.

He repudiated the idea of sending federal troops into the South—even as he made contingent plans for doing it.

The House passed the civil rights bill again in 1957, so the fight was thrown into the Senate—with its endless delays.

Ike and his team developed a clever way to bypass the racist-dominated Senate Judiciary Committee and force the bill onto the floor. Ike worked with Lyndon Johnson to avert the threat of a filibuster.

Ike knew that LBJ was working both sides of the street when it came to civil rights—he knew that modus operandi.

LBJ had presidential ambitions, and he wanted to burnish his image as a civil rights reformer. But he would also cater to the South by forcing compromises that would weaken the bill. One such "compromise" was the tacking on of amendments that would guarantee trial by jury—thus gutting the bill.

Ike was enraged when that happened.

He condemned the Senate Republicans who broke with the administration, and he chastised liberals in both parties who convinced themselves that a weak civil rights bill was better than none.

He was fighting mad, and he threatened to veto the watered-down legislation. On August 13, 1957, Ike said that he was "in favor of fighting it out to the end to prevent the pseudo liberals from getting away with their sudden alliance with the Southerners on a sham bill."[46] At a cabinet meeting, he said there was "not much forgiveness in my soul. We've taken political defeats in the past four years, but this one is the worst."[47] White House aides remembered that he was "angrier than at any time before in his four and one-half years in the White House."[48]

Ike's veto threat forced Johnson to the bargaining table: he signaled he was ready to strengthen the bill—just a bit.

So the Justice Department came up with a compromise formula. Jury trials were restored, but *only if the penalty for contempt of court should exceed $300 and sixty days in jail.* LBJ bargained them down to forty-five days in jail, and the deal was struck.

The Civil Rights Act of 1957—weak, but the very first piece of civil rights legislation to emerge from Congress since Reconstruction—was passed on August 29.

In 1957, the school board of Little Rock, Arkansas, approved a plan for the gradual integration of public schools over seven years. The first step would be the admission in the fall semester of a few Black students to Little Rock's Central High School.

The "Mothers' League of Central High School" filed suit and asked the state's demagogic governor, Orval Faubus, to intervene.

Faubus got an injunction from the Pulaski County Chancery Court blocking the integration plan, but Thurgood Marshall of the NAACP got the plan reinstated by Judge Ronald N. Davies of the U.S. District Court for the Eastern District of Arkansas.

On September 4, Faubus ordered the Arkansas National Guard to surround Central High School. Their presence was augmented by a screaming mob of five hundred racists. Faubus called integration a threat to public order and safety, and the nine Black students who tried to enter the school were turned away.

Press coverage of the incident featured photographs showing the bestiality of the white mob in such vivid terms that the incident became news around the world.

Judge Davies requested the Justice Department to intervene, and this gave Brownell a chance to send FBI agents and federal marshals.

Brownell followed up by announcing that Faubus could be cited for contempt of court or even prosecuted for a federal crime. If nothing else worked, the president could send in troops.[49]

This was probably the occasion that Brownell, the Lincoln Republican, had been hoping for. Sherman Adams would remember later on that Brownell was "a man of great tenacity… who could not be shaken when his mind was firmly made up."[50]

Faubus fired off a telegram to Ike protesting the intervention of federal authorities. Ike supported Brownell, and he promised to back up the integration edict "by every legal means at my command."[51]

Meanwhile, on September 9, Ike signed into law the Civil Rights Act of 1957, which covered voting rights only. The subsequent Civil Rights Act of 1960, which Ike would also introduce, gave slightly better protection.

On September 10, Brownell requested Judge Davies to issue an injunction against the use of the Arkansas National Guard to block integration.

Meanwhile, Congressman Brooks Hays of Arkansas requested Ike to meet with Faubus. So the meeting was arranged to take place on September 14 at the naval base in Newport, Rhode Island, where Ike was on vacation. He had gone there for the purpose of playing golf at the Newport Country Club. For several years, Newport had been serving as his "summer White House."

Brownell, Sherman Adams, and Hays attended the meeting.

Ike told Faubus that "where the federal government has assumed jurisdiction and this is upheld by the Supreme Court, there can only be one outcome: the state will lose. I don't want to see any governor humiliated."[52] He told Faubus to command the National Guardsmen to protect the right of the Black children to enter the high school. Faubus seemed to agree.

But then Faubus broke his word when he returned to Arkansas, and Ike was furious. Brownell advised him to wait until Judge Davies issued a court order commanding integration. If Faubus defied it, Ike could intervene.

Davies ordered Faubus to cease interfering with desegregation, whereupon Faubus withdrew the National Guard. But then the governor left the state: he departed for the Southern Governors Conference at Sea Island, Georgia.

On September 23, a mob of over a thousand shrieking racists descended on Central High School. City police held them off as the Black students entered the school, but then the mob broke through the barricades and invaded the school building. The deputy police chief rescued the children and evacuated them. The mayor of Little Rock sent a telegram to Ike pleading for assistance.

Ike prepared to send in the army.

No less than at Normandy, he would use massive power. "In my career," he told Brownell, "I have learned that if you have to use force, use overwhelming force."[53] He told army chief of staff Maxwell Taylor to prepare the 101st Airborne at Fort Campbell, Kentucky, to be flown into Little Rock.

That was the very same unit whose paratroopers were dropped behind enemy lines on the eve of D-Day.

Ike announced that "the Federal law and the orders of a United States District Court cannot be flouted with impunity by any individual or any mob of extremists. I will use the full power of the United States including whatever force may be necessary to prevent the obstruction of the law."[54]

Ike issued a proclamation calling upon the mob to disperse, but the mob did not disperse.

Instead, an armed riot spread through Little Rock, and the city was out of control. So on September 24, Ike federalized the Arkansas National Guard—thus depriving Faubus of its use—and ordered the 101st Airborne to occupy the city.

As the troops arrived, John Chancellor of NBC News recorded his impressions: "As they marched in, the clean, sharp sound of their boots clacking on the street was a reminder of their professionalism. There was something majestic about the scene: it was a moment at once thrilling and somehow frightening as well."[55]

Ike's action was audacious.

And it was fitting for a Republican president—a president from Lincoln's party—to send the army into a southern state to protect Blacks. During Reconstruction, Ulysses S. Grant had sent the army to suppress the Ku Klux Klan. It can be argued the army should have been kept in the South for many decades after that.

Hundreds of lives would be lost or ruined because federal force was withdrawn from the former Confederate states too soon. From the 1870s onward, lynchers murdered hundreds of Blacks with impunity. Like the Nazis, they deserved to be forced into total surrender and put on trial for their crimes.

It is one of the outrages of our nation's history that that never happened.

Ike couldn't make up for all the many years of abdication, but he did take a powerful step to enforce the rule of law and command justice.

Martin Luther King Jr. wrote to Ike proclaiming that "the overwhelming majority of southerners, Negro and white, stand firmly behind your resolution."[56] Jazz musician Louis Armstrong was more emotional. "Daddy," he wrote to Ike, "if and when you decide to take those little Negro children personally into Central High School along with your marvelous troops, take me along."[57]

Senator Richard Russell of Georgia sent Ike an absurd letter comparing the troops of the 101st Airborne to Nazi stormtroopers. Ike had no intention of letting him get away with that, and he sent an indignant reply.[58]

Characteristically, though, Ike sought to keep the nation calm. "I know," he said, "that the overwhelming majority of the people of the South—including those of Arkansas and Little Rock—are of good will, united in their efforts to preserve and respect the law even when they disagree with it."[59]

Earl Warren would complain years later that such gestures of conciliation toward the South were unwise. But Ike's methods were different from Warren's, and his hidden-hand techniques had other sources.

Some have viewed the conciliatory statements that Ike made about southern white attitudes as evidence of cowardice—or even racism. That evidence deserves to be compared with his *deeds* on behalf of integration.[60]

It is true that a rift between Warren and Ike would develop in the aftermath of *Brown*. A near-pervasive legend holds that Ike resented *Brown* and called Warren's appointment the biggest mistake he ever made.

There can be no question that the early good relations between them disintegrated. And there is no question either that Ike chose to dodge the civil rights issue whenever he deemed it expedient during his second term.

But his actions on behalf of civil rights in 1957 consisted of *deeds*—deeds stronger than any other president had performed since Reconstruction.

Sputnik and its Aftermath

In the Suez and Little Rock crises, Ike had been at the zenith of his powers—poised, in charge, a commander in chief who decided what he wanted, faced up to opposition, used maximum force, and held his ground. He never went further than he needed to go to gain his objectives, which were justice, safety, and peace.

He acted out on the global scale the epiphany that came to him in childhood: he would emulate the lawmen who made his hometown safe.

He always followed up with goodwill, since his goal was an age of good feelings.

Americans were overwhelmingly in favor of what he was doing, and American popular culture in the mid-1950s was rife with the themes of his leadership.

Hollywood poured out a steady stream of the westerns that Ike loved to watch: stories devoted to the never-ending challenge of establishing a safe haven for yourself and your family, civics lessons on the range.

Ike was par excellence the leader whom Americans felt they had to have: the old guardian who knew what the rising generation needed, a leader who would give them a world in which it was safe to fall in love, get married, have children.

A world without war.

Rock 'n' Roll culture—a paean to youth—was in a roundabout way a secret tribute to the leader who had once been a crazy kid himself, who had gotten into trouble when he danced the wrong way with the girls, and who remembered all that. There was something in the smile of Dwight Eisenhower that made you want to be carefree and to savor the sweetness of living—made you want to *relax*.

Ike *knew* what it took to make Americans happy, so Americans... *liked* him.

Many loved him.

Americans loved him at the height of his powers, but they were suddenly shaken in October 1957.

The Russians took the world by surprise when they "beat America into space," and Ike was on the spot.

He recovered: his popularity surged again, and he could have won a third term easily in 1960, if the Constitution had not been amended to preclude the option.

Still, something fundamental was changing, and the sureness of Ike's command seemed open to question. He was after all approaching seventy, and he would not remain at the height of his powers forever. The twilight of his presidency was coming.

On October 4, 1957, the Russians launched the first Earth satellite, Sputnik I, and panic spread over America. The effect was like another Pearl Harbor, and the questions that people asked were full of urgency: Could the satellite pose a military threat? Was the missile that launched it a threat? Was it

A presidential portrait of Ike that projects his public persona.

stronger and better than the rockets America possessed? Had Americans fallen behind in scientific preeminence? Was there a "missile gap?"

Should there be a "space race?"

At a news conference on October 9, Ike sought to calm the nation down. There was no need to worry, he said. The satellite was no threat, and the United States was keeping up in the development of guided missiles.

369

But then the Russians launched a second and larger satellite on November 3.

The navy, in conjunction with the National Science Foundation, had been given the responsibility for putting an American research satellite into orbit for International Geophysical Year. This was the Vanguard project. But when the navy tried to launch its satellite on December 8, the Vanguard rocket lost thrust, tumbled, and exploded on the launch pad at Cape Canaveral, Florida.

It was a humiliating spectacle.

The army, which had already developed rockets that could launch a satellite, came to rescue. On January 31, 1958, the army launched Explorer I, but the damage to America's prestige and self-confidence had been done.

The Democrats were swift to take advantage as they warmed up for the midterm and presidential elections. Ike would not be running again in 1960, but the depiction of him as an out-of-touch leader was good politics for them.

The rocket that launched Sputnik I, the R-7 Semyorka, had been in development since 1953, and it was an ICBM—an intercontinental ballistic missile. The United States had been developing its own ICBM, the Atlas, since 1951. The Atlas and the R-7 were *both* introduced in 1957, which meant that the rival nations were keeping pace with one another.

The Soviets were *not* ahead of the United States in missile development.

The U-2 overflights of Russia had commenced on July 4, 1956, and Ike was delighted by the clarity of the photographs.

The Russians filed a diplomatic protest. Given the delicacy of the situation, Ike insisted on approving all the overflights himself, and he plotted their routes with Richard Bissell, the CIA official whom Allen Dulles put in charge of the program.

In truth, *it suited Ike's secret purposes to have the Soviets launch the first satellite*. Why? *Because it set the precedent for "freedom of space,"* and the Russians would have no basis for complaining about the *surveillance* satellites—the spy satellites—that Ike was developing. The fact that the Russians had launched their own satellite first implied that they took it for granted—they *presumed*—that they *had the right* to send objects into orbit above other nations, and above their air space.

Lockheed—the same company that had developed the U-2 spy plane—was also developing reconnaissance satellite designs for America.

Their satellite program was first dubbed "SAMOS," and two different ideas were explored: the idea of a satellite designed to beam electronic images back to Earth and the idea of sending film to Earth in capsules.

The capsules would plunge through the atmosphere, deploy parachutes, and then get plucked from midair by planes that would be using an ingeniously designed harness system. The concept was developed at RAND and adopted by the air force WS-117L program in August 1957.[61]

The reconnaissance team at Lockheed developed these two alternative ideas—direct transmission of images versus the conveyance of film that was sent back to Earth in recovery capsules—into rival satellite designs: SAMOS, which would beam electronic images to Earth, and CORONA, which would send film to Earth in capsules.

These concepts were explained to Ike in a White House meeting on February 7, 1958.[62]

CORONA turned out to be the better design.

Ike had put the reconnaissance mission under CIA control, with the air force providing support by launching the satellites and picking up the capsules.[63]

A Thor–Agena rocket combination would be used for the reconnaissance program. The rockets were launched from Vandenberg air force base in California, and the public was told that these satellite launches were part of an innocuous air force project: a "DISCOVERER" program whose satellites were purely scientific. This was a cover story.

In order to maintain the fiction and preserve deniability, some of the so-called "DISCOVERER" satellites were scientific. But the others were CORONAs, and the two craft were indistinguishable. The hidden components were tucked into the second-stage Agena rocket, and the whole craft went into orbit.

On the Defensive

On November 25, 1957, Ike walked into his office and felt alarmingly dizzy. When he sat down, he found that he could not read the papers in front of him. He buzzed for Ann Whitman, and the words that he tried to speak to her were unintelligible. He felt panic. "It was impossible for me to express any coherent thought whatsoever," he remembered. "I began to feel truly helpless."[64]

General Goodpaster decided to call in some neurological specialists, who quickly determined that Ike had suffered a spasm in the capillaries of the brain—a minor stroke.

The next day he felt better, but he was still not back to normal. He was due to attend a NATO conference, and Foster Dulles suggested sending Nixon instead. Ike decided to go himself, and he resolved to resign the presidency if he could not perform successfully.

He did fine.

But it was a sign—and in 1958, at the midway point of his final term in office, it was time to complete his life's work. He sent a letter to Nixon setting forth the conditions under which he should assume presidential powers if Ike were disabled. "You will decide," he instructed Nixon, when the time to take over had arrived, and "the decision will be yours only."[65]

The post-Sputnik panic kept getting worse.

Its sources had been building for a long time, not least of all because of the civil defense program. People had begun to build "fallout shelters"— underground bunkers to help them survive a thermonuclear blast and its radioactive aftermath.

After Sputnik, these fears of nuclear war became pervasive, and the fear reached the point of hysteria when Khrushchev started bragging about how far his new missiles could strike, and how many of them the Russians intended to produce. He said that they would be turning them out "like sausages."

A new novel, On the Beach, by Neville Shute, depicted the aftermath of a nuclear war: everyone dies.

Many had been advocating an enormous federal construction program to build fallout shelters. Ike was opposed, but he decided to confront the issue by appointing a citizens' commission to consider the nuclear threat.

The decision backfired.

Ike appointed H. Rowan Gaither, former head of the Ford Foundation, to run the commission. Gaither chaired the RAND Corporation, and the commission's report was presented to the National Security Council on November 7, 1957. The principal author was Paul Nitze, the hard-liner who had written NSC-68 back in 1950.

Deterrence and Survival in the Nuclear Age—Nitze's report—predicted that the United States would be vulnerable to a Soviet ICBM attack by 1959, and that the risks would increase every year unless the United States spent vast amounts of money on additional missiles and bombers, supplemented by a program to build fallout shelters.

The report was supposed to be secret, but its recommendations were leaked. "Enormous Arms Outlay Is Held Vital for Survival," blared the headline of a *Washington Post* story on December 20, 1957, authored by Chalmers Roberts.

Three Democratic senators who were planning to seek their party's presidential nomination in 1960—Lyndon Johnson, Stuart Symington, and John F. Kennedy—started harping on the theme that America was behind in missile development due to Ike's negligence.

Johnson chaired the Preparedness Subcommittee of the Senate Armed Services Committee. On November 25, 1957, he began to hold hearings on the theme of America's preparedness. Impressive witnesses—Edward Teller (a physicist who had designed the hydrogen bomb), Vannevar Bush (a presidential science adviser during World War II), and Wernher von Braun (the army rocket scientist who ran the German V-2 program)— warned that the Soviets were ahead of the United State in missile technology.

Then Allen Dulles chimed in.

On November 26, he gave top-secret testimony warning that the Soviets might indeed be getting ahead. He followed up with a secret warning to the National Security Council on December 17: the Gaither Commission, he speculated, might have *under*-stated the risk of a Soviet ICBM attack. He said that America could be hit by Soviet nuclear-armed missiles as early as 1958.[66]

Worst-case contingency planning is always a good idea in principle: it is integral to sound strategic thinking. But there is all the difference in the world between responsible forms of worst-case planning and alarmism.

Allen Dulles, as usual, was floating with the tide, like the opportunist that he was. He knew from experience that he would never pay a price when Ike was boss.

As William Hitchcock has said, "Dulles knew exactly what he was doing" from the standpoint of politics: "a dire report about a Soviet lead in the missile race would prompt congressional outcry and lead to increased dollars for the CIA."[67]

Nine months later, Dulles had to revise his estimates downward; on August 27, 1958, he admitted that the Soviets were not even close to having an operational ICBM capability. In a National Intelligence Estimate codenamed NIE 11-5-58, he projected that the Soviets would not possess such a capability before 1960 at the earliest.

Then he had to backtrack again: he admitted in October that "we have no conclusive evidence that a Soviet ICBM production program of the type estimated in NIE 11-5-58 is being accomplished."[68]

As Evan Thomas has written, "the director of Central Intelligence, Allen Dulles, was caught between military analysts who were quick to credit Khrushchev's claim that Soviet factories would soon be stamping out missiles 'like sausages' and more cautious analysts who saw no evidence that the Soviets had deployed even one missile."[69]

The truth of the matter was that no one knew for sure how quickly the Soviets were progressing with their ICBM deployment.

The U-2 plane had the capability to film a strip of territory two hundred miles wide by twenty-five hundred miles long.[70] But definitive knowledge of the Soviet nuclear arsenal would not arrive until the advent of the CORONA reconnaissance satellite—which would give defense planners a chance to take a look at the entire vastness of Russia.

What Ike *did* know—and what the American people could *not* know—was what *he himself* had done. There was no way for Ike to tell the American people how hard he had been working to protect them.

So much of it was ... secret.

Ike redoubled his efforts.

He created a new "President's Science Advisory Committee," and he tapped the reliable James Killian to head it.

He gave a vigorous 1958 State of the Union address in which he proclaimed that America could master the Cold War's challenges. He proposed a new education bill designed to bolster the teaching of science in the nation's public schools. This legislation would become the epochal National Defense Education Act of 1958.

He created NASA—the National Aeronautics and Space Administration—to channel the civilian side of the space race into an arena that would be fully visible to the public.

He sponsored the Defense Reorganization Act to reduce interservice rivalries and increase the coordination of space-age military efforts.

In short, he responded to the American public's concerns with vigorous *actions*. He continued to create an ever-newer technological infrastructure for American development.

But the post-Sputnik hysteria would not let up.

Talk of a "missile gap" became pervasive when columnist Joseph Alsop claimed on August 1, 1958, that America was losing the Cold War and that time was running out.

"At the Pentagon," he proclaimed in the *New York Herald Tribune*, "they shudder when they speak of the 'gap,' which means the years 1960, 1961, 1962, and 1963" when "the American government will flaccidly permit the Kremlin to gain an almost unchallenged superiority in the nuclear striking power that was once our specialty."[71]

Alsop projected that the U.S. would have zero operational ICBMs in 1959 compared to one hundred for the Soviet Union. Then the gap would get worse: in 1960, he asserted, the U.S. would have only thirty ICBMs compared to five hundred for the Soviets.

These numbers were pulled from thin air—the whole thing was nonsense—but Alsop was not entirely to blame.

He had been fed a lot of cooked-up estimates by Lyndon Johnson and his fellow hawk in the Senate Stuart Symington—who was apparently fed misinformation by a friend in the Convair Corporation, one of the contractors that manufactured the Atlas missile and which (of course) had a vested interest in stoking the demands for more production.

Symington had served as secretary of the air force under Truman, and he still had contacts there.

And the Convair leaker was apparently prompted by some other leakers in the air force who wanted bigger budgets. They were joined by leakers in the CIA who were after the very same thing.

It is tempting to speculate what a better CIA director might have done to help Ike with these problems.

Ike had been warned about Allen Dulles—first by James Doolittle in 1954. At Doolittle's suggestion, Ike had set up a secret advisory board to oversee the CIA's operations and report to him. It was called the President's Board of Consultants on Foreign Intelligence. In the aftermath of the CIA's performance in the Hungary and Suez crises of 1956, two members of that group—David Bruce and Robert Lovett—told Ike that the agency was badly led. Lovett had served as secretary of defense from 1951 to 1953.[72]

Ike's reticence to fire Allen Dulles was perhaps reinforced by the fact that by 1959 John Foster Dulles was dying. Ike visited him at Walter Reed Hospital, where George Marshall, in another room just down the hall, was also dying. In this morbid atmosphere, Ike reflected on the imminent loss of "Foster," whom he had come to regard as a friend.

Before Sputnik, it was the sneering literati and the Stevenson Democrats who tried to pillory Ike as a "do-nothing" president. But after Sputnik, as William Hitchcock has noted, Ike came across to more people as "a man unable to make decisions, passive, complacent," an "amateur" who was "more interested in golf than governing."[73]

Admirers of Senator John F. Kennedy—like Joseph Alsop—spread this malevolent fiction. But the symptoms of fatigue in Ike's performance were not entirely illusory.

It showed on the economic front: Ike failed to take sufficient action to counteract a new recession in 1958, and his standing in the polls declined. The contrast with his masterful and vigorous performance in 1954 should be noted.

Even so, he did his best to stay focused as the bad news continued to arrive.

Instability developed in Lebanon, whose president appealed to Ike for troops to maintain order. Arab refugees from Palestine had upset the delicate balance in Lebanon between Christians and Muslims. Street fighting broke out, and on July 14, 1958, the overthrow of the Iraqi government by radical nationalists created even more instability.

So on July 15, 1958, Ike invoked the Eisenhower Doctrine by sending to Lebanon marines from the Sixth Fleet and airborne army groups from Germany. This intervention did not lead to fighting, and the troops were quickly withdrawn.

A few months later, there was trouble again in the Formosa Strait. Chiang had sent reinforcements to Quemoy and Matsu, and the Chinese communists resumed their shelling of the islands.

Foster Dulles and the Joint Chiefs requested Ike to give the commander of the U.S. Seventh Fleet authority to use nuclear weapons, and Ike said no.

Then the crisis began to blow over. Perhaps Mao began the bombardment to bolster his position at home. Perhaps the nuclear threat was a factor in persuading him to call it off. When Ike was asked at a press conference on August 27 if he intended to use nuclear weapons, he hedged—as usual. When he instructed Foster Dulles to announce, on September 4, that the U.S. was willing to negotiate, the communists responded. The crisis passed, and Chiang reduced his forces on the islands at the prompting of Ike.

Once again, a hot war had been averted. Ike's patience had protected the world.

Nikita Khrushchev had eclipsed Bulganin as the leader of the Soviet Union. He could sometimes be a swaggering bully, but he could also be moderate and reasonable depending upon the vicissitudes of Soviet politics and his own shifting moods.

Thousands of East German refugees had been fleeing through Berlin, which was not yet divided by the infamous Berlin Wall. Walter Ulbricht, the Soviets' puppet leader in East Germany, demanded in October 1958 that Allied occupation forces should withdraw. Khrushchev supported this demand, and he laid down a six-month timetable after which—he said—the Soviets would act unilaterally to force Allied troops out of West Berlin.

John F. Kennedy would inherit this situation, which became steadily more dangerous.

West German leaders—Chancellor Konrad Adenauer and West Berlin mayor Willy Brandt—stood firm, as did the leaders of NATO. Foster Dulles and the foreign ministers of Britain and France told the Soviets that their nations would not comply with the ultimatum.

Khrushchev let the deadline of his withdrawal ultimatum pass without incident.

The members of the team that Ike had assembled back in 1953 were beginning to depart. George Humphrey and Charles Wilson had resigned in 1957, and so did Herbert Brownell in the aftermath of Little Rock. Foster Dulles was dying of cancer.

Sherman Adams, Ike's chief of staff, was accused of influence peddling in 1958—he had accepted some gifts from a New Hampshire industrialist and friend named Bernard Goldfine—and the episode was awkward for Ike: after all, it put the gifts that he had accepted from the gang in a very bad light.

Republican leaders warned Ike that Sherman Adams had to go, and Ike took some steps to make it happen.

His emotional condition grew worse as these events played out.

The diaries of Dr. Snyder and Ann Whitman reveal that his moods became more apoplectic. His consumption of alcohol increased, and Snyder was finding it necessary to prescribe heavier doses of sedatives to help him sleep. His chronic illnesses grew worse.

And then the Democrats made tremendous gains in the midterm elections. People drew the conclusion that the Eisenhower administration was repudiated and that Ike was a spent force in politics.

So Ike began to look for a transcendent mission to perform in 1959 and 1960: an achievement that would let him retire in a blaze of glory.

In discussions with speechwriter Emmet Hughes and with press secretary Jim Hagerty, the grand theme emerged: Ike would take some new initiatives to secure his place in history as a guardian of peace.

He would take a few steps in the direction of Cold War détente.

In 1956, he had corresponded with Richard Simon of Simon & Schuster about the challenge of "man against war."

Nuclear brinksmanship had been taking such a toll upon his mind that he called *war itself* the enemy. His oracular statements on behalf of disarmament were deeply interwoven with his actions as commander in chief.

He had practiced nuclear brinksmanship, and yet he thought all the time about the danger.

He was being swept along in a process he abhorred, and the contradictions grew apace. Was there any way out?

Was there any way for this soldier to guide the world into an era when security did not require terror—or the threat of extinction?

He fondly hoped it could be done.

It was time, Ike declared, to reach "the understanding that the era of armaments has ended."[74] In Evan Thomas's opinion, "Eisenhower's ultimate, if distant, aim was disarmament—to rid the world of these 'terrible' weapons."[75]

A noble objective—but did this soldier believe it was attainable?

Or was it just a daydream?

Ike's conversations with Hughes and Hagerty led to three ideas for new initiatives. First, Ike would try to negotiate a nuclear test-ban treaty with the Soviets. Second, he would travel the globe urging de-escalation of tensions. Third, he would seek to engage himself more directly with Khrushchev in pursuit of a Cold War détente. He told Goodpaster that he hoped to get Khrushchev thinking about his own place in history.

The test-ban idea was already in wide circulation. People were concerned about the fact that contamination from nuclear testing was entering America's food chain. A new radioactive poison—Strontium-90—was threatening everyone. Discussions with the Soviets about a possible test-ban treaty were initiated in the summer of 1958.

But Ike faced enormous pushback at home from his own administration.

Lewis Strauss, the hawkish chairman of the Atomic Energy Commission, refused to cooperate. The very idea of de-escalating Cold War tensions seemed to elicit a wave of insubordination in the national security sector.

When Ike ordered a temporary halt to nuclear testing after Lewis Strauss stepped down as AEC chairman, John McCone, his successor, asked Ike to approve just "one more test."

Ike approved—and then nineteen additional tests were conducted without presidential permission.[76]

In the final year of Ike's presidency, Henry Luce wrote an editorial in *Life* observing that the president was a lenient manager: "he has tended to assume, as you can in the army but not in the White House, that an order once given is self-executing.... He has been an easy boss."

Delegation of authority was indeed a method that Ike had learned in the army. He was powerfully influenced in 1942 when George Marshall told him that he needed "assistants who will solve their own problems and tell me later what they have done."

Ike wrote back to Luce as follows: "I plead guilty to the general charge that many people have felt I have been too easy as a boss." But he went on to explain that one of his foremost "problems has been to control my temper—a temper that I have had to battle all my life."[77] So he avoided confrontations with subordinates.

Personal Diplomacy

Ike invited Khrushchev to visit the United States in September 1959.

Just before this visit, he flew off to Europe to meet with his NATO partners: Harold Macmillan, Konrad Adenauer, and Charles de Gaulle. He was greeted by vast throngs of well-wishers everywhere he went; people lined the parade routes to cheer him.

De Gaulle was especially delighted to see Ike again; "whatever may come in the future," he told Ike, "you will for us forever be the generalissimo of freedom."[78]

Khrushchev came to the United States on September 15, 1959, and then he stayed for thirteen days. He was sometimes in high spirits—gregarious, effusive, on his best behavior. But at other times he was irritable and even unpleasant; he lost his temper when, for security reasons, his request to visit Disneyland was denied.

Ike brought him to Camp David, and their private discussions continued at the Gettysburg farm. When Khrushchev admired a young Angus bull, Ike told him he could have it. They watched Hollywood westerns together.

When Ike introduced his grandchildren to Khrushchev, the Soviet leader became sentimental, and the possibility of establishing real rapport—a real person-to-person breakthrough—seemed to be at hand.

Ike asked Khrushchev how the Soviets decided on their military spending—confiding he was under constant pressure from the top brass to spend more than he thought was necessary. Khrushchev replied that he was in the very same position, which gave Ike the chance to say, "We really should come to some sort of an agreement in order to stop this fruitless, really wasteful rivalry."[79]

They talked about Berlin, and Ike observed that the real issue was *Germany's* division. He said that the ultimatum for withdrawal of troops had made things needlessly difficult, and Khrushchev replied that he did not wish to take unilateral action and that the issues could probably be resolved in a friendly manner.[80]

The "spirit of Geneva" appeared to be returning—at least to some extent. The men discussed a nuclear test-ban treaty and reductions in military spending. They agreed to meet in Paris with Macmillan and de Gaulle on May 16, 1960.

In December 1959, Ike embarked on a goodwill tour of the world that took him to eleven nations. Everywhere he went, he encountered immense crowds who hailed him as the champion of peace.

He made another goodwill tour, this time to South America, in February 1960. The Cold War had been spreading to Latin America: Fidel Castro, a revolutionary leader, had prevailed in a long guerilla war that he had been fighting since 1953 to depose Cuba's dictator, Fulgencio Batista.

Castro denied being a communist, and Eisenhower recognized his new government. But before very long, it was clear enough that Castro *was* a communist and that hostility with the United States was inevitable.

1960

The CORONA reconnaissance satellite program was launched in 1959, but the craft had not yet succeeded as the Paris summit approached. The

U-2 spy plane, though approaching obsolescence, was still the primary aerial reconnaissance tool for the United States, and Allen Dulles pressed Ike to approve more overflights of the Soviet Union in the early months of 1960.

Ike had misgivings. In February, he told Goodpaster that Khrushchev had revealed the extent of Soviet capabilities in a candid moment at Camp David and that "every bit of information I have seen from the overflights corroborates what Khrushchev told me." In light of that, and in light of the upcoming summit, Ike believed that it would be foolhardy to continue the overflights.

Goodpaster wrote in his notes of the meeting that "if one of these aircraft were lost when we were engaged in apparently sincere deliberations, it could be put on display in Moscow and ruin the President's effectiveness."[81]

But Allen Dulles persisted—at the behest of Richard Bissell, who had become his most reckless subordinate. Ike made the mistake of indulging them. Bissell had become like a kid with a toy when it came to the U-2.

And it wasn't only Dulles and Bissell. Defense officials were badgering Ike almost constantly to permit more overflights. No one could predict when the CORONA reconnaissance satellite would succeed. And Alsop was at it again with his inflammatory allegations of a missile gap.

So against his better judgment, Ike gave in.

He permitted more overflights of the Soviet Union in the months before the May summit.

Ike had banned the U-2 overflights in 1958 because the world situation had become so tense. These missions could be viewed as being tantamount to acts of war, and the problem was inherent in covert CIA operations.

The nature of war itself had been fundamentally changing.

Under constitutional law, there was a distinction between "peacetime" and "wartime," but that distinction at times became blurry.

It blurred when Woodrow Wilson permitted sales of armaments to belligerent powers in 1915 when the United States was "neutral." It blurred when FDR got Congress to authorize the Lend-Lease program in 1941 when America was neutral—"at peace."

Congress declared war on Japan after Pearl Harbor. That was—and it remains to this day—the last time that Congress has exercised its power to declare war.

After World War II, the distinction between war and peace became tenuous. Harry Truman acted under the authority of the United Nations Participation Act of 1945 when he sent American troops into combat in Korea without a declaration of war.

In the age of nuclear weapons, total war could erupt in an instant.

Moreover, the CIA's provocations could employ *force*.

In 1949, Congress passed the Central Intelligence Agency Act, which exempted the agency from accounting for its expenditures.

In effect—though not in so many words—the agency was given enough leeway to perpetrate warlike acts.

So when Ike contemplated the U-2 missions from a different perspective in 1959, he asked himself how he would react if the Soviets conducted overflights of the United States.

And he reflected that "nothing would make him request authority to declare war more quickly than the violation of our air space by Soviet aircraft."[82]

On May 1, the Soviets used their newly enhanced ground-to-air missile capability to shoot down a U-2. And though the plane crashed, its pilot, Francis Gary Powers, survived, as did the reconnaissance film. On May 5, Khrushchev made a preliminary announcement about the incident, and he did it with predictable theatrics.

NASA announced that the plane was one of its own craft that had strayed off-course—an obvious cover-up—and the White House issued a denial of any authorized reconnaissance overflights of Russia. But Khrushchev announced the pilot's name and showed copies of the pictures that were taken.

So Ike instructed the State Department to acknowledge the U-2 flights. Milton Eisenhower—now president of Johns Hopkins—urged Ike to disavow responsibility, and John Eisenhower urged his father to fire Allen Dulles.

For Ike, that was out of the question.

He probably remembered the message that he had written so many years ago on the eve of D-Day—that message declaring that he alone would be responsible if the invasion failed.

He took the blame.

"We will now just have to endure the storm," he told some aides.[83]

And the storm was bad: the incident ruined the summit and destroyed any hopes for a test-ban treaty. Khrushchev himself was disappointed: the U-2 incident had destroyed his own hopes for détente.

His response was dictated by Kremlin politics. Ever since his "secret speech" about Stalin, the hard-liners had scrutinized him. He had to keep proving his toughness.

Khrushchev made it clear through diplomatic channels that he hoped the summit would succeed. He said that Ike could save face very easily if he blamed the overflights on subordinates, and such a course of action would allow Khrushchev himself to save face.

Ike could not do it. It would make him look like the out-of-touch leader the Democrats accused him of being.

When the summit convened on May 16, Khrushchev subjected the participants to a long and incontinent tirade. De Gaulle pointed out that Russian satellites were passing over France all the time, and they might very well contain cameras—for all he knew—since a Soviet satellite had snapped pictures of the far side of the moon, which the Soviets had released with great fanfare.

And Ike pointed out that the U-2 flights were not aggressive; they merely gathered information to protect against surprise attacks.

But it was no use: Khrushchev's denunciations continued. He pointed his finger at Ike and yelled. He demanded that Ike apologize and punish those responsible for the U-2 missions. He withdrew his invitation for an Eisenhower visit to the Soviet Union. At last, the Soviet delegation walked out.

De Gaulle told Ike that "I want you to know that I am with you to the end."[84] Ike tried to take it in stride, but he was not consoled.

He had come so close to achieving the legacy he wished to bequeath, but the achievement had slipped from his grasp.

His mood became defiant.

"No one wants another Pearl Harbor," he declared when he confessed the truth about the U-2.[85] Spying, he said, was a necessity, and the Soviets spied upon America relentlessly. So he would not apologize. Looking back years later in his memoirs, he said that if he had the whole thing to do over again, "I know of no decision that I would make differently."[86]

Did he really have no regrets? Or was he being dishonest with himself?

Meanwhile, the CORONA reconnaissance satellite succeeded. CORONA 14, launched on August 18, 1960, performed to perfection: the film from its panoramic camera was conveyed by a take-up spool to the reentry capsule, and the capsule was successfully snagged in midair by the air force near Hawaii.

After the film was taken to the Eastman Kodak Company to be processed, it was presented to Ike in the Oval Office on August 24. Edwin Land did the honors, saying, "Here are your pictures, Mr. President!"[87]

CORONA would prove that the "missile gap" was nonexistent; America was far ahead of the Soviets in the number of its operational ICBMs.

But Ike couldn't tell the American people the truth: that Joe Alsop and the Pentagon hypesters had been wrong.

In the 1960 election, Ike pointedly declined to endorse any candidate for the Republican nomination. This worsened Nixon's deep insecurity, and it probably contributed to his terrible behavior when at last he did become president.

When Ike addressed the Republican National Convention on July 26, 1960, he never mentioned Nixon. He devoted himself to a recitation of his own accomplishments.

At a press conference on August 24, his answers to questions about Nixon's contributions to decision-making were vague. Worst of all, when Charles Mohr of *Time* magazine asked Ike to "give us an example of a major idea of his [Nixon's]" that was adopted, Ike's answer was this: "If you give me a week, I might think of one. I don't remember."[88]

The relationship between the men became icy, and Nixon would get his revenge when, in 1969, just after Ike's death, he began to systematically destroy the civic culture that Ike had tried so hard to create.

Michael Korda has called the Ike–Nixon relationship "Oedipal," and the point is worth pondering.[89] The distant behavior of Ike's own father had prompted him to seek a long series of surrogate fathers—Bob Davis, Fox Conner, and the rest.

Was Ike unconsciously reenacting his father's bad behavior in his attitude toward Nixon—to say nothing of his relationship with his own son John, who kept striving with such touching fidelity to live up to his father's stern expectations?

We can certainly wonder how things would have played out for Ike as a father if Icky had lived. Ike had been a loving father to Icky—he had doted upon the little boy—but the death of the child may have frozen up something in Ike that was deep and fundamental.

As to Nixon: Ike's reluctance to admit to himself the challenging days of his presidency would soon be coming to an end—that he was, in short, an old man—would have probably made him averse to letting *any* Republican successor in 1960 take the limelight and promise new beginnings for the country.

Because Ike was too busy in the work of immortalizing his own legacy.

His defiance increased when he heard that John F. Kennedy accused him of having "lost" Cuba. He would show this upstart who was boss.

And that was why he approved enthusiastically when Allen Dulles presented him with a plan for a covert operation to topple Castro.

Which of course would lead to the Bay of Pigs fiasco.

And he approved enthusiastically when Allen Dulles proposed an operation to topple the left-leaning president of the Congo, Patrice Lumumba.

But for all of Ike's defiance in the 1960 election, he behaved very differently when it was time to step down.

He took Nixon's defeat as a personal affront, and yet his anger subsided to depression—and reflectiveness.

As he prepared to take his last bows, the editor Norman Cousins encouraged him to give a farewell address—as George Washington had done.

And the result was one of the famous items in the Eisenhower legend.

He decided to warn about the "military-industrial complex," a theme that derived not only from his many years of fighting for frugality in military spending but from deeper patterns of reflection.

Assisted by his brother Milton and speechwriter Malcolm Moos—a political science professor on leave from Johns Hopkins—Ike composed the speech that for many people would become the most symbolic part of his legacy. On January 17, 1961, he addressed the nation on television.

He observed that "we have been compelled" by necessity "to create a permanent armaments industry of vast proportions." He noted that this "conjunction of an immense military establishment and a large arms industry is new to the American experience." The Cold War and the advent of nuclear weapons had made the development inevitable—indeed, imperative.

But it was also fraught with menace.

"In the councils of government," Ike warned, "we must guard against the acquisition of unwarranted influence, whether sought or unsought, by the military-industrial complex. The potential for the disastrous rise of misplaced power exists and will persist."[90]

Then, after John F. Kennedy's inauguration on January 20, 1961, Ike and Mamie departed for Gettysburg. He settled into life in his retirement home, and he was given an office at Gettysburg College.

Farewell

Perhaps the situation reminded him of the days when he had lived at the college with Mamie and Icky in 1918.

He had been so frustrated then, because he simply couldn't get a combat assignment in the final days of World War I. Yet how could he have known at the time that those days would seem so poignant later—so bittersweet—for another reason: he was delighted by the little family that he was creating.

Icky was alive.

In 1961, Ike and Mamie established a winter residence at the Eldorado Country Club in California's Coachella Valley, and they would live there for five months out of every year until 1968. They had a home on the

Eldorado golf course constructed exclusively for them by the Texas oil millionaire Robert McCulloch.

Ike and President John F. Kennedy sparred about the latter's defense spending, which Ike deplored, and the abandonment of the New Look in defense, which was scrapped in favor of additional conventional forces that would give the United States "flexible response." But Ike was deeply impressed by JFK's handling of the Cuban missile crisis.

After Kennedy's assassination, Ike and Truman found themselves reunited at the funeral. Realizing they would have to ride together in the same limousine to Arlington National Cemetery, they shared a glass of scotch at Blair House, and the old animosities vanished, at least temporarily. They reminisced about things they had in common and reflected upon the experience of being president. "We know what we did," said Truman, and Ike replied, "We surely do."[91]

Alarmed by the possibility that Goldwater might get the Republican presidential nomination in 1964, Ike tried to prevent it. But he was careful to maintain a posture of neutrality, and he refrained from public declarations.

He helped to establish the Republican Critical Issues Council, a twenty-four-member group of Republican moderates and liberals. His brother Milton agreed to serve as chairman.[92]

The CIC disseminated policy papers in the hope of shaping the 1964 Republican platform. These manifestos endorsed civil rights and voting rights legislation, job-creation programs, and equal educational opportunity.

Goldwater criticized the CIC, and he tried to strike back by recruiting Ike's conservative brother Edgar—who in turn tried to pressure Milton into watering down the CIC recommendations.

Milton refused, and he went on to nominate the moderate William Scranton at the 1964 Republican convention.

When Goldwater won the nomination, Ike's very worst fears about the future of his party seemed to be coming true.

Ike forced Goldwater to promise—if he became president—to enforce the epochal Civil Rights Act of 1964, which Ike supported. A year later, Ike supported Lyndon Johnson's definitive Voting Rights Act of 1965.

Ike found satisfaction in Goldwater's massive defeat, and there was reason to hope that a moderate Republican might take the helm in 1968.

But he had to watch America's tranquility erode as the United States got trapped in the war that he avoided back in 1954.

He had to watch as American society was convulsed by furious divisions: he beheld the antiwar protests (some of them violent), the inner-city riots, and the rise of an alienated "counterculture," all of which shattered the Middle Way that he had tried to create for America.

What consolation could he have had up in Gettysburg as he pondered the ironies of history?

As he dictated his final volumes of memoirs—*Mandate for Change* and *Waging Peace*, which covered his presidency, followed by the charming book *At Ease*, which became a bestseller—nothing improved.

In 1965, he suffered another heart attack. He suffered yet another one in April 1968. A Gallup poll had just rated him the most admired man in America.

By 1968, when Richard Nixon made a comeback, America was more divided and embittered than at any other time in Eisenhower's life.

When Nixon won the 1968 election, Ike nursed a few hopes that his former vice president would mend things. After Earl Warren resigned as chief justice, Ike recommended the appointment of Herbert Brownell to replace him. Nixon, of course, paid no attention.

But Ike never lived to see it. And he never lived to see the way that Nixon and his vice president Spiro Agnew spread hatred, creating such polarization that it stood for half a century—until the time of Donald Trump—as the worst since the Civil War.

What Ike did live to see was the wedding of his grandson, David, to Nixon's daughter Julie. He saw it on closed-circuit television from his bed at Walter Reed Hospital—the hospital from which he would never return, for he was mortally ill.

After such a life, what perspective?

The way that he said goodbye—beginning with a special in-hospital Thanksgiving dinner that was carefully arranged by Mamie—was extended through months.

389

Mamie herself was quite ill in the days leading up to his death, but she did what she needed to do. Ike was ravaged by recurrent heart disease and ileitis.

He had the gratification of receiving a copy of his son's new book about the Battle of the Bulge that was on its way to becoming a bestseller. But increasingly, as his illnesses worsened, he prayed for release.

"Don't forget," he told Mamie, "that I have always loved you."[93]

On the day of his death, on March 28, 1969, his family gathered around him in the hospital. His final words consisted of an order—an order to lift him up higher to a sitting position—then a prayerful request: "I want to go; God take me."

He had risen with astonishing speed to be a world-historical figure.

He was a strange man—so likable in so many respects, but so selfish at times and so distant. He was a man of moods, mischievous, furious, cold, enraged, peaceful, and contemplative by turns. His power of analysis was formidable. But the emotions that drove him were mysterious. He could be honest and deeply deceptive.

His path had taken him from one gifted mentor to another as the opportunities came. There was no plan most of the time: he just made things up as he went. But in other respects, he was guided all his life by a vision.

He had acted out the synthesis that dawned upon him in childhood. He would deliver his mother's fondest wish—peace—by becoming a fighter who was good enough to *keep* the peace, a guardian upon whom everyone else depended.

But his happiness had to be sacrificed at times because of the way in which his love life evolved. He was often full of pain.

Gladys Harding could well have been his, and yet he never discovered it in time, so he looked elsewhere.

Mamie Doud was the woman whom he took to the altar, and they settled down together quickly. But their needs were extraordinarily different, and the loss of little Icky seemed to ruin things. They drifted.

Kay Summersby was ready to give him whatever he needed and to follow him anywhere. But he left her.

A photograph of Ike in retirement, lost in some wistful reflections.

He wandered away into misery and looked around for answers, finding none.

Tough-minded as he was, the force of destiny that he finally accepted after years of evasion almost ruined him. But he conquered it with help from some friends and went on to his life's consummation.

He enjoyed himself immensely at the height of his powers as he cultivated thoughts and reveled in success. He was a gifted commander, and he loved the exercise of power. Gone were the days right after the war when he was led astray by illusions—except for one. He trusted certain people who did not deserve his confidence.

Even so, he was a visionary leader who could look far over the horizon—a masterful president.

He put from his mind all the sadness that lingered down below. He avoided contemplation of beautiful things that would never come to pass, the unrealized dreams that came once and would never come again.

But there were things that saddened him so much that he could never quite expunge them from his mind, like the death of poor Icky. He and Mamie had needed each other so desperately then, and their sorrow defeated them.

"The greatest disappointment and disaster of my life" was what he called the little boy's death.[94]

He had never gotten over it.

After World War II, his admirers created a museum in his honor out in Abilene, and the Kansas legislature appropriated funds for a presidential library. The complex now bears the name of the Dwight D. Eisenhower Presidential Library, Museum, and Boyhood Home. Ike and Mamie decided to be buried there.

In 1966, Ike exhumed the body of Icky and had it interred in the plot where he would soon lie with Mamie.

They are there now, united in death.

So many of his goals had been achieved, but so many good things had slipped away. Some of this resulted from his choices. He had sacrificed some things to get others, and the blame—if any—was his.

But the loss of little Icky had been different. The poor child was attacked and cut down. Life is war—and Eisenhower knew it.

And he knew how to bury the dead.

He was a soldier.

EPILOGUE

In 1999, Congress passed a bill to create a memorial to Dwight Eisenhower, and support was overwhelming.

A bipartisan commission—the Dwight D. Eisenhower Memorial Commission—was created with members of Congress and presidential appointees serving as commissioners.

The founding chairman of the commission was the late Rocco C. Siciliano, a public servant who worked in the Eisenhower White House. He was a combat veteran of World War II, as were two other commissioners, the late Senators Ted Stevens (R-Alaska) and Daniel Inouye (D-Hawaii), whose states were admitted to the Union when Ike was president.

The executive director of the commission was Brigadier General Carl W. Reddel (USAF, Ret.).

The Dwight D. Eisenhower Memorial was dedicated in 2020 on a four-acre tract of land across the street from the National Air and Space Museum in Washington, D.C. This location—approved by Congress after a review of twenty-six sites—made good sense.

An average of eight million people visit the National Air and Space Museum—as well as the neighboring Museum of the American Indian—every year, so the Eisenhower Memorial will be visited by many Americans.

What its creators hoped to achieve was to show the American people why Eisenhower *matters*.

The memorial is only beginning to achieve its potential because its creation was hindered for twenty years.

In the first place, the memorial was initially controversial among members of the Eisenhower family, even though President Clinton took the important step of putting Ike's grandson, David, on the memorial commission. Politicians hesitated to move ahead with funding until these controversies were resolved. In addition, the great public plaza that architect Frank Gehry designed for the memorial was subjected to vehement attack by design traditionalists, who complained that it was ill-suited to its setting.

These complaints were extremely misguided, for the memorial has taken its place on the Mall as a dignified presence. The design traditionalists have nothing to say anymore—they are completely silent—and the members of the Eisenhower family profess unanimity in favor of Frank Gehry's design.

When it was time for the memorial to be dedicated, two other factors interfered: (1) the onset of COVID led to a drastic reduction in the number of invited participants who were able to come to the dedication ceremony, and (2) the memorial was dedicated at a time when the presidential incumbent, Donald Trump, epitomized everything that Dwight D. Eisenhower loathed.

But the irony of this latter circumstance shows *precisely* why Eisenhower matters.

More on that momentarily.

Successful as Ike had been in his mission to heal the divisions of America, his success—though it guaranteed him immense popularity during his presidential years—hurt his short-term reputation. One price to be paid for his hidden-hand methods was the empowerment of critics who called him a "do nothing" president, a duffer who "snoozed" in the White House, an old man who wasted time on the golf course.

Adlai Stevenson and many other liberal Democrats attempted to pillory Ike in that manner, and the stereotype would flourish among American liberals in the years that followed. As late as the 1990s, a writer in the *New York Times* sneered that "Harry S. Truman was followed by eight years of Dwight D. Eisenhower, who was rumored to have died early in his term without there being any visible change in his style of governing."[1]

Given the immensely visible changes that would come in the administrations of John F. Kennedy and Lyndon Johnson, it was to some extent understandable that Ike's governing style might look pale by contrast.

Many of his greatest achievements had been kept deliberately hidden, and his visible actions were deliberately understated.

Over time, the force of scholarship began to reveal the magnitude of what Ike had done.

It began with Stephen Ambrose, who cultivated Ike in the years before his death and was commissioned in 1964 to write an authorized biography. It came out in the 1980s as a two-volume set.

Then the editing and publishing of Eisenhower's papers was commenced at Johns Hopkins University—under the initial editorship of Ambrose and then under the successive editorship of Alfred D. Chandler Jr. and Louis Galambos —and the twenty-one-volume series, now complete, was published by Johns Hopkins University Press. Eisenhower's diaries (in the collection of the presidential library) were edited by Robert H. Ferrell and published in 1981.

Path-breaking books began to reveal many hidden details of Eisenhower's presidency. Blanche Wiesen Cook, in *The Declassified Eisenhower: A Divided Legacy of Peace and Political Warfare* (1981), used presidential library records to trace Ike's political development and his covert interventions as president. Fred Greenstein's book *The Hidden-Hand Presidency: Eisenhower as Leader* (1982) opened larger vistas by showing that Eisenhower's low-key demeanor was a deception created to facilitate brilliant acts behind the scenes.

The continuing study of Ike's secret methods and their results has proceeded ever since, and this story has become more fascinating by the decade.

A series of monographic books by historian David Nichols shed additional light on behind-the-scenes activities of Ike: *A Matter of Justice: Eisenhower and the Beginning of the Civil Rights Revolution* (2007), *Eisenhower 1956: The President's Year of Crisis* (2011), and *Ike and McCarthy: Dwight Eisenhower's Secret Campaign Against Joseph McCarthy* (2017). Journalist Philip Taubman's book *Secret Empire: Eisenhower, the CIA, and the Hidden Story of America's Space Espionage* (2003) revealed the way in which Ike created space-based intelligence-gathering.

Journalist Evan Thomas's brilliant book *Ike's Bluff* (2012) probed the paradoxical methods Ike used to keep the peace.

The Dwight D. Eisenhower Memorial Commission tapped these new revelations from the outset. It now appears that no other presidential memorial has relied so heavily on the findings of historical scholars.

Dwight Eisenhower in his presidential years was a guardian: he aimed to protect Americans while preparing the nation for challenges that were far beyond the power of other people to foresee. He planned much of the infrastructure that would guide and support the nation's development for decades to come.

He put in place a strategic "architecture" to undergird American prosperity and safety in many ways: through the interstate highways that would quickly transform the continent, through space-based surveillance that would guard the country against future military threats, by transforming the judiciary to support great advances in civil rights. Many of these transformations were hidden, and even the great highway program was launched with minimal fanfare.

The quotations that follow show the findings that convinced the members of Congress to honor the contributions of Ike through a national memorial.

The aerial reconnaissance program that Eisenhower engineered was revolutionary. As Philip Taubman has said, Eisenhower's presidency "was a time of landmark advances in defense, a record unequalled by nine subsequent presidents." Ike was always "open to new ideas [and] respectful of the contributions that science could make."[2]

Historian R. Cargill Hall has observed that Ike's reconnaissance satellites made his "Open Skies" proposal a reality. The Soviets opposed it, but Ike went ahead and created it anyway—for everybody's good. An extended quotation is in order:

> With the SALT I Treaty of 1972, reconnaissance satellites would be recognized formally as the "national technical means" for policing the terms of international arms control agreements. By that date, these remarkable overhead technical systems provided the strategic "transparency" that a prescient leader had sought: they helped ensure that the Cold War remained "cold." In fact, by that date American

reconnaissance satellites had turned Eisenhower's "intelligence problem" of the early 1950s, when virtually no reliable information about Soviet military capabilities could be obtained, upside down. Now intelligence officers faced an avalanche of satellite data, nearly all of it totally reliable.... On leaving office on 20 January 1961 Eisenhower surely could take satisfaction in the knowledge that he and his advisors had engineered a revolution in intelligence.[3]

Eisenhower did these things for the purpose of keeping people *safe*. As historian Dennis Showalter has observed,

a steadily growing body of evidence [is] establishing just how dangerous the Eisenhower years and their aftermath to 1963 really were. At several points World War III could have happened and almost did.... Public opinion stampeding in any direction might trigger global thermonuclear destruction. Eisenhower's calm public demeanor... played no small role in helping the United States, and the world, develop a sense of perspective.[4]

It was an *architectonic mind* that was able to do such things for America and the world. Another latter-day appraisal put the Eisenhower achievement in a psychological perspective that was panoramic. Michael Korda reflected that

Ike had a genius for logistics [and] a deep conviction that America should fight only wars in which its industrial superiority guaranteed victory with the minimum loss of lives. It was not for nothing that Ike and Patton had stripped an early tank to pieces in 1920 and put it back together again.... Machinery, industrial capacity, and technology interested Ike, both as a general and president. Though his role in it is hardly even remembered, Ike regarded his determination to build the interstate highway system as one of the great achievements of his presidency.... It is hard for most Americans to even imagine what the country was like before the late 1950s, when road travel from state to state was still an adventure, and when small towns all across the nation still remained comparatively isolated from each other.[5]

Ike was a visionary. He was a man who was in some respects ahead of his time, and right now—when the times, so to speak, have been getting ahead of our leaders—that fact is extremely important.

Of surpassing importance was the way that Ike stabilized America's long-term role as a superpower and came to terms with the nuclear menace.

There was no way for him or for anyone else to "put the nuclear genie back in the bottle," but the system of deterrence that Ike pioneered has succeeded—to date—in averting nuclear war. On one occasion after another, he restrained the impulsive.

He did, however, practice "brinksmanship" with Foster Dulles, which made people wonder.

He told aides in the Suez crisis that "if those fellows [the Soviets] start something, we may have to hit them...with everything in the bucket." Was he justified in saying that—justified in *thinking* it?

Only the cold-as-steel sensibility that Eric Larrabee attributed to Ike made the difference.

"Ike could never admit," wrote Evan Thomas, "that he had pulled off a giant bluff, that he had kept the peace by threatening all-out war. His all-or-nothing strategy worked brilliantly." And while Eisenhower probably "had no intention of ever using nuclear weapons it was vitally important that "the president never said as much."

He told no one.

He made a famous boast when he was asked about his presidential achievement years later: "The United States never lost a soldier or a foot of ground in my administration.... People ask how it happened—by God, it didn't just happen, I'll tell you that."[6]

The world that Ike made for himself and for others took shape through the course of his life.

Korda was right: Ike's knack for logistics, his compulsion to dissect the tank with Patton, his work at the Industrial College, and the genius that led him to anticipate structures that were needed to keep the world safe for generations were part of a vision that grew in him throughout adulthood.

To some extent, this vision grew without anticipation or planning; Ike jumped at opportunities, and never reached out for promotions. But the promotions kept *coming to him* because he was *industrious*—a trait that his mother had instilled.

His rise to world fame had been hectic, serendipitous, unplanned in a great many ways. But pervading it all was a vision. It dawned upon him in his childhood as he reacted to the personalities of his parents.

His father had been stern on the surface but weak down below, and so his mother—the finest person he had ever known—became the dominant parent.

He went looking for surrogate fathers, and he found a long series. He strove to rebel and assert himself, but he was driven to reconcile the things that he learned in the target practice sessions with the pacifist ideals of his mother.

The role of Bill Hickok set the pattern for him: he would *make things safe for everyone* by learning to fight.

His mother taught him to be virtuous and self-controlled, and Ike knew that he *should* be. But he needed to rebel now and then if he wished to break free of maternal constraint—if he wished to avoid being a "mama's boy." FDR had faced the same problem.

Ike tried to rebel at West Point, with all his rule-breaking and heedlessness. He reveled in male camaraderie.

But the abiding vision never left him.

One of his final chances to rebel had been with Kay, who could offer him spontaneous happiness—a chance to *yield* to his visceral needs and let the world take care of itself.

But it was no use.

He had to *render service*, not merely as a teacher but through the active work of protecting his fellow men and women. We are all his beneficiaries.

There was *solitary* fulfillment for Ike as he performed this self-imposed role, and he made the most of it. He rose to the challenge of putting that remarkable mind of his to maximum use as he stretched his gifts as a planner and strategist to their utmost limits.

His *ambition*—his drive to follow his *ego* wherever it led him—had been sublimated in a purpose that transcended all else.

But it was lonely business.

The long-term achievements of Ike are extremely important.

But the evanescent nature of his *short-term* achievement is also (unfortunately) relevant.

For the age of good feelings that he worked so hard to create would be short-lived. The Middle Way that he created would unravel. The pressure of events and the baleful influence of Richard Nixon corroded it.

By 1969, the American mood had reverted to the poisonous state that Ike confronted when he ran for the presidency in 1952.

This shows us something else that is important about Ike's legacy: not only the guardianship but the challenge of effectuating repairs when things go very wrong.

As they surely will.

Civility and decency—like civilization—are frail, and the dangers to them are ever-present. Which brings us to the issue of Ike, Donald Trump, and the times in which we find ourselves living.

As William Hitchcock has argued, Ike's bipartisan appeal looks better and better over time: even when the "voters put Democrats in charge of Congress, they loved Eisenhower…. Over eight years, 50 percent of *Democrats* approved of his performance. In our more polarized times, such cross-party affinity is rare."[7]

It is indeed.

The divisions and the rage that are currently tearing away at our culture make the Nixon era look benign. America has never been more at odds with itself since the Civil War, and the presidency of Trump worsened everything—he spread hatred with malevolent glee. Recovery from this may take a long time.

So there could be few spectacles more grotesque—more obscene—than the dedication of a memorial to Eisenhower by President Donald Trump.

When the memorial was dedicated, it felt as if Joe McCarthy had been in the White House for four years. And the association was substantial since McCarthy's henchman Roy Cohn had been one of Trump's mentors.

Donald's father—Fred Trump—was the dominant parent for him, and Fred was a cruel predator. He taught his son to humiliate others to prove that he was a "winner."

And the world could go to hell.

Trump degraded his office by behaving like a vile guttersnipe. Mere weeks after the dedication of the Eisenhower Memorial, Trump turned a presidential debate into a farce by interrupting his opponent with rant. Throughout his presidency he dished out a never-ending torrent of abuse on social media. He insulted those who dared to question him by giving them crude nicknames.

He defiled almost everything he touched.

Millions of people asked themselves, "What happened to the America we thought we knew?"

Ike's strategy for defeating McCarthy was to give the American people a chance to see him on television. Ike was confident that once Americans could see this mean demagogue in action, they would be revolted.

And they were.

Now consider this comparison: in the election of 2016, Trump's behavior was *televised for months on end*, and his supporters *loved* it. What manner of historical and cultural transformation could account for such declension?

Whereas Ike promoted science, Trump responded to COVID by suggesting that Americans ingest antiseptics like bleach.

When Trump lost the 2020 election, he attempted a brazen coup to overturn the election results, and he incited a violent mob to invade the United States Capitol.

Is it *already too late* for us to hope that the legacy of Eisenhower can help the American people?

Time alone will tell.

In the final days of Ike's life, he witnessed his legacy unravelling. He never lived to see Nixon's fate.

Likewise, the Eisenhower Memorial was dedicated at a moment when the deeds of Nixon and McCarthy were being reenacted on a much larger scale by America's very worst president.

The poignancy of these events forms a theme: it suggests both the possibilities and limitations of history.

A master manager, Ike created new structures of security and a wholesome new civic culture. But the ironies of history can thwart the most gifted of leaders. The standard Ike set will be studied by a multitude of others—by the leaders who will follow in his footsteps. As things go wrong, new servants of the people will correct them, fix them, put them right.

Ike's legacy will guide them forever.

Endnotes

Preface

1 Fred I. Greenstein, *The Hidden–Hand Presidency: Eisenhower as Leader* (Baltimore: Johns Hopkins University Press, 1982).

2 Dwight D. Eisenhower, *Mandate for Change, 1953–1956: The White House Years* (Garden City, NY: Doubleday, 1963), 478.

3 Louis Galambos, *Eisenhower: Becoming the Leader of the Free World* (Baltimore: Johns Hopkins University Press, 2018), IX, passim.

4 Dwight D. Eisenhower to Henry Luce, August 8, 1960, Dwight D. Eisenhower Presidential Library.

5 Theodore Roosevelt to Sydney Brooks, November 20, 1908, in Theodore Roosevelt, *The Letters of Theodore Roosevelt: The Big Stick, 1905-1909*, Elting E. Morison, ed. (Cambridge, MA: Harvard University Press, 1951), VI, 1369. For analysis of Eisenhower's place in a tradition of left–right political synthesis, see Richard Striner, *Lincoln's Way: How Six Great Presidents Created American Power* (Lanham: Rowman & Littlefield, 2010).

6 Dwight D. Eisenhower, *Crusade in Europe* (Garden City, NY: Doubleday, 1948), 21–22.

7 Dwight D. Eisenhower to James Forrestal, January 17, 1949, cited in Greenstein, *The Hidden–Hand Presidency*, 48, 257 n. 68.

8 Allan H. Meltzer, *A History of the Federal Reserve* (Chicago: University of Chicago Press, 2003), I, 591.

9 Anthony Solomon, quoted in William Greider, *Secrets of the Temple: How the Federal Reserve Runs the Country* (New York: Simon & Schuster, 1987), Touchstone edition, 121.

10 David Eisenhower and Julie Nixon Eisenhower, *Going Home to Glory: A Memoir of Life with Dwight D. Eisenhower, 1961-1969* (New York: Simon & Schuster, 2010), 65.

Chapter One

1 Eric Larrabee, *Commander in Chief: Franklin Delano Roosevelt, His Lieutenants and Their War* (New York: Harper & Row, 1987), 412.

2 Robert J. Donovan, oral history, Dwight D. Eisenhower Presidential Library, cited in Jean Edward Smith, *Eisenhower in War and Peace* (New York: Random House, 2013), 545.

3 Major General Howard Snyder, quoted in Don Van Natta Jr., *First Off the Tee: The Presidential Hackers, Duffers, and Cheaters from Taft to Bush* (New York: PublicAffairs, 2003), 58.

4 See Thomas Branigar, "No Villains—No Heroes: The David Eisenhower–Milton Good Controversy," *Kansas History* (Autumn 1990): 168–179.

5 Michael Korda, *Ike: An American Hero* (New York: HarperCollins, 2007), 64.

6 Dwight D. Eisenhower, *At Ease: Stories I Tell to Friends* (Garden City, NY: Doubleday, 1967), 80, 70.

7 Ibid., 73.

8 Ibid., 32.

9 Ibid., 78–79.

10 Ibid., 68.

11 Ibid., 65.

12 Ibid.

13 Ibid., 69.

14 Ibid., 65–66.

15 Ibid., 39.

16 Ibid., 93–94.

17 Ibid., 95.

18 Ibid., 76.

19 Ibid., 52.

20 Ibid.

21 Ibid., 30.

22 Ibid., 89–90.

23 Ibid., 88.

24 Ibid., 88.

25 Dick Taylor, "Tom 'Bear River' Smith," *Kansas Collection Articles*, https://www.kancoll.org/articles/tomsmith.htm.

26 John E. Long letters, Box 4, Eisenhower Library, cited in Carlo D'Este, *Eisenhower: A Soldier's Life* (New York: Henry Holt and Company, 2002), 39.

27 Dwight D. Eisenhower, *At Ease*, 43.

28 Ibid., 100.

29 Dwight D. Eisenhower, "The Student in Politics," November 18, 1909, in Dwight D. Eisenhower, *Eisenhower: The Prewar Diaries and Selected Papers, 1905–1941*, Daniel D. Holt and James W. Leyerzapf, eds. (Baltimore: Johns Hopkins University Press, 1998), 5–7. See also Robert H. Ferrell, "Eisenhower Was a Democrat," *Kansas History* 13 (Autumn 1990): 134–38.

30 Francis Trevelyan Miller, *Eisenhower: Man and Soldier* (Philadelphia: John C. Winston, 1944), 81.

31 Dwight D. Eisenhower, *At Ease*, 108.

32 Ibid.

33 Ibid., 4.

34 Ibid.

35 The Recollections of Charles Herrick, Class of 1915, United States Military Academy Archives, cited in D'Este, *Eisenhower: A Soldier's Life*, 66.

36 Korda, *Ike: An American Hero*, 92.

37 Dwight D. Eisenhower, interview by Edgar F. Puryear Jr., May 2, 1963, in Edgar Puryear, *19 Stars: A Study in Military Character and Leadership* (Orange, VA: Green Publishers, 1971), 13, quoted in Smith, *Eisenhower in War and Peace*, 21.

38 Dwight D. Eisenhower, *At Ease*, 19–20.

39 Eisenhower to Col. J. Franklin Bell, February 14, 1967, Box 20, Post–Presidential Papers, Secretary's Series, Eisenhower Library.

40 Alexander M. "Babe" Weyand, "The Athletic Cadet Eisenhower,"*Assembly*, Spring 1968, cited in D'Este, *Eisenhower: A Soldier's Life*, 69.

41 Eisenhower to Ruby Norman, cited in Stephen E. Ambrose, *Eisenhower: Soldier, General of the Army, President–Elect, 1890–1952* (New York: Simon & Schuster, 1983), Touchstone edition, 50.

42 Joseph C. Haw, "Eisenhower's West Point," United States Military Academy Archives, CU#5377.

43 Eisenhower to Ruby Norman, November 5, 1913, Ruby Norman Lucier Papers, Eisenhower Library.

44 Gordon R. Young Papers, U.S. Army Military History Institute, Carlisle Barracks, Pennsylvania, cited in D'Este, *Eisenhower: A Soldier's Life*, 78.

45 Ibid.

46 Ibid.

47 Kenneth S. Davis, *Dwight D. Eisenhower: Soldier of Democracy* (New York: Doubleday, Doran & Company, 1945), 130–131.

48 Dwight D. Eisenhower, *At Ease*, 24–25.

49 Ibid., 26.

50 J. Earl Endacott, "The Ike I Remember and Other Stories," Endacott Papers, Eisenhower Library.

51 See Cole Kingseed (Col., U.S. Army, Ret.), "Ike and Gladys Harding—The Summer of 1915," Dwight D. Eisenhower Vertical File, United States Military Academy Archives, and Gladys Harding Brooks Papers, Dwight D. Eisenhower Presidential Library, cited in D'Este, *Eisenhower: A Soldier's Life*, 86–89.

52 D'Este, *Eisenhower: A Soldier's Life*, 97–98.

53 Dwight D. Eisenhower, *At Ease*, 113.

54 Eisenhower to Ruby Norman, January 17, 1916, in Dwight D. Eisenhower, *Eisenhower: The Prewar Diaries and Selected Papers*, 7.

55 Merle Miller, *Ike: The Soldier as They Knew Him* (New York: G.P. Putnam's Sons, 1987), 130–131; D'Este, *Eisenhower: A Soldier's Life*, 103.

56 J. Earl Endacott, *Washington Post*, October 16, 1953, quoted in Six McDonnell, oral history, Dwight D. Eisenhower Presidential Library, D'Este, *Eisenhower: A Soldier's Life*, 89.

Chapter Two

1 Dwight D. Eisenhower, *At Ease*, 118.

2 Korda, *Ike: An American Hero*, 123.

3 For a lengthy examination of Wilson's incompetence as a wartime leader, see Richard Striner, *Woodrow Wilson and World War I: A Burden Too Great to Bear* (Lanham: Rowman & Littlefield, 2014).

4 Dwight D. Eisenhower, *At Ease*, 129.

5 Dwight D. Eisenhower, *Eisenhower: The Prewar Diaries and Selected Papers*, 13.

6 Lieutenant Edward C. Thayer to his mother, January 1918, Eisenhower Library, cited in Smith, *Eisenhower in War and Peace*, 40.

7 Dwight D. Eisenhower, *At Ease*, 138.

8 Ike made the statement to Major Norman Randolph, who reminded him about it years later in a letter he that sent to Ike on June 20, 1945, Dwight D. Eisenhower Presidential Library.

9 Dwight D. Eisenhower, *At Ease*, 152.

10 Ibid., 153–154.

11 Ibid., 155.

12 Ibid., 166–167.

13 Dwight D. Eisenhower, unpublished assessments of World War II personalities, Box 7, Post–Presidential Papers, A–WR Series, Eisenhower Library, quoted in D'Este, *Eisenhower: A Soldier's Life*, 153.

14 Ibid., 170.

15 Ibid., 171.

16 John S. D. Eisenhower, *General Ike: A Personal Reminiscence* (New York: Free Press, 2003), 2.

17 Dwight D. Eisenhower, *At Ease*, 173.

18 Mamie Doud Eisenhower, oral history, Eisenhower Library, cited in Smith, *Eisenhower in War and Peace*, 57.

19 Susan Eisenhower, *Mrs. Ike: Memories and Reflections on the Life of Mamie Eisenhower* (New York: Farrar, Straus, Giroux, 1996), 64.

20 Ibid., 181.

21 Smith, *Eisenhower in War and Peace*, 59.

22 Julie Nixon Eisenhower, *Special People* (New York: Simon & Schuster, 1977), 198–99.

23 Dwight D. Eisenhower, *At Ease*, 183.

24 Lester David and Irene David, *Ike and Mamie: The Story of a General and His Lady* (New York: G. P. Putnam's Sons, 1981), 90, quoted in Smith, *Eisenhower in War and Peace*, 65.

25 Virginia Conner, *What Father Forbad* (Philadelphia: Dorrance, 1951), 120–121.

26 Dwight D. Eisenhower, *At Ease*, 186.

27 Susan Eisenhower, *Mrs. Ike*, 83.

28 Korda, *Ike: An American Hero*, 167.

29 Ibid., 166.

30 Dwight D. Eisenhower, *At Ease*, 198.

31 Ibid., 199.

32 D'Este, *Eisenhower: A Soldier's Life*, 178.

33 Smith, *Eisenhower in War and Peace*, 76.

34 See Richard Rayner, "Channelling Ike," *New Yorker*, April 19, 2010, https://www.newyorker.com/magazine/2010/04/26/channelling-ike. See also Irwin F. Gellman, *The President and the Apprentice: Eisenhower and Nixon, 1952-1961* (New Haven: Yale University Press, 2015).

35 Interviews with Dwight D. Eisenhower and Milton Eisenhower, in Ambrose, *Eisenhower: Soldier, General of the Army, President–Elect*, 83.

36 John J. Pershing to Major General Robert H. Allen, August 15, 1927, Dwight D. Eisenhower 201 File, Eisenhower Library, cited in Smith, *Eisenhower in War and Peace*, 80.

37 Dwight D. Eisenhower, efficiency report, June 30, 1928, Eisenhower Library, cited in Smith, *Eisenhower in War and Peace*, 81.

38 Mamie Doud Eisenhower, oral history, cited in D'Este, *Eisenhower: A Soldier's Life*, 193.

39 John S. D. Eisenhower, *Strictly Personal: A Memoir* (New York: Doubleday & Co., 1974), 9.

40 Dwight D. Eisenhower, *At Ease*, 195.

41 Ibid., 200–201.

42 James C. Humes, *Confessions of a White House Ghostwriter: Five Presidents and Other Political Adventures* (Washington, D.C.: Regnery, 1997), 39.

43 Dwight D. Eisenhower, diary entry, November 9, 1929, labeled "Chief of Staff Diary," Eisenhower Library, cited in Smith, *Eisenhower in War and Peace*, 93.

44 Ambrose, *Eisenhower: Soldier, General of the Army, President-Elect*, 88.

45 See Richard Striner, *Hard Times: Economic Depressions in America* (Lanham: Rowman & Littlefield, 2018), 65–78, and John Kenneth Galbraith, *The Great Crash, 1929* (Boston: Houghton Mifflin, 1954). Some historians have questioned the causal link between the crash and the Depression, but I find their arguments completely unconvincing.

46 Gary M. Walton and Hugh Rockoff, *History of the American Economy* (Stamford, CN: South–Western/Thomson Learning, 2002), 497–499.

47 John Maynard Keynes, "The World's Economic Outlook," *Atlantic Monthly*, May 1932, 525.

48 Smith, *Eisenhower in War and Peace*, 116.

49 Ibid., 54, 95.

50 Smith cites this statement from Moseley's unpublished memoir, "One Soldier's Journey," in the Moseley Papers at the Library of Congress. Moseley's bitter invective against Jews may be found in volume four, pages 215–219. Smith, *Eisenhower in War and Peace*, 95, 785 n. 14.

51 Ibid., 95.

52 George Marshall to George Moseley, September 9, 1938, in George C. Marshall, *The Papers of George Catlett Marshall: "The Soldierly Spirit,"* Larry L. Bland, ed. (Baltimore: Johns Hopkins University Press, 1986), III, 626.

53 Dwight D. Eisenhower, diary entry, June 14–August 10, 1932, in Dwight D. Eisenhower, *The Prewar Diaries and Selected Papers*, 225–226.

54 Smith, *Eisenhower in War and Peace*, 94.

55 Dwight D. Eisenhower, *At Ease*, 213.

56 Vernadette Vicuña Gonzalez, *Empire's Mistress, Starring Isabel Rosario Cooper* (Chapel Hill: Duke University Press, 2021); William Manchester, *American Caesar: Douglas MacArthur, 1880–1964* (New York: Little, Brown, 1978), 158–159; Smith, *Eisenhower in War and Peace*, 116 fn.

57 Douglas MacArthur to Dwight D. Eisenhower, November 4, 1931, Eisenhower Library.

58 Dwight D. Eisenhower, diary entry, February 15, 1932, in Dwight D. Eisenhower, *The Prewar Diaries and Selected Papers*, 214–215.

59 Dwight D. Eisenhower, *At Ease*, 214.

60 Ibid., 213.

61 Korda, *Ike: An American Hero*, 202.

62 T. H. Watkins, *The Hungry Years: A Narrative History of the Great Depression in America* (New York: Henry Holt & Co., 1999), 43–44.

63 Ibid., 45.

64 Ibid., 57.

65 Arthur M. Schlesinger Jr., *The Crisis of the Old Order: 1919-1933, The Age of Roosevelt* (Boston: Houghton Mifflin, 1957), 250.

66 Watkins, *The Hungry Years*, 131–141; Smith, *Eisenhower in War and Peace*, 106–115.

67 Ambrose, *Eisenhower: Soldier, General of the Army, President–Elect*, I, 98.

68 Dwight D. Eisenhower, *At Ease*, 217.

69 Ibid., 216–217.

70 Geoffrey Perret, *Eisenhower* (New York: Random House, 1999), 112–113; Miller, *Ike: The Soldier*, 266–267; D'Este, *Eisenhower: A Soldier's Life*, 223–224; and Smith, *Eisenhower in War and Peace*, 112–116.

71 Dwight D. Eisenhower, diary entry, August 10, 1932, Dwight D. Eisenhower, *The Prewar Diaries and Selected Papers*, 233.

72 Dwight D. Eisenhower, "To Secretary of War," August 15, 1932, Pre–Presidential Papers, Bonus March File, Eisenhower Library, in Dwight D. Eisenhower, *The Prewar Diaries and Selected Papers*, 241.

73 Jkircher314, "Bonus Army: US military attacks demonstrating American War Veterans," YouTube video, 6:53, https://www.youtube.com/watch?v=sNOsIB5VMSQ.

74 Dwight D. Eisenhower, diary entry, April 26, 1934, Dwight D. Eisenhower, *The Prewar Diaries and Selected Papers*, 268–269.

75 Dwight D. Eisenhower, *At Ease*, 215.

76 Dwight D. Eisenhower, diary entry, November 30, 1932, Dwight D. Eisenhower, *The Prewar Diaries and Selected Papers*, 247.

77 Ibid., February 28, 1933, 248–249.

78 Ibid., December 9, 1933, 256.

79 Manchester, *American Caesar*, 166. See also Mark Perry, *The Most Dangerous Man in America: The Making of Douglas MacArthur* (New York: Basic Books, 2014).

80 Arthur M. Schlesinger Jr., *The Politics of Upheaval: 1935-1936, The Age of Roosevelt* (Boston: Houghton Mifflin, 1960), 83.

81 Korda, *Ike: An American Hero*, 202.

82 Ibid., 207.

83 Mamie Doud Eisenhower to her parents, June 25, 1935, Box 2, Barbara Thompson Eisenhower Papers, Eisenhower Library, cited in D'Este, *Eisenhower: A Soldier's Life*, 232.

84 Smith, *Eisenhower in War and Peace*, 125.

85 Dwight D. Eisenhower, diary entry, January 20, 1936, Dwight D. Eisenhower, *The Prewar Diaries and Selected Papers*, 302.

86 Ibid., May 29, 1936, 311.

87 Dwight D. Eisenhower, interview with Peter Lyon, August 1967, quoted in Peter Lyon, *Eisenhower: Portrait of the Hero* (Boston: Little, Brown, 1974), 78.

88 Unpublished memoir of Lt. General Robert L. Eichelberger, Eichelberger Papers, United States Army Military History Institute, cited in D'Este, *Eisenhower: A Soldier's Life*, 237.

89 Susan Eisenhower, *Mrs. Ike*, 137.

90 Smith, *Eisenhower in War and Peace*, 135.

91 Susan Eisenhower, *Mrs. Ike*, 143.

92 Mamie Doud Eisenhower to her parents, March 9, 1938, Eisenhower Library.

93 Douglas MacArthur to Malin Craig, August 22, 1937 and September 10, 1937, MacArthur Memorial Bureau of Archives, cited in Smith, *Eisenhower in War and Peace*, 140.

94 Dwight D. Eisenhower, diary entry, Oct. 8, 1937, Dwight D. Eisenhower, *The Prewar Diaries and Selected Papers*, 363.

95 Ibid., October 8, 1937, 363.

96 Ibid., November 10, 1938, 410–412.
97 Dwight D. Eisenhower, *At Ease*, 229–230.

Chapter Three

1 Dwight D. Eisenhower to Mark Clark, September 23, 1939, Dwight D. Eisenhower, *The Prewar Diaries and Selected Papers*, 447.
2 Dwight D. Eisenhower, diary entry, September 3, 1939, Ibid., 446.
3 John S. D. Eisenhower, *General Ike*, 38.
4 Dwight D. Eisenhower to Leonard Gerow, August 23, 1940, Dwight D. Eisenhower, *The Prewar Diaries and Selected Papers*, 489–490; Dwight D. Eisenhower, *At Ease*, 237.
5 George S. Patton to Dwight D. Eisenhower, October 1, 1940, in Martin Blumenson, *The Patton Papers: 1940–1945* (Boston: Houghton Mifflin Harcourt, 1972), II, 15.
6 Dwight D. Eisenhower to Leonard Gerow, July 18, 1941, Eisenhower Library.
7 Walter Krueger to George C. Marshall, June 11, 1941, cited in Smith, *Eisenhower in War and Peace*, 162.
8 Hanson W. Baldwin, "Paratroopers Drop in New Exploit: 'Men from Mars' Tumble upon Blue Army Area in Louisiana War Games," *New York Times*, September 29, 1941.
9 Dwight D. Eisenhower, *Crusade in Europe*, 14.
10 Walter Krueger, *From Down under to Nippon: The Story of the Sixth Army in World War II* (Washington, D.C.: Combat Forces Press, 1953), 4.
11 Dwight D. Eisenhower, *Crusade in Europe*, 18.
12 Ibid., 21–22.
13 Forrest Pogue, *George C. Marshall* (New York: Viking, 1963–1987), II, 239.
14 Dwight D. Eisenhower, diary entry, January 4, 1942, in Dwight D. Eisenhower, *The Eisenhower Diaries*, Robert H. Ferrell, ed. (New York: W.W. Norton, 1981), 40.
15 Dwight D. Eisenhower, *At Ease*, 249.
16 Meeting of the U.S.–British chiefs of staff, December 25, 1941, United States Department of State, *Foreign Relations of the United States, The Conferences at Washington, 1941–1942, and Casablanca, 1943* (Washington, D.C.: U.S. Government Printing Office, 1968), 93.
17 Pogue, *George C. Marshall*, II, 276–277.
18 Dwight D. Eisenhower, diary entry, January 1, 1942, in Ferrell, ed., *The Eisenhower Diaries*, 40.
19 Ibid., January 22, 1942, 44.
20 Dwight D. Eisenhower, *Crusade in Europe*, 46.
21 Ibid.
22 Dwight D. Eisenhower, *At Ease*, 249–250.
23 Ibid., 250.
24 Memorandum for the Chief of Staff, February 28, 1942, Dwight D. Eisenhower, *Papers of Dwight D. Eisenhower: The War Years*, Alfred D. Chandler, ed. (Baltimore: Johns Hopkins University Press, 1970), I, 149–155.
25 Ibid., 47.
26 Nigel Hamilton, *The Mantle of Command: FDR at War, 1941–1942* (Boston: Houghton Mifflin Harcourt, 2014), passim; Idem, *Commander in Chief: FDR's Battle with Churchill, 1943*, 35–38.

27 Memorandum for the Chief of Staff, "Critical Points in the Development of Coordinated Viewpoint as to Major Tasks of War," March 25, 1942, Chandler, ed., *Papers: The War Years*, I, 205–207.
28 Winston Churchill, *The Hinge of Fate* (Boston: Houghton Mifflin, 1950), 323.
29 Hastings Ismay, *The Memoirs of General Lord Ismay* (New York: Viking, 1960), 249–250.
30 Mark Clark, *Calculated Risk* (London: George G. Harrap & Co. Ltd., 1951), 19.
31 Mark Clark, quoted in Miller, *Ike: The Soldier*, 363, and Mark Perry, *Partners in Command: George Marshall and Dwight Eisenhower in War and Peace* (New York: Penguin Press, 2007), 89.
32 H. H. Arnold, *Global Mission* (New York: Harper and Brothers, 1949), 315.
33 D'Este, *Eisenhower: A Soldier's Life*, 306.
34 Dwight D. Eisenhower to George C. Marshall, "Command Arrangements for Bolero," June 3, 1942, in Chandler, ed., *Papers: The War Years*, I, 327–328.
35 Directive for the Commanding General, ETO, June 8, 1942, Chandler, ed., *Papers: The War Years*, I, 334–335.
36 Dwight D. Eisenhower, diary entry, June 8, 1942, in Ferrell, ed., *The Eisenhower Diaries*, 62.
37 Ibid., June 11, 1942.
38 Alden Hatch, *Red Carpet for Mamie Eisenhower* (New York: Henry Holt, 1954), 180–181.
39 Churchill, *The Hinge of Fate*, 345.
40 Ibid., 381–382.
41 Ibid., 382.
42 Winston Churchill, *Their Finest Hour* (Boston: Houghton Mifflin, 1949), 173.
43 Winston Churchill, *The Grand Alliance* (Boston: Houghton Mifflin, 1950), 264–265.
44 Norman Rich, *Hitler's War Aims: Ideology, the Nazi State, and the Course of Expansion* (New York: W. W. Norton, 1973).
45 Conor Cruise O'Brien, *The Siege: The Saga of Israel and Zionism* (New York: Simon & Schuster, 1986), 251–252.
46 Quoted in Henry L. Stimson and McGeorge Bundy, *On Active Service in Peace and War* (New York: Harper & Brothers, 1948), 425.
47 Dwight D. Eisenhower to George C. Marshall, June 30, 1942, Chandler, ed., *Papers: The War Years*, I, 366–367.
48 Dwight D. Eisenhower, diary entry, July 22, 1942, in Ferrell, ed., *The Eisenhower Diaries*, 73.
49 Harry Butcher, *My Three Years with Eisenhower: The Personal Diary of Captain Harry C. Butcher, U.S.N.R* (New York: Simon & Schuster, 1946), 29.
50 Smith, *Eisenhower in War and Peace*, 212.
51 Dwight D. Eisenhower, *Crusade in Europe*, 71.
52 Pogue, *George C. Marshall*, II, 328.
53 Major General Richard W. Stephens, "Northwest Africa: Seizing the Initiative in the West," *U.S. Army in World War II: Mediterranean Theater of Operations* (Washington, D.C.: Government Printing Office, 1956), 15.
54 Gen. Walter Bedell Smith, memo for JCS, August 1, 1942, notes of Conference held at White House, 8:30 p.m., July 30, 1942, Smith, *Eisenhower in War and Peace*, 213 n34.
55 Mark Perry, *Partners in Command: George Marshall and Dwight Eisenhower in War and Peace* (New York and London: Penguin Books, 2007), 319.

ENDNOTES

56 Dwight D. Eisenhower, diary entry, September 2, 1942, in Ferrell, ed., *The Eisenhower Diaries*, 76.
57 Ibid., 77.
58 Ibid., 78.
59 Quoted in Miller, *Ike: The Soldier*, 388.
60 Dwight D. Eisenhower, *Letters to Mamie*, John S. D. Eisenhower, ed. (Garden City, NY: Doubleday, 1978), 40–41.
61 Smith, *Eisenhower in War and Peace*, 220.
62 Susan Eisenhower, *Mrs. Ike*, 206.
63 D'Este, *Eisenhower: A Soldier's Life*, 341–342.
64 Dwight D. Eisenhower to George C. Marshall, October 20, 1942, Chandler, ed., *Papers: The War Years*, I, 626–628.
65 Kay Summersby Morgan, *Past Forgetting: My Love Affair with Dwight D. Eisenhower* (New York: Simon & Schuster, 1976), 78.
66 Dwight D. Eisenhower to George C. Marshall, October 29, 1942, Chandler, ed., *Papers: The War Years*, I, 639–643.
67 Dwight D. Eisenhower, *Letters to Mamie*, 50–52.
68 Franklin D. Roosevelt, State of the Union address, January 6, 1942, Franklin D. Roosevelt, *The Public Papers and Addresses of Franklin D. Roosevelt: Humanity on the Defensive, 1942*, Samuel Rosenman, ed. (New York: Harper and Brothers, 1950) XI, 32.
69 Bureau of the Census, U.S. Department of Commerce, *Historical Statistics of the United States, Colonial Times to 1957* (Washington, D.C.: U.S. Government Printing Office, 1960), 711.
70 Alvin H. Hansen, *The American Economy* (New York: McGraw–Hill, 1957), 26.
71 *The Federal Reserve System: Its Purposes and Functions* (Washington, D.C.: U.S. Government Printing Office, 1939), 85.
72 Seymour E. Harris, "Fiscal Policy," *American Economic History*, Seymour E. Harris, ed. (New York: McGraw–Hill, 1961), 151, 155.
73 Anthony Solomon, quoted in Greider, *Secrets of the Temple*, 121.
74 This interview with FDR may be seen and heard in the documentary film *FDR*, directed by David Grubin for the PBS "American Experience" series and broadcast in 1994.

Chapter Four

1 Dwight D. Eisenhower to Walter Bedell Smith, November 9, 1942, Eisenhower Library.
2 Everett Hughes, diary entry, October 27, 1942, Manuscripts Division, Library of Congress, cited in Smith, *Eisenhower in War and Peace*, 234.
3 Smith, *Eisenhower in War and Peace*, 235.
4 William Manchester, *The Last Lion: Winston Spencer Churchill: Alone, 1932–1940* (Boston: Little, Brown, 1988), 263.
5 Dwight D. Eisenhower to Mark Clark, November 12, 1942, Chandler, ed., *Papers: The War Years*, II, 698.
6 Churchill, *The Hinge of Fate*, 637.
7 Dwight D. Eisenhower to John S. D. Eisenhower, December 20, 1942, Chandler, ed., *Papers: The War Years*, II, 855–856.

8 Robert Sherwood, *Roosevelt and Hopkins: An Intimate History* (New York: Harper, 1948), 651–652.

9 Larrabee, *Commander in Chief*, 426.

10 Dwight D. Eisenhower to Walter Bedell Smith, November 8, 1942, Chandler, ed., *Papers: The War Years*, II, 677.

11 Dwight D. Eisenhower to Winston Churchill, November 14, 1942, cited in D'Este, *Eisenhower: A Soldier's Life*, 357.

12 Blumenson, *The Patton Papers*, II, 137–138.

13 Arthur Bryant, *Turn of the Tide: A History of the War Years Based on the Diaries of Field-Marshal Lord Alanbrooke, Chief of the Imperial General Staff* (Garden City, NY: Doubleday, 1957), 430.

14 George C. Marshall to Dwight D. Eisenhower, December 22, 1942, Marshall, *Papers of George Catlett Marshall*, 488.

15 "Joint Chiefs of Staff Minutes of a Meeting at the White House," January 7, 1943, *Foreign Relations of the United States, The Conferences at Washington, 1941–1942, and Casablanca, 1943* (Washington, D.C.: Government Printing Office, 1968), 509–510.

16 Diaries of William Lyon Mackenzie King, Library and Archives Canada, Ottawa, Ontario, entry of December 6, 1942, cited in Nigel Hamilton, *Commander in Chief: FDR's Battle with Churchill, 1943* (Boston: Houghton Mifflin Harcourt, 2016), 37.

17 Everett Hughes, diary entry, December 30, 1942.

18 D'Este, *Eisenhower: A Soldier's Life*, 315.

19 Dwight D. Eisenhower to Mamie Eisenhower, December 31, 1942, in Dwight D. Eisenhower, *Letters to Mamie*.

20 Butcher, *My Three Years with Eisenhower*, 243.

21 Sherwood, *Roosevelt and Hopkins*, 689.

22 Hamilton, *Commander in Chief*, 90.

23 Ibid., 213.

24 Perry, *Partners in Command*, 191.

25 Korda, *Ike: An American Hero*, 362.

26 Perry, *Partners in Command*, 188.

27 Summersby Morgan, *Past Forgetting*, 104–105.

28 Dwight D. Eisenhower to Adjutant General, War Department [AGWAR], February 13, 1943, quoted in Rick Atkinson, *An Army at Dawn: The War in North Africa, 1942–1943* (New York: Henry Holt, 2002), 337.

29 Korda, *Ike: An American Hero*, 367.

30 Hamilton, *Commander in Chief*, 169.

31 Butcher, *My Three Years with Eisenhower*, 278–279; Hamilton, *Commander in Chief*, 171.

32 Dwight D. Eisenhower to Charles Moreau Harger, publisher of *Abilene Reflector*, April 23, 1943, Chandler, ed., *Papers: War Years*, II, 1099–1100.

33 Dwight D. Eisenhower to Leonard Gerow, February 24, 1943, Ibid., 985–987.

34 Smith, *Eisenhower in War and Peace*, 266.

35 Harold MacMillan, *War Diaries: Politics and War in the Mediterranean* (New York: St. Martin's Press, 1984), 260.

36 Dwight D. Eisenhower to Mamie Eisenhower, March 2, 1943, Dwight D. Eisenhower, *Letters to Mamie*, 104–105.

37 Everett Hughes, diary entry, February 12, 1943.

38 D'Este, *Eisenhower: A Soldier's Life*, 325.

39 Korda, *Ike: An American Hero*, 282.

40 Ibid., 283.

41 Merle Miller, *Plain Speaking: An Oral Biography of Harry S. Truman* (New York: Berkeley, 1974), 24.

42 Ibid., 339–340.

43 Robert H. Ferrell, "Plain Faking?" *American Heritage Magazine* 46, no. 3, (May–June 1995).

44 Smith, *Eisenhower in War and Peace*, 546, fn.

45 Ibid., 441.

46 Ibid., fn.

47 Omar N. Bradley and Clay Blair, *A General's Life: An Autobiography* (New York: Simon & Schuster, 1983), 133.

48 Anna Roosevelt Boettiger to John Boettiger, December 19, 1943, Franklin D. Roosevelt Library, Hyde Park, cited in Smith, *Eisenhower in War and Peace*, 315.

49 James Gavin, *On to Berlin: Battles of an Airborne Commander, 1943–1946* (New York: Viking, 1978), 142.

50 Smith, *Eisenhower in War and Peace*, 315.

51 Summersby Morgan, *Past Forgetting*, 117.

52 Ibid., 128.

53 Ibid., 131.

54 Ibid., 132.

55 Ibid., 137.

56 Susan Eisenhower, "Hardly an Affair," *Washington Post*, June 22, 1997.

57 Lloyd Shearer, "Kay Summersby and Dwight Eisenhower: The True Story of Their Friendship," *Parade*, January 2, 1977.

58 Hamilton, *Commander in Chief*, 221.

59 William D. Leahy, diary entry, May 13, 1943, William D. Leahy Papers, Library of Congress, cited in Hamilton, *Commander in Chief*, 209.

60 "Meeting of the Combined Chiefs of Staff, May 13, 1943," *Foreign Relations of the United States, The Conferences at Washington and Quebec, 1943*, (Washington, D.C.: Government Printing Office, 1970), 45.

61 King diaries, May 19, 1943, "Memorandum re: questions asked Mr. Churchill by members of the Senate of the U.S. and representatives of the Foreign Committee and answers given by Mr. Churchill," cited in Hamilton, *Commander in Chief*, 239.

62 Henry Stimson, diary entry, May 27, 1943, Henry L. Stimson Papers, Yale University Library, quoted in Hamilton, *Commander in Chief*, 253.

63 D'Este, *Eisenhower: A Soldier's Life*, 428.

64 Stimson, diary entry, August 10, 1943.

65 Dwight D. Eisenhower to George C. Marshall, August 24, 1943, Chandler, ed., *Papers: War Years*, II, 1353.

66 Dwight D. Eisenhower to George C. Marshall, September 6, 1943, Ibid., 1387–1390.

67 Hamilton, *Commander in Chief*, 313–314.

68 D'Este, *Eisenhower: A Soldier's Life*, 447.

69 Ibid., 423.

70 Korda, *Ike: An American Hero,* 411.

71 Butcher, *My Three Years with Eisenhower,* 420.

72 George C. Marshall to Dwight D. Eisenhower, September 22, 1943, Marshall, *Papers of George Catlett Marshall,* 136.

73 Stimson, diary entry, May 25, 1943.

74 Summersby Morgan, *Past Forgetting,* 156–157.

75 D'Este, *Eisenhower: A Soldier's Life,* 443.

76 Summersby Morgan, *Past Forgetting,* 146–149.

77 Dwight D. Eisenhower, *Crusade in Europe,* 147.

78 Summersby Morgan, *Past Forgetting,* 152.

79 Ibid., 153.

80 Sherwood, *Roosevelt and Hopkins,* 770.

81 Pogue, *George C. Marshall,* III, 307.

82 Elliott Roosevelt, *As He Saw It* (New York: Duell, Sloan, and Pearce, 1946), 144–145.

83 Summersby Morgan, *Past Forgetting,* 161.

84 Pogue, *George C. Marshall,* III, 321–322.

85 James Roosevelt, *My Parents: A Differing View* (New York: Playboy Press, 1976), 176.

86 Harry Butcher,, diary entry, Eisenhower Library, cited in Smith, *Eisenhower in War and Peace,* 323.

87 Bernard Law Montgomery, "First Impression of Operation OVERLORD, made at the request of the Prime Minister by General Montgomery," January 1, 1944, Montgomery Papers, British War Museum.

88 See William Safire, "Indeed a Very Dear Friend," *New York Times,* June 6, 1991.

89 John S. D. Eisenhower, *Strictly Personal,* 51.

90 Summersby Morgan, *Past Forgetting,* 168–172.

91 Dwight D. Eisenhower, Memorandum for the Record, March 22, 1944, Chandler, ed., *Papers: War Years,* III, 1782–1785.

92 Dwight D. Eisenhower to Brehon Somervell, April 4, 1944, Ibid., III, 1806–1807.

93 Dwight D. Eisenhower to Mamie Doud Eisenhower, May 12, 1944, Dwight D. Eisenhower, *Letters to Mamie,* 179.

94 Montgomery Papers, quoted in Smith, *Eisenhower in War and Peace,* 344.

95 Dwight D. Eisenhower, *Crusade in Europe,* 246–247.

96 Walter Bedell Smith, *Eisenhower's Six Great Decisions: Europe, 1944–1945* (New York: Longman, Greens, 1956), 55.

97 John S. D. Eisenhower, *Allies: Pearl Harbor to D–Day* (Garden City, N.Y.: Doubleday, 1982), 469.

98 Dwight D. Eisenhower, undated note, Eisenhower Library.

99 Summersby Morgan, *Past Forgetting,* 190–193.

Chapter Five

1 Korda, *Ike: An American Hero,* 430.

2 Dwight D. Eisenhower to Edgar Eisenhower, April 10, 1944, Chandler, ed., *Papers: The War Years,* III, 1816.

3 Summersby Morgan, *Past Forgetting,* 194.

4 Ibid., 194–196.

5 Robert A. Taft, "Liberalism—Real or New Deal," *Young Republican*, May 1936, 6–7, and *New York Times*, July 5, 1936, cited in James T. Patterson, *Mr. Republican: A Biography of Robert A. Taft* (Boston: Houghton Mifflin, 1972), 156.

6 Robert A. Taft to Sumner Keller, February 18, 1941, Keller Papers, Yale University, cited in Ibid., 243.

7 Robert A. Taft to Herbert Hoover, June 26, 1941, Hoover Papers, cited in Ibid., 246.

8 James MacGregor Burns, *Roosevelt: The Soldier of Freedom* (New York: Harcourt Brace Jovanovich, 1970), 511.

9 Korda, *Ike: An American Hero*, 449–451.

10 Bradley criticized Ike for blaming Monty in his memoirs for moving too slowly in the capture of Caen. He claimed that the agreed–upon plan "called for Monty not to 'break out' but to hold and draw the Germans to his sector." See Bradley and Blair, *A General's Life*, 265.

11 Dwight D. Eisenhower, *Crusade in Europe*, 269.

12 Dwight D. Eisenhower to George C. Marshall, June 20, 1944, Chandler, ed., *Papers: The War Years*, III, 1938.

13 Korda, *Ike: An American Hero*, 497.

14 Dwight D. Eisenhower to George C. Marshall, August 11, 1944, Chandler, ed., *Papers: The War Years*, IV, 2066–2067.

15 Dwight D. Eisenhower, *Crusade in Europe*, 279, and Martin Blumenson, *Breakout and Pursuit: U.S. Army in World War II: The European Theater of Operations* (Washington, D.C.: Office of the Chief of Military History, Department of the Army, 1961), 558.

16 Quoted in D'Este, *Eisenhower: A Soldier's Life*, 576.

17 John S. D. Eisenhower, *General Ike*, 175.

18 Dwight D. Eisenhower, *Letters to Mamie*, 193.

19 Gil Troy, "With Ike, Rumors were Steamier than Facts," *Washington Post*, Outlook, March 1, 1998, C–3.

20 Korda, *Ike: An American Hero*, 493.

21 Summersby Morgan, *Past Forgetting*, 178.

22 Abraham Lincoln to Don C. Buell, January 7, 1862, Abraham Lincoln, *Collected Works of Abraham Lincoln*, Roy P. Basler, ed. (New Brunswick, N.J.: Rutgers University Press, 1953), V, 98.

23 Bernard Law Montgomery, *Normandy to the Baltic* (Boston: Houghton Mifflin, 1948), 193.

24 Larrabee, *Commander in Chief*, 474–475.

25 Smith, *Eisenhower in War and Peace*, 398, 400–401.

26 Hans Speidel, *We Defended Normandy*, Ian Colvin, trans. (London: Herbert Jenkins, 1951), 152–153

27 Ambrose, *Eisenhower: Soldier, General of the Army, President–Elect*, 337.

28 Forrest Pogue, *The Supreme Command* (Washington, D.C.: U.S. Department of the Army, 1954), 245.

29 Roland G. Ruppenthal, *United States Army in World War II, The European Theater of Operations: Logistical Support of the Armies* (Washington, D.C.: Office of the Chief of Military History, United States Army, 1953), II, 8–10.

30 Francis De Guingand, *Operation Victory* (London: Hodder and Stoughton, 1947), 411–413.

31 "Interview with Major General Sir Miles Graham," January 19, 1949, Wilmot Papers, Liddell Hart Centre for Military Archives, Kings College, London, cited in Larrabee, *Commander in Chief,* 479.

32 Dwight D. Eisenhower, *Crusade in Europe,* 332–333.

33 Bradley and Blair, *A General's Life,* 343.

34 Bernard Law Montgomery to Alan Brooke, December 7, 1944, quoted in Nigel Hamilton, *Monty: Final Years of the Field Marshal, 1944–1976* (New York: McGraw-Hill, 1987), 162.

35 Arthur Bryant, *Triumph in the West: A History of the War Years Based on the Diaries of Field-Marshal Lord Alanbrooke, Chief of the Imperial General Staff* (Garden City, NY: Doubleday, 1959), 258.

36 Ibid., 257.

37 Summersby Morgan, *Past Forgetting,* 214.

38 Lord Alanbrooke, "Notes from My Life," November 14, 1944, quoted in D'Este, *Eisenhower: A Soldier's Life,* 631.

39 Dwight D. Eisenhower to Mamie Eisenhower, November 12, 1944, Dwight D. Eisenhower, *Letters to Mamie,* 219–220.

40 Doris Kearns Goodwin, *No Ordinary Time: Franklin and Eleanor Roosevelt, The Home Front in World War II* (New York: Simon & Schuster, 1994), 517–521.

41 The rank of "General of the Army" was created in 1866 for Ulysses S. Grant. It was surpassed by the rank of "General of the Armies," created for John J. Pershing and conferred posthumously on George Washington.

42 Among the multiple sources for the things that were said by both Ike and Patton at this Verdun meeting, see D'Este, *Eisenhower: A Soldier's Life,* 797, n22.

43 Ibid.

44 SHAEF office diary, December 20, 1944, Eisenhower Library, quoted in Stephen Ambrose, *Eisenhower: Soldier and President* (New York: Simon & Schuster, 1990), 174.

45 Smith, *Eisenhower in War and Peace,* 415.

46 Korda, *Ike: An American Hero,* 520–521.

47 John S. D. Eisenhower, *The Bitter Woods: The Battle of the Bulge* (New York: Putnam, 1969), 381–383.

48 Butcher, *My Three Years with Eisenhower,* 763.

49 Merle Miller, diary entry, February 26, 1945, quoted in Miller, *Ike: The Soldier,* 752.

50 Dwight D. Eisenhower, *Crusade in Europe,* 379–380.

51 Summersby Morgan, *Past Forgetting,* 217.

52 Omar N. Bradley, *A Soldier's Story* (New York: Popular Library, 1951), 535.

53 Dwight D. Eisenhower to Joseph Stalin, March 28, 1945, Chandler, ed., *Papers: The War Years,* IV, 2551.

54 Franklin D. Roosevelt to Winston Churchill, April 4, 1945, Franklin D. Roosevelt, *Churchill and Roosevelt: The Complete Correspondence,* Warren F. Kimball, ed. (Princeton, N.J.: Princeton University Press, 1984), III, 603–604.

55 Erich Fromm, *The Anatomy of Human Destructiveness* (New York: Holt, Rinehart & Winston, 1973), Fawcett edition, 362–474.

56 Dwight D. Eisenhower to George Marshall, April 15, 1945, Eisenhower Library.

57 Dwight D. Eisenhower to the Combined Chiefs of Staff, May 7, 1945, Chandler, ed., *Papers: The War Years,* IV, 2696.

58 Harry S. Truman, *Memoirs by Harry S. Truman, 1945: Year of Decisions* (Garden City, N.Y.: Doubleday, 1955), I, 214.

59 *London Times,* June 13, 1945.

60 Field Marshal Lord Alanbrooke, *War Diaries 1939–1945,* Alex Danchev and Daniel Todman, eds. (Berkeley: University of California Press, 2001), 697.

61 Miller, *Ike: The Soldier,* 781.

62 Butcher, *My Three Years with Eisenhower,* 869.

63 Ibid., 870.

64 Ambrose, *Eisenhower: Soldier, General of the Army, President-Elect, 1890-1952,* 413.

65 *New York Times,* June 20, 1945, quoted in Ibid., 412.

66 Butcher, diary entry, June 21, 1945, quoted in Ibid.

67 Dwight D. Eisenhower to George Allen, October 28, 1943, quoted in Ibid., 413.

68 Dwight D. Eisenhower, *Ike's Letters to a Friend, 1941–1958,* Robert W. Griffith, ed. (Manhattan, KS: University Press of Kansas, 1984), 33.

69 Dwight D. Eisenhower, *Crusade in Europe,* 444.

70 Dwight D. Eisenhower to Neill Bailey, August 1, 1945, quoted in Ambrose, *Eisenhower: Soldier, General of the Army, and President-Elect,* 414.

71 Miller, *Plain Speaking,* 339–340.

72 Ambrose, *Eisenhower: Soldier, General of the Army, and President-Elect,* 415.

73 Dwight D. Eisenhower to George Marshall, June 4, 1945, Chandler, ed., *Papers: The War Years,* V, 126–127.

74 Ambrose, *Eisenhower: Soldier, General of the Army, and President-Elect,* 417.

75 Korda, *Ike: An American Hero,* 591.

76 Smith, *Eisenhower in War and Peace,* 546.

77 Korda, *Ike: An American Hero,* 589.

78 Smith, *Eisenhower in War and Peace,* 441–442.

79 Ibid., 440.

80 Perry, *Partners in Command,* 364.

81 Summersby Morgan, *Past Forgetting,* 241.

82 Ibid.

83 Dwight D. Eisenhower to Kathleen McCarthy–Morrogh Summersby, November 22, 1945, Chandler, ed., *Papers: Occupation,* VI, 546–547.

84 Smith, *Eisenhower in War and Peace,* 443.

85 Summersby Morgan, *Past Forgetting,* 251.

86 Quoted in Davis, *Soldier of Democracy,* 547.

87 *New York Times,* August 15, 1945.

88 The Vaughan interview with the Associated Press generated significant news coverage. Writer Susan Wittig Albert found the following example of a front-page story in the course of her research for a 2017 novel based upon the Ike–Kay Summersby relationship: "Ike's Divorce Letter Still Exists, Says Former HST Aide," *High Point Enterprise,* High Point, NC, November 27, 1973, 1. Vaughan's claims were back referenced in a *Washington Post* story about the discovery of the Ike–Marshall correspondence about bringing Mamie over to Europe. See Robert J. Donovan, "Ike's 'Lost Letters' Dispute Divorce Claim," *Washington Post,* July 2, 1977.

89 Dr. John R. Steelman, oral history interview by Niel M. Johnson, February 29, 1996, Harry S. Truman Presidential Library and Museum, National Archives, 202–205, https://www.trumanlibrary.gov/library/oral-histories/steelm2b. Here are some excerpts from the interview.

Johnson: He wanted you to be a witness. Steelman: He was critical of Eisenhower I remember that. I can't remember his chauffeur's name now. Johnson: It's Kay Summersby. Steelman: Kay Summersby, yes. Johnson: Was that what the issue was about when you were with Marshall? Steelman: Yes. Johnson: In the Oval Office. Steelman: That's right. Johnson: What do you remember about that? Steelman: Marshall wanted to criticize Eisenhower and he was afraid that Truman was too prejudiced in favor of Eisenhower and so he wanted me as a witness that.... Johnson: But was it a letter? Did he have two letters with him, one letter from Eisenhower to him and then a letter that he was going to send Eisenhower? Steelman: That's right. Yes, he was going to burn Eisenhower up, you know. Johnson: Because of what? Steelman: Oh, Eisenhower had said he was going to divorce Mamie and marry Kay, and Marshall told him, "If you do that, I'll bust you out of the army, so help me. Don't you dare do that." Johnson: What did he advise Marshall to do with those two letters, to burn them or save them? Steelman: Oh, yes. Truman said, "Take the letters over and burn them." And so on the way out, Marshall said to me, "This is one time I'm going to defy the President. I ain't going to burn them; I'm going to file them."

90 Ibid., 238.
91 "Kay Summersby Morgan Dies, Eisenhower Confidante in War," New York Times, January 21, 1975.
92 Summersby Morgan, Past Forgetting, 248.
93 Ibid., 16.
94 Ibid., 250–251.
95 Dwight D. Eisenhower, diary entry, December 2, 1947, Ferrell, ed., The Eisenhower Diaries, 145.

Chapter Six

1 Ibid., March 8, 1947, 140.
2 Dwight D. Eisenhower to Swede Hazlett, August 25, 1947, Griffith, ed., Ike's Letters to a Friend, 42–43.
3 Dwight D. Eisenhower, diary entry, December 31, 1947, Ferrell, ed., The Eisenhower Diaries, 145.
4 Ibid., January 15, 1948, 147.
5 Ibid., November 25, 1949, 166.
6 Ibid., January 1, 1950, 170.
7 Korda, Ike: An American Hero, 629.
8 Perry Miller, Errand into the Wilderness (Cambridge, MA: Belknap Press of Harvard University Press, 1956), Harper Torchbook edition, 15.
9 Summersby Morgan, Past Forgetting, 136–137.
10 Ibid., 178.
11 Ibid., 244–245.
12 Kay took the Berlin job that Lucius Clay had offered. Then she returned to the United States in October, 1946, and was ordered to serve as an army public

relations official in California. She did not return to the East Coast until the next summer. She and Ike exchanged letters in 1946—some of which are in the pre-presidential papers at the Eisenhower Library and some of which were auctioned at Sotheby's in 1991 and 2008. She visited Harry Butcher in California—Harry, who divorced his wife, Ruth, so he could marry his wartime girlfriend, and who wrote a memoir, *My Three Years with Eisenhower*. This book caused Ike embarrassment because of some things it disclosed. Harry told Kay that she ought to write a memoir of her own. This would be her first memoir, *Eisenhower was My Boss*, which was published in 1948. It would be interesting to know how much tension the knowledge of this impending publication might have caused for Ike. In any case, this information about the postwar life of Kay Summersby was gleaned by the writer Susan Wittig Albert in the course of preparing to write her 2017 novel, *The General's Women*. Ms. Albert has posted a guide to this research under the title *Kay Summersby, Missing Person: A Biographical Epilogue*, and the guide is annotated. It is accessible via https://susanalbert.com/wp–content/uploads/2019/04/Biographical–Afterword–TGW.pdf.

13 Korda, *Ike: An American Hero*, 600.

14 House Committee on Military Affairs, Hearings on H.R. 515, 79th Cong., 1st Session, 1945, 77–78, cited in Smith, *Eisenhower in War and Peace*, 457.

15 Dwight D. Eisenhower, diary entry, June 11, 1949, Ferrell, ed., *The Eisenhower Diaries*, 160.

16 Ibid., May 16, 1946, 136–137.

17 Ibid.

18 Ibid., December 2, 1946, 139.

19 Ibid., November 12, 1946, 138.

20 Ibid.

21 Ibid., 139.

22 Ibid., 138.

23 Ibid., September 16, 1947, 143.

24 Theodore Roosevelt to George Otto Trevelyan, October 1, 1911, in Theodore Roosevelt, *Cowboys and Kings: Three Great Letters of Theodore Roosevelt*, Elting E. Morison, ed. (Cambridge, MA: Harvard University Press, 1954), 93–94.

25 Dwight D. Eisenhower, *Mandate for Change*, 81.

26 Dwight D. Eisenhower to Walter Bedell Smith, July 3, 1947, Chandler, ed., *Papers: The War Years*, VIII, 1799–1800.

27 Robert J. Donovan, *Conflict and Crisis: The Presidency of Harry S. Truman, 1945–1948* (New York: W.W. Norton, 1977), 338. Donovan confirmed the Truman offer to Ike in oral history interviews with Samuel Rosenman, John Steelman, John Snyder, and Milton Eisenhower. See idem, 457, fn 1–4.

28 Robinson memo of April 1, 1948, Robinson to Leo Perpen, June 12, 1948, Robinson Papers, cited in Ambrose, *Eisenhower: Soldier, General of the Army, and President-Elect*, 478.

29 Dwight D. Eisenhower, inaugural address, Columbia University, October 12, 1948, in Travis Beal Jacobs, *Eisenhower at Columbia* (New Brunswick, N.J.: Transaction Publishers, 2001), 120.

30 Dwight D. Eisenhower, diary entry, January 14, 1949, Ferrell, ed., *The Eisenhower Diaries*, 153.

31 Dwight D. Eisenhower, "Address to first Columbia 'Forum on Democracy,'" February 12, 1949, Eisenhower Library.

32 Dwight D. Eisenhower, diary entry, September 27, 1949, Ferrell, ed., *The Eisenhower Diaries*, 164.

33 Ibid., January 1, 1950, 170.

34 Ibid., April 5, 1950, 173.

35 Ibid., October 29, 1951, 203.

36 Ibid., March 22, 1950, 173.

37 William Robinson to Helen Rogers Reid, June 21, 1948, William Robinson Papers, Box 9, Eisenhower Library, cited in Blanche Wiesen Cook, *The Declassified Eisenhower* (New York: Doubleday, 1981), Penguin edition, 77–78.

38 Dwight D. Eisenhower, diary entry, May 15, 1951, Ferrell, ed., *The Eisenhower Diaries*, 193.

39 Summersby Morgan, *Past Forgetting*, 246.

40 Whittaker Chambers, *Witness* (New York: Random House, 1952), 471–472.

41 Ira Henry Freeman, "Eisenhower of Columbia," *New York Times Magazine*, November 7, 1948, cited in Smith, *Eisenhower in War and Peace*, 481.

42 Richard Rovere, *Harper's Magazine*, November, 1948.

43 Jacques Barzun, interview by Travis Beal Jacobs, April 7, 1979, quoted in Jacobs, *Eisenhower at Columbia*, 144.

44 Dwight D. Eisenhower to Swede Hazlett, August 12, 1949, Griffith, ed., *Ike's Letters to a Friend*, 61–62.

45 Dwight D. Eisenhower to Louis Graham Smith, May 25, 1948, Galambos, ed., *Papers: Columbia University*, X, 84–87.

46 Harry J. Carman, interview with Travis Beal Jacobs, December 1, 1961, in Jacobs, *Eisenhower at Columbia*, 87.

47 Summersby Morgan, *Past Forgetting*, 247.

48 Clifford Roberts, interview, September 12, 29, 1968, Columbia Oral History Project, cited in Smith, *Eisenhower in War and Peace*, 479.

49 Dwight D. Eisenhower to James Forrestal, November 4, 1948, Galambos, ed., *Papers: Columbia University*, X, 283.

50 Dwight D. Eisenhower, diary entry, February 4, 1949, Ferrell, ed., *The Eisenhower Diaries*, 156–157.

51 Dwight D. Eisenhower to Milton Eisenhower, May 13, 1949, Galambos, ed., *Papers: Columbia University*, X, 580–581.

52 Dwight D. Eisenhower, diary entry, July 7, 1949, Ferrell, ed., *The Eisenhower Diaries*, 161–162.

53 John Krout, interview, Eisenhower Library, cited in Ambrose, *Eisenhower: Soldier, General of the Army, President Elect*, 480.

54 Richard Rovere, "The Second Eisenhower Boom," *Harper's Magazine*, May 1950, 31–39.

55 Dwight D. Eisenhower, diary entry, October 14, 1949, Ferrell, ed., *The Eisenhower Diaries*, 164.

56 Ibid., November 25, 1949, 166.

57 Ibid., January 1, 1950, 168.

58 Dwight D. Eisenhower to A. Andrews, September 29, 1950, quoted in Ambrose, *Eisenhower: Soldier, General of the Army, President–Elect*, 482, and Cook, *The Declassified Eisenhower*, 83–84.

59 Richard Rovere, *Senator Joe McCarthy* (Cleveland: World Publishing Company, 1960), 11.

60 Quoted in Manchester, *American Caesar*, 535.

61 Dwight D. Eisenhower to Philip C. Jessup, March 18, 1950, Galambos, ed., *Papers: Columbia University*, XI, 1014.

62 Ibid., June 30, 1950, 175.

63 William E. Jenner, *Congressional Record*, 81st Congress, 2nd Session, 14914–14917, cited in Dean Acheson, *Present at the Creation: My Years in the State Department* (New York: W.W. Norton, 1969), 365.

64 *Congressional Record*, 81st Congress, 1st Session, 6602.

65 Dwight D. Eisenhower, October 16, 1950, Galambos, ed., *Papers: Columbia University*, XI, 1383.

66 Dwight D. Eisenhower, diary entry, October 28, 1950, Ferrell, ed., *The Eisenhower Diaries*, 180.

67 Ibid.

68 Ibid., November 6, 1950, 181.

69 Ibid., November 29, 1950, 182.

70 Cook, *The Declassified Eisenhower*, 88–89.

71 Dwight D. Eisenhower, diary entry, November 6, 1950, Ferrell, ed., *The Eisenhower Diaries*, 181.

72 Ibid., December 16, 1950, 183.

73 Oren Root, "Why We Wanted Willkie," *Constitution*, Spring–Summer 1990, 50–57.

74 Robert A. Taft, quoted in Alonzo Hamby, *Liberalism and Its Challengers: From F.D.R. to Bush* (New York: Oxford University Press, 1985), 106.

75 Hamby, *Liberalism and Its Challengers*, 110.

76 Korda, *Ike: An American Hero*, 624.

77 Dwight D. Eisenhower, *At Ease*, 372.

78 Ibid., 372.

79 C. L. Sulzberger, *A Long Row of Candles: Memoirs and Diaries, 1934–1954* (New York: Macmillan, 1969), 702.

80 Minutes, Columbia University Board of Trustees, February 8, 1951, Carl W. Ackerman manuscript collection, Library of Congress, cited in Smith, *Eisenhower in War and Peace*, 496.

81 Dwight D. Eisenhower to Swede Hazlett, June 21, 1951, Griffith, ed., *Ike's Letters to a Friend*, 85.

82 Dwight D. Eisenhower, diary entry, March 17, 1951, Ferrell, ed., *The Eisenhower Diaries*, 190.

83 Ibid., April 23, 1951, 191–192.

84 Ibid., March 13, 1951, 189.

85 Cook, *The Declassified Eisenhower*, 109.

86 Hoover and Taft quoted in Justus Doenecke, *Not to the Swift: The Old Isolationists in the Cold War Era* (Lewisburg, PA: Bucknell University Press, 1979), 198–199, 202.

87 Douglas MacArthur, Senate Committees on Armed Services and Foreign Relations, 82nd Congress, 1st Session, Hearings to Conduct an Inquiry into the Military Situation in the Far East and the Facts Surrounding the Relief of General of the Army Douglas MacArthur from his Assignments in that Area, 3544, cited in Acheson, *Present at the Creation*, 520.

88 Lucius D. Clay to Dwight D. Eisenhower, April 13, 1951, Dwight D. Eisenhower Personal Papers, Box 22, Eisenhower Library.

89 Swede Hazlett to Dwight D. Eisenhower, June 1, 1951, Box 51, Eisenhower Library.

90 Dwight D. Eisenhower, diary entry, June 5, 1951, Ferrell, ed., *The Eisenhower Diaries*, 194.

91 Dwight D. Eisenhower to members of Congress, June 19, 1951, Box 91, Eisenhower Library.

92 Cook, *The Declassified Eisenhower*, 109.

93 Dwight D. Eisenhower, diary entry, April 27, 1951, Ferrell, ed., *The Eisenhower Diaries*, 192–193.

94 Stanley Rumbough Jr., *Citizens for Eisenhower* (McLean, VA.: International Publishers, 2013), 20–23.

95 Dwight D. Eisenhower to Lucius D. Clay, September 27, 1951, Galambos, ed., *Papers: NATO and the Campaign of 1952*, XII, 580.

96 Lucius D. Clay to Dwight D. Eisenhower, September 29, 1951, *Ibid.*, XII, 607, n5.

97 Dwight D. Eisenhower, diary entry, October 4, 1951, Ferrell, ed., *The Eisenhower Diaries*, 199.

98 Ibid., October 5, 1951, 200.

99 Truman's offer to Ike was revealed by Arthur Krock in the *New York Times* on November 8, 1951.

100 Henry Cabot Lodge Jr., interview with Jean Edward Smith, May 5, 1971, cited in Smith, *Lucius D. Clay: An American Life* (New York: Henry Holt & Co., 1990), 585.

101 Dwight D. Eisenhower, diary entry, December 11, 1951, Ferrell, ed., *The Eisenhower Diaries*, 206.

102 Dwight D. Eisenhower to Lucius D. Clay, December 19, 1951, Personal File, Eisenhower Library.

103 Harry S. Truman to Dwight D. Eisenhower, December 18, 1951, cited in David McCullough, *Truman* (New York: Simon & Schuster, 1992), 888.

104 Dwight D. Eisenhower to Lucius D. Clay, December 27, 1951, Galambos, ed., *Papers: NATO and the Campaign of 1952*, XII, 817–818.

105 Dwight D. Eisenhower to Henry Cabot Lodge Jr., December 29, 1951, Ibid., 829.

106 Dwight D. Eisenhower to Clifford Roberts, January 11, 1952, Eisenhower Library, cited in Ambrose, *Eisenhower: Soldier, General of the Army, President Elect*, 522.

107 C. L. Sulzberger, "Larger Duty Cited; But General Precludes any Political Action before Convention," *New York Times*, January 8, 1952.

108 Dwight D. Eisenhower to George A. Sloan, January 3, 1952, Galambos, ed., *Papers: NATO and the Campaign of 1952*, XII, 836–838.

109 Dwight D. Eisenhower, *Mandate for Change*, 20.

110 Dwight D. Eisenhower, diary entries, February 11, 1952, and February 12, 1952, Ferrell, ed., *The Eisenhower Diaries*, 214.

111 Jean Edward Smith, *Lucius D. Clay*, 603.

112 Albert, *Kay Summersby, Missing Person*, 10.

113 Rumbough, *Citizens for Eisenhower*, 40.

114 Jacqueline Cochran, interview, Eisenhower Library, cited in Smith, *Eisenhower in War and Peace*, 512.

115 Ambrose, *Eisenhower: Soldier, General of the Army, President Elect*, 525.

116 Marquis Childs, *Eisenhower: Captive Hero* (New York: Harcourt, Brace, 1958), 134.

117 Ambrose, *Eisenhower: Soldier, General of the Army, President Elect*, 536.

118 Ibid., 537–538.

119 Smith, *Eisenhower in War and Peace*, 518–519.

120 Leo Egan, "Taft Gives Winner his Pledge of Aid," *New York Times*, July 12, 1952.

121 Herbert Brownell, interview by Jean Edward Smith, April 7, 1971, cited in Smith, *Eisenhower in War and Peace*, 520–521.

122 Henry Cabot Lodge Jr., interview by Jean Edward Smith, May 5, 1971, Ibid., 522.

123 Brownell, interview, Ibid., 521.

124 Ambrose, *Eisenhower: Soldier, General of the Army, President Elect*, 543.

125 Smith, *Eisenhower in War and Peace*, 531.

126 Dwight D. Eisenhower to Harry S. Truman, August 14, 1952, Galambos, ed., *Papers: NATO and the Campaign of 1952*, XIII, 1322–1323.

127 Harry S. Truman to Dwight D. Eisenhower, August 16, 1952, Ibid., 1327 n1.

128 Dwight D. Eisenhower, *Mandate for Change*, 318n.

129 "Text of Eisenhower Talk Scoring 'Barefaced Looters,'" *New York Times*, September 10, 1952.

130 Emmet John Hughes, *The Ordeal of Power: A Political Memoir of the Eisenhower Years* (New York: Atheneum, 1963), 41.

131 *New York Post*, September 18, 1952.

132 Roger Morris, *Richard Milhous Nixon: The Rise of an American Politician* (New York: Henry Holt, 1990), 770–771.

133 Smith, *Lucius D. Clay*, 605.

134 Ibid., 606.

135 Garry Wills, *Nixon Agonistes: The Crisis of the Self-Made Man* (Boston: Houghton Mifflin, 1970), 102.

136 Morris, *Richard Milhous Nixon*, 822–823.

137 Gladwin Hill, "Nixon Leaves Fate to G.O.P. Chiefs," *New York Times*, September 24, 1952.

138 Smith, *Lucius D. Clay*, 606.

139 "Text of Eisenhower Talk in Cleveland Praising Nixon," *New York Times*, September 24, 1952.

140 Hughes, *The Ordeal of Power*, 42.

141 David A. Nichols, *Ike and McCarthy: Dwight Eisenhower's Secret Campaign Against Joseph McCarthy* (New York: Simon & Schuster, 2017), 5.

142 Ambrose, *Eisenhower: Soldier, General of the Army, President Elect*, 561.

143 Cook, *The Declassified Eisenhower*, 81.

144 "Text of General Eisenhower's Speech on 'Middle Way,'" *New York Times*, August 21, 1952, 8.

145 Bernard Shanley diaries, Eisenhower Library, cited in William I. Hitchcock, *The Age of Eisenhower: America and the World in the 1950s* (New York: Simon & Schuster, 2018), 82.

146 Curt Gentry, *J. Edgar Hoover: The Man and his Secrets* (New York: Norton, 1991), 402–403; Athan Theoharis, *From the Secret Files of J. Edgar Hoover* (Chicago: Ivan R. Dee,

1991), 284–286; David K. Johnson, *The Lavender Scare: The Cold War Persecution of Gays and Lesbians in the Federal Government* (Chicago: University of Chicago Press, 2004), 122–123; Marquis Childs, *Witness to Power* (New York: McGraw–Hill, 1975), 67–68.

147 Smith, *Eisenhower in War and Peace*, 546.

148 "Text of General Eisenhower's Speech in Detroit on Ending the War in Korea," *New York Times*, October 25, 1952.

Chapter Seven

1 Evan Thomas, *Ike's Bluff: President Eisenhower's Secret Battle to Save the World* (New York and Boston: Little, Brown, 2012), 412.

2 Acheson, *Present at the Creation*, 706.

3 Herbert Brownell, *Advising Ike: The Memoirs of Attorney General Brownell* (Lawrence, KS: University Press of Kansas, 1993), 131–132.

4 John Foster Dulles, "Evolution of Foreign Policy," speech to the Council on Foreign Relations, January 12, 1954, Department of State Press Release 8, 1954, cited in Smith, *Eisenhower in War and Peace*, 643.

5 Dwight D. Eisenhower to John Foster Dulles, September 8, 1953, cited in Ambrose, *Eisenhower: The President*, 124.

6 John Foster Dulles to Dwight D. Eisenhower, September 10, 1953, Ibid.

7 Ibid., I, 443.

8 Conference, October 19, 1954, Ann Whitman administrative series, Eisenhower Library, cited in Ambrose, *Eisenhower: The President*, 227. The unfitness of Allen Dulles was brought to Ike's attention more forcefully by an ex-CIA official named Jim Killis, who told Ike in a letter dated May 24, 1954, that the CIA was "in a rotten state" and that Allen Dulles was a "ruthless, ambitious, and utterly incompetent government administrator." Anne Whitman file, Eisenhower Library.

9 William Bragg Ewald Jr., *Eisenhower the President: Crucial Days, 1951–1960* (Englewood Cliffs, N.J.: Prentice–Hall, 1981), 32.

10 Dwight D. Eisenhower, diary entry, February 7, 1953, Ferrell, ed., *The Eisenhower Diaries*, 227.

11 Dwight D. Eisenhower to Cliff Roberts, July 29, 1952, Galambos, ed., *Papers: NATO and the Campaign of 1952*, XIII, 1283–1285.

12 Ibid.

13 Herbert S. Parmet, *Eisenhower and the American Crusades* (New York: Macmillan, 1972), 176.

14 Mark Clark, oral history, Columbia University, cited in Smith, *Eisenhower in War and Peace*, 559.

15 Dwight D. Eisenhower, *Mandate for Change*, 95.

16 Stephen Ambrose, *Eisenhower: The President* (New York: Simon & Schuster, 1984), 33.

17 "Texts of Eisenhower's Statements on Trip to Korea," *New York Times*, December 15, 1952.

18 Ambrose, *Eisenhower: The President*, 35, 680, fn.51.

19 Dwight D. Eisenhower, interview, Dulles Oral History Project, Princeton, cited in Ibid., 35, 680, fn. 52.

20 Peter Lyon, *Eisenhower: Portrait of the Hero* (New York: Little Brown and Company, 1974), 472.

21 Nichols, *Ike and McCarthy*, 81.

22 David A. Nichols, *A Matter of Justice: Eisenhower and the Beginning of the Civil Rights Revolution* (New York: Simon & Schuster, 2007), 40.

23 Nichols, *Ike and McCarthy*, 15.

24 Dwight D. Eisenhower, diary entry, January 21, 1953, Ferrell, ed., *The Eisenhower Diaries*, 225.

25 J. B. West and Mary Lynn Kotz, *Upstairs at the White House: My Life with the First Ladies* (New York: Coward, McCann, and Geoghegan, 1973).

26 Dwight D. Eisenhower, diary entry, February 1, 1953, Ferrell, ed., *The Eisenhower Diaries*, 226.

27 L. Arthur Minnich, notes of cabinet meeting, January 23, 1953, cited in Ambrose, *Eisenhower: The President*, 45.

28 Robert J. Donovan, *Confidential Secretary: Ann Whitman's 20 Years with Eisenhower and Rockefeller* (New York: Dutton, 1988), 14; Susan Eisenhower, *Mrs. Ike*, 205–210.

29 Quoted in Arthur Krock, *Memoirs: Sixty Years on the Firing Line* (New York: Funk and Wagnalls, 1968), 281.

30 Thomas, *Ike's Bluff*, 73.

31 Ibid., 74.

32 NSC meeting, March 31, 1953, *Foreign Relations of the United States, 1952–1954*, XV, 825–827.

33 Hitchcock, *The Age of Eisenhower*, 104.

34 Thomas, *Ike's Bluff*, 79–80.

35 Dwight D. Eisenhower, *Mandate for Change*, 230.

36 Allan R. Millett, "Eisenhower and the Korean War: Cautionary Tale and Hopeful Precedent," in *Forging the Shield: Eisenhower and National Security for the 21st Century*, Dennis E. Showalter, ed. (Chicago: Imprint Publications, 2005), 51.

37 Hughes, *The Ordeal of Power*, 105.

38 NSC notes, April 9, 1953, Eisenhower Library, cited in Ambrose, *Eisenhower: Soldier and President*, 327.

39 Dwight D. Eisenhower, "The Chance for Peace," April 16, 1953, *Public Papers of the Presidents of the United States: Dwight D. Eisenhower, 1953* (Washington, D.C.: Government Printing Office, 1958), 179–188.

40 Philip Taubman, *Secret Empire: Eisenhower, the CIA, and the Hidden Story of America's Space Espionage* (New York: Simon & Schuster, 2003), 12–13.

41 R. Cargill Hall, "Clandestine Victory: Eisenhower and Overhead Reconnaissance in the Cold War," in Showalter, ed., *Forging the Shield*, 124.

42 Taubman, *Secret Empire*, 70, 199.

43 Ibid., 197.

44 Ibid., 202.

45 Dwight D. Eisenhower, Radio–Television Address on National Security and Its Costs, May 19, 1953, *Public Papers: Eisenhower, 1953*, 306–316.

46 Dwight D. Eisenhower, *At Ease*, 31.

47 Lewis Douglas to Franklin D. Roosevelt, November 28, 1934, Franklin D. Roosevelt Library, President's Personal File, 1914, cited in William E. Leuchtenburg, *Franklin D. Roosevelt and the New Deal: 1932-1940* (New York: Harper & Row, 1963), Harper Torchbooks, 91.

48 *Historical Statistics of the United States, Colonial Times to 1957*, Bureau of the Census, U.S. Department of Commerce (Washington, D.C.: Government Printing Office, 1961), 714.

49 Walton and Rockoff, *History of the American Economy*, 552.

50 Accessible via http://www.law.cornell.edu/supremecourt/text/79/457#writing-type-1 -STRONG.

51 Robert J. Donovan, *Eisenhower: The Inside Story* (New York: Harper and Brothers, 1956), 209.

52 Dwight D. Eisenhower, diary entry, May 1, 1953, Galambos, ed., *Papers: The Presidency*, XIV, 195–197.

53 Dwight D. Eisenhower, diary entry, January 18, 1954, Ferrell, ed., *The Eisenhower Diaries*, 269.

54 Quoted in Kai Bird, *The Chairman: John J. McCloy, The Making of the American Establishment* (New York: Simon & Schuster, 1992), 468.

55 Dwight D. Eisenhower, Remarks at Dartmouth College Commencement Exercises, June 14, 1953, *Public Papers: Eisenhower, 1953*, 411–415.

56 Dwight D. Eisenhower, Radio and Television Address Announcing the Signing of the Korean Armistice, July 26, 1953, *Public Papers: Eisenhower, 1953*, 520–522.

57 Thomas, *Ike's Bluff*, 107.

58 See Robert R. Bowie, "Bowie's Commentary," in *American Cold War Strategy: Interpreting NSC 68*, Ernest May, ed. (Boston: Bedford Books of St. Martin's Press, 1993), 113–114, and William B. Pickett, *George F. Kennan and the Origins of Eisenhower's New Look: An Oral History of Project Solarium* (Princeton, N.J.: Princeton Institute for International and Regional Studies, 2004).

59 Hitchcock, *The Age of Eisenhower*, 110.

60 NSC 162/2, "A Report to the National Security Council by the Executive Secretary on Basic National Security Policy," accessible via https://irp.fas.org/offdocs/nsc-hst/nsc-162-2.pdf.

61 Emmet Hughes, diary entry, September 15, 1953, Hughes Papers, Seeley G. Mudd Manuscript Library, Princeton University.

62 Dwight D. Eisenhower to John Foster Dulles, September 8, 1953, Galambos, ed., *Papers: The Presidency*, XIV, 505.

63 Notes of National Security Council meeting, September 24, 1953, Eisenhower Library, cited in Thomas, *Ike's Bluff*, 103.

64 Memorandum of conversation, December 4, 1953, Eisenhower Library, in Hitchcock, *The Age of Eisenhower*, 111.

65 "Speech before the United Nations," December 12, 1953, Ann Whitman file, Eisenhower Library, cited in Thomas, *Ike's Bluff*, 111.

66 Thomas, *Ike's Bluff*, 112.

67 Hall, "Clandestine Victory," in Showalter, ed., *Forging the Shield*, 120.

68 Conference with William Knowland, November 23, 1954, Ann Whitman administration series, Eisenhower Library, cited in Ambrose, *Eisenhower: The President*, 226.

69 Quoted in Stephen Kinzer, *All the Shah's Men: An American Coup and the Roots of Middle East Terror* (Hoboken, N.J.: John Wiley and Sons, 2003), preface.

70 James Chace, *Acheson: The Secretary of State Who Created the American World* (New York: Simon & Schuster, 1998), 353.

71 Harry S. Truman to Henry Grady, Grady Papers, Truman Presidential Library, quoted in Smith, *Eisenhower in War and Peace*, 619.

72 Dwight D. Eisenhower, diary entry, January 6, 1953, Ferrell, ed., *The Eisenhower Diaries*, 223.

73 Anthony Eden to Winston Churchill, March 6, 1953, Anthony Eden, *Full Circle: The Memoirs of Anthony Eden* (Boston: Houghton Mifflin, 1960), 235.

74 Ambrose, *Eisenhower: The President*, 111.

75 Kinzer, *All the Shah's Men*, 161.

76 Ibid.

77 Memorandum of Telephone Conversation, by the Secretary of State, July 24, 1953, 10:55 a.m., *Foreign Relations of the United States, 1952–1954, Iran*, X (Washington, D.C.: U.S. Government Printing Office, 1989), 737.

78 Editorial Board, "Land Reform in Guatemala," *New York Times*, May 21, 1952, 26.

79 Dwight D. Eisenhower, diary entry, June 11, 1951, Ferrell, ed., *The Eisenhower Diaries*, 195.

80 Quoted in Parmet, *Eisenhower and the American Crusades*, 192.

81 Dwight D. Eisenhower, diary entry, October 27, 1953, Ferrell, ed., *The Eisenhower Diaries*, 257.

82 Conversation between Eisenhower and Gabriel Hauge, February 13, 1956, in Ann Whitman, diary entry, Box 8, Eisenhower Library, cited in Cook, *The Declassified Eisenhower*, 155.

83 Dwight D. Eisenhower, *Mandate for Change*, 139.

84 Ambrose, *Eisenhower: The President*, 197.

85 Donovan, *Eisenhower: The Inside Story*, 154–163.

86 Nichols, *A Matter of Justice*, 26–42.

87 Ibid., 43.

88 Brownell, *Advising Ike*, 193–194.

89 Nichols, *A Matter of Justice*, 56.

90 Adam Clayton Powell, speech, February 28, 1954, *New York Times*, March 1, 1954.

91 Quoted in Jack Harrison Pollack, *Earl Warren: The Judge Who Changed America* (Englewood Cliffs, NJ: Prentice Hall, 1979), 160–161.

92 Dwight D. Eisenhower to Edgar Eisenhower, October 1, 1953, and Dwight D. Eisenhower to Milton Eisenhower, October 9, 1953, Galambos, ed., *Papers: The Presidency*, XIV, 551–552, 576–578.

93 Dwight D. Eisenhower, diary entry, October 8, 1953, Ibid., 564–570.

94 Dwight D. Eisenhower, diary entry, April 1, 1953, Ibid., 136–139.

95 Henry Cabot Lodge Jr. to Dwight D. Eisenhower, February 9, 1954, Henry Cabot Lodge Papers, Lodge–Eisenhower Correspondence, 1950–1955, cited in Nichols, *Ike and McCarthy*, 132.

96 Memorandum of Discussion at the 194th Meeting of the National Security Council, April 29, 1954, United States Department of State, *Foreign Relations of the United States,*

1952–1954, *Indochina*, XIII (Washington, D.C.: U.S. Government Printing Office, 1982), 1431–1445.

97 Ambrose, *Eisenhower: The President*, 184.

98 *Foreign Relations of the United States, 1952–1954*, XIII, 1431–1445.

99 Statements by John Foster Dulles, June 23, 1954, and July 23, 1954, Eisenhower Library, cited in Hitchcock, *The Age of Eisenhower*, 203–204.

100 Nichols, *Ike and McCarthy*, 96–97.

101 Ibid., 10, 47.

102 Swede Hazlett to Dwight D. Eisenhower, March 25, 1954, Eisenhower Library, cited in Ibid., 213.

103 Henry Cabot Lodge Jr. to Dwight D. Eisenhower, February 23, 1954, Henry Cabot Lodge Papers, cited in Nichols, *Ike and McCarthy*, 149.

104 Nichols, *Ike and McCarthy*, 158.

105 Ibid., 121–123; Brownell, *Advising Ike*, 257–258.

106 I have transcribed Welch's statement from Emil de Antonio's film *Point of Order* (1964). This documentary film about the army–McCarthy hearings used archival television footage for its value as cinéma vérité.

107 President's Radio and TV Address to the American People on the Administration's Purposes and Accomplishments, January 4, 1954, *Public Papers: Eisenhower, 1954*, 2–23.

108 Donovan, *Eisenhower: The Inside Story*, 213.

109 Ibid., 214.

110 Ibid. See also Jean Edward Smith, *Lucius D. Clay*, 618–619.

111 Dwight D. Eisenhower, diary entry, April 8, 1954, Ferrell, ed., *The Eisenhower Diaries*, 278.

112 Ambrose, *Eisenhower: The President*, 159.

113 Ibid., 301.

114 Alvin Hansen, *The American Economy* (New York: McGraw-Hill, 1957), 118.

115 Dwight D. Eisenhower, "Address at Eisenhower Day Dinner Given by the Citizens for Eisenhower Congressional Committee of the District of Columbia," October 28, 1954, *Public Papers: Eisenhower, 1954*, 983.

116 Dwight D. Eisenhower to Edgar Newton Eisenhower, November 8, 1954, Galambos, ed., *Papers: The Presidency*, XV, 1386.

117 Dwight D. Eisenhower, speech in Wheeling, West Virginia, September 24, 1952, quoted in Steven Wagner, *Eisenhower Republicanism: Pursuing the Middle Way* (DeKalb: Northern Illinois University Press, 2006), 5.

118 Dwight Eisenhower, "Statement by the President Concerning the Need for a Presidential Commission on Federal–State Relations," February 26, 1953, *Public Papers: Eisenhower, 1953*, 17.

119 Smith, *Eisenhower in War and Peace*, 654.

120 Dwight D. Eisenhower, diary entry, February 24, 1954, Ferrell, ed., *The Eisenhower Diaries*, 276.

121 Dwight D. Eisenhower, "Remarks for the White House Conference on Education," November 28, 1955, accessible via http://www.presidency.ucsb.edu/ws/index.php?pid =10391.

122 Chandler, ed., *Papers: The Presidency*, March 26, 1955, XVI, 1636.

123 Evan Thomas, *Ike's Bluff*, 159.

ENDNOTES

124 Press conference, March 16, 1955, *Public Papers: Eisenhower, 1955*, 332.
125 Ibid., 477–478.
126 Press conference, March 23, 1955, Ibid., 358.
127 James C. Hagerty, *The Diary of James C. Hagerty: Eisenhower in Mid-Course, 1954–1955*, Robert Ferrell, ed. (Bloomington: Indiana University Press, 1983), 219.
128 Thomas, *Ike's Bluff*, 205–206.
129 Nichols, *A Matter of Justice*, 78–88.
130 Hagerty, *The Diary of James C. Hagerty*, 181–184.
131 Taubman, *Secret Empire*, 202–203; Hall, "Clandestine Victory," in Showalter, ed., *Forging the Shield*, 129.
132 Taubman, *Secret Empire*, 199.
133 Hall, "Clandestine Victory," in Showalter, ed., *Forging the Shield*, 134.
134 Taubman, *Secret Empire*, 203–204.
135 Hall, "Clandestine Victory," in Showalter, ed., *Forging the Shield*, 131.
136 Ibid., 126.
137 Taubman, *Secret Empire*, 71–109.
138 Hall, "Clandestine Victory," in Showalter, ed., *Forging the Shield*, 130–131.
139 Dwight D. Eisenhower, Statement on Disarmament Presented at the Geneva Conference, July 21, 1955, *Public Papers: Eisenhower, 1955*, 713–716.
140 "Eisenhowers Worship in Denver," *New York Times*, August 29, 1955, and James Reston, *Sketches in the Sand* (New York: Alfred Knopf, 1967), 420.
141 Dwight D. Eisenhower, Radio and Television Address, July 19, 1955, *Public Papers: Eisenhower, 1955*, 701–705.
142 Dana Adams Schmidt, "Eisenhower, Back in U.S., Cites 'New Friendliness;' Talks to Nation Tonight; Greeted by 5,000," *New York Times*, July 25, 1955.
143 *Los Angeles Times*, August 4, 1955.
144 Dwight D. Eisenhower, diary entry, November 20, 1954, Ferrell, ed., *The Eisenhower Diaries*, 288–289.
145 Arthur Larson, *A Republican Looks at His Party* (New York: Harper and Row, 1955).
146 Neil Sheehan, *A Fiery Peace in a Cold War: Bernard Schriever and the Ultimate Weapon* (New York: Vintage, 2010), 283; Thomas, *Ike's Bluff*, 184–186.
147 Memorandum of Discussion, National Security Council meeting, August 5, 1955, Eisenhower Library.
148 Clarence G. Lasby, *Eisenhower's Heart Attack: How Ike Beat Heart Disease and Held On to the Presidency* (Lawrence: University Press of Kansas, 1997), 71.
149 Leonard Hall, interview by Jean Edward Smith, April 4, 1971, in Smith, *Lucius D. Clay*, 681.
150 Lucius D. Clay, Columbia Oral History Project, Smith, *Lucius D. Clay*, 682.
151 Smith, *Lucius D. Clay*, 626–627.

Chapter Eight

1 Dwight D. Eisenhower, diary entry, January 10, 1956, Ferrell, ed., *The Eisenhower Diaries*, 356.
2 Dwight D. Eisenhower to Swede Hazlett, March 2, 1956, Griffith, ed., *Ike's Letters to a Friend*, 161.

3 James Shepley, "How Dulles Averted War," *Life*, January 16, 1956.

4 Vernon A. Walters, *Silent Missions* (Garden City, NY: Doubleday, 1978), 491.

5 National Security Council meeting, January 12, 1956, Eisenhower Library, cited in David A. Nichols, *Eisenhower 1956: The President's Year of Crisis: Suez and the Brink of War* (New York: Simon and Schuster, 2011), 58.

6 Dwight D. Eisenhower, acceptance address, August 23, 1956, *Public Papers: Eisenhower, 1956*, 702–715.

7 Memorandum for the Record, January 23, 1956, *Foreign Relations of the United States 1955–1957*, XIX, 188–192, cited in Nichols, *Eisenhower 1956*, 63–64, 78–79, 278.

8 Civil Defense meeting, April 19, 1956, Ibid., 96; Guy Oakes, *The Imaginary War: Civil Defense and American Cold War Culture* (New York: Oxford University Press, 1994), 92–95.

9 Dwight D. Eisenhower to Swede Hazlett, August 20, 1956, Griffith, ed., *Ike's Letters to a Friend*, 167–169.

10 Dwight D. Eisenhower, State of the Union address, January 5, 1956.

11 "Text of Eisenhower Foreign Policy Speech to Newspaper Editors," *New York Times*, April 22, 1956.

12 Hughes, *The Ordeal of Power*, 173.

13 Press conference, May 23, 1956, *Public Papers: Eisenhower, 1956*, 522.

14 Press conference, June 6, 1956, Ibid., 554–555.

15 Nichols, *Eisenhower 1956*, 154.

16 Eugene Black, interview, Dulles Oral History Project, Princeton University, quoted in Smith, *Eisenhower in War and Peace*, 693.

17 Nichols, *Eisenhower 1956*, 170.

18 Ibid., 233.

19 Dwight D. Eisenhower to Anthony Eden, July 31, 1956, Galambos, ed., *Papers: The Presidency*, XVII, 2222–2225.

20 White House conference, July 31, 1956, Eisenhower Library, cited in Smith, *Eisenhower in War and Peace*, 695.

21 Nichols, *Eisenhower 1956*, 172, 182.

22 Donald Neff, *Warriors at Suez: Eisenhower Takes America into the Middle East* (New York: Simon & Schuster, 1981), 404.

23 Dwight D. Eisenhower, *Waging Peace 1956–1961: The White House Years* (Garden City, NY: Doubleday, 1965), 95.

24 Dwight D. Eisenhower, interview with Kennett Love, November 25, 1964, in Kennett Love, *Suez: The Twice-Fought War* (New York: McGraw-Hill, 1969), 503.

25 Conference, October 29, 1956, Eisenhower Library, quoted in Smith, *Eisenhower in War and Peace*, 697.

26 Dwight D. Eisenhower, Address in Convention Hall, Philadelphia, November 1, 1956, *Public Papers: Eisenhower, 1956*, 1066–1074.

27 Dwight D. Eisenhower to Anthony Eden, November 5, 1956, Galambos, ed., *Papers: The Presidency*, XVI, 2361–2362.

28 Dwight D. Eisenhower to Lewis Douglas, November 3, 1956, Eisenhower Library, quoted in Nichols, *Eisenhower 1956*, 236.

ENDNOTES

29 Harold Macmillan, *Riding the Storm, 1956–1959* (New York: Harper & Row, 1971), 163–164; Diane B. Kunz, *The Economic Diplomacy of the Suez Crisis* (Chapel Hill: University of North Carolina Press, 1991), 131–133.

30 Nichols, *Eisenhower 1956*, 244.

31 Hughes, *The Ordeal of Power*, 224.

32 White House statement, November 5, 1956, Eisenhower Library, cited in Nichols, *Eisenhower 1956*, 246.

33 Snyder Medical Diary, November 5, 1956, Snyder Papers, Eisenhower Library, cited in Ibid., 247.

34 Conference, November 6, 1956, Eisenhower Library, cited in Ibid., 250.

35 Nichols, *Eisenhower 1956*, 355; Smith, *Eisenhower in War and Peace*, 704. Eden repeated Ike's statement and the warning it contained to the French prime minister, Guy Mollet, who repeated it to his foreign minister, Christian Pineau, who revealed it to the world.

36 Hughes, *The Ordeal of Power*, 198–199.

37 Memorandum, November 8, 1956, Eisenhower Library, cited in Nichols, *Eisenhower 1956*, 264.

38 Dwight D. Eisenhower, *Waging Peace*, 178.

39 Henry Cabot Lodge Jr. to Dwight D. Eisenhower, October 31, 1956, Eisenhower Library, cited in Smith, *Eisenhower in War and Peace*, 705.

40 Hitchcock, *The Age of Eisenhower*, 323.

41 Cabinet Meeting notes, March 23, 1956, Eisenhower Library, cited in Nichols, *A Matter of Justice*, 130.

42 Dwight D. Eisenhower, *Mandate for Change*, 229.

43 Nichols, *A Matter of Justice*, 130.

44 Ibid., 107.

45 Emmet John Hughes, diary entry, September 9 or 10, 1956, cited in Nichols, *A Matter of Justice*, 106.

46 Handwritten notes on Legislative Leaders Meeting, August 13, 1957, Eisenhower Library, cited in Ibid., 164.

47 Handwritten notes of Cabinet Meeting, August 2, 1957, Eisenhower Library, cited in Ibid., 161.

48 W.H. Lawrence, "Eisenhower Irate," *New York Times*, August 3, 1957.

49 Nichols, *A Matter of Justice*, 172.

50 Sherman Adams, *First-Hand Report: The Story of the Eisenhower Administration* (New York: Harpers and Brothers, 1961), 346–351.

51 Dwight D. Eisenhower to Orval Faubus, September 5, 1957, Eisenhower Library, cited in Smith, *Eisenhower in War and Peace*, 717.

52 Dwight D. Eisenhower, *Waging Peace*, 166.

53 Brownell, *Advising Ike*, 211.

54 Dwight D. Eisenhower, public announcement, September 23, 1957, *Public Papers: Eisenhower, 1957*, 689.

55 David Halberstam, *The Fifties* (New York: Villard Books, 1993), 687.

56 Martin Luther King Jr. to Dwight D. Eisenhower, September 25, 1957, Galambos, ed., *Papers: The Presidency*, XVIII, 479.

57 Louis Armstrong to Dwight D. Eisenhower, September 24, 1957, Eisenhower Library.

58 Dwight D. Eisenhower to Richard Russell, September 27, 1957, Galambos, ed., *Papers: The Presidency*, XVIII, 462–464.

59 Dwight D. Eisenhower, Radio and Television Address to the American People on the Situation in Little Rock, September 24, 1957, *Public Papers: Eisenhower, 1957*, 689–694.

60 Nichols, *A Matter of Justice*, 103–108.

61 Hall, "Clandestine Victory," in Showalter, ed., *Forging the Shield*, 135.

62 Ibid., 136.

63 Ibid., 136–137.

64 Dwight D. Eisenhower, *Waging Peace*, 227.

65 Dwight D. Eisenhower to Richard Nixon, February 5, and February 10, 1958, Ibid., 233–235.

66 SNIE 11-10-57, "The Soviet ICBM Program," December 17, 1957, cited in Hitchcock, *The Age of Eisenhower*, 385.

67 Ibid., 385.

68 Ibid., 399.

69 Thomas, *Ike's Bluff*, 366.

70 Ibid., 173.

71 Joseph Alsop, "The Gap," *New York Herald Tribune*, July 30, 1958.

72 Thomas, *Ike's Bluff*, 236–238, 304–305; Anne Karalekas, *History of the Central Intelligence Agency* (Laguna Hills, CA: Aegean Park Press, 1977), 51.

73 Hitchcock, *The Age of Eisenhower*, xii–xiii.

74 Ibid., 284–285.

75 Thomas, *Ike's Bluff*, 109.

76 Ibid., 292–293.

77 Ibid., 401–402.

78 Walters, *Silent Missions*, 489.

79 Nikita Sergeyevich Khrushchev, *Khrushchev Remembers: The Last Testament*, Strobe Talbott, ed. and trans. (Boston: Little, Brown, 1974), 412.

80 United States Department of State, *Foreign Relations of the United States, 1958–1960* (Washington, D.C.: Government Printing Office, 1993), X, 462–467.

81 White House Memo for Record, February 8, 1960, Eisenhower Library, cited in Smith, *Eisenhower in War and Peace*, 751.

82 Memorandum for the Record, February 12, 1959, cited in Hitchcock, *The Age of Eisenhower*, 458.

83 Dwight D. Eisenhower, *Waging Peace*, 552.

84 Walters, *Silent Missions*, 346.

85 "The President's News Conference," May 11, 1960, quoted in Hitchcock, *The Age of Eisenhower*, 466.

86 Dwight D. Eisenhower, *Waging Peace*, 558.

87 Hall, "Clandestine Victory," in Showalter, ed., *Forging the Shield*, 138–139.

88 Dwight D. Eisenhower, press conference, August 24, 1960, *Waging Peace*, 646–658.

89 Korda, *Ike: An American Hero*, 716–717.

90 Dwight D. Eisenhower, Farewell Radio and Television Address, January 17, 1961, *Public Papers: Eisenhower, 1960–1961*, 1035–1040.

91 David Eisenhower and Julie Nixon Eisenhower, *Going Home to Glory*, 122.

ENDNOTES

92 Ron Wolk, "2016 A Reminder of the Goldwater–Eisenhower Convention," *The Morning Call*, April 5, 2016, https://www.mcall.com/opinion/mc–trump–eisenhower–yv–0506–20160405–story.html.

93 David Eisenhower and Julie Nixon Eisenhower, *Going Home to Glory*, 275.

94 Dwight D. Eisenhower, *At Ease*, 181.

Epilogue

1 Viki Goldberg, "The Cars were Big and Elvis was Young, *New York Times*, February 20, 1998, B–35.

2 Taubman, *Secret Empire*, xii–xiii.

3 Hall, "Clandestine Victory," in Showalter, ed., *Forging the Shield*, 141.

4 Dennis E. Showalter, Ibid., 3.

5 Korda, *Ike: An American Hero*, 718.

6 Lyon, *Eisenhower: Portrait of a Hero*, 851.

7 Hitchcock, *The Age of Eisenhower*, xx.

Acknowledgments

Many people have contributed to this book. Thanks to my old friend Philip Terzian for suggesting many years ago that Ike was an important and underrated figure. Profound thanks to Carl Reddel for giving me a chance to help commemorate the Eisenhower legacy at the Dwight D. Eisenhower Memorial Commission and for opening many doors in the world of Eisenhower scholarship. I will always remember our conversations at the Tabard Inn and Jaleo. Thanks also to Collette Reddel, whose beneficence encouraged me, and to the late Jann Hoag for introducing me to Carl. I am grateful to my colleagues at the Commission, especially the late J.T. Dykman, Samuel Holt, and Louis Galambos for their suggestions. At Post Hill Press, my editor Alex Novak and my copyeditor Kate Post provided invaluable support. Finally, thanks to my agent Maryann Karinch, a resourceful lady.

Index

Citizens for Eisenhower, 234, 258, 261, 263, 264.

civil defense program, 344, 372-373.

Civilian Conservation Corps (CCC), 79.

civil rights, 290, 313-316, 332-333, 358-367, 388, African American leadership and, 290, 314, 359, 362, Brownell and, 279, 313, *Brown v. Board of Eduction* and, 332-333, 359, Ike and, 290, 313-316, 332-333, 358-367, 388, judicial appointments and, 332-333, Warren and, 279-280.

Civil Rights Act of 1957, 362-363, 364.

Civil Rights Act of 1960, 364.

Civil Rights Act of 1964, 388.

Clark, Mark, 36, 74, 76, 84, 94, 96, 97, 102, 110, 117, 118, 125, 142, 147, 287, abilities as commander, 125, ETO and, 96, Giraud-Ike negotiations and, 117, Italian campaign and, 142, 147, North African campaign and, 117, 118, 125, Korean War and, 287.

Clark-Darlan agreement, 118.

Clay, Lucius, 129, 176, 188, 194, 196, 222, 238, 243, 255-256, 258-260, 262, 264, 266, 270, 271-272, 277, 279, 285, 317, 322, 326, 338, 341, Allied occupation of Germany and, 188, 222, 238, Dewey's relationship with, 258-260, 264, Ike's 1952 presidential campaign and, 255-256, 258-260, 264, 266, 270, 271-272, 277, Ike's relationship with, 129, 196, 243, 255-256, 258-260, 277, 338, interstate highway system and, 326, Nixon's Checkers speech and, 271-272, selection of Eisenhower cabinet and, 279-280, 285, Summersby-Ike relationship and, 129, 196, views about Ike of, 196, 262, 338.

Cohn, Roy, 302, 323, 400, and Army-McCarthy hearings, 323, as McCarthy henchman, 302, as mentor to Donald Trump, 400.

Cold War, xi, 221-223, 237-238, 245, 247-248, 295-297, 336-338, 348, 373-376, 378-387, arms race and, 245, 373-376, CIA and, 382-383, defense budget and, 247, 282, Ike's national security concerns and, 216, 218, 221, 225, 242, 247, 249-257, 295-297, Korea and, 246-247, 295-297, military-industrial complex and, missile gap and, 375-376, 385, New Look defense policy and, 282, 284, 288, 336, nuclear weapons and, 281, 287-288, 294-295, 304-306, 319-320, 329-331, 343-345, public opinion and, 247, 336-338,

Russia-U.S. relations and, 216, 218, 237-238, 295-297, 336-338, 378-387.

Collins, J. Lawton "Lightning Joe," 151, 161, 170.

Columbia University, 224-226, 228-229, 232, 237, 239-242, 243, 245, 253, academic freedom issues at, 240, faculty at, 239, 243, football at, 239, fund-raising at, 240-241, Ike as president of, 228-229, 231, 236, 237, 239-242, 243, 245, 253, Ike's leaves of absence from, 242, 250, 253, Ike's popularity at, 239, 243, presidential search committee of, 224-226.

Combined Chiefs of Staff (CCS), 89, 103, 121-122, 183, 188, creation of, 89, at Casablanca conference, 121-125, command structure of, 89, Ike's relations with, 121-125, 183, 188, members of, 89, North African campaign and, 103, 121-125, at QUADRANT conference, 141, TORCH invasion and, 103, at TRIDENT conference, 136-137.

Command and General Staff School (CGSS), 44, 45, 77.

communism, 216-220, 238, 240, 245-246, 256, 274, 311-312.

concentration camps, 187.

Congress, 12, 28, 34, 48, 58, 60-61, 81, 84, 87, 163, 190-191, 222, 225, 230, 245, 253, 321-324, 357, 362-363, 383.

Conner, Fox, 39-40, 43-44, 45, 46, 51.

conservatism, xii-xiii, 48, 55-56, 218-219, 231-232, 245, 286, evolution of, 55, 218-219, varieties of, 218-219.

Cook, Blanche Wiesen, 255, 257, 274, 395.

Cooper, Isabel Rosario, 58, 197, 201.

CORONA satellite, 371, 374, 381, 385.

Corwin, Edward S., 317.

COSSAC, 148, 165, 174.

Council on Foreign Relations, 240, 249.

Cousins, Norman, 386.

Craig, Malin, 69, 71, 79.

Cronkite, Walter, xi, 277.

cross-channel invasion, 90-91, 92-93, 96-98, 101, 120, 124, 13 5-136, 145-157, 160-163, BOLERO, 93, Churchill's attitudes toward, 92-93, 97, 124, 135-136, COSSAC and, 148, German preparations for, 160, Ike/OPD proposal for, 90-91, 92-93, landing craft for, 94, 99, 149, 152, 161, logistics for, 92-94, 151, 152, 160-161, Marshall's attitudes toward, 91, 94, 97-101, 120, 124, Montgomery and,

Morrow, E. Frederic, 313.
Moseley, George Van Horn, 52, 55-56, 66.
Mossadegh, Mohammad, 308-310.
Mountbatten, Louis, 96, 101, 148.
Mulberries, 148, 166.
Murphy, Robert, 105, 110, 115, 117, 118.
Murrow, Edward R., 118.

N

Nasser, Gamal Abdel, 312, 347-351, 353.
National Aeronautics and Space Administration
   (NASA), 375, 383.
National Defense Education Act of 1958,
National Security Act of 1947, 222.
National Security Council (NSC), 222, 294,
   295, 296, 297, 304, 319, 334, 337, 340, 343,
   349, 357, 373.
NATO, 238, 249-250, 253-254, 256-257, 263,
   356, communism and, 238, creation of, 238,
   Ike as commander of, 249-257, Ike's head-
   quarters for, 254, Ike's staff at, 254, Russia
   and, 238, 356.
Navy, U.S., 94, 98, 104, 137, 225, 242, 244, U.S.
   Air Force rivalry with, 242, Army rivalry
   with, 225, Formosa Strait crisis and, 329,
   331, Operation OVERLORD and, 148, 161,
   Operation TORCH and, 106, 107, segrega-
   tion in, 315.
Nazism, 64, 74-75, 187, 188.
New Deal, 64-65, 79, 218, 243, 299.
"New Look" defense policy, 282, 284, 288, 298,
   306, 333.
Newport, Rhode Island, 365.
New York City, 17, 228-229, 236-237.
Nichols, David A., 314, 321, 333, 348-349, 352,
   361, 395.
Nielsen (Aksel) ranch, 267, 340.
Nitze, Paul, 247, 303, 373.
Nixon Eisenhower, Julie. See Eisenhower, Julie
   Nixon.
Nixon, Richard M., 238, 265, 266, 271-273,
   319, 340, 345-346, 372, 385-386, 389, 400,
   Checkers speech of, 272, fund scandal of,
   271, election of 1952 and, 265, 266, 271-273,
   election of 1956 and, 345-346, election of
   1960 and, 385-386, election of 1968 and,
   389, Ike's health and, 340, 372, Ike's relationship with, 271-273, 345-346, 372, 385-386,
   389, Ike's views of, 345-346, 385-386.
Normandy campaign, 161, 165-167, 169-170.

Normandy invasion. *See* Operation
   OVERLORD.
Norman, Ruby, 13, 16, 22, 24.
North Africa campaign, 89-90, 92, 99, 100, 101,
   103, 104-107, 110-111, 115-120, 122, 125,
   126-127, Allied disagreements about, 90,101,
   103, 122, Churchill and, 89, 99, 101, 105,
   Clark-Darlan agreement and, 118, command
   structure of, 106-107, 110, 126-127, decision
   to launch, 103, France and, 104-105, 115-117,
   German operations in, 100, 119, 122, 125,
   GYMNAST and, 89-90, 99, Ike as supreme
   commander of, 103, 104-107, 110-111,
   115-117, 122-125, 126-127, Kasserine Pass
   and, 125, 126, Marshall and, 90, 101, 122-
   123, Patton and, 110-111, 125, planning for,
   106-107, 110-111, Roosevelt and, 89, 92, 102,
   118, 121-125, SATIN and, 122, TORCH
   invasion armada and, 110-111, TORCH
   landing zones and, 110, 117.
NSC 162-2, 304.
NSC-68, 247, 303, 373
nuclear weapons, 81, 199, 221, 245, 281, 287-
   288, 294-295, 304-306, 319-320, 329-331,
   339-340, 343-345, 356-357, 372-376, 377,
   398, brinksmanship and, 294-295, 320,
   329-331, 343-345, 356-357, destructive
   power of, 221, 304, 330, 339-340, 343-344,
   Ike's views regarding, 199, 281, 287-288,
   294-295, 304, 329-331, 339-340, 343-345,
   356-357, 372-376,

O

oil, as factor in Iran coup, 308-309, as factor in
   Suez crisis, 355, 358.
Omaha Beach, 161.
"Open Skies" proposal, Eisenhower's, 336-338.
Ord, James G., 68, 69, 73.
OVERLORD, Operation, 147-157, 159, 160-163,
   ANVIL and, 152, British misgivings about,
   148, buildup in Britain for, 148, 151-152,
   160-161, COSSAC planning for, 148, de
   Gaulle and, 155, FORTITUDE deception
   and, 148, German operations during, 160,
   166-167, Ike named commander of, 147,
   Ike's headquarters in France and, 147, 170,
   Ike's visit with troops during, 156-157, logis-
   tics of, 148, 151, 153, 160-161, Marshall and,
   145-147, Montgomery and, 147, 151, 154,
   Normandy breakout campaign (COBRA)

Snyder, Howard, 340, 356-357, 378.
socialism, 219-220, 308, 311-312, 348.
Social Security, 219, 327.
SOLARIUM, 303-304.
Soviet Union. See Russia.
Spaatz, Carl "Tooey," 101, 153.
space race, 369-370.
Speidel, Hans, 175.
Sputnik, 368-370.
spy satellites. See reconnaissance satellites.
St. Lawrence Seaway, 326.
stag dinners, Eisenhower's, 293.
Stalin, Joseph, 64-65, 98, 143, 200, 238, 295.
Stark, Harold, 89,
State Department, U.S., 105-106, 222, 223, 245, 280-283, 348-349.
Steelman, John R., 202-203, 226.
Stevenson, Adlai, 200, 266, 267, 275, 343.
Stewart, Potter, 332.
Stimson, Henry L., 80, 93, 199.
Strategic Air Command (SAC), 297.
Strauss, Lewis, 379.
Suez crisis, 347-358.
Sulzberger, Cyrus, 253.
Summersby, Kay, 95, 102, 108-110, 111, 121, 124, 127-135, 143, 144-145, 146, 149-150, 151, 156-157, 162-163, 171-173, 185, 188, 192-207, 212-213, 214-215, 236-237, 241, 262, 278-279, 390, 399, 418-419, n. 12.
Supreme Court, U.S., 279-280, 315-316, 317, 332, 365.
Supreme Headquarters, Allied Expeditionary Force (SHAEF), 151-152, 175, 176-177.
surveillance satellites. See reconnaissance satellites.
Sutherland, Richard K., 73-74.
Symington, Stuart, 373, 375.

T

Taft, Robert A., 129, 164, 202, 229-230, 250-252, 256, 262, 264-265, 270, 290-291, 301-302.
Taft, William Howard, 39, 250, 265.
tanks, 30, 36-38, 40.
Taubman, Philip, 395.
Taylor, Maxwell D., 140, 365.
Tedder, Arthur, 142, 143, 153, 182.
Teheran Conference (November, 1943), 144.
Telegraph Cottage, 108, 151.

Teller, Edward, 373.
test-ban treaty, nuclear, 379-380.
Thomas, Evan, 294, 295, 303, 305-306, 320, 331, 340, 374, 379, 395, 398.
Thurmond, Strom, 230, 361.
Till, Emmett, 359, 360.
Tobruk, 99-100.
TORCH, 103-108, 110-111, 115-116, 117, 119-120.
TRIDENT Conference (Washington, May, 1943), 135-137.
Tripartite Declaration, 352.
Troy, Gil, 172.
Truman, Harry S., 129, 165, 188, 189, 191, 195, 201-203, 220, 221, 226, 230, 238, 242, 247-248, 249, 250, 256, 258-259, 263, 268, 269, 275, 279, 283, 288-289, 388, Cold War and, 220, 238, 247-248, 283, Democratic Party and, 226, 230, 258-259, 263, election of 1948 and, 226, 230, election of 1952 and, 258-259, 263, Ike's political career and, 191, 202, 226, 258-259, 263, Ike's relationship with, 188, 191, 195, 226, 242, 249, 250, 259, 263, 268, 269, 275, 279, 288-289, 388, Korean War and, 247, 256, 288, MacArthur and, 247, 256, 288, Marshall and, 192, 222-223, 245, 248, NATO and, 238, 249, NSC-68 and, 247, nuclear weapons and, 238, Potsdam conference and, 191, presidential leadership of, 220, 247-248, Russia-U.S. relations and, 238, Summersby-Ike relationship and, 129, 193-197, 201-203, 275, Taft and, 258.
Trump, Donald, 400-401.

U

U-2 spy plane, 307, 334-335, 370, 374, 382-385.
Ubico, Jorge, 310.
ULTRA, 149.
unemployment, 33-34, 53-54, 60, 163, 324-326.
United Fruit Company, 310-313.
United Nations, 247, 353, 356.

V

Vaughan, Harry, 129, 202.
VE Day, 188.
Vichy government, 104, 115, 117-118.
Vietnam, 254, 318-321.
Vinson, Fred M., 315.